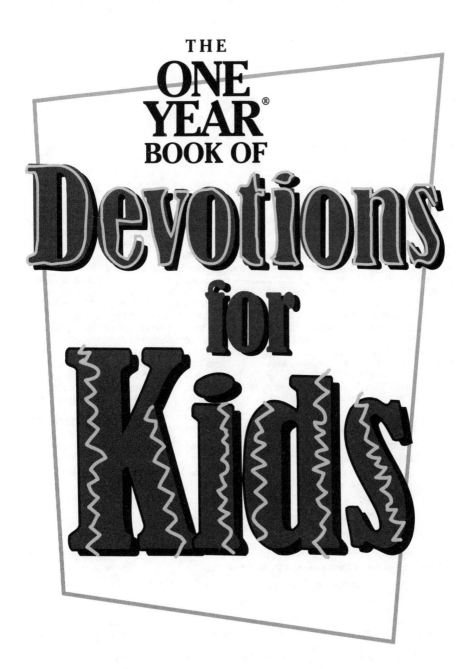

THE ONE YEAR® BOOK OF Devotions for Kids

Tyndale House Publishers, Inc., Wheaton, IL

Stories written by: Katherine Ruth Adams, Gina L. Anfenson, Esther M. Bailey, Stephanie Blair, Judi Boogaart, Carol Brookman, Jean Burns, David C. Carson, V. Louise Cunningham, Carol A. DeCesare, Ann K. Dunkerton, Harriett A. Durrell, Donna Edinger, Dean Fowler, Stephanie E. Frantz, Cathy Garnaat, Carolyn Gaston, Jonnye R. Griffin, Ruth Hamel, Sue A. Haub, Alicia Hekman, Shelley Janofski, Joyce Jentes, Pam Jones, Bernice Karnop, Nance E. Keyes, Dorothy R. King, Phyllis Klomparens, Daryl Knauer, Linda E. Knight, Sherry Kuyt, Donna L. Lawless, Donna A. LeBlanc, Joyce Lee, Delores A. Lemieux, Kevin Licht, Amy Linde, April Lymer, Dawn Ellen Maloney, Blanche Manos, Deborah Marett, Hazel Marett, Lorna B. Marlowe, Roseann Mayhle, Ruth McQuilkin, Sara Nelson, Matilda Nordtvedt, Miriam K. Nowak, Della R. Oberholtzer, Ellen C. Orr, Mary Rose Pearson, Linda Prince, Victoria L. Reinhardt, Lynn Stamm Rex, Janet Rhine, Glenna Roberts, Phyllis Robinson, Catherine Runyon, A. J. Schut, Sheri Shaw, Marie Shropshire, Dorellen Smith-Belleau, Sam L. Sullivan, Lois A. Teufel, Juanita Urbach, Trudy VanderVeen, Elisient M. Vernon, Joyce Voelker, Lyndel Walker, Linda Weddle, Barbara Westberg, Lola M. Williams, Carolyn Yost, Pauline Youd, and Sarah P. Zaengle. Authors' initials appear at the end of each story. All stories are taken from issues of *Keys for Kids,* published bimonthly by the Children's Bible Hour, Box 1, Grand Rapids, Michigan 49501.

Scripture quotations marked NKJV are from *The Holy Bible,* New King James Version. Copyright © 1979, 1980, 1982, Thomas Nelson Inc., Publishers.

Scripture quotations marked TLB are from *The Living Bible.* Copyright © 1971 owned by assignment by KNT Charitable Trust. All rights reserved.

Scripture quotations marked NIV are from *The Holy Bible,* New International Version®. Copyright © 1973, 1978, 1984 by International Bible Society. Used by permission of Zondervan Publishing House. All rights reserved.

The One Year is a registered trademark of Tyndale House Publishers, Inc.

Copyright © 1993 Children's Bible Hour.

Library of Congress Cataloging-in-Publication Data

The One year book of devotions for kids.
     p.   cm.
    Includes indexes.
    Summary: A collection of devotions for each day of the calendar year, including readings, illustrative stories, memory verses, and questions to internalize the messages.
    ISBN 0-8423-5087-X (pbk.)
    1. Devotional calendars—Juvenile literature. 2. Children—Prayer books and devotions—English. [1. Devotional calendars. 2. Prayer books and devotions. 3. Christian life.]
BV4870.064 1993
242'.682—dc20
                        93-15786

Table of Contents

MAY

1 Grounded
2 The Brick House
3 The Brick House (Part 2)
4 The Brick House (Part 3)
5 Wade's Secret Project
6 Trusty
7 Just like the Kings
8 The Safety Pin
9 Trapped
10 In the Dark
11 The Bottom Line
12 The World's Best Baby-Sitter
13 Jonathan's Bath
14 A Dead Stick or a Living Tree
15 Sweeter than Chocolate
16 Like Grandpa

17 Lessons from the Garden
18 Junior Bridesmaid
19 What Do You See?
20 The Sad Night
21 The Memory Box
22 Riding on Clouds
23 Puzzle Pieces
24 Do You Hear?
25 God's People
26 The Needy Baby
27 Grandma's Coming
28 A Different Beat
29 Cobwebs and Cables
30 Carmel and David
31 God's Flower Garden

JUNE

1 A Special Poem
2 The Woodpecker
3 Keep Knocking
4 Picking up the Pieces
5 The Dirty Socks
6 Flying Is for Birds
7 The Bald Eagle
8 Breakthrough
9 Hidden Dirt
10 Sea Lion Ears
11 Minced Oaths
12 The Abscessed Tooth
13 Audible Repetitions
14 Try It! You Might Like It!
15 Obedient Rex

16 Baby Birds
17 Sand Castles
18 Big Sister
19 Scars to Remember
20 Adjustments
21 What's in the Well
22 Run
23 Fresh Air
24 A Torn Sail
25 Catch Me, Daddy!
26 Press On
27 A Bit of Beauty
28 A Very Special Day
29 Building Bridges
30 Firmly in Place

JULY

1 Blind Bats
2 No More Dust
3 The Beautiful Apple
4 A Reason to Celebrate

5 Proper Care
6 It Takes Two
7 The Prison Breakout
8 In God's Care

A U G U S T

S E P T E M B E R

DECEMBER

Introduction

For many years Children's Bible Hour has published *Keys for Kids,* a bimonthly devotional magazine for kids. Their fine ministry to parents and kids has been much appreciated over the years, and Tyndale House is proud to present this collection of stories from *Keys for Kids.*

The One Year Book of Devotions for Kids has a full year's worth of stories that illustrate the day's Scripture reading. Following each story is a "How About You?" section, which asks children to apply the story to their lives. There is also a memory verse for each day, usually taken from the Scripture reading. We have quoted the memory verses from the New International Version, the New King James Version, and *The Living Bible.* However, you are free to have your children memorize the verses as they appear or use whichever Bible translation your family prefers. And the devotion ends with a "key," a two-to-five-word summary of the lesson.

The stories in this devotional are geared toward children between the ages of eight and fourteen. Kids can enjoy these stories by themselves as they develop their own daily quiet time (with any degree of parental involvement), or they can be used as part of family devotions. Like the many stories in the Bible that teach valuable lessons about life, the stories here will speak not only to children but to adults. They are simple, direct, and concrete, and, like Jesus' parables, they speak to all of us in terms we can understand.

This book contains a Scripture index for both daily readings and memory verses as well as a topical index. The Scripture indices are helpful if you want to locate a story related to a passage that you want to draw attention to. The topical index is included because concerns arise unexpectedly in any family—such as moving, illness, or the loss of a friend or family member. We hope you will use this book every day, but the indexes are here so you will not feel locked into any one format. Please use any story at any time you feel it relates to a special situation in your family.

The Broken Eggshell (Read James 3:2-10)

"I hate you, Allen!" Tom shouted. "Don't ever come in my room again! You're a thief!"

"Whoa, there," called Grandpa, coming down the hall. "What's all this yelling about?"

"Tom says I stole his scissors, but I didn't," Allen called from his room. "He's a liar, and he better stay out of my room, too!" Allen slammed his door.

With a sigh, Grandpa checked into the incident. It wasn't long before he discovered Tom's scissors on the hall table. With angry words, both boys insisted the other had left them there.

"Quiet!" ordered Grandpa. He motioned for them to follow him and headed for the kitchen, where he placed an egg and an empty teacup on the counter. "Allen, you crack this egg into the cup," said Grandpa. The boys wondered what he was getting at, but Allen obeyed. "Now," said Grandpa, "Tom, you put the egg back into the shell again, please—just the way it was."

Tom frowned. "What do you mean?" he asked. "That's impossible, Grandpa. You can't fix a broken egg."

"Like Humpty Dumpty, eh?" Grandpa chuckled. Then he became serious. "The point is, there's something else like Humpty Dumpty—something that can't be easily mended. I'm thinking of feelings. You boys said some ugly things to each other. Taking words back is just as impossible as mending an egg." Both boys felt bad. "Never forget how harmful words can be," cautioned Grandpa. "God says the tongue is like a fire that cannot be put out. That's how much damage words can do. Even saying you're sorry doesn't make them disappear."

"I am sorry, though," Tom told his brother.

"Yeah . . . well . . . me too," replied Allen. "You can come in my room, if you want." *D.F.*

HOW ABOUT YOU?

Are you careful about the words you speak, or do you say things before you think? Even when you say you're sorry, the other person may still remember those words you said. Ask God to help you tame your tongue.

MEMORIZE:

"Don't use bad language. Say only what is good and helpful to those you are talking to, and what will give them a blessing." *Ephesians 4:29, TLB*

 Think before You Speak

Afraid of the Dark (Read 2 Corinthians 4:3-6)

2

Kim did her best to comfort Billy, the little boy she was baby-sitting, but he was terrified. A nightmare had awakened him, and he was sure that monsters were hiding in his room. "There's no such thing as a monster, Billy," Kim said as she sat on his bed and hugged him.

When she tried to tuck him under the covers, he clutched at her frantically. "I want my mommy!" he choked out between sobs.

"Listen, Billy," Kim soothed, "your mommy and daddy will be home later, but you're safe with me. I'll tell you what—why don't I leave the door open and turn on the hall light. I'll be right outside the door."

"I want my bear," Billy whimpered.

"All right." Kim placed the scruffy teddy in his arms. She dried his tears and then quietly left the room. "Please let him sleep," Kim prayed. And after Billy called out to her for reassurance several times, he did sleep.

Kim was tired when Billy's parents finally came home, but she perked up when they apologized for being late and paid her overtime. The extra money meant she would be able to buy the camera she'd been wanting.

At church the next day, a missionary showed slides of his work in India. The sound of the eerie pipe music filled the room. Kim saw people, their faces twisted by fear, offering sacrifices to cruel-looking idols. *Why,* she thought suddenly, *they're just like Billy. They're scared of the dark—only the darkness they're afraid of is the darkness of evil. They need to know there's Someone to take care of them. They need the light of Jesus.* Then something occurred to her. She had money. She could give some of it to help send them the gospel. The camera could wait for a while. *A.L.*

HOW ABOUT YOU?

Have you been afraid of the dark? Can you imagine how much worse it would be to be surrounded by the darkness of evil, with no knowledge that God loves you or that Jesus died for you? Think about what you can do to help send the light of the gospel to the people who live in such darkness.

MEMORIZE:

"The people walking in darkness have seen a great light; on those living in the land of the shadow of death a light has dawned." *Isaiah 9:2, NIV*

➤ *Reach Those in Spiritual Darkness*

In His Arms (Read Isaiah 40:28-31)

Lesa tore open the door and stumbled down the hallway. "Mother! Mother!" she called. "Is it true?"

"Settle down there, Lesa." Dad met her and put an arm around her shoulders. "What's wrong?"

"David said his mom doesn't have a job anymore, and that all the plant workers have been laid off. It must be true—you're home, too!" exclaimed Lesa. "Daddy, if you don't have your job anymore, how will we pay Kari's doctor bills?"

3

JANUARY

Just then, Mom came down the steps with baby Kari. Kari's eyes lit up when she saw Lesa, and she eagerly reached out her hands. Dad let Lesa out of his bear hug so that she could take Kari. Lesa couldn't help remembering when Kari was sick and had to go to the hospital so often. She was such a quiet and dull baby then, not at all like the bright, happy baby she was now. She squeezed her little sister even tighter in her arms.

Dad saw the tight hug Lesa gave Kari. "Lesa, whose arms are holding Kari?" he asked.

"That's a funny question," said Lesa. "My arms are. Why did you ask that?"

"Well," said Dad, "is she really safe in your arms? Maybe I should take her."

Lesa looked puzzled. "But, Dad, you and Mom have taught me to be very careful with Kari. I'm in fourth grade, you know. Why don't you trust me with Kari now?"

Dad smiled. "Actually, I do," he said. "I'll leave her with you. But think about this—you're worried because I'm out of work. I know it's a scary thought, and I'll admit that Mom and I feel a little shaky about it, too. But we decided to leave it in the arms that are holding us."

Lesa stared blankly at her father for a minute, and then she smiled. "God's arms," she said simply. Yes, it was true. God's arms were underneath her family. He would hold them tight, no matter what happened with Dad's job. *P.J.*

HOW ABOUT YOU?

Are you worried about your future? Has your mom or dad been laid off or lost a job? Remember, God knew it was going to happen before you did, and he knows what to do about it. Trust him.

MEMORIZE:

"The eternal God is your refuge, and underneath are the everlasting arms."

Deuteronomy 33:27, NKJV

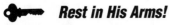

Rest in His Arms!

Mystery Soup (Read 1 Samuel 16:6-13)

4

JANUARY

The front door slammed, signaling that John was home from school. When he didn't burst into the kitchen as usual, Mother checked on him. "What's wrong?" she asked the glum-faced boy sitting on the sofa.

John scowled. "I have to work on a social studies project with that new boy, Stefan," he mumbled. "You should see him. His pants are too short, his socks never match, and his hair's always a mess."

"But what makes you think he wouldn't be a good project partner?" asked Mother.

"I just told you," grumbled John. "If you could see him, you wouldn't ask that question."

Just then there was a loud *clunk* in the kitchen. They both hurried to the kitchen, where they found John's two-year-old brother, Travis, surrounded by cans from the cupboard, many with the labels peeled off. "Oh, no," moaned Mother, looking at the mess. After thinking a moment, she said, "John, you can help me. Would you tape the labels back on these cans, please? I want them done neatly."

"But which label goes on which can?" asked John.

"Don't worry about that," Mother said. "Just make sure it looks nice. Then let's have one that says 'Corn' for dinner."

"But, Mom," protested John, "if you just slap the labels on any old can, the outside might not match what's inside."

"So the outside appearance isn't really important, is it?" asked Mother. She smiled at John. "That's something I think you should remember. You've already judged Stefan because of how he looks. You've slapped a label on him without knowing what's on the inside. Find out what Stefan is like as a person—don't just judge him on his looks."

John thought about it. "Maybe I should get to know him," he decided. "But what are you going to do about those cans?"

Mother laughed. "I guess we'll be having mystery soup for a while." *S.P.Z.*

HOW ABOUT YOU?

Do you judge people by the way they look or dress? Do you label them without finding out what is inside? God doesn't judge on outward appearances, and neither should you. Try to discover what's in the heart.

MEMORIZE:

"The Lord does not see as man sees; for man looks at the outward appearance, but the Lord looks at the heart."

1 Samuel 16:7, NKJV

Don't Judge by Appearance

Battered Bears (Read 1 Timothy 5:1-4)

As Jenny gave her battered old teddy bear a hug before setting him on her pillow, her brother, Adam, walked past her bedroom door. "Why don't you give that ratty old thing a decent burial—in the garbage can?" asked Adam, laughing at his own joke.

"Be quiet, Adam," shouted Jenny. "You're not funny."

Mother appeared in the doorway. "Let's go, kids," she said. Jenny made a face. They were going to visit Great-Aunt Catherine at the nursing home. Her mind was no longer alert, and the children hated visiting her.

5

JANUARY

At the nursing home, they found Great-Aunt Catherine sorting through ancient photographs, as usual. Mother talked gently to her about the past while the children drew pictures. Jenny sketched a funny picture of her great-aunt and some of the other old folks and showed it to Adam, and they snickered together in the corner. They didn't notice Mother until she pulled the sketch from Adam's hand.

Back home, Mother steered the children to Jenny's room. She took the teddy bear from the bed. "Jenny, you didn't like Adam making fun of your bear," she said. "I guess you still love it, even though its fur is rubbed off and one eye is missing, right?" Jenny nodded. "Well," said Mother, "I love Great-Aunt Catherine, even though she's old. She raised me after my parents died. It hurts me to see you make fun of her—just like it hurt you, Jenny, when Adam made fun of this bear."

"I'm sorry," murmured Jenny. Both children were ashamed of their attitude that morning.

"God commands us to honor and respect old people, even though they may have broken bodies and childlike minds," continued Mother. "They have spent their lives in service to their families and friends. Now it's our turn to be of service to them. Will you both please try to remember that?"

Jenny and Adam nodded solemnly. Adam even gave the old teddy bear a gentle pat as he left the room. *E.C.O.*

HOW ABOUT YOU?

Have you ever made fun of older people? Do you get impatient with the elderly members of your church or family when they cannot move fast or when they tell the same stories over and over? Proverbs 16:31 says that gray hair is a crown of glory. Treat older people with honor and respect.

MEMORIZE:

"You shall rise before the gray headed and honor the presence of an old man." *Leviticus 19:32, NKJV*

 Respect the Elderly

Allen's Allergies (Read Psalm 34:12-16)

6

"Mom, the itchy spots are back on my skin," Allen said, holding out his arms. "I have bumps on my legs, too."

"Oh, Allen," said Mother, "your allergies are acting up again. I haven't changed the laundry detergent or any of our soaps. I can't imagine what caused this reaction, can you?"

Allen scratched his arms as he thought. "When I was over at Bob's this morning, his mom had some stuff out to the send to the mission," he said. "Bob and I dressed up in some of his dad's old camouflage clothes. I suppose they were washed in something I'm allergic to."

"I suspect that's it," said Mother. "Go take a shower, and then we'll get your prescription refilled."

As Allen and his mother drove home after picking up the medicine, Allen sighed. "It's hard to remember that I need to be careful about what touches my skin," he said. "We were having so much fun that I didn't even think about it." He rubbed his arms. "My allergies remind me, though," he added. "It's too bad they don't remind me ahead of time!"

"Isn't that the truth!" agreed Mother. She smiled at her son. "You know," she added, "dressing in those clothes was innocent fun, and it's too bad you have to avoid things like that. But you do, or you get this negative reaction. There are other things that we need to be very careful to avoid, too, even though they seem like innocent fun. We need to think about the consequences before getting involved in those things."

"Like what?" asked Allen.

"Well, . . . like watching bad TV shows, or reading dirty books, or going places where we'll be tempted to do wrong," said Mother. "Those kinds of things, like any sinful activity, will stir up a negative reaction in our lives. We need to ask the Lord to remind us to avoid things that will harm us." *N.E.K.*

HOW ABOUT YOU?

Are you allergic to anything—foods, bees, medicine, weeds, soap? If so, you know it's best for you to avoid those things. Sin can cause a very bad reaction in your life as well. Try to avoid sinful things so you can avoid their consequences, too.

MEMORIZE:

"Keep away from every kind of evil." *1 Thessalonians 5:22, TLB*

 *Avoid Sinful Activity*

Blind Leaders (Read 1 John 4:1-6)

7

JANUARY

"But, Mom," argued Mary Beth, "what's wrong with joining that club? They just play games and do crafts. And they help poor children, too. Some of my Christian friends have joined. After all, it's a church club. Does it matter that it's not our church?"

"It isn't a church, Mary Beth," answered Mom. "It's a cult. The leaders and teachers don't believe that Jesus is God, or that he died for the sins of the world and rose again. I understand they include a lesson time at the club, and that's the kind of false teaching you would hear."

"Oh, Mom," protested Mary Beth, "I know better than to believe that stuff. I'll just go for the fun times and the charity projects."

"Don't be so sure of yourself," said Mom. She paused, then added, "Let me tell you a true story. When I was young, some friends and I decided to explore some trails in the woods behind our house. I thought I knew those woods so well that I could never get lost, but before we knew it, we were lost. I was relieved when Sally, one of the other girls, said she knew the way back home. So she led the way, but you know what? She just led us farther and farther into the woods. The sun went down, and we wandered around in the dark. We weren't rescued until the next day."

"How awful!" exclaimed Mary Beth.

Mother nodded and smiled. "When my father found us, he quoted something Jesus said: 'If the blind lead the blind, both will fall into a ditch.' Mary Beth, unsaved teachers are 'blind'—they can't understand Scripture. They will lead you astray."

Mary Beth sighed. "OK," she agreed. She grinned at her mother. "I don't want to fall into any ditches!" *M.R.P.*

HOW ABOUT YOU?

Are you careful about what kind of Bible teachers you listen to? Beware of those who deny any part of God's Word. Be sure your teachers believe and teach that all of God's Word is true.

MEMORIZE:

"If the blind leads the blind, both will fall into a ditch."

Matthew 15:14, NKJV

 Follow Bible-Believing Teachers

Dead Religion (Read Matthew 28:1-9)

8

JANUARY

"Is not!" Michael's voice rang throughout the house.

"Is too!" Sandy shouted back at her older brother.

"Oh, Sandy, just wait till you're older and have learned more about the world," said Michael crossly. "Then you'll be more broad-minded."

"Well, Dad's older than you, and I bet he agrees with me!" Sandy replied.

"Whoa! What's all the shouting about?" asked Dad, coming into the room.

"Michael's been learning about different religions, and he thinks they're as good as ours," explained Sandy. "But Jesus is the only way to heaven. Isn't that right, Dad?"

"Well, some of the leaders we've been learning about were real good people," muttered Michael.

"Better not be too broad-minded, Michael," Dad cautioned. "Have they told you about Mohammed's tomb? Or Buddha's grave?"

"What do you mean, Dad?" Michael was a little puzzled. "We did learn about Buddha and Mohammed."

"Well, if you wanted to, could you visit the graves, or tombs, of those men?" asked Dad.

Michael shrugged. "I suppose so," he said. "I could visit Jesus' grave, too."

"If you did, what would you find in those graves?" asked Dad.

"I know!" cried Sandy, almost jumping from her seat. "Just like Mary and the disciples on Easter morning, you'd find nothing in Jesus' grave. At least, not a body like in those other graves."

Dad nodded. "Sandy's right, Michael," he said. "Jesus not only died to pay the price for our sins, but he rose again so that we can have eternal life. Those men you are learning about may have been wise teachers. In fact, many of them mimic the teachings of Jesus. But not one of them took our sins upon himself, died, and then came back to life in order to save us. They are still dead. If you choose to trust in any of them, you are choosing death, not life."

L.W.

HOW ABOUT YOU?

Has anyone ever told you that you should be "broad-minded" and believe there are other ways to God? The Bible says there is no other way than through Jesus Christ. He died, but he rose again. Trust only in him, and praise God for a living Savior.

MEMORIZE:

"Jesus said to him, 'I am the way, the truth, and the life. No one comes to the Father except through Me.'" *John 14:6, NKJV*

 *Jesus Is Alive*

Plenty of Time (Read Mark 13:32-37)

"Come on in, guys," invited Larry. "My folks are gone, so we can do anything we want. They won't be home until five today."

"Party hearty!" the boys yelled, charging into the house. Larry searched through the cabinets for an assortment of munchies. As the boys sat around talking and laughing and eating, Larry turned the radio to a station his friends recommended and turned up the volume. Then he propped his feet on the coffee table.

9

JANUARY

"Lawrence Louis Brown!" Dad's voice boomed over the music. Larry jumped up, trembling. His parents weren't supposed to be home yet. "What is going on here?" Dad asked after turning off the radio. "You know your friends are not allowed in this house when we're away." Dad showed Larry's friends out the door. "You also know we don't pig out between meals," continued Dad. "And what's with the music? Start explaining, Son!"

Larry felt sick. "I . . . I . . . ," he stammered. "I didn't think you'd be home until five." Dad sent Larry straight to his room without another word.

After Mom and Dad talked, they went to Larry's room. "Your mother and I have decided on your punishment for disobeying us," said Dad. Larry didn't dare ask what was going to happen. He didn't need to. His father went into full detail.

Dad looked sad as he finished. He saw Larry's Bible on the dresser, and he turned to Matthew 24:44-51. "What happened today reminds me that many people think they have plenty of time before Jesus returns," he said. "They think they can live in sin and do as they please, and then clean up their act just before Jesus comes. But Jesus will appear at an unexpected time, just like we did today." He held out Larry's Bible. "Read this," he said, "and think about it. What will you be doing when Jesus comes again?"

N.E.K.

HOW ABOUT YOU?

When Jesus returns, what do you want him to find you doing? If you live for him each day, you won't be ashamed when he comes. Ask him to help you live a godly life.

MEMORIZE:

"Therefore you also be ready, for the Son of Man is coming at an hour you do not expect."

Matthew 24:44, NKJV

 There's No Time for Sin

Four Pennies nor a Dollar (Read 1 Peter 1:18-21)

10

JANUARY

Jill and Jenny tagged along with Curt to the toy store. While Curt looked at model trains, the girls walked away and found stuffed bears. Little Jill hugged them close. "Jill wants this one," she said, holding a big, soft one. Walking to the counter where she'd seen people pay for things, she held up the bear along with four pennies. "Here's money for my bear," she said.

"I'm sorry, but that won't buy this bear," said the clerk. "Do you have any more money?" Jill shook her head.

Six-year-old Jenny spoke up. "I have a dollar. Is that enough?" she asked.

When the clerk shook her head, Jill and Jenny ran back to Curt. With tears in her eyes, Jill told him about the bear. "Please," she pleaded, "will you buy it for me?"

Curt looked thoughtful. "Well, OK," he agreed. "I was going to buy you a birthday present anyway."

Back home, Jill played with her bear all afternoon. She loved to tell how Curt bought the bear for her. "I couldn't pay for it," she repeated at the dinner table. "Jenny couldn't pay for it, either."

"I came closer than you," Jenny put in.

"But only Curt could pay for it," Jill looked adoringly at her big brother. "Curt bought my bear for me."

Mother smiled. "That makes a good object lesson," she said. "Some people do a few good things, and they think that will be enough to save them. Others might do more. But the Bible says that all have sinned and come short of the glory of God. Just as neither of you girls had enough money to buy the bear, no one is ever good enough to buy salvation."

"Jesus paid for our salvation by dying on the cross, didn't he?" asked Curt.

"Yes," agreed Mother. "Only Jesus could do that, for he is sinless. He bought our salvation with his precious blood. All we need to do is to receive the free gift." *M.R.P.*

HOW ABOUT YOU?

Do you think the good things you do will buy eternal life? No matter how good you are, it will never be enough to buy salvation. Salvation is a free gift, purchased for you by Jesus with his blood. Trust him to save you, and receive your free gift now.

MEMORIZE:

"For the wages of sin is death, but the gift of God is eternal life in Christ Jesus our Lord."

Romans 6:23, NKJV

 *Salvation Is God's Gift*

Something Stinks! (Read 2 Corinthians 6:14-18)

11
JANUARY

"Come on, Angela, try it," coaxed Carol after taking a puff from a cigarette Jane had passed to her.

Angela shook her head. "No, thanks." She knew that smoking was harmful to the body and displeasing to God, but she didn't say anything about that. Carol and Jane were popular at school, and Angela was thrilled to be considered part of their gang.

Later, Angela held her hand over her nose as she entered her grandparents' kitchen. "What's that horrible smell?" she wanted to know.

"Smell?" asked Grandpa as he seated himself at the kitchen table. "Oh, you must smell the sauerkraut we had for lunch. It has a strong odor, but we've gotten so used to it that we don't smell it anymore."

"What's sauerkraut?" asked Angela.

"*Sauerkraut* is a German word that means 'sour cabbage,'" replied Grandma.

"It smells awful!" declared Angela. "I think I need a clothes pin for my nose."

Grandpa laughed. Then he said thoughtfully, "It reminds me of sin, Angela. When we're first saved, we often are very aware of sin—it's as though we can 'smell' how horrible it is. But if we stay around it long enough, we get used to the 'smell,' and it doesn't bother us anymore."

"And another thing," added Grandma, "the smell of sauerkraut can get into our clothes, and it gets on my hands when I prepare it. Sin is like that, too. The 'stink' of sin can rub off on us if we're around it long enough."

Angela suddenly remembered that occasionally, without meaning to, she would say a swear word she heard her friends use. Could this be a sin she couldn't "smell" anymore, one that had rubbed off on her? In fact, Carol and Jane did quite a few things Angela knew were wrong. Maybe being around them was dulling her "sense of smell." Being part of their gang might not be so great after all. *E.C.O.*

HOW ABOUT YOU?

Do you have friends who are doing things you know are wrong? Maybe you find yourself doing those same things so they'll accept you. If that's the case, perhaps you should reconsider whom you should have for close friends.

MEMORIZE:

"Don't be teamed with those who do not love the Lord, for what do the people of God have in common with the people of sin?" *2 Corinthians 6:14, TLB*

 **Sin Stinks!**

The Dusty Doll (Read Romans 8:31-39)

12

JANUARY

As Kara said good-night one evening, her mother noticed that she seemed upset. "I've been kind of worried lately, Mom," Kara confided hesitantly. "After I asked Jesus to save me, I was really happy for a while. But . . . I've sinned lots of times since then—like when I got so mad at Jason tonight. I asked God to forgive me, but I'm sure he isn't happy with me. And what about the times I sin without realizing it, or when I forget to ask God to forgive me? Am I still saved?"

Mother hugged Kara. "Jesus' death paid for *all* our sins," she said. "And Jesus himself said, 'No man is able to take them'—Christians—'out of my Father's hand.' He won't disown you after you've trusted in him."

"I guess that's true," said Kara with a sigh, but she didn't look convinced.

As Mother glanced around the room, she noticed a porcelain doll on Kara's dresser. "I see you've cleaned up that doll," she said. "Tell me again where it came from."

Kara smiled. "You know, Mother," she replied. "Mrs. Knott put it out with the trash. It was covered with mud and garbage. I cleaned it up and dressed it in new clothes. It looks great now, don't you think?"

"Yes," Mother agreed. "It's beautiful—enjoy it while you can. This room gets pretty dusty this time of year, you know. Soon your doll will be covered with dust, and then I suppose you'll throw it away."

"Throw it away!" exclaimed Kara. "Are you kidding? Even if it did get dusty, it could never look any worse than it did when I found it. I'd never throw it away after all the work I did to get it cleaned up. I'll just clean it off whenever it needs it."

Mother smiled. "I thought you'd say that," she said. "Honey, God loves you much more than you love that doll. He's not going to just 'throw you out' now—not after all he's done for you." *S.K.*

HOW ABOUT YOU?

Have you accepted Jesus Christ as your Savior from sin? If so, you don't need to worry about losing your salvation. Trust God and believe his promises so that you can always know the peace of forgiveness and the joy of fellowship with him.

MEMORIZE:

"Neither height nor depth, nor anything else in all creation, will be able to separate us from the love of God that is in Christ Jesus our Lord."

Romans 8:39, NIV

 Salvation Is Forever

Clean Glasses (Read Psalm 19:7-14)

"Brad, please take the dishes out of the dishwasher and put them away," said Mother one afternoon. "And would you be sure to check the glasses? I've noticed water spots on them lately. If you hold them up to the light, you'll be able to see if they're clean or spotted."

Brad carefully checked each glass by holding it up to the light coming in the window. As Mother had mentioned, there were spotted ones. "What shall I do with these?" asked Brad.

13

JANUARY

"If there are spots, just leave them in the dishwasher, and I'll wash them over again," replied Mother.

Brad finished his work and was closing the dishwasher when Dad came into the kitchen. "Hold it, Son," said Dad. "Put the rest of those glasses away before you quit!"

Brad grinned as he pulled a spotted glass from the dishwasher. "You're sure I should put these away?" he asked as he held the glass up to the light.

Dad grinned back. "Hmmmm," he murmured as he put down his Saturday morning paper. "Son, you just made a good illustration about something."

"What's that, Dad?" asked Brad.

"If we're not sure if a glass is clean or dirty, we hold it up to the light to find out," replied Dad. "And if we aren't sure whether something we want to do is right or wrong—if it's 'clean' or 'spotted'—we should hold it up to the light of God's Word. We should see if there are principles there to help us make the right decision. If it looks good when God's truth shines on it, then we may believe it is good." *C.G.*

HOW ABOUT YOU?

Are there any activities you do that have "spots"? Anything you do that when held against the light of God's Word is shown to be wrong? You can know what is right and clean by reading your Bible.

MEMORIZE:

"How can a young man cleanse his way? By taking heed according to Your word."

Psalm 119:9, NKJV

 Check Activities with God's Word

Sammy Squirrel Christians

(Read Deuteronomy 18:9-14)

14

"You know my friend Sammy?" asked Bart one evening. "I think I'll call him 'Sammy Squirrel.' Every day his mom packs him a nice lunch, but he always wants to have something from everybody else's lunch, too."

"Huh," snorted Bart's brother, Mark. "What's that got to do with squirrels?"

"Sammy makes me think of the squirrel that stole the bird seed from our bird feeder even though he had plenty of his own," explained Bart. "Like that squirrel, Sammy isn't satisfied with what he has."

"Well, that's no reason for you to call him names," Mom scolded mildly.

Later that evening, Bart was looking through a book on witchcraft he had taken from the library. *This is wild,* he thought. *These guys do real magic! It would be fun to see it done.*

Bart closed the book quickly when Dad came into the room. "What do you have there?" asked Dad.

"Just a book," said Bart, feeling uneasy.

"The Magic in Witchcraft?" asked Dad, noticing the title. "Isn't one Sammy Squirrel enough, Son?"

"What?" asked Bart. "Sammy doesn't have anything to do with this."

"You wanted to call him 'Sammy Squirrel' because he had everything he needed right in front of his face, but he still reached out for more—and for things that don't belong to him," Dad reminded Bart. "As a Christian, you have everything you need for living. You have the Bible as your guide. You have our loving Lord Jesus to forgive sins. You have the Holy Spirit to work in your life." Dad paused, then added, "May I ask why you are reaching out for more—and for things that don't belong to you, but to the devil?"

"I just thought I'd take a look," said Bart sheepishly.

"Don't even dabble in it," said Dad sternly. "God has filled you to overflowing. You don't need anything else." *N.E.K.*

HOW ABOUT YOU?

Are you satisfied with all the wisdom and knowledge God has displayed in his Word? Or do you dabble in the things of the world? Don't be a "Sammy Squirrel Christian." Be content with the Christian life God has given you.

MEMORIZE:

"We have not received the spirit of the world but the Spirit who is from God, that we may understand what God has freely given us." *1 Corinthians 2:12, NIV*

 Be a Contented Christian

Guilty (Read Psalm 130)

15

JANUARY

Monica's heart felt like lead. *I shouldn't have done it. Oh, why did I?* As she opened the front door, she pasted on a smile. "Hi, Mom. I'm home." There was no answer. She started down the hall. "Friskie?" she called. "Here, boy." Where was Friskie? He always met Monica at the door. Then she saw it—a trail of tissue paper from the bathroom down the hall. "You did it again, you naughty boy!" scolded Monica. "Where are you, Friskie? Come out."

A white ball of fur came slinking out from under Monica's bed, tail tucked between his legs. Monica laughed. "You know you're guilty," she said, picking up the pup, "but I love you anyway, and I forgive you. Let's get this cleaned up before Mother sees it."

That night Monica tossed and turned. She kept asking herself, *Why did I do it?* She pulled the blanket over her head to hide! It seemed like Jesus was standing beside her bed, looking through the blanket, right into her heart. She shivered. It seemed . . .

"Mama! Mama!" she screamed, sitting up in bed.

The light came on. "What's wrong?" asked Mother.

Wide-eyed, Monica looked around. "I thought . . . it seemed like . . . I mean . . . Jesus is right here."

Mother smiled. "He is," she agreed. "He's always with us. But why does that frighten you? He loves you."

Monica shivered. "I . . . I . . . just . . . . Oh, Mama, I stole five dollars from Sue. It was on her desk and . . ."

Mother put her arms around Monica. "And that's why you're afraid," she said. "The presence of the Lord is frightening only when we have sin in our life. It makes us want to hide." Monica remembered Friskie hiding under the bed and nodded. "When we confess our sins, his presence comforts us," continued Mother. "The Lord Jesus loves you, honey, and he wants to forgive you."

After Monica and her mother prayed, Monica snuggled under the covers. "I'll return the money," she said. "I can sleep now. Thanks, Mom." She knew God had forgiven her, just like—no, even more than she had forgiven Friskie. Soon she was asleep. *B.W.*

HOW ABOUT YOU?

Does it comfort you or make you afraid to know that the Lord is with you? No matter what you have done, Jesus loves you. Confess your sin and ask his forgiveness. He wants to give you peace.

MEMORIZE:

"But there is forgiveness with You." *Psalm 130:4, NKJV*

 Confession Brings Peace

A Clean Environment (Read Romans 6:1-2, 11-14)

16

JANUARY

"To preserve our environment we must look for the best ways to protect it. Thank you." Sharon concluded her speech. The applause of the audience echoed in the gym, and Sharon smiled. *I'm sure to get a high grade,* she thought.

After the meeting, Sharon's family found her sitting on the stage. "Hi, Sharon," said her little sister, Carrie. "You're baby-sitting Cory and me tonight."

"Oh, Dad," moaned Sharon, "do I have to?"

Dad nodded. "You did promise," he reminded her.

Sharon sighed and slapped her papers together. "If it's not one thing, it's another," she grumbled. "Come on then." She grabbed Carrie's hand, and Cory followed them. "Everybody else has fun," mumbled Sharon, "but not me. I have to baby-sit."

At home, Sharon sat at the table, writing out an environmental petition for her school group. "Will you play a game with us?" Carrie pleaded for the third time.

"P-lee-ease?" added Cory.

"Can't you see I'm doing something?" snapped Sharon. "Play your game and quit bothering me."

The twins went to play, but soon they were back. "We're hungry, Sharon," they called in unison.

Sharon sighed loudly. "Why can't you make your own peanut butter and jelly sandwiches?" she grumbled. Cory began crying. "Oh, stop your bawling," snarled Sharon. "I'll get your stupid sandwich." When Cory did not stop immediately, Sharon slammed her hands down on the counter. "I told you to stop bawling."

Cory sniffled. "You try to make everything nice on earth," he whimpered, "but maybe Jesus doesn't think your heart is nice."

Sharon's eyes dropped to the petition. Then she looked at Carrie and Cory. She felt so guilty! She was a Christian, but she knew she wasn't acting like one. Leaning down, Sharon whispered to the twins, "I'm sorry." Silently she prayed, "Dear God, please forgive me. Help me remember that it's even more important to have a clean life than it is to have a clean environment." *D.A.L.*

HOW ABOUT YOU?

Do you care about the environment? If so, that's good—it's important. But what about the environment of your heart? Is it in the condition it should be in? That's a matter of even greater importance.

MEMORIZE:

"I, the Lord, search the heart."

Jeremiah 17:10, NKJV

 *A Clean Heart Is Important*

Ready Brakes (Read Ephesians 6:10-18)

"Are you sure you're OK?" Mother asked again. The car's brakes had failed when they came to a stop sign, and the car had kept going slowly across the road and into a pole.

"We're fine," Brian and Chris assured her. They were more interested in watching the truck tow their car away than in answering Mother.

17

JANUARY

Later that afternoon, the boys went over to play at a neighbor's home. When Mark, the neighbor boy, suggested they watch a video, Brian looked at the title. *Everyone's been talking about this movie,* he thought. *But we probably shouldn't watch it.*

Chris was uneasy about the video, too. *There's going to be language and stuff in this that Christians shouldn't watch,* he told himself. But when Mark slipped the tape into the VCR, neither of the boys said anything. Although they winced now and then at the language they heard, they were soon engrossed in the story.

At the supper table, their accident was the main topic of conversation. "I meant to have those brakes checked," said Dad regretfully, "but I put it off. That was a mistake. Car maintenance is very important." Then, just as Brian and Chris started to leave the table, Dad reached for the family Bible. "Just a minute," he said. "This accident reminds me that maintenance of our spiritual life is even more important—so starting today, we're going to take time for family devotions right after dinner. When we don't spend time in the Word, we don't maintain a close walk with the Lord, and our own 'brakes' might fail when we need to apply them."

"Our own brakes?" Chris asked, puzzled.

Dad nodded. "When our spiritual life is maintained through time spent with the Lord, we're more prepared to apply our 'spiritual brakes'—we're more likely to call on the Lord for help, or to recite a Bible verse that stops us from giving in to temptation," he explained.

"I think we understand what you mean," Brian said, nudging Chris under the table. They knew their "spiritual brakes" had failed just that afternoon. *N.E.K.*

HOW ABOUT YOU?

Do you find it hard to resist temptation? Pay close attention to God's Word during family and personal devotions. It will help you be stronger and better able to say no when you're tempted.

MEMORIZE:

"Put on the full armor of God so that you can take your stand against the devil's schemes."

Ephesians 6:11, NIV

 Maintain Your Spiritual Life

Suffering Persecution (Read 1 Peter 4:12-16)

18

JANUARY

Tom picked up his lunch tray and headed for a table of talking, laughing boys. But before he could sit down, one of the boys plopped his jacket onto the empty chair. "Sorry," he said with a sneer. "This seat is taken." Then as Tom turned to leave, he heard someone say, "We don't want that *Christian* to sit here!" The way he said "Christian" made it sound like something bad.

In math later that day, Mrs. Brown announced, "The winning team in the local math competition next week gets a trophy and goes to the state contest next month. The students who will represent our school are Amy, Rita, Bob, and Tom."

"Lucky bums," growled one of the students.

"Luck had nothing to do with it," said Mrs. Brown. "Hard work did. These students have put out the necessary effort to get ready for the competition. I know I can count on them to do their best."

Back home, Tom told Mother about being chosen for the contest. Then he told her what had happened at lunchtime. "Sometimes I wish I could be like the other kids so they wouldn't make fun of me," he confessed.

Mother frowned slightly. "Think about what Mrs. Brown said," she suggested. "The reward comes to those who can hold up even when the going gets tough. Tell me, have you always felt like studying your math?" Tom shook his head. "But you studied anyway," Mother pointed out. "You earned the privilege of entering that contest. And just as you wouldn't want to exchange math averages with boys in your class, I don't think you would really want to be like them in other ways. I know it seems hard when they reject you, but the reward for serving the Lord is much greater than the reward for studying math. Don't let them get to you. Keep doing what God wants you to do." *S.L.S.*

HOW ABOUT YOU?

Do you sometimes get the feeling that living the Christian life is too hard? Do you wish you could do what everyone else does so no one will make fun of you? God has promised that he will not allow you to be tempted more than you can bear. Ask him to give you strength to be faithful to him.

MEMORIZE:

"You can trust God to keep the temptation from becoming so strong that you can't stand up against it, for he has promised this and will do what he says."

1 Corinthians 10:13, TLB

Be Strong in Christ

Good Advice (Read Romans 13:8-10)

Kim walked home, her eyes brimming with tears. A cold ache filled her. "No one even sees me," she thought as her schoolmates ran by, laughing. That night she cried herself to sleep.

"Daddy, please, let's move back to Miami. I hate it here!" she begged the next morning.

"But, honey, we can't," her father replied. "I'm sorry you're so unhappy, but I can't quit my job."

19

JANUARY

Tears rolled down Kim's cheek. "We've been here six weeks, and I still don't have one friend—not one!"

Mother looked up. "Kim, long ago I learned a little poem. Listen," she said. "I went looking for a friend, but not one could be found; I went out to be a friend, and friends were all around."

Kim wiped her face with a napkin. "What does that mean?"

Mother explained gently. "It means that you shouldn't worry about finding a friend. Instead, look for someone who needs a friend."

Dad stood up. "The Bible gives the same advice in the book of Proverbs," he said. He squeezed her shoulder. "You've been feeling sorry for yourself, honey. It's time to think about others. Now grab your books, and I'll give you a free ride to school."

When they got to school, Kim jumped from the car. "Do what God says—be friendly today," encouraged Dad. "He knows what he's talking about."

As Dad drove away, Kim noticed a girl going up the walk. *That looks like the girl who sits across from me in homeroom,* Kim thought. *What's her name? Oh, yes—Nadine. I wonder where all her friends are. Maybe . . .*

"Nadine, wait up," Kim called. "Could I walk with you?"

Nadine looked up, and a smile spread over her face. "You sure can. I've been here for seven weeks, and you're the first person who has even noticed me."

A warm feeling filled Kim, driving out the cold lonely ache. *Dad's right,* she thought. *God does know what he's talking about.*

B.W.

HOW ABOUT YOU?

Do you feel lonely? Left out? Do you always wait for others to speak to you first? Instead of waiting for someone to be a friend to you, do what God says—start today to be a friend. You'll find friends everywhere.

MEMORIZE:

"A man who has friends must himself be friendly."

Proverbs 18:24, NKJV

 ***Be a Friend***

20/20 Vision (Read Matthew 28:16-20)

20 JANUARY

"That missionary was good today," Cheryl told her mother as they arrived home from church. "I think missionaries have such an exciting life—traveling far away and seeing strange places and different people. And they get to give the gospel to people who've never heard it before. That would be neat! Maybe I'll be a missionary some day. I hope God calls me to Japan."

Just then the phone rang, and Mother answered. After a moment, she held her hand over the mouthpiece. "Cheryl," she said, "Mrs. Fisher would like you to go with her on youth visitation next Friday. She wants to visit some girls who have just moved into our neighborhood."

"I want to go skating Friday," said Cheryl. "Anyhow, I don't know what to say to those girls. Do I have to go?"

Mother spoke into the phone, "Cheryl will call you later, Mrs. Fisher." Hanging up the phone, she turned to her daughter. "Remember what the optometrist said when you had an eye examination a week ago?" asked Mother.

Cheryl nodded. "He said I had 20/20 vision," she replied, "and that means I have perfect eyesight. At twenty feet I can see what the normal person sees from that distance."

"Right," said Mother, "and I'm glad you have 20/20 vision in your eyes. But I've just been thinking about your missionary vision. It seems to me that you're farsighted."

Cheryl beamed. "You mean because I'm interested in mission work in faraway places? That's good, isn't it?"

Mother shook her head. "Not exactly," she replied. "A person whose eyes are farsighted can't see objects up close very well. You're excited about going far away to tell people about Jesus, but you aren't interested in some girls on the next block. If you can't be a good witness here, do you suppose you'd make a good missionary far away?" *M.R.P.*

HOW ABOUT YOU?

Are you interested in someday taking the gospel to a faraway place? That's wonderful! But are you so farsighted that you don't see the people around you who need to hear about Jesus? Ask the Lord to open your eyes to see the souls you should reach here and now. Get 20/20 mission vision!

MEMORIZE:

"Do you not say, 'Four months more and then the harvest'? I tell you, open your eyes and look at the fields! They are ripe for harvest." *John 4:35, NIV*

 Witness Here and Now

Science Project (Read Romans 14:11-13; 15:1-2, 5-6)

As Mother tapped on Timothy's door, she could hear him talking. "If I didn't know better, I'd think you were talking to yourself," she said as she came into the room.

"Just chatting with my plants," Timothy said with a grin. "It's going to be interesting to see if talking to them affects their growth."

21
JANUARY

Mother nodded. "What did you learn in Sunday school today?" she asked.

Timothy frowned; then he grinned. "Well, for one thing, I learned that Pete doesn't know nuthin' when it comes to Bible stories."

Mother raised her eyebrows. "Looks like you've been doing some comparing," she said as she picked up a plant. "Are you using the same food, soil, and amounts of light with the plants you're talking to and the ones you're not talking to?" she asked.

"Of course," said Timothy. "Otherwise I won't know if the difference in their growth is because of being talked to or something else. The ones in the basement get a different amount of light, though, and I'm talking to those in the laundry room but not those in the freezer room. I have to take all that into account when I make my report."

Mother nodded. "I should think so," she said. "And you know what? I think you should think about differences when you compare the growth of kids in your class." She set the plant down. "Pete hasn't been coming to Sunday school for very long, remember?" she asked. "He's a new Christian, and he hasn't had time to learn a lot of Bible stories and what God expects of him as a Christian. Most of the kids have heard these things over and over since they were tiny. Besides, God has given some the ability to learn more quickly than others. So do you think it's fair to expect the same amount of growth in each one?" Timothy shook his head. "I don't think so, either," continued Mother, "so take differences into account. Or better yet, don't judge your friends at all. Leave that to God. He's the only one who can make fair judgments, anyway."

S.S.

HOW ABOUT YOU?

Do you compare your friends? Don't expect them all to be the same or to grow at the same rate. Remember that they all have different backgrounds and capabilities. Leave it to God to judge them, and concentrate on making your own life pleasing to him.

MEMORIZE:

"Judge not, that you be not judged." *Matthew 7:1, NKJV*

 Don't Judge Others

Science Project (continued from yesterday)

(Read Philippians 1:2-6, 9-11)

22

JANUARY

Timothy scowled when his mother asked how he enjoyed his Sunday evening youth meeting. "I learned how much more everyone else knows than me," he mumbled. "I don't know why I was laughing at Pete for not knowing anything this morning. I don't know much more. We played Bible baseball tonight, and I got out every time I was up."

"Hmmmm," murmured Mother. "Don't forget the things we talked about earlier today. [See yesterday's story.] You need to apply them when you're tempted to compare yourself to other people as well as when you're tempted to judge your friends." She looked thoughtful as she motioned toward the plants Timothy was raising for his science project. "Are you disappointed that these plants are so small?" she asked.

Timothy shrugged. "It doesn't matter," he said. "They're growing good." He picked up a notebook. "This is the plant growth chart," he explained. "I write everything down in here—how much I water them and talk to them—stuff like that. I can check here and see how they've done over a period of time."

"That's a good idea," approved Mother. She smiled at Timothy. "Maybe you should try keeping a spiritual growth chart, too," she suggested. "Keep a notebook of some of the things that happen in your life—like how you react when you're told to do something or when something makes you angry, a special thing God has taught you, your response to a lesson that challenged you—things like that. Then when you wonder how you're doing, you can check your notebook. That way you can compare yourself to yourself by looking at how you used to behave and how you do now. That would be much better than comparing yourself to others." S.S.

HOW ABOUT YOU?

Do you compare yourself to others? To how they dress? How they act? How much they know? God just wants you to be you. He made you just the way you are and promises to keep working in you. If you feel you must compare yourself to something, look at how far God has brought you. Don't look at anyone else.

MEMORIZE:

"For God is at work within you." *Philippians 2:13, TLB*

⌐━ *Don't Compare Yourself with Others*

Rekindled Fire (Read 2 Timothy 1:6-14)

Chris gazed at the fire as it became smaller and smaller. Sitting in front of the fireplace usually made him feel contented, but not tonight. His father sat next to him and asked, "What's bothering you, Chris?"

23

JANUARY

Chris felt stupid when tears came to his eyes, but he couldn't stop them. "I may have just lost my best friend. I was with some guys in the hallway at school today when John walked by. One guy made a nasty remark about John—loud enough for him to hear. Then they all laughed. John looked right at me . . . and I just stood there and laughed with them."

Dad put his arm around Chris. "I see," he said.

"I don't know why I did it . . . except that . . . these were the popular guys, and I guess I wanted them to like me," continued Chris miserably. He stared ahead at the fireplace.

Dad spoke softly. "Chris, you remind me of that fire."

"What do you mean?" asked Chris. All that was left of the fire was a dull orange glow beneath the charred logs.

Dad crouched in front of the fireplace and blew on the glowing embers. While he blew, he added a few scraps of paper and small pieces of wood. Soon the fire was roaring brightly again. "You're a Christian, Son," said Dad, "but you failed the Lord as well as your friend John. When we become weak and fail, we need God's forgiveness and help. Just as I had to rekindle that fire, you need to ask God to rekindle your spiritual fire." Dad patted Chris's shoulder. "Talk to the Lord—tell him all about what you did. Talk to John, too. An apology is in order."

Chris settled back and prayed silently while he basked in the warmth of the crackling fire. In a few minutes he would leave the warm fire and make that difficult phone call to John. But he was sure the warm feeling in his heart would remain. *A.J.S.*

HOW ABOUT YOU?

Do you need your spiritual fire "rekindled"? Ask God for strength to help you correct some specific problem or to help you continue doing what is right. Read God's Word often and ask him for the power to do what he expects of you.

 Ask God for Spiritual Strength

MEMORIZE:

"Fan into flame the gift of God, which is in you through the laying on of my hands. For God did not give us a spirit of timidity, but a spirit of power, of love and of self-discipline."

2 Timothy 1:6-7, NIV

Turn It On (Read James 1:19-27)

24

JANUARY

"What time did you put dinner in the oven, Dad?" asked Mark, coming into the living room. "I'm ready to eat. It seems like we've been waiting a long time for that frozen lasagna to be ready."

Dad looked up from his newspaper. "The package said it needs to cook for fifty-five to sixty minutes," he said. "An hour is almost up."

"But I don't even smell it cooking yet," observed Mark.

"Oh no!" Dad exclaimed, jumping up and hurrying to the kitchen. "I read the directions and put it in the oven, but I never turned it on! Looks like dinner will take another hour."

"But I'm starving!" Mark complained.

"And I'm sorry," Dad apologized. "Let's have an apple to take care of some of those hunger pangs." He and Mark each chose a shiny red apple. "This mistake reminds me of what Pastor Tom was teaching us last Sunday," added Dad. "Do you remember his message? He talked about how we so often take God's Word but don't turn it on in our life."

"Just like you put the lasagna in the oven but didn't turn it on, huh?" said Mark.

Dad nodded. "Many times in Sunday school or church—or in our own devotions—we take in the truths about how to live as Christians. We even memorize key verses, but then we forget to 'turn on' the lessons and live them out in our life. The material just sits there cold."

"Like our lasagna," said Mark.

"And when it sits there cold, we get into situations where we need to draw on certain principles, only to find that we've forgotten them," continued Dad. "Then we're left . . ."

"Hungry," finished Mark.

"And unforgiving," added Dad. "And unkind. And accusing."

Mark grinned at his father. "OK, Dad," he said, "you're forgiven, and I'll try to remember to 'turn on' the lessons I've learned."

N.E.K.

HOW ABOUT YOU?

Do you know lots of lessons from God's Word? Be sure to "turn them on" in your life so you're ready to do his will when you need to each day.

MEMORIZE:

"But be doers of the word, and not hearers only, deceiving yourselves." *James 1:22, NKJV*

 Apply Lessons from God

A Cover-Up Expert (Read Luke 12:1-3)

Kevin quietly shut the door behind him and started down the hall. "Kevin?" He jumped as Mother came up behind him. "Get ready. We're going to Aunt Betty's for Uncle Phil's birthday dinner. Dad's meeting us there."

All the way to Aunt Betty's, Kevin's conscience tormented him. *Why did you do it? You know better.* Silently, he argued back. *No one knows. Dad will never miss it. I had to pay my debt, and Dad wouldn't understand—he doesn't believe in betting.*

25

JANUARY

At Aunt Betty's, everyone remarked about her spotless house—they always told her she was a wonderful housekeeper. But after dinner, something happened.

Aunt Betty brought out the birthday cake. "We need a picture of this," she declared. "I forgot the camera. It's in the hall closet."

Kevin jumped up. "I'll get it," he offered.

Aunt Betty hesitated. "OK," she agreed, "but you better wear your hard hat." When Kevin opened the closet door, he stared in amazement. It was so cluttered he was afraid he'd start an avalanche if he touched anything.

"Can't you find it?" asked Aunt Betty, coming up behind him. She laughed at his expression. "Surprised? I'm a cover-up expert," she told him, "but you can get away with hiding things only so long. I got caught this time, didn't I?"

That night, Kevin couldn't sleep. Finally he got up and went into his parents' room. "Dad," he whispered as he sat on the edge of the bed, "I've got a confession to make." Dad flipped on the lamp as Kevin continued. "I stole five dollars from your billfold," continued Kevin. "I made a bet with Joe, and I lost. I know it's wrong to steal and to bet. I'm sorry. I'll pay you back."

"You certainly will," said Dad. He sat up and slipped an arm around his son. "What made you confess?" he asked.

"Aunt Betty's closet," Kevin replied promptly. "You can hide things by covering them up only so long."

"True," agreed Dad. "And you know what? You can never hide things from God!" *B.W.*

HOW ABOUT YOU?

Is there something in your life you're hiding? Something that needs to be confessed? Don't wait. Now is the time to "clean house." Confess the matter to God and also to any person you have wronged.

MEMORIZE:

"There is nothing concealed that will not be disclosed, or hidden that will not be made known." *Matthew 10:26, NIV*

 Confess Your Sins

Antibiotics (Read Matthew 4:1-11)

26

JANUARY

Candy took the pill Mother handed her. "My throat doesn't hurt anymore," she said. "Why do I have to keep taking this medicine?"

"Dr. Binns said to take these antibiotics for two weeks, until the bottle is empty," said Mother. "If you quit too soon, your sore throat might come back."

Later that afternoon Candy stubbed her toe. "Ouch!" she exclaimed loudly. Then, almost before she knew it, some crude, nasty words slipped out of her mouth.

"Candy!" exclaimed Mother. "I know you've been working hard not to talk like that anymore, and you've been doing well. But what happened today? Did you forget the memory verse I taught you to recite when you're tempted to say such things?"

"Ecclesiastes 10:12, 'The words of a wise man's mouth are gracious,'" murmured Candy. "I know the verse, but I don't say it much anymore," she confessed. "I used to practice it over and over in my mind, but lately I haven't needed it."

"Hmmmm," murmured Mother. "Looks like you quit taking your 'antibiotic' too soon."

"I took one of my pills just a little while ago," said Candy in surprise. "Don't you remember?"

"I meant your spiritual 'antibiotic'—your Scripture verse," explained Mother. "You see, even after your throat starts feeling better, you need the antibiotic to control the germs that remain there. In a similar way, you still need to rely on the Word of God to help you fight against your habit of using bad language. One or more doses of Scripture a day can give your heart and mind strength to fight against temptation."

Candy nodded slowly. "So even though I seem to be doing better, I still need to use God's Word to keep from having a relapse."

N.E.K.

HOW ABOUT YOU?

Do you fill your heart and mind with God's Word so you can stand against temptation? Even when things are going well, you need God's Word to help keep you from sin.

MEMORIZE:

"**Direct my footsteps according to your word; let no sin rule over me.**" *Psalm 119:133, NIV*

God's Word Fights Sin

Around and Around (Read Psalm 116:1-9)

27

JANUARY

"How come all the exits are blocked?" asked Robbie as the car circled around and around, climbing from one level to another in the nearly empty indoor parking lot.

"Yeah!" murmured Anna. "I don't like this place—it's spooky. It makes me nervous." It was getting dark outside, and Baby Sally was beginning to whimper, too.

"Well, there's no need to be nervous," Dad assured Anna, "but I can't imagine why they have those exits blocked. This is ridiculous. I'm heading back—we'll go out at the entrance."

When they reached the entrance, the attendant wasn't on duty, and Dad drove right on out. "Well," said Robbie, "that was easy enough. We just had to go back to where we started."

"Right. Going back to the beginning is often a good idea," said Dad thoughtfully. "You know, sometimes we get so involved in our problems that we feel as if we're going in circles. We may even become nervous and afraid. Just as the parking lot exits were blocked, we often find that our efforts to solve our problems are 'blocked'—nothing seems to work. We need to stop our efforts and go back to the beginning."

"But how can we do that?" asked Robbie.

"Well," said Dad, "as Christians, Jesus is our beginning—the doorway into eternal life. Isaiah 30:15 (*NKJV*) says, 'In returning and rest you shall be saved.' We need to turn to Christ and ask for wisdom and comfort when we're feeling confused and don't know what to do. He's always ready to help us." *C.B.*

HOW ABOUT YOU?

Are things at school going badly for you? Is something at home upsetting you? Do you feel lost, afraid, or confused? Remember God's goodness to you in the past. Even when it seems that everything you tried has failed, you can turn back to Jesus. He promised to comfort and lead his children.

MEMORIZE:

"Return to your rest, O my soul, for the Lord has dealt bountifully with you."

Psalm 116:7, NKJV

 Return to Jesus

Bless Everyone (Read Nehemiah 1:4-11)

28

JANUARY

"God bless everyone. Amen," Carla prayed. She opened her eyes and saw a slight frown on her mother's face.

"What do you mean by 'God bless everyone'"? asked Mother. "Exactly who is everyone?"

"Well," said Carla, "I mean Grandma, Scott, my friends, my Sunday school teacher, the missionaries—everyone."

"What do you want God to do for them?" Mother asked.

"Bless them," Carla said. "You know—Grandma needs help with her eyes, and Scott's having trouble sleeping. Those kinds of things."

"Then why not tell those things to God?" asked Mother.

Carla shrugged. "I don't know," she said. "I guess it's easier to say, 'Bless everyone.' God knows what I mean."

That afternoon Mother and Carla went shopping. "Would you please show my daughter something to wear?" Mother asked a clerk.

"A coat?" asked the clerk. "Jeans? Tops?"

"Just something to wear," Mother answered.

"I need a red sweater," Carla said quickly, "and I need a pair of jeans." She told the clerk what size she needed, and soon she was busy in the fitting room.

"Why did you do that?" Carla asked as she tried on the clothes. "That was so embarrassing! Why didn't you say what I needed?"

"It was so much quicker and easier not to go into detail," Mother answered. Carla looked at her suspiciously. "I thought you knew that," added Mother. Carla still looked puzzled, so Mother explained. "I'm thinking of your quick 'God-bless-everyone' prayers," she said, handing Carla another sweater to try on. "I wanted you to see how important complete communication is. Take your time when you talk to God, being specific about who you're praying for as well as listing their needs. That will also help you know when the specific prayers are answered." *N.E.K.*

HOW ABOUT YOU?

When you pray, are you specific with God, or do you hurry through your prayers? Take time to communicate. It's true that God knows what you need before you ask, but he wants you to talk with him, telling him all about your needs as well as your blessings.

MEMORIZE:

"Pray about everything; tell God your needs, and don't forget to thank him for his answers." *Philippians 4:6, TLB*

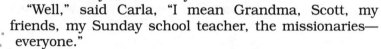

Pray with Specific Requests

The Puppet (Read Ephesians 2:1-7)

29

JANUARY

Jeffrey was so excited he could hardly open his birthday gift. He was pretty sure it was a puppet—something he'd been wanting ever since he'd seen an evangelist perform with one at church. He tore off the wrappings and opened the box. Sure enough, there was a puppet inside! His little sister, Debbie, looked on with wide-eyed wonder. "A doll?" she asked. "You're going to play with dolls?"

"No way," said Jeffrey. "This is a puppet, like the one the preacher had at church. Remember?"

"His puppet was alive," said Debbie. "It could move and talk, but yours just lies there. I still think it's a doll."

"Just wait," replied Jeffrey. "Mine will come to life, too. I'm going to learn to be a ventriloquist, like that preacher. I'm going to name my puppet Andy."

After Jeffrey had practiced for several weeks, Debbie declared, "Andy is alive now, just like the preacher's puppet." Then Jeffrey knew he was truly becoming a good ventriloquist.

One morning at family devotions, Dad turned to the second chapter of Ephesians (see today's Scripture). "And you He made alive, who were dead in trespasses and sins," read Dad. He looked up. "Let me explain what this means. For example, Jeffrey's puppet, Andy, is entirely limp and lifeless, except when Jeffrey slips his hand inside him and operates the controls and speaks for him." Dad lifted the Bible. "God tells us that as sinners we're spiritually dead. Just as Andy needs Jeffrey to bring him to life, sinners need Jesus as personal Savior to give them spiritual life."

M.R.P.

HOW ABOUT YOU?

Have you been trying to live the Christian life but finding you can't do it? If you've never accepted Christ as Savior, you're dead in sins. Trust Jesus to save you, and you'll begin to live.

MEMORIZE:

"And you He made alive, who were dead in trespasses and sins." *Ephesians 2:1, NKJV*

 Be Made Alive through Christ

Alicia Finds a Way (Read Proverbs 4:20-27)

30

JANUARY

As Alicia browsed in Mrs. Elliott's craft shop, she spotted a cross-stitch sampler kit that pictured a teddy bear holding two balloons. Stitched below the teddy bear was a baby's name and birth date. *That sampler would be a nice gift for Aunt Melissa's new baby,* thought Alicia, *and it looks quite easy, too.* She looked to see Mrs. Elliott beside her.

"Hello, Alicia," Mrs. Elliot said brightly. "I see you found something you like."

"Yes," replied Alicia. "This sampler would be a great gift for my aunt's new baby."

"Well," said Mrs. Elliot, "the kit contains everything you'll need—fabric, floss, needles, and a work chart. All you need to provide are the skills and patience."

"The patience might be the problem," said Alicia with a sigh. "I never seem to finish a project."

Mrs. Elliott smiled. "Alicia," she said, "Proverbs 4:26 says, 'Ponder the path of your feet, and let all your ways be established.' I memorized that verse long ago, and I still quote it often. It reminds me that I need to plan carefully what I'm going to do, and then I find that it generally turns out right. I think that would be a good verse for you to remember, too."

Alicia thought about it. A plan—that was just what she needed to finish the sampler! She decided to buy the kit. As she walked home she asked the Lord to help her make a plan and carry it out.

The next day Alicia was thumbing through an old magazine and came across a picture of a smiling baby. Suddenly she had an idea. Quickly, she cut out the picture and taped it to the mirror above her dresser. Now every time she looked at her mirror, she would see the picture of the smiling baby. This would be a reminder to her to work on the sampler instead of wasting time.

It worked for Alicia. "I didn't give up, Lord," Alicia prayed when the sampler was finished. "I made a plan and carried it out. Thank you for helping me find the way." *D.R.K.*

HOW ABOUT YOU?

Do you have a problem finishing projects? Plan carefully and ask God to help you. You'll be surprised at how much you can get done.

MEMORIZE:

"Ponder the path of your feet, and let all your ways be established." *Proverbs 4:26, NKJV*

 Work Hard and Be Patient

The J-Bar (Read Psalm 25:4-10)

31
JANUARY

Dana and Jim were excited about their ski trip. "That rig over there that looks like a bunch of *J*'s going up the hill is called the J-bar," said Dad when they got to the slopes. They skied over to it. "It's not a chair—you don't sit on it," added Dad. "Just let it guide you up the hill." He helped Dana get in position. She grabbed the bar and headed up the hill. Next, Dad got Jim on track, and then he started up the slope.

Shortly before they reached the top of the hill, Dana plopped into the snow. The J-bar groaned to a stop, and Dad came to rescue Dana as quickly as possible. "What happened?" he asked, as he helped his daughter up.

"I didn't know how long it would take to get off," she said. "I moved too soon."

"Quite a bit too soon," agreed Dad. "Just wait, Dana. You'll know when to get off—it'll be easy."

The J-bar began to climb again, but soon it had another stop. This time it was Jim! Dad helped Jim out of the soft snow while the other skiers grumbled.

"You're too anxious—just be patient, Jim. You'll see where to let go," Dad repeated. When they reached the top of the hill, Dana and Jim were glad to find how easy it was to get off.

After skiing a while, they enjoyed a snack in the lodge. "Were you mad at us, Dad?" asked Dana.

Dad chuckled. "No, kids," he said. "Actually, the whole experience reminded me of myself."

"Did you jump off too soon, too?" asked Jim.

Dad shook his head. "No, but I've often jumped into other things before the time was right," he explained. "It's not always easy to wait for the plans the Lord has for us. We can't always see the 'top of the hill,' but if we wait patiently for the Lord to guide us, we'll make the right move at the right time." *D.E.M.*

HOW ABOUT YOU?

Are you wondering what the future holds for you? Do you want God's guidance? Read your Bible every day and pray often. God knows what tomorrow will bring and sees what you cannot see. Ask him to guide you. Hang on to his promises and trust him. Don't go off on your own.

MEMORIZE:

"Guide me in your truth and teach me, for you are God my Savior, and my hope is in you all day long." *Psalm 25:5, NIV*

 God Gives Guidance

Pray and Pray (Read Luke 11:5-13)

1

FEBRUARY

"That was Arnie again," Bill complained as he hung up the phone. "I wish he'd quit calling to ask if I'll come help him with his model airplane. I'm not interested! I don't like model planes."

The following day Arnie called again—and the day after that, and the day after that. Finally Bill agreed to help. "If nothing else, we'll get the plane done so Arnie won't keep after me anymore," Bill told his mother. Mom nodded, and Bill headed out the door.

"Well, persistence scored again," observed Mother when Bill returned home. "Just like the man in the Bible."

Bill frowned. "What are you talking about?" he asked.

Mother laughed. "Jesus told about a man who helped his friend because he was so persistent," she explained. "That reminds me of Arnie. He kept calling and calling until you finally agreed to help him." She paused and looked at her son. "Christians shouldn't give up when they pray about things, either," she told him. "We should keep asking—keep praying in God's will, and he'll answer our persistent prayers of faith."

"I gave in even though I didn't really want to," said Bill thoughtfully. "What if I'd keep begging for something God doesn't want? Would he give in, like I gave in to Arnie?"

"No," replied Mother, "but if you're persistent in prayer, God will answer by showing you a better way."

Just then the phone rang. It was Arnie again. "It was fun making the airplane today," said Arnie. Bill cringed—he was afraid Arnie might have another model ready to build. "I just wanted to say thanks for your help, Bill," added Arnie.

As Bill hung up the receiver, he felt good. *It was nice of Arnie to call and say thanks,* he thought. Then he thought of one more thing—*it's important to say thanks when God answers, too.*

N.E.K.

HOW ABOUT YOU?

Do you pray and pray and pray? Or do you give up when you don't get instant answers? Be persistent. God will answer in his special time and perfect way when you remain faithful in your prayers. And then be sure to tell him thank you.

MEMORIZE:

"Ask, and it will be given to you; seek, and you will find; knock, and it will be opened to you." *Luke 11:9, NKJV*

 **Be Persistent in Prayer**

Mrs. McGinn's New Rule

(Read Exodus 20:3-17; James 2:10)

"Mrs. McGinn posted a new list of class rules today," Greg complained to his parents. "She says she's tired of everyone acting up. But these rules are impossible. And she's really coming down hard on us if we break a rule."

"Well, then you better be sure to know the rules and follow them," replied Dad.

2
FEBRUARY

The following day at school, Greg's pencil point broke. He glanced at Mrs. McGinn. She wasn't looking his way, so he tapped his friend Brad on the shoulder. "Do you have an extra pencil?" Greg whispered.

"Greg Harris," thundered Mrs. McGinn, "You shall not whisper in class! You broke a rule, and you'll have to take the punishment. You'll stay after school for three days, starting tomorrow." Greg tried in vain to explain.

When Greg's parents heard about it, Mother shook her head. "That's too bad," she said sympathetically, "but you did know the rule, so you really can't complain."

Dad took out his Bible. "Tonight let's read some of the rules God gave," he said. Turning to Exodus 20, he read the laws found there. "No one could ever keep these rules," said Dad. "And God also told what punishments were to be given for disobeying his rules."

"Were they as bad as Mrs. McGinn's?" Greg asked.

"Sometimes the punishment was death," replied Mom. "Sin is a terrible offense to God. And the ultimate judgment for sin is eternal death, which is punishment in hell forever."

"But Jesus paid the penalty for our sin," added Dad. "We now may experience God's grace rather than the punishment we deserve. We need to simply accept what Jesus did for us."

Mother nodded. "Although God does expect his children to do their best to obey him, we don't need to fear eternal punishment. Jesus took the punishment for us."

"I wish someone would take my punishment from Mrs. McGinn, too," added Greg with a grin. *N.E.K.*

HOW ABOUT YOU?

Are you aware that you have broken God's rules? You deserve the punishment that follows disobedience, but Jesus took that punishment on himself. The "rule" now is that you must accept what he has done for you. Have you done that?

MEMORIZE:

"Therefore, there is now no condemnation for those who are in Christ Jesus."

Romans 8:1, NIV

 Jesus Took Your Punishment

Junk Food (Read Psalm 119:97-104)

3

FEBRUARY

"Uh-oh, I've gotta go, Brad!" exclaimed Jerry. "It's dinner-time. I was having so much fun that I didn't watch the clock. Thanks for the snacks. Bye." Jerry dashed out the door.

At the dinner table, Jerry ate almost nothing. "I'm just not hungry—I had potato chips, cookies, and pop at Brad's house," he explained.

"Jerry Allen Byron! You know you're not supposed to eat near dinnertime," scolded Mother. "Actually, we don't want you to eat many snacks of that sort at any time. That's junk food—mostly empty calories that do almost nothing to help you grow a strong body. Eating too much junk food dulls your appetite for the good food you need."

Dad frowned slightly. "I'm afraid you're getting too much junk food in another area, too," he said. "So often lately we've had to get after you for spending too much time on things like TV shows and video games and comic books. They're 'spiritual junk food.' They don't help you grow as a Christian."

"I agree," said Mother. "We do want you to have a strong, healthy body, but we're even more concerned that you grow as a Christian."

"But I only look at comic books you approve of," protested Jerry, "and there's nothing wrong with my video game, is there?"

"No," agreed Dad, "unless it dulls your desire for the things of God or takes time you should use for other things. You know, there are many books, cassettes, and radio or TV programs that have a Christian message—many are meant especially for children. They're interesting and fun, and they'll help your Christian growth. How about spending more time with them, OK?"

Slowly Jerry nodded. "OK," he agreed. *M.R.P.*

HOW ABOUT YOU?

Have you ever compared the amount of time you spend on having fun to the time you give to your spiritual growth? It's right for you to have fun and play games, but don't neglect the things that build your Christian character and make you more like Christ.

MEMORIZE:

"As newborn babes, desire the pure milk of the word, that you may grow thereby."

1 Peter 2:2, NKJV

 *Desire Spiritual Food*

Best Friend (Read John 13:34-35; 14:2-3)

4

"Hell is a terrible place, Daddy," seven-year-old Kathryn announced one day. "It's not a place I'd like to go to."

"That's right, honey," agreed her father, who was a pastor. "That's what the Bible tells us."

"That's what I told Jackie yesterday, and she said her mother doesn't believe there are any such places as heaven and hell," said Kathryn. "She doesn't even think God is real, Daddy." Kathryn looked concerned.

"And what do you think?" asked Daddy.

"I think God is real," said Kathryn.

"Because I say so, and because I tell all the people who come to church to believe in God?" asked Daddy.

"Yes," said Kathryn, "but I talk to him, too, and he answers my prayers." Her father smiled. "Jackie says her mother thinks prayer is silly," added Kathryn. Then she had a terrible thought. "Oh, Daddy, Jackie won't go to hell, will she?" she exclaimed. "She's my best friend!"

"I'm glad God gave Jackie a good friend like you," her father answered, giving Kathryn a big hug. "She needs to know God loves her and that he sent his Son Jesus to die for her sins."

"I told her," Kathryn said. "I think Jackie wants to believe me, but she wants to believe her mother, too."

"You said that you talk to God and that he answers your prayers," said Daddy, "so let's talk to God about Jackie and her mother. Remember, God loves Jackie even more than you do. He'll help you show her his love, and he's the only One who can change her heart—and her mother's!" *P.Y.*

HOW ABOUT YOU?

Do you have friends who don't know Jesus? You can show them God's love by being kind, and you can tell them about Jesus. But if you really love them, you will also pray for them, because only God can change their hearts.

MEMORIZE:

"Greater love has no one than this, that he lay down his life for his friends." *John 15:13, NIV*

 Pray for Your Friends

Tight Braces (Read 2 Corinthians 7:4-11)

5
FEBRUARY

"Oooh! Oww! That hurts!" moaned Janie, rubbing her mouth. "Why do my braces have to hurt so much?" She and her mother were driving home from the orthodontist's office.

"I'm sorry, honey," said Mother. "You know it always hurts for a while when you have the braces tightened. If they weren't tight enough to cause a little discomfort, they wouldn't be tight enough to relocate your crooked teeth. It will feel better soon, and just think of how nice your teeth will look after they're straight."

"Yeah, I know," grumbled Janie, "but they sure do hurt now." She looked up at the sound of a horn, and she and her mother both waved as they saw their pastor go around a corner.

"Pastor Martin is sort of like your orthodontist, Dr. Peters," murmured Mother.

Janie frowned. "He is?"

Mother nodded. "Pastor Martin preaches right out of the Bible, you know, and he often speaks about our sinfulness and our need for obedience to God's commandments," she said. "That makes us feel uncomfortable sometimes, doesn't it?"

"Yeah, I guess so," admitted Janie slowly.

"We enjoy hearing about God's greatness and his love for us, but we also need to think about his commandments—even if they are uncomfortable at first," continued Mother. "Now do you see how Pastor Martin is like your orthodontist?"

"I get it." Janie smiled. "It's kind of like Pastor Martin puts tight braces on us, too, isn't it?"

"That's right," agreed Mother. "The braces of God's commandments."

"Well, I'm glad we go to a good church," said Janie, "and I'm also glad I can have braces on my teeth. Pastor Martin and Dr. Peters both 'hurt' me sometimes, but I know the results will be worth it!" *S.K.*

HOW ABOUT YOU?

Do you think life should always be fun? Do you complain about the pastor's sermons or even your parents' instructions? Learning and growing is not always enjoyable, but it is important. Don't rebel against God. Be willing to let him correct you. The results will be worth it!

MEMORIZE:

"God sometimes uses sorrow in our lives to help us turn away from sin and seek eternal life." *2 Corinthians 7:10, TLB*

 *Accept God's Correction*

The Broken Doll (Read Exodus 4:11; Psalm 139:13-18)

"Hi, Mom!" called Brenda as she came in from school.

"Hi, honey," replied Mother. "Sara called and wanted to know if you would come over and play later."

"I don't have time to play with Sara today," said Brenda. "I told Margie I'd ask if I could have her come over to play. Can I?"

6

FEBRUARY

Mother ignored Brenda's question. "You never seem to have time to play with Sara anymore," she said. "She really misses playing with you. Sara doesn't have many friends."

"You know how it is, Mom," pleaded Brenda. "Sara can't really do anything but play baby games. I'm too old for that kind of stuff."

Mother frowned. "You never minded playing with Sara before. In fact, you always had a good time together."

"I know," admitted Brenda. She hesitated before adding, "But she's handicapped. My friends at school just wouldn't understand if they knew I played with her." She picked up an apple. "Do you know where my doll Alicia is?" Brenda wanted to change the subject. "Margie and I want to play with our dolls today. Margie can come over, can't she?"

"Why do you want to play with that doll?" asked Mother. "She's broken. What will Margie say if she sees you playing with a broken doll?"

"I don't care what she says. Alicia is my favorite doll," declared Brenda. "Besides, she's not broken so bad I can't play with her."

"I see," said Mother. "It's all right to use some *thing*, even if it's broken. But if a person is 'broken,' we just throw her away, right?"

Brenda blushed. "I . . . I never thought about it that way before," she said slowly. After a moment, she added, "I do like Sara, and I bet Margie would, too. Would it be all right if I asked both Margie and Sara to come over?"

Mother smiled. "I think that would be a good idea." *S.A.H.*

HOW ABOUT YOU?

Do you include people even if they look different or are disabled in some way? God created every person, and he loves each one. We don't understand why he made some one way and some another, but they're all created in his image, and they're all special to him. Treat each one as somebody worthwhile.

MEMORIZE:

"So God created man in His own image; in the image of God . . . He created them."

Genesis 1:27, NKJV

⚷ _All Are Special and Worthwhile_

A Real Offering (Read 2 Samuel 24:18-25)

7

FEBRUARY

"Do you have your offerings to put in the collection plate?" Mother asked Joanne and Betsy.

Joanne nodded, but Betsy shook her head. "I spent all my allowance," she confessed. "Will you give me some money for the offering, Mom?" Mother frowned, but she reached into her wallet, took out some quarters, and handed them to Betsy.

That afternoon, Betsy had a suggestion for her mother. "If you can't think of anything to get me for my birthday, I have some ideas," she said.

"I've been thinking about that," replied Mother, "and I've decided to see if Joanne has any extra socks in her drawer that I can give you." She smiled brightly at Betsy. "Or maybe she has something else she wouldn't mind giving up."

"Mom!" said Betsy. "I'm serious."

"What's wrong with that idea?" Mother asked, pretending to be surprised.

"It's . . . it's leftovers," said Betsy. "Besides, it wouldn't really be from you if you gave me something that belonged to Joanne." Betsy frowned, and then she added, "It seems like a thoughtless present."

"You're right," agreed Mother. "It wouldn't truly be giving if I wrapped something that didn't belong to me in the first place— something I didn't put any thought, effort, or money into, now would it?" Betsy shook her head. Mom continued, "This morning at church you were satisfied to offer God a gift that wasn't really from you," Mother reminded her.

"But you always used to give us money for church," argued Betsy.

"When you were too young to have your own money I gave you some so you'd get in the habit of giving to God," Mother said. "Now that you have a little of your own cash, it's up to you to willingly give some of that to the Lord. Then you'll be giving a real offering instead of simply dropping some of my money in the plate."

N.E.K.

HOW ABOUT YOU?

Do you give back to the Lord some of the money you receive? When you give, give from your heart and from your blessings rather than borrowing from your parents.

MEMORIZE:

"Each man should give what he has decided in his heart to give, not reluctantly or under compulsion, for God loves a cheerful giver." *2 Corinthians 9:7, NIV*

 **Give to God**

The Accident (Read Romans 14:7-13)

Kim lay in the dark thinking about Uncle Dale. He was in the hospital, possibly dying. "Judy," Kim whispered, "are you asleep?"

"No," came the answer from the other bed. "I wish Mom and Dad would get home from the hospital."

"Dad said the driver of the other car was drunk." Kim's voice broke. She sobbed softly. "How dare that man drink and drive! Now Uncle Dale might be dying, and the other man is walking around perfectly OK."

8

FEBRUARY

When their parents finally arrived home, the girls were still awake. Dad came and knelt between their beds. "First," he said, "I want you to know that Uncle Dale is doing a little better. And I met the driver of the other car tonight. He's very sorry and upset."

"He should be! That man should be put in jail—forever!" stormed Judy.

"He may go to jail." Dad took Judy's hand in his. "He said he's a Christian—"

"I don't believe it!" interrupted Kim.

"He said his friends talked him into drinking," Dad explained. "He could have chosen not to, but he didn't. Now he's very sorry, but he can't take back what happened tonight. He knows he deserves punishment."

"But no Christian would do what he did!" protested Kim.

"Christians do sin," Dad reminded her. "Remember last year when you stole candy from the corner store?"

"Yes," admitted Kim, "but that's not the same! I didn't hurt anybody!"

"Why didn't your friend Sally come to Sunday school with us for a long time?" asked Dad.

Kim didn't want to answer. "She said I was no different from her, since I stole that candy," she said finally. She sighed. "No matter what our sin is, it affects others, doesn't it, Dad?"

"It surely does," Dad replied. "Always remember that." *A.L.*

HOW ABOUT YOU?

Do you think your sin isn't hurting anyone? Every sin you commit influences others. Alcohol, drugs, and robbery have ruined whole families. But things like white lies, cheating, and unfriendliness have caused hurts, too. One sin could hurt your testimony and make it difficult for someone to come to Jesus.

MEMORIZE:

"We are not our own bosses to live or die as we ourselves might choose." *Romans 14:7, TLB*

 Sin Influences Others

The Accident (continued from yesterday) (Read Colossians 3:12-15)

9
FEBRUARY

Kim and Judy were visiting Uncle Dale in the hospital. As they were playing a board game the girls had brought along, a man entered the room. "Hi, Joe!" said Uncle Dale cheerfully.

"Hello," Joe replied.

"Kim, Judy, meet Joe Turner." Uncle Dale introduced his nieces. "Joe comes to see me every day, and we have a Bible study," he explained to the girls.

"Don't let me interrupt you," said Joe. "I have some errands to run. I'll come back in a little while."

"That will be fine." Uncle Dale smiled and added, "Don't forget."

"No chance," replied Joe as he left.

The girls were silent for a while. "Joe is the man who caused your accident, isn't he?" said Kim at last. "Why are you friends with him? It's his fault you can't walk."

"I was angry right after the accident," Uncle Dale admitted. "Then one day I read Colossians 3:13. Judy, will you find that in my Bible?"

Judy quickly found the verse in Uncle Dale's Bible and began reading. "Be gentle and ready to forgive; never hold grudges. Remember, the Lord forgave you, so you must forgive others."

"Shortly after I finished my devotions that day," continued Uncle Dale, "Joe came into my room. I sure had a grudge against him! But he asked me to forgive him." Uncle Dale cleared his throat. "God used the accident to bring both Joe and myself closer to him," he added quietly.

Kim had tears in her eyes. "I just don't think I can forgive Joe," she said. "Is there something the matter with me, Uncle Dale?"

"Nothing God can't cure," Uncle Dale assured her. "It's just that you love me, so you don't like to see me hurt. That's natural. But listen—why don't you girls stay for our Bible study today? Then you can get to know Joe better. It's easier to forgive someone when he's your friend." *A.L.*

HOW ABOUT YOU?

Has someone hurt you so badly that you can't forgive him? Be nice to him even when he isn't nice to you. Get to know him better—you may even become friends. Above all, remember how much God has forgiven you; then it may not be so hard to forgive someone else.

MEMORIZE:

"**Be gentle and ready to forgive; never hold grudges. Remember, the Lord forgave you, so you must forgive others.**"

Colossians 3:13, TLB

 **Forgive As Christ Does**

I Said That? (Read 1 Peter 3:8-12)

10

FEBRUARY

"Listen to this, Mom!" Ruthie exclaimed as she came in from school. "Warren, Millie, and I taped a radio script for our English project. It has a Christian message; we wanted to make a testimony to all the unsaved kids in our class."

Ruthie played the tape while Mother finished preparing dinner. As the tape ended, Ruthie glanced down the hall. "What are you doing in my room?" she screamed at her brother, Pete. As Ruthie raced toward her room, Mother quickly flipped the tape over and set it to record. "You hog!" Ruthie yelled. There was a *thump* as she hit her brother, then pounding footsteps as he chased her back into the kitchen. "You look like a pig, and you act and smell like one, too. Oink, oink," continued Ruthie.

"Oh! Poor baby has to name call," Pete sang out. He looked at Mother, who usually would have stopped the fighting by now.

"I can't stand you!" Ruthie said in disgust. "You belong in a barn."

The arguing continued for a few more minutes until Dad came in and firmly said, "Enough!" While the children washed for dinner, Mother rewound the tape.

"Can I play my tape for part of our devotions?" Ruthie asked when the table was cleared. "It has a Christian message."

"Good. I'd like to hear that," said Dad.

Ruthie pushed the play button. "You hog! . . . You look like a pig. . . ."

Ruthie quickly pressed stop. "My tape!" she gasped.

"Your project is on the other side," Mother assured her, "but let's hear the rest of this."

"But, Mom," Ruthie whined. She could see that Mother wasn't going to change her mind. "Dad?" she pleaded. At her parents' insistence, she again played the cassette. Soon she pressed stop, very embarrassed. "I said *that?*" All eyes were on her. "I'm sorry."

"Your rehearsed tape had a good Christian message," observed Mother, "but what if we could play your unrehearsed words and thoughts during the day? How much would glorify God?" *N.E.K.*

HOW ABOUT YOU?

Would you be more careful if you had to hear yourself over again at the end of the day? Ask God to help you say words that glorify him.

MEMORIZE:

"Whoever would love life and see good days must keep his tongue from evil and his lips from deceitful speech."

1 Peter 3:10, NIV

 Watch Your Words

Redeeming the Time (Read Ephesians 5:14-17)

11

FEBRUARY

At the first meeting of his church youth group, Jimmy was given a quiet-time diary. At first he was very faithful in reading his Bible and writing responses to the questions. One day, however, Jimmy's father bought a video game for the family. Jimmy loved it. He never seemed to grow weary of rescuing princesses or shooting down enemy planes. He often had to be told to turn the game off and do his homework or finish his chores.

One day as Jimmy's father was walking past his son's room he noticed the diary on the dresser. He stopped, "Mind if I look at this, Son?" he asked.

Jimmy shrugged. "Go ahead," he said on his way out.

As Dad thumbed through the book he noticed that no questions had been answered since the day he had bought the video game. Still holding the diary, Dad went to the family room, where Jimmy was about to rescue the princess. Receiving no reply when he spoke to Jimmy, Dad went over and turned off the monitor.

Jimmy was shocked. "Son, I'm sorry I ever bought that game," said Dad as Jimmy was about to object. "I can see it has had a bad effect on you. We're going to put it away for a while."

"Aw, Dad," protested Jimmy, "there's nothing wrong with this. What's it hurting?"

Dad looked very solemn. "There's nothing wrong with the game," he agreed. "The problem is with you. You're obsessed with it, and that's wrong." Jimmy was about to argue when he noticed the quiet-time diary in his father's hand. "A little recreation is good," continued Dad, "but something good can become bad when it takes the place of what is best."

Jimmy took the diary from his father's hand and mumbled something about trying to do better. A few minutes later, he sat on his bed staring down at the diary. The memory verse for the day was Ephesians 5:16, "Redeeming the time, because the days are evil." Reading the verse over again, he knew God was speaking to him. *D.C.C.*

HOW ABOUT YOU

Does God have first place in your time schedule? Decide right now that you will set aside a time to read the Bible and pray each day. Then do it. If you fail, ask God's forgiveness and start over, but never let anything take his place.

MEMORIZE:

"Redeeming the time, because the days are evil."

Ephesians 5:16, NKJV

 Give Your Time to Jesus

Captivity (Read Proverbs 23:29-35)

Chris sat on the stool by the workbench, watching his father build a shelf. "Dad, why don't you drink beer?" asked Chris. "A lot of the kids—even some from church—say it's OK to have one drink."

"Why get started?" asked Dad. "It's so easy to become captive to sin."

12

FEBRUARY

"What do you mean?" Chris wanted to know.

"When we—*Ouch!*" Blood spurted from Dad's finger. "That saw blade slipped! Ouch!" he said again, quickly wiping his finger with a cloth. "I guess we'd better make a trip to the emergency room. I think I'm going to need stitches and a tetanus shot."

Twenty minutes later, Chris sat in the lounge at the hospital waiting for his dad. As he waited, two men walked in side by side. Chris noticed that the first man wore a uniform with "Daley Correctional Center" written on it. *He must be a prisoner, and that other man must be a guard,* Chris thought. When the prisoner needed to go to the desk to answer some questions, the guard went with him.

"I can't imagine someone following me everywhere I go!" Chris told his dad as they drove home later.

Dad looked thoughtful. "Remember what I said about becoming captive to sin?" he asked. "That prisoner is a picture of what I meant. He was free, but because he made a bad choice and broke the law, he is now a prisoner, a captive. In Christ, we are free, but when we choose to mess around with bad things, we may become captive, too. We say we'll take just one drink or listen to just one dirty joke, but so often we find ourselves being captivated by those things, and soon we're doing them over and over." Chris listened thoughtfully. "We have the choice of staying out of captivity," added Dad. "I want to make the right choices and rejoice in the freedom I have in Christ." *L.W.*

HOW ABOUT YOU?

Do you sometimes "mess around" with sin, thinking you'll do something just once? It's hard to take only one drink, try drugs just once, or listen to only one dirty joke. These things can quickly become habits. If you're a Christian, you are free in Christ! Don't become a captive of sin!

MEMORIZE:

"But I see another law in my members, warring against the law of my mind, and bringing me into captivity to the law of sin which is in my members."

Romans 7:23, NKJV

 Live Free in Christ

Guilt by Association (Read Philippians 2:13-16)

13

FEBRUARY

"I didn't do anything wrong!" Sara yelled at Lisa as she slammed her lunch tray down on the table. Lisa's expression indicated that she wasn't sure she believed what Sara was saying. "I didn't!" Sara cried. Several students at surrounding tables turned to see what the shouting was about.

Things settled back to normal as Sara and Lisa began to devour their slices of pepperoni pizza. After a few moments, Lisa leaned toward Sara and spoke quietly. "I'm not the only one who knows you were at Tina's last night. And everyone knows about the drinking and stuff that goes on at Tina's parties."

"Just because I was there doesn't mean I was drinking," retorted Sara.

"Remember when we were in the fourth grade and some money was stolen from Mrs. Smith's desk?" asked Lisa. Sara nodded. "Becky and Clara both got into a lot of trouble," continued Lisa. "Clara was the one who took the money. But Becky had gone in at lunchtime to get something, and someone saw them go into the room together."

"Yeah, and it was a long time before anyone trusted Clara or Becky again," replied Sara.

"You believed Becky was guilty at first, too," said Lisa. "What's so different about that and about people thinking you do the bad things Tina and her gang do if you hang around with them?" She looked solemnly at her friend. "They'll believe it whether it's true or not."

Sara stopped eating. Suddenly the pizza didn't taste so good any more. "Maybe you're right," she admitted. "Well, I can't change where I was last night," she added. "But you can bet I won't be going to any more of Tina's parties. *S.L.S.*

HOW ABOUT YOU?

Do you go to places a Christian should not go? Do you think it's OK to spend time with people who drink, smoke, or swear? Even if you don't do what they do, people may think you're guilty, too.

MEMORIZE:

"You are to live clean, innocent lives as children of God in a dark world full of people who are crooked and stubborn. Shine out among them like beacon lights." *Philippians 2:15, TLB*

Avoid the Appearance of Evil

Saying Good-Bye (Read John 14:1-6, 16-17)

14

FEBRUARY

Phil stood watching the big plane disappear into the night sky. His dad was leaving to go overseas with his army unit. Mom stood beside Phil, her arm around his shoulders. They had tearfully kissed Dad good-bye. No one knew how long he would be gone.

When the plane was no longer in sight, Phil and his mom trudged back to their car. "How will we manage without Dad?" fretted Phil. "I'm going to miss him so much."

"I know, Phil. We'll both miss him," Mom replied, "but we can be thankful we have each other. Maybe we can remind each other of the things Dad has been saying to us. Remember what he said this morning at breakfast?"

So many things had happened that day. Phil had to think a while. "Do you mean about God being with us?" he asked. "Dad said, 'When you think of me, remember that the heavenly Father is with me. And he's also with you.'"

"That's it, Phil," replied Mom. "That's something we'll want to remember every day."

All the way home Phil and his mother talked about how they would get along without Dad. Talking about it made Phil feel a little better.

Just before Phil got ready for bed that night, Mom picked up the family Bible. "Do you remember the story Dad read last night?" she asked.

Phil had to think again. Then he remembered. "It was about Jesus telling his disciples he was going to leave them and go back to heaven," he said.

"Right. The disciples were sad about Jesus leaving," said Mom, "but Jesus told them not to be sad. He promised to send the Holy Spirit to comfort them and be with them forever."

"Let's read that same story tonight," Phil suggested. "I need some comforting." Mom gladly turned to John 14. *M.S.*

HOW ABOUT YOU?

Has someone you loved gone away for some reason? Do you feel lonely or worried or sad? You need to remember that you are never alone. It's often when you miss someone that you can feel most strongly that the Spirit of Jesus is with you.

MEMORIZE:

"I will never leave you nor forsake you." *Hebrews 13:5, NKJV*

God Is Your Ever-Present Comforter

Grandmother's Journey (Read John 6:30-35)

15

FEBRUARY

Jason was trying to figure out the answers to a Sunday school assignment when his parents came in. They had been at the hospital to see Jason's grandmother. Mother knelt beside Jason, her eyes bright with tears. "Son, you know Grandma has been ill for a long time," she said. Jason nodded slowly. "Well, she has gone to be with Jesus," added Mother. Dad held Jason and Mother close as they cried together.

The next Wednesday, after his grandmother's funeral, Jason let out a long sigh. "I feel sad," he said. "I miss Grandma." Dad nodded and placed his arm around Jason's shoulders. Then Jason added, "Grandma used to say life was like a journey and that she couldn't wait to reach the promised land. Did she mean heaven?"

"That's right," answered Dad, "and now she's there."

Jason sighed. "That reminds me of my Sunday school lesson," he said. "Our last lesson was about God giving the Israelites manna to eat when they were traveling to the land God had promised them. Our next lesson is about Jesus being the Bread of Life. Mrs. Carson asked us to compare Jesus with the manna, and I didn't get it. But now I do. Manna was kind of like bread, and the Israelites needed it so they could get to their promised land. We need Jesus, the Bread of Life, so we can get to heaven."

"That's it exactly," agreed Dad. *A.L.*

HOW ABOUT YOU?

Have you accepted Jesus, the Bread of Life? Is he your Savior and friend? Are you looking forward to going to heaven? Accept Jesus as your Savior today and let him be your companion through your journey of life.

MEMORIZE:

"I am the bread of life. He who comes to me will never go hungry, and he who believes in me will never be thirsty."

John 6:35, NIV

 Accept the Bread of Life

The U-Turn Sign (Read Deuteronomy 18:9-14)

16
FEBRUARY

Carla waited impatiently for Jeannine to come to the door. "Oh, hi," Jeannine greeted her. "Come in and meet my new sitter. Mrs. Johnson couldn't come, but she recommended Glenda. She's neat."

The girls found Glenda reading a book in the family room. She looked up as they came in. "Hi. What sign are you?" she asked Carla.

"Sign?" Carla asked. "I don't know." She pushed her right hand out in front of her. "A stop sign, I guess."

"No silly," said Jeannine. "She means a sign like Gemini or Libra. You know—astrology."

"If you tell me your birthday, I can tell you about your personality and your future," offered Glenda.

"My Sunday school teacher says the only place we can find out about the future is in the Bible," Carla argued.

"Oh, brother!" exclaimed Glenda. "A Jesus freak."

"I'm a Scorpio," Jeannine told Carla. "Glenda read my horoscope just before you came." Then she and Glenda talked about Jeannine's horoscope and what it could mean for Jeannine's life.

Carla was uncomfortable, but she didn't leave. "Let's go play something," she suggested.

"Oh, let Glenda read your horoscope first," begged Jeannine. "You don't have to believe it. Make it a game." But Carla shook her head, and the girls finally went out to play.

When Carla got home, she told her mother about Glenda and the horoscopes. "I'm proud of you, Carla," Mother said. "I'm glad you said you were a stop sign and acted like one—you stopped Glenda from reading your horoscope. But next time you're confronted with this, I want you to be a U-turn sign. The minute the subject comes up, U-turn—do an about-face and get out of there. Those things may seem harmless, but they are a tool of the devil. Many people are led astray by them."

"OK, Mom," agreed Carla, "I will." *N.E.K.*

HOW ABOUT YOU?

Do you read your horoscope in the newspaper? It seems harmless, but it's best to not get involved in any way with astrology. Christians do not need the devil's games to tell them how to live. Turn away from any kind of fortune-telling. You have God's Word to guide you.

MEMORIZE:

"The nations you will dispossess listen to those who practice sorcery or divination. But as for you, the Lord your God has not permitted you to do so." *Deuteronomy 18:14, NIV*

 Turn Away from Fortune-Telling

Mending the Rip (Read Colossians 3:12-17)

17

FEBRUARY

Heidi darted out of Stacy's house, slamming the door behind her. "Some friend Stacy is!" she fumed as she walked home. "I'm never going to play with her again!"

As she stomped up the steps to her house, Heidi stumbled and fell. She wasn't hurt, but when she picked herself up, she saw a tear in her skirt. Tears filled her eyes, and she ran into the house to find her mother. "Oh, Mom," she cried, "this is the very worst day of my life! I fell on the steps and tore my best skirt. Just look at it!"

Mother examined the skirt carefully. "This isn't a bad tear," she said. "I'll mend it right now, before it gets worse, and you'll never know it was torn." Heidi changed clothes, and her mother got busy with needle and thread.

As Mother worked, Heidi told her about the quarrel with Stacy. "You should have heard what she called me," whined Heidi.

"And what did you call her?" Mother asked.

"Uh—well, I don't exactly remember what I said," stammered Heidi. "I was pretty mad."

Soon the ripped skirt was mended. "It's just as good as new," Mother told Heidi, holding up the skirt. "I'm glad you showed it to me right away, though. If it had ripped further, it would have been a lot harder to fix."

"Thanks, Mom," said Heidi, managing a smile. "I'm glad you could mend it. This is my favorite skirt."

"And what about your friendship with Stacy, your favorite friend?" Mother asked. "Shouldn't that be mended, too?" Heidi looked down at the floor. "Isn't that a great deal more important than fixing your ripped skirt?" persisted Mother. "Why don't you go and mend that ripped friendship before it gets worse? Think about it." Slowly Heidi nodded. *M.R.P.*

HOW ABOUT YOU?

Have you had a quarrel with a friend or relative? Isn't your relationship with that person important enough for you to forgive and forget about the hurt you feel? Perhaps that will be easier to do if you'll remember how much God has forgiven you.

MEMORIZE:

"**Be gentle and ready to forgive; never hold grudges. Remember, the Lord forgave you, so you must forgive others.**" *Colossians 3:13, TLB*

 *Patch Quarrels Quickly*

Fairy Tales (Read Genesis 1:1, 31; 2:1-3)

18

"I didn't know you were going to choose evolution for our project!" Carrie exclaimed in dismay.

"Well, we voted to do it," replied Desmond, one of Carrie's classmates. "Now you'd better do your share of the work!"

"But I don't believe in that stuff," Carrie argued. She felt the other group members' eyes upon her as she turned away.

After school, Carrie plopped down on a chair in the family room just in time to hear the ending of a story her mother was reading to Ellen, Carrie's little sister. "And they all lived happily ever after," finished Mother. She closed the book. "That was a fun story," she added, "but it was just make-believe. Which book's stories are always true?"

"The Bible," Ellen answered promptly.

"Sometimes people believe fairy tales," put in Carrie. "Like scientists who believe in evolution. My study group is doing a project about it. Desmond is going to give an oral book report. Jenny plans to draw a mural. And Tom is making up the front page of a newspaper from day one—the beginning of the world."

"And you?" asked Mother.

Carrie shrugged. "I don't want to do anything," she replied. "But we're graded as a group, so if I don't, it will hurt everyone."

Mother frowned. "But if you teach false theory, it will hurt you and anybody who might believe it," she said. After a moment, she added, "When I read fairy tales to your sister, I always remind her that they aren't true, and that the place to find truth is in the Bible. Perhaps you could do the same thing."

Carrie sat up straight. "I've got an idea!" she exclaimed after a moment. "I could make a once-upon-a-time story about the theory of evolution! After I read it to the class, I could tell them it's a fairy tale and that the Bible tells the true story. What do you think?"

"I think that's a great idea," approved Mother. "I'm glad you're standing up for the truth about creation while still fulfilling your responsibility to your class at school." *N.E.K.*

HOW ABOUT YOU?

Have you studied evolution or other theories about man's origin? Learn the truth in Genesis 1 and 2. God created all things. That's a fact, not a fairy tale.

MEMORIZE:

"In the beginning God created the heavens and the earth."

Genesis 1:1, NKJV

 God Is the Creator

Copy-Cats (Read Ephesians 5:1-2; 1 Peter 1:13-16)

19

FEBRUARY

Kevin slammed the front door, making his Dad jump. "Dad, tell Brian to quit copying me," he said, crossing his arms over his chest. "He's always following me around." As Dad put down the evening paper, Brian appeared around the corner. He marched into the living room, stood beside Kevin, and promptly crossed his arms, also. "See what I mean?" complained Kevin as Brian stared up at him.

"Brian copies you because he wants to be like you," said Dad, smiling.

Kevin frowned. "Brian's a copy-cat," he said.

"Well, maybe we should all be copy-cats," suggested Dad as he reached over and picked up his Bible. "Come here." Dad patted a spot on the couch. Shuffling to the couch, Kevin plopped down. Brian immediately did the same.

"Read this verse—Ephesians 5:1." Dad held out his Bible.

Kevin read where his dad indicated. "Therefore be imitators of God as dear children."

"We're to imitate, or copy, what God does," Dad explained. "We show our love for God that way." Brian was grinning at Kevin, and Dad smiled. "Brian cares for you, Kevin, and he shows it by wanting to do the same things you do." *C.A.D.*

HOW ABOUT YOU?

Do you get frustrated when others imitate you? They might repeat what you say, act the way you act, or even try to look the way you do by wearing similar clothes. Remember, we imitate those we love. Copy Jesus by being patient and kind. Others will see Jesus in you and want to copy him, too.

MEMORIZE:

"Therefore be imitators of God as dear children."

Ephesians 5:1, NKJV

 *Be Imitators of God*

"Salty" Christians (Read Matthew 5:13; Colossians 4:2-6)

"This sure is a good breakfast, Grandma," exclaimed Andy as he took another helping of ham and eggs.

"Yeah," agreed his sister Julie. "I wish we lived out here in the country. At home there are so many things Mom and Dad won't let us do with other kids. I'm glad I'm a Christian, but sometimes I wish Christians didn't have to be so different. Why do they?"

20
FEBRUARY

"You may find the answer in that ham on your plate," answered Grandpa. Andy and Julie looked puzzled. "You see," Grandpa went on, "I cured this ham myself. One main ingredient in the curing process is salt. It helps keep the ham from going bad. Jesus said Christians are to be the salt of the earth. Do you know what that means?"

"Does it mean we're supposed to keep other people from going bad?" asked Andy. "How could we ever do that?"

"We'll never change the whole world of sinners," said Grandpa, "but we can witness wherever we are. We can set an example of right living, too. Then at least some of those around us may be saved from sin."

"I sure would like to win Jeremy to Jesus," Andy said. "He's my best friend."

"Then be a 'salty' Christian, Andy," said Grandpa. "Cheerfully obey God's rules and those of your parents. Jesus said that if salt has lost its savor—its saltiness—it's good for nothing. It becomes tasteless. In the same way, a believer who falls into sin loses his testimony, making the Christian life seem tasteless, or undesirable, to sinners."

"Grandma, may I have some more milk?" asked Julie. "This ham makes me thirsty."

"And why do you suppose it does that?" asked Grandma.

"Because of the salt," answered Julie. "Hey, I think I get it! If we're 'salty' Christians, we make others thirsty for Jesus!" Grandma nodded as she filled Julie's glass. *M.R.P.*

HOW ABOUT YOU?

Is it hard for you to live the way a Christian should? Do you sometimes wish you could do the things others do? Be a "salty" Christian by cheerfully being an example of what a believer should be.

MEMORIZE:

"Don't let anyone look down on you because you are young, but set an example for the believers." *1 Timothy 4:12, NIV*

 **Be a "Salty" Christian**

The Best Bullfrog (Read Romans 12:3-11)

21

FEBRUARY

Mother waited until she and Julie were alone in the kitchen washing the dishes. Then she asked gently, "Did something go wrong in Sunday school today, honey? You've been so quiet since we got home from church."

"Oh, class was OK, I guess," Julie muttered, "but Mrs. King assigned parts for the Sunday school program. I'm supposed to sing in a trio, but you should hear my part! It's awful! I sing only two different notes the entire song. I sound like a . . . like a fog horn or a bullfrog or something!"

Mother smiled. "Who's singing with you?" she asked.

"Laurie and Suzy. They sing the pretty parts while I drone on like a broken record. It's not fair!" Julie stormed. "I don't want to sing in that dumb old program at all."

Mother put her arm around her daughter. "Honey," she said quietly, "I'm sure your part sounds nice with the other parts. And I think God is pleased when you use your voice to praise him."

"But my part is ugly," protested Julie. "How can that honor God?"

"Even bullfrogs sing praises to their Creator," Mother said with a smile.

Julie giggled. "All right, Mother," she said after a moment. "I'll do my part—and be the best bullfrog the church has ever heard!"

A.K.D.

HOW ABOUT YOU?

Do you feel jealous of other people who seem to get more fun or more important jobs than you? All of God's children have a necessary place in the body of Christ. To us, some may seem more special than others, but everyone is equally important to God.

MEMORIZE:

"We have different gifts, according to the grace given us."

Romans 12:6, NIV

  *Do Your Part*

One Very Small Thing (Read 2 Timothy 2:19-22)

22

FEBRUARY

"Aw, Dad, how could one cigarette hurt a guy?" pleaded Jeremy. "I only wanted to give it a try. Can't we just forget it?"

Dad shook his head. "Jeremy, remember when you asked me for a dollar the other day because you wanted to send for some CDs?" he asked.

Jeremy nodded. "Sure I remember, but what does that have to do with all this?"

"Well, after you asked for the dollar, we read the fine print in the advertisement and found that you weren't just buying ten CDs for a dollar," replied Dad. "You were also obligating yourself to purchase a certain number of discs within a certain period of time. Once we counted the true cost of buying those first ten 'bargain discs,' you decided you really couldn't afford them."

"Yeah—that advertisement was just a come-on to get me to spend more money," agreed Jeremy.

"Well, Son, that's the way sin can be, too," said Dad. "It can seem like one very small thing—like smoking just one cigarette. But often we're buying into so much more when we choose to sin. When you smoked that cigarette, you also made the decision to disobey and to deceive your parents. And if you had gotten away with that first cigarette, you might have decided to try it again and again. Each time, you would have more and more to hide from your parents. I love you too much, Jeremy, to let you get away with smoking 'just one cigarette.' I hope the next time you're tempted to disobey, you'll count the cost a little more carefully."

Jeremy nodded. "And don't go for the bargain, right? Are you sure I haven't learned my lesson well enough to skip the grounding?" he asked hopefully.

"I'm sure," said Dad. *L.W.*

HOW ABOUT YOU?

Have you ever found yourself much further into sin than you expected to be? One sin often leads to another, and then another. Don't take that first step—don't "just try" something that is wrong. Instead, flee from it.

MEMORIZE:

"Flee the evil desires of youth."

2 Timothy 2:22, NIV

 Don't Try Sinful Things

Cereal War (Read Romans 12:17-21)

23
FEBRUARY

Travis reached for the cereal box at the same instant his younger brother, Blake, picked it up. "Hey, I had it first," Travis yelled while he tried to yank the box back.

"You didn't!" retorted Blake, pulling even harder. "I did."

The box flipped from their hands, and cereal flew in all directions. "See what you did!" they yelled at each other.

Dad looked stern. "Quiet!" he ordered. "You boys do enough fighting for a whole army. We're going to have to figure out a way to bring peace into this house."

Mom nodded. "I just read in the newspaper about the peacekeeping force sent to work overseas," she said. "Maybe we could start our own peacekeeping force right here. The Bible tells us we must live peaceably, as much as possible. Now let's figure out a peacekeeping plan. What could you do to keep peace?"

Travis scowled at Blake and said, "I'd make Blake share."

Dad shook his head. "That's not the idea," he said. "The idea is to make peace by changing yourself, not the other person. How could you have prevented the fight over the cereal?"

Travis scratched his head, trying to think. "Well, I could have let go and let Blake pour his cereal first," he admitted. "I guess it wouldn't have hurt me to wait a minute."

"We could take turns," suggested Blake. "One day Travis could pour first; the next day I could."

"Excellent peacekeeping plan," approved Dad.

Travis went to the cupboard for another box of cereal. He set it on the table. "You go first today," he told his brother.

"Hold it!" ordered Mom. "Before you start sharing the cereal, there's something else you need to share—clean-up duties. Before you eat your breakfast, you can both clean up the cereal you spilled." *C.Y.*

HOW ABOUT YOU?

Do you fight a lot with your brother or sister? You can do much to keep the peace. You can learn to be polite, thoughtful, and willing to share and take turns. Not all conflict can be avoided, but God wants you to live in peace with others. When you do disagree with someone, do it in a pleasant way.

MEMORIZE:

"Don't quarrel with anyone. Be at peace with everyone, just as much as possible."

Romans 12:18, TLB

 *Get Along with Others*

Survival Kit (Read Psalm 1:1-6)

"We played a fun game in science," David told his mom as he packed for a weekend at his grandparents' house. "We had to get into small groups and decide which items we would include in our survival kit if we made a trip to the moon. Our teacher gave us a list of twenty items that we had to narrow down to eight things for our kit."

"Sounds interesting," said Mom. "Did everyone agree on the same eight items?"

24
FEBRUARY

David shook his head. "One of the girls in my group kept insisting on a map of the earth. What good would that do on the moon? Some kids wanted a compass. Personally, I was disappointed that chocolate wasn't even on the master list. But since it wasn't, I thought vitamins should be in the first spot."

Mom chuckled. "You and your chocolate!" she said. "But vitamins? We don't even take vitamins at home."

"I know," said David, "but I would if I went to the moon because all the good, healthy food we get here might not be available there."

A little later, David said that he was ready for his visit to his grandparents. "Did you pack your pajamas?" asked Mom.

"Of course," answered David.

"Toothbrush?" asked Mom.

"Check," said David. "Don't forget, Mom—I worked on a survival kit at school today. My mind is in gear to pack."

"What about your daily vitamins?" Mom asked.

David laughed. "Grandma will see that I eat well," he said. "I won't need vitamins there."

"What I actually meant by daily vitamins was your Bible," Mom told him. "It's important to read your Bible every day for spiritual nutrition. It helps keep you spiritually healthy." David looked at the Bible on his bedside table. He hadn't thought to pack that. "I'm sure it wasn't on your master list at school," added Mom, "but whether you're going to the moon or just to your grandparents' house, you need a daily dose of God's Word." David opened his suitcase and made room for his Bible. *N.E.K.*

HOW ABOUT YOU?
If you prepared a survival kit, would the Bible be included? Reading God's Word faithfully is important for spiritual growth.

MEMORIZE:
"But his [the godly man's] delight is in the law of the Lord, and in His law he meditates day and night."
Psalm 1:2, NKJV

 Keep a Bible Handy

False Worshipers (Read Psalm 95:1-7a)

25

On the way home from church, Todd and Susan told their parents about the missionary who had spoken to their Sunday school department. "He told us the people he works with worship a false god," said Todd. "They run around and around their temple, and each time around they drop a piece of wood into a box. By the time they finish, they're dead tired. But they go home happy, because they think they've done a great service to their god."

"Isn't that silly?" asked Susan. "That's not worshiping at all. I'm glad we know the true God. We worship him each time we go to church, don't we?"

"Maybe not," replied their father. He went on to explain. "While the pastor was preaching, Todd, I caught you and Jeffrey starting to write notes, didn't I? Do you think you can worship the Lord while writing notes?" Todd slowly shook his head. "As for me, I'll have to confess that at one point, I was thinking about a problem at work instead of listening to the sermon," added Dad.

"I'm sometimes guilty, too," confessed Susan. "Last Sunday I whispered to Laurie during our prayer time. After class, Mrs. Smith talked to me about it, and I was really embarrassed. Did she tell you about it, too?"

Mother shook her head. "No, but now I guess it's my turn," she said. "The Bible says we're to sing with the spirit and with the understanding. In other words, we should sing with real praise to the Lord, thinking about the words. Sometimes I catch myself thinking about something else while singing the old, familiar hymns."

"We could all improve in our worship, couldn't we?" asked Dad. "Let's determine that each time we go to church, we'll really worship God in every part of the service. If we don't, I can't see that we're much better than the heathen in their rituals and ceremonies. In fact, we're worse, because we know better." All the family nodded in agreement. *M.R.P.*

HOW ABOUT YOU?

What do you think about when you sing hymns? When someone prays, do you quietly pray, too? Do you try to understand the sermon? Worship God at church and center your thoughts on him and his Word.

MEMORIZE:

"I will pray . . . [and] sing with the spirit, and . . . with the understanding."

1 Corinthians 14:15, NKJV

 Worship God at Church

Jimmy Wants More (Read Matthew 20:1-15a)

Lauren and Jimmy ran next door to show their report cards to their grandmother. Grandma gave them each a quarter. "I'm proud of your hard work," she told them.

"It's not fair. Lauren gets the same thing for *B*s and *C*s that I got for *A*s," Jimmy complained when they returned home. "I should have gotten more for doing better."

"That decision was really up to Grandma," replied Mother. "She knows you both did your best."

26
FEBRUARY

After dinner Mother baked cookies. When she pulled the first pan out of the oven, Jimmy raced into the kitchen. "Anyone who wants to try my cookies must help clean up the kitchen first," Mother said. Jimmy started washing the dishes.

"Ummmm! Cookies." Lauren followed her nose into the kitchen.

"Anyone who wants to eat cookies must help clean my kitchen," Mother said again. There wasn't a whole lot left to do, but Lauren dried a few items.

"Are the cookies ready yet?" Dad asked a little later.

"Anyone who wants to eat cookies has to help clean my kitchen," repeated Mother.

Dad looked around. Even the cookie sheets had been washed. Taking a sponge, he wiped the counter.

Mom handed each person two cookies.

"Two for everybody?" Jimmy exclaimed. "They didn't clean as much as I did! Why do they get the same amount as me?"

"They did all they could," said Mother. Jimmy still scowled.

"Time for family devotions," Dad said a little later. "I think we'll read from Matthew 20 tonight (see today's Scripture). Jimmy, how about reading for us?"

When Jimmy had finished reading, Dad nodded. "Grandma and Mother gave equal rewards today—not for equal work, but for equal effort and willingness to work," he said. "God is like that, too. He knows each person's ability and opportunity. Equal faithfulness to those opportunities is equally rewarded by him. Aren't you glad he treats everyone fairly?" *N.E.K.*

HOW ABOUT YOU?

Do you get upset when you think you deserve more than others but they get just as much as you do? Be happy with what you get. And be thankful that rewards for serving God will be given fairly. Remember that God rewards faithfulness.

MEMORIZE:

"**A faithful man will be richly blessed.**" *Proverbs 28:20, NIV*

 Faithfulness Is Rewarded

Hardened Modeling Clay (Read Ecclesiastes 11:9–12:1)

27

FEBRUARY

Tim had just settled down with a good book when his father walked into the room. "What is this, Tim?" asked Dad, as he held out a hardened, shapeless mass of clay. "Weren't you supposed to mold something out of this and take it back to school?"

"Oh, I forgot all about my art project!" exclaimed Tim, jumping up. "I'll have to hurry and finish that before the clay hardens too much."

"I'm afraid it's too late—it's already too hard," replied his father. He sighed and continued, "Tim, I've noticed that you're always putting off what you're supposed to do." He added, "You need to learn to finish what you start."

Tim frowned. "I really do mean to get things done," he said. "Only tomorrow always seems like a better time to work than today. But I'm going to do better."

Dad smiled. "Starting tomorrow?" he asked. Then he became serious. "I used to put things off, too," he told Tim, "but then I began to realize that I was wasting my life away. You see, each day is a gift to us from God—one which we must use wisely, for it will never come our way again. It's like a mass of fresh, soft clay which, with God's help, we may shape into something useful and beautiful. I know it's hard to believe, but your youthful days will soon be gone. What do you suppose you'll have to show for them?"

Tim fingered the unsightly mass of hardened clay. "If I waste my time, I'll end up with an ugly old nothing," he said. "Right?"

"Yes," agreed Dad. "God gives you 24 hours every day in which you may work, play, and sleep. You can waste these hours, or you can use them to learn God's Word, to serve him and grow closer to him, and to prepare yourself to be the best you can be when you grow up." *M.R.P.*

HOW ABOUT YOU?

How much time do you waste each day? It's OK to have a good time—everyone needs to relax. But ask God each day to help you spend your time wisely. Ask the Holy Spirit to mold your days into something beautiful and worthwhile for the Lord's honor and glory.

MEMORIZE:

"Redeeming the time, because the days are evil."

Ephesians 5:16, NKJV

 *Use Time Wisely*

The Spider Bite (Read Ephesians 4:17-24)

28
FEBRUARY

Susan slumped in her chair, a sour look on her face. "Why can't I see the movie with Jenny?" she asked. "All my friends have seen it. It won't affect me. I just want to know what it's about. Everybody's talking about it." Susan knew how her parents felt about horror movies, but she just couldn't understand what the big deal was.

After a moment of thought, her father began rolling up his sleeve, and Susan saw the big, ugly scar close to his elbow. He pointed to the scar and said, "Do you know how that got there?" Susan had heard the story before, but she just shrugged. "It was caused several years ago by a bite from a poisonous spider," continued Dad. "A spider bite is a small thing—so small that I didn't pay any attention to it when it happened. But after a couple of days, it started to swell, and the flesh around the bite literally rotted and fell away. Now I have this big scar. And you know something? I don't have any feeling at all there. The poison killed the nerves around the bite."

"But what does that have to do with a movie?" asked Susan, pouting.

Her father looked her in the eye. "Susan, you already know that what's in that movie is not pleasing to God. It's sinful, and sin is like a spider's poison. It often doesn't seem like much at first, but in the end it leaves dreadful scars on your life, and it destroys your sensitivity toward the things of God. The more you allow yourself to be scarred by sin, the less able you will be to hear God when he speaks to you. Is that what you want?"

Slowly Susan shook her head. "No, I guess not," she said with a sigh. "I'd better call Jenny and tell her I can't go." *D.C.C.*

HOW ABOUT YOU?

Do you avoid sinful things? Or do you think they won't have any long-lasting effect on you? If you have been playing with sin, ask Jesus to forgive and cleanse you, and then begin seeking his will in all you do.

MEMORIZE:

"Come out from them [unbelievers] and be separate, says the Lord. Touch no unclean thing, and I will receive you."

2 Corinthians 6:17, NIV

 Sin Causes Scars

Foreign Words (Read Psalm 119:33-40)

1

"We had the neatest guests in our social studies class today," Doug told his parents one evening. "Mrs. Berg invited a Vietnamese family to talk to us about their culture and to tell us what it's like to fit into the American way without losing their heritage."

"Sounds interesting," said Dad. "What was the hardest thing for them?"

"Learning English," replied Doug. He got up and took a paper from one of his school books. "This is what their language looks like."

Mother looked at the foreign words. "I know it would be hard for me to learn this," she said. "And it would be confusing and scary not to be able to talk to people or to understand what others are saying or writing."

"It sure would," agreed Dad. He reached for the family Bible. "Time for devotions together."

Doug shrugged. "Sometimes the Bible is just as hard for me to understand as the foreign words on these papers," he observed. "I know it's written in English, but some parts still don't make sense to me."

"Tell me . . . how did your social studies guests figure out what the English words meant?" asked Dad.

"They studied and studied," Doug said. "They got help from different organizations and people who taught them."

"In other words, they were persistent—they kept at it," said Dad. "We need persistent Bible study, too. The more we study, the more we'll understand."

"And we need to ask for help," added Mother. "Your dad and I can help. Pastor Bertrom and your Sunday school teacher can help. But, most importantly, God can help. Ask him." *N.E.K.*

HOW ABOUT YOU?

Do you find it difficult to read the Bible because parts are hard to understand or the words are too big? Keep reading. Ask God to help you understand what he wants you to learn. The more time you spend with him, the more you will understand what he is saying to you.

MEMORIZE:

"Open my eyes that I may see wonderful things in your law."

Psalm 119:18, NIV

 God Gives Understanding

Dad's Coming Home! (Read Mark 13:32-37)

When Mandy came in from school, her mother smiled and said, "I got a letter from your father today. And guess what? He's coming home!"

"Ooohh, goody!" squealed Mandy. "When is he going to be here?"

"Within the next week or so," replied Mom. "He's on a special mission for the government, and he can't tell us when he'll be finished. I guess we won't know he's back until we see him at our door."

2 MARCH

That night Mandy lay awake in her bed, thinking. She hadn't seen her father in six months, and now he could be home any day! She would help Mom clean the house and yard. She would make sure her clothes were clean, and she'd shampoo and curl her hair. And another thing—she must be sure to obey Mom. Once she'd been naughty just before Dad came home, and he had to hear about it first thing. She didn't want that to happen this time.

As the days went by, Mandy helped her mother prepare for Dad's return. "You've been very good and helpful," Mom told her with a smile. "Dad will be so proud!"

The next day, Mandy's friends wanted her to go with them to buy some candy after school, but Mom had said to come straight home. It would only take a few minutes, and Dad probably wouldn't come today. She started for the store with the others, but suddenly she stopped. "No," she declared. "I can't go. Dad may come today."

When Mom heard about it, she gave Mandy a hug. "If you had disobeyed, and Dad had come, you'd have been ashamed instead of happy to see him," she told Mandy. She smiled and added, "You know, all this reminds me that we should always be ready for Jesus to come back, too." As Mandy nodded she glanced out the window. It was a taxi—Dad was home! *M.R.P.*

HOW ABOUT YOU?

If you knew Jesus was coming today, what things would you do in order to be ready? Confess some sin? Ask somebody for forgiveness? Witness to an unsaved friend? Read your Bible and pray? Ask Jesus to come into your heart as your Savior? Whatever you'd do, do it now. Jesus could come today!

MEMORIZE:

"And now, little children, abide in Him, that when He appears, we may have confidence and not be ashamed before Him at His coming." *1 John 2:28, NKJV*

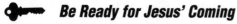 *Be Ready for Jesus' Coming*

Saturday Every Day? (Read Philippians 4:11-13)

Betsy smiled as she looked at her baby brother, still asleep. *Robbie's really cute,* she thought, *but I'm glad I'm not a baby. All he does is eat and sleep. What a boring life. I have lots more fun playing and even going to school.*

"Breakfast is ready," called Mother.

Seated beside her brother Jimmy, Betsy watched Mom make breakfast for their father. Betsy wondered if her mother knew how boring her life looked. Always doing things for everyone else—like scrambling eggs just right, and checking schoolwork, and telling Dad he needed a haircut. Could anything be more dull?

Dad glanced at the clock; it was almost 7:30. "I better go," he said. "Traffic is always heavy on Monday."

Betsy's thoughts turned to her father's life. *Dad does the same thing Monday through Friday—eat breakfast, grab his briefcase, drive to the office to spend the day doing whatever he does. Then he comes home until the next day, when he does it all over again. Does he ever wish every day could be Saturday?* Betsy's thoughts all had question marks this morning.

"Betsy, you'll have to catch the bus soon. Shall we read our verse for today?" Mom opened her Bible as she spoke. "First Corinthians 13:11 (*NIV*): 'When I was a child, I talked like a child, I thought like a child, I reasoned like a child. When I became a man, I put childish ways behind me,'" read Mom. "What does that verse say to you, honey?"

Betsy thought a minute. "I guess it's that children think differently from grown-ups," she answered.

"That's right." Mom smiled. "God has special things for us our whole life. When we're young, life is often exciting and fun. As we grow older, there are more responsibilities and less playtime, but adults can be as happy working as children are playing. Aren't you glad Jesus gives us contentment whether we're eight or eighty?"

Betsy smiled as she grabbed her books. "Have a good day, Mom," she called as she heard the school bus. *P.K.*

HOW ABOUT YOU?

Do you ever wish that every day could be Saturday? God has given days to work and days to play. He knows what is best, so be content with each day. Each one is a special gift from him.

MEMORIZE:

"I have learned to be content whatever the circumstances."

Philippians 4:11, NIV

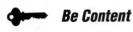

Be Content

Just like Dad (Read Ephesians 4:30-32; 5:1-8)

One day when Nathan and his father were shopping, an elderly man walked up to them. "Excuse me," the man said. "I'm Bill Cook. I've been watching the two of you, and I can't help noticing how much both of you look like a school chum I had years ago. His name was Nathan Noble. Are you related to him?"

4

MARCH

"That's my name, and my dad's, too!" blurted out Nathan. "He's Nathan Noble, Jr., and I'm the third," he added proudly. "But you look too old to have gone to school with Dad."

The two men laughed. "I'm sure this gentleman is talking about your grandfather, Nathan," explained Dad.

"I just knew you must be related," said Mr. Cook after they had talked a few minutes. "Your boy here, with his red hair and freckles, looks very much like old Nate did in grammar school. Both of you walk and talk like him, too."

After Mr. Cook left, Dad smiled at Nathan. "It was a real compliment, Nathan, to be recognized as my father's son," he said. "I've always admired him very much, and I guess I've copied his ways more than I realized. I'm really proud to be just like Dad."

"Yeah, wasn't that something?" asked Nathan. "Mr. Cook hasn't seen Grandpa in years, and yet he recognized how much we were like him."

Dad looked very thoughtful. "There's someone else we should be like, Nathan," he said. "The Bible says we should be 'followers of God as dear children.' People should be able to tell that God is our Father just by watching our actions and hearing our words."

"But God's perfect, and he can do all kinds of miracles," said Nathan. "We can't be exactly like him."

"That's true," agreed Dad, "but with God's help, we can show his kind of love, kindness, and forgiveness to others. We should also do our best to live without sin. Then surely some people will say, 'There goes a child of God.'" *M.R.P.*

HOW ABOUT YOU?

Have you been told that you look, sound, or act like one of your parents? Can people also tell by watching you that you're a child of God? In every way possible, Christians are to be like their heavenly Father. After all, that's the only way some people will see what God is really like.

MEMORIZE:

"Be imitators of God as dear children." *Ephesians 5:1, NKJV*

 Be like Your Heavenly Father

False Teeth (Read 1 John 4:1-6)

"Aaagh!" squealed Claudine when she looked on Grandma's bathroom counter. "There are teeth in this cup!" Grandma chuckled as she stopped at the bathroom door. "I forgot that you wear false teeth," Claudine added. "They don't look false in your mouth."

"Good," said Grandma. "Then maybe only I and my dentist know for sure." She gave Claudine a toothless grin. "And you," she added.

The following week, Claudine became friends with Virginia, a new student who talked about God. "We all have God in us, so we can all determine our own right and wrong," said Virginia. "You may think certain things are wrong, but I may think they're OK. And that's fine. We should each decide for ourself." Claudine was so glad to find a friend who wasn't afraid to talk about God that she blindly accepted whatever Virginia said.

One day Claudine got into trouble for hitting her brother Stan. "Well, Virginia says we're all a part of God and can decide for ourselves what's right," stated Claudine, "and I think it's OK for me to hit Stan when he teases me."

"Oh, you do," said Mother dryly. "Who's Virginia?"

"She's my new Christian friend at school," explained Claudine.

"Are you sure she's a Christian?" asked Mother. "The things she says sound like New Age thinking, and that's man-centered, not Christ-centered. You see, many people use words that sound biblical, but they really aren't." Claudine looked confused. "Those words are like Grandma's teeth," added Mother.

"Grandma's teeth!" exclaimed Claudine. "What's that supposed to mean?"

"You told me Grandma's teeth looked real, but they were false," said Mother. "In a similar way, some people use words that may seem 'Christian,' but they're false—they disagree with what God says. I think you'll have to listen carefully to what Virginia says." Mother added sternly, "God definitely does *not* say you can decide for yourself what is right or wrong. His standard is perfect and holy. It's always right, whether we like it or not." *N.E.K.*

HOW ABOUT YOU?

When you hear someone talk about God, do you think that such a person must be a Christian? Don't be fooled by false teaching. Compare what is said with what God says in his Word so you will not be tricked.

MEMORIZE:

"Beware of false teachers who come disguised as harmless sheep, but are wolves and will tear you apart."

Matthew 7:15, TLB

 Beware of False Teachings

Stolen Seed (Read Mark 4:3-4, 13-15)

A-choo! Alan sneezed loudly, and the children in his Sunday school class giggled. Miss Larkin paused before beginning the lesson. "Bless you," someone said.

Miss Larkin once more started to speak, but . . . *A-choo!* Again, all eyes were on Alan. Some students faked coughs and sneezes, causing the class to laugh.

After the children had settled down again, Miss Larkin led in prayer. "Lord, You know the thief is here again today," she prayed. "He's trying to steal your treasure. We trust you to protect it. In Jesus' name. Amen." Then she directed the kids to open their Bibles to the parable of the sower, and they read it together.

6

MARCH

"God's Word is like seed," said Miss Larkin. "Our hearts are like soil. This first kind of soil—the first kind of heart—described here is the 'wayside.' Before God's Word has time to grow here, Satan quickly steals it. Satan, who wants only weeds of sin to grow in our life, uses many things to snatch the seed away. Some thieves look innocent, but while one holds your attention, others steal the seed. For example, this morning a thief came to class disguised as a sneeze. Alan couldn't help it, but his sneezing took our minds off our lesson. Can you think of other disguises Satan's thieves might use?"

A girl raised her hand. "In church they might come as hiccups or crying babies," she suggested. "Or sleepiness."

"When we have devotions at home, it seems like the telephone or doorbell often rings," offered Alan.

"Something we've seen on TV or read could make us think about silly or bad things instead of good things," said another class member.

"Right," Miss Larkin said. "Let's be on our guard so we're not distracted by such things."

Alan raised his hand. "We should be careful not to distract other people, too," he said. As he finished talking, he grabbed his handkerchief and quickly smothered another big sneeze. This time no one giggled or faked sneezes. *J.R.*

HOW ABOUT YOU?

Do you try hard to keep your mind on God's Word when it's being read or taught? Do you try not to do things that might keep others from hearing what God has to say? Be careful! Don't let Satan use you to steal God's Word from others.

MEMORIZE:

"The thief comes only to steal and kill and destroy; I have come that they may have life."

John 10:10, NIV

 Don't Distract Others

Panic Messages (Read Matthew 24:36-42)

7

MARCH

Kitty always left the answering machine on when she got home from school because she wasn't supposed to answer the phone when her mother wasn't home. When calls came in, she listened to the speaker. If it was her mother calling, she would pick up the phone. Otherwise, she'd let the person leave a message.

"Kitty," Mom called over the speaker one afternoon. "Pick up the phone, honey." But Kitty was looking for something in the basement, and she missed the call.

"Kitty," Mom called a little later, "where are you?" Again Kitty didn't hear the phone. She also missed her mom's next two calls. "Kitty, answer me!" Mom called once more. By this time Kitty was back upstairs, so she picked up the phone. "What's wrong? Where have you been? Are you OK?" Mom asked all at once.

"I'm here. I'm fine," said Kitty.

Later, Mom and Kitty listened to messages friends had left earlier in the day. Then they heard Mom's messages. "I certainly sounded shook up," Mom said. "I couldn't understand why you didn't answer." She hugged Kitty.

During devotions, Mom read a passage that talked about Jesus coming again. "Mom," Kitty said, "when Jesus takes us to heaven, will our friends who aren't Christians try to find us and leave panic messages on the answering machine like you did today?"

Mom looked concerned. "I don't know," she said, "but your question makes me wonder. It's sad to think some of our friends will be left here, possibly crying out, 'Where are you? Did you leave me behind? Why didn't you tell me so I could have come?' Kitty, we have a responsibility to get busy and tell them about Jesus, his gift of salvation, and his second coming."

Kitty nodded as she imagined some of her classmates' voices on the answering machine, calling out to her after she'd gone. "We have a lot of work to do," she agreed. *N.E.K.*

HOW ABOUT YOU?

Can you think of someone who might be left behind if Jesus came back today? Take time right now to pray for his or her salvation. And remember that although you can't make others choose the Lord, it's your job to tell them about Jesus.

MEMORIZE:

"And he will send his angels with a loud trumpet call, and they will gather his elect from the four winds, from one end of the heavens to the other."

Matthew 24:31, NIV

 Tell Others about Jesus Now

Traffic Lights (Read Romans 13:1-5; 1 Timothy 1:18-19)

"Slow down, Dad," warned Philip. He pointed to a cluster of bushes. "I see a cop hiding back there."

"I don't need to slow down, Phil," Dad answered. "I'm not going over the speed limit."

"Yeah, but don't you feel sort of uneasy when you see a cop, like maybe he'll get you for something you don't even know about?" asked Philip.

Dad shook his head. "Not a bit," he said, stopping for a red light. "I have no reason to have a guilty conscience."

"My Bible club teacher says your conscience is kind of like a traffic light, flashing red when you're about to do something wrong, and green when you're doing right," observed Philip. "Of course, it doesn't actually flash red or green in front of your eyes, but we knew what she meant."

Dad nodded. "God has given each person a conscience," he said, "and your conscience works according to your knowledge of right and wrong. That's why you need to train your conscience while you're young. Studying the Bible and listening to the advice of older Christians are good ways to do that."

"Well, I know a kid who does wrong even though he knows better, but he says his conscience doesn't bother him," stated Philip. "My teacher says kids like him have run through the red light of their conscience so many times that they're becoming color blind."

The traffic light turned green, and Dad drove on. "When you run a red light—with your car, or by ignoring your conscience—you're likely to have a wreck," he said. "And wrecking your life is much more serious then wrecking a car."

Philip nodded. "Yeah," he agreed, "but you know something, Dad? Sometimes I'm not sure what color my conscience is flashing."

"When you're not sure what's right, observe the yellow caution light and slow down until you know what to do," advised Dad. "Play it safe. Don't go ahead unless you're sure it's OK." *M.R.P.*

HOW ABOUT YOU?

Have you ever had a tug at your heart or an uneasy feeling when you started to do wrong? Then thank God for a tender conscience that was flashing a red light. When you get those warnings, pay attention and do what's right.

MEMORIZE:

"I strive always to keep my conscience clear before God and man." *Acts 24:16, NIV*

 Keep a Clear Conscience

The White Cabinets (Read Ephesians 5:6-16)

9 MARCH

"See, Mom, I told you you shouldn't have painted those cabinets white," said Jason as he sat at the kitchen table watching his mother wipe the cabinets with a cleaning cloth. "If you had painted them brown or something, they wouldn't show the dirt, and you wouldn't have to be cleaning them all the time."

Mother smiled. "But this way I can see the dirt and wipe it off before there's so much that it's really a big chore to get them clean," she told him.

"Hmmmm. Like sin," murmured Dad, looking up from his morning paper.

"Huh?" asked Jason. "You're not making sense, Dad."

Dad chuckled. "My thoughts are," he said. "It occurred to me that just as dark cabinets hide the dirt, darkness in our lives hides the sin that may be there, and that's not good. By darkness in our lives, I mean not walking close to Jesus, who is the Light."

"Good thought," chimed in Mother as she rinsed her cleaning rag. "And if dark cabinets are like lives dark with sin, these white cabinets are like our lives when we walk in God's light. Then when we sin, we see it more quickly and clearly. We can confess those sins and get them cleaned up immediately."

"What do you think our lives are like when we're like these white cabinets, Jason?" asked Dad.

Jason shrugged. "I guess we'd go to church and Sunday school and read our Bibles and pray," he suggested.

"I think you're right, Jason," agreed Mother. "When we're close to God's people and his Word, it's easier for us to see when we've done something wrong. Then we can clean it up quickly." *L.W.*

HOW ABOUT YOU?

Are you able to see the "dirt" in your life quickly? Or do you need more light? Read God's Word, listen to his servants at church, talk with him in prayer. Take care of the "dirt"—the sin in your life—by confessing it to the Lord and asking him to wash you and keep your life clean.

MEMORIZE:

"Walk as children of light."

Ephesians 5:8, NKJV

Walk in Jesus' Light

Two Ordinary Shoes (Read 1 John 3:18-23)

"Mom! I can't find my shoes," yelled Bill, "and I'm going to be late for the bus." He pulled up his bedspread to look under the bed for what he thought was the hundredth time. "I've looked everywhere," he added.

"Have you prayed about it?" Mom asked, appearing in the doorway. "Bill, have you prayed yet?" she repeated.

"No, Mom. I don't think God has time to worry about two ordinary shoes," replied Bill crossly. "Besides, I'm late. I don't have time to stop and pray." Immediately, he knew it was the wrong thing to say.

10

MARCH

Bill's mother held him gently by his shoulders and stared into his brown eyes. "Bill," she said, "when you have to get something from the basement at Grandma's house, you slow down on her steps and hold on to her railing. Why is that?"

"Because the steps are steep, and it's dark down there," Bill said, and he shivered as he remembered the rickety, gloomy stairway.

"But you've never fallen down those steps because you're careful to take your time," said Mom. "On the other hand, last week you fell down our new, well-lit stairs that had railings on both sides. You run up and down those steps a dozen times a week, so you didn't think you had to be careful. They're just our regular, ordinary steps, right?"

Bill slowly nodded. He was trying to understand what his mother's point was.

"So the difficult ones didn't cause you trouble, but the ordinary ones did," said Mother. "In life, often the big scary things that happen cause us less trouble than ordinary ones do. Maybe that's because we seem to take time to pray about the big, scary things, but not about the small, simple, ordinary things."

"Like shoes?" Bill asked, and he grinned sheepishly.

"Like shoes," Mom answered.

"OK, Mom. I'm ready to ask God where my shoes are," said Bill with a grin, "and I think I'll ask him for a ride to school, too." *J.J.*

HOW ABOUT YOU?

Do you pray about your "little" concerns—things like having a good time at a friend's house, or getting chosen to play on your best friend's baseball team? God is waiting to hear even the little prayers of his people.

MEMORIZE:

"Don't worry about anything; instead, pray about everything; tell God your needs and don't forget to thank him for his answers." *Philippians 4:6, TLB*

 Pray about Everything

Cleaned Up (Read 1 John 1:5-9)

11

MARCH

"But, Mom . . ." began Sean.

"Sean, you're the oldest. I don't want to hear any more about it," said Sean's mother. She handed him a scrub brush and a bucket. "I want it all cleaned up," she said.

Sean groaned as he stomped down the basement stairs. He stared glumly at the paint splatters on the floor. *I wouldn't have to clean up this mess if Bobby had been more careful painting the walls,* Sean thought. *Mom should make him help.* The fresh latex paint washed off the cement easily enough. Still, he was upset over having to clean up a mess that he felt was more his little brother's fault than his.

After a while, Sean heard his mother come down the stairs. She sat on the bottom steps. "How is it coming?" she asked.

"OK," mumbled Sean.

"You may be right that Bobby got more paint on the floor than you did," said Mother, "but you're not the first person who's ever had to clean up someone else's mess. I've had to do that often myself, and I used to be resentful about it, too. But then I realized that when I make a mess of my life and can't clean it up myself, Jesus is always ready to help me." Sean stopped scrubbing and looked at his mother. "Think about it," she said. "Jesus takes all our sins and makes us clean. When we come to him for help, he takes all our mistakes and straightens them out. We don't stop to thank him for that very often."

Sean dunked his brush and started scrubbing again. Somehow, he wasn't angry anymore.

"You know why I made you do this and not your brother?" asked Mother. Sean looked at her and shook his head. "Because I wanted it done well." Mother squeezed his shoulder and went back upstairs. *M.K.N.*

HOW ABOUT YOU?

Have you thought about how Jesus is not only willing, but also able, to straighten out your life and make you clean? When you sin, you can decide not to do it again, and you can ask God to forgive you. When you have a problem, you can give it to God, and he'll help you. And he does all things perfectly—thank him for that.

MEMORIZE:

"To Him [Jesus] who loved us and washed us from our sins in His own blood . . . to Him be glory." *Revelation 1:5-6, NKJV*

 *Jesus Makes You Clean*

The Silent Treatment (Read 1 Timothy 2:1-8)

"Doesn't Justin ever quit talking?" complained Joanne. "He's always bothering me. I wish he'd leave me alone."

"We've talked about this before," said Mother. "Why don't you pray about it and then confront your brother?"

"Oh," grumbled Joanne, "you always want to pray about everything! I have an idea that will work faster."

12

MARCH

When Justin ran into the house a little later, Joanne retreated to her room. Soon Justin banged on her door and called out to her, but she turned the volume of her radio up so she couldn't hear what he said. After several attempts to get her attention, Justin gave up and walked away.

As Joanne was watching TV later, Justin began to tell her something, but Joanne took both hands and covered her ears and began to hum. *I'll teach him,* she thought. All afternoon she refused to hear anything he said.

At dinnertime, Joanne went to the kitchen. She noticed that Justin had changed clothes. "Are you going somewhere, Justin?" asked Dad, who had just arrived home.

Justin nodded. "I'm going with the Kehoes for pizza and skating," he said. "They got discount tickets."

"Sounds like fun," said Dad. He looked at Joanne. "Why aren't you going?" he asked.

"I wasn't invited," Joanne answered crossly.

"You were too!" said Justin as the Kehoes' car came up the driveway. "I tried to tell you, but you wouldn't listen."

Joanne stormed to her room. A little later, Mother went to talk to her. "Well, how do you feel now about giving Justin the silent treatment?"

"I wanted to teach him a lesson and make him feel bad," said Joanne with a sigh, "but I'm the one who feels bad."

"I think you're also the one learning the lesson," said Mother. "It concerns me that you not only cut off communication from your brother, but also from the Lord. By refusing to pray about the problem, you missed out on the blessing God would have given. It hurts God when we don't talk to him." *N.E.K.*

HOW ABOUT YOU?

Do you keep open communication with the Lord? Don't give God the silent treatment and try to work things out in your own way. Seek the Lord's help in everything.

MEMORIZE:

"I want men everywhere to lift up holy hands in prayer, without anger or disputing."

1 Timothy 2:8, NIV

 **Talk to God**

Out of Gas (Read Acts 2:42-47)

13

MARCH

Carrie sat in the back seat of the family car with her brother Blake and their younger brother, Jody. They had moved to town just that week, and they were going to drive past a couple of churches and choose one to visit the next day. "I wish Dad's company didn't transfer us so often," murmured Carrie. "I hate going to strange Sunday schools. I always have to introduce myself, and say where I'm from, and what grade I'm in. What a pain!"

"Pain," little Jody echoed.

"Yeah," agreed Blake. He sighed. "We went to Sunday school last week, so can't we skip it tomorrow?" he asked. "Couldn't we just sing a few hymns and pray at home? We could read something from the Bible, too."

"Well, yes, we could—and we will," said Dad, "but that's family devotions, not church. We need fellowship with God's people. Right now, though, we'd better watch for a gas station—we're nearly empty."

Mother smiled. "Oh, we don't have to worry," she said, "we got gas last week."

"Last week?" asked Dad, puzzled. Then he caught on. "Oh, that's right," he said, "and it's a pain to pump gas in a new place, isn't it? Why don't we wait till we're used to this town? We can get gas then."

Blake sighed. "OK," he said. "I get the message."

"What message?" Jody wanted to know.

Carrie turned to face her little brother. "What Mom and Dad are saying, Jody, is that a car needs fuel to keep running and we need spiritual fuel to keep running. And church is a good place to get it. Right, Mom?"

"Right," agreed Mom. "I know it can be hard to go to a new church and Sunday school, but let's ask the Lord to help us be friendly as we go, and I think we'll find friendly people in return. Personally, I enjoy meeting other Christians."

Dad nodded as he pulled off the street and into a gas station, and Jody clapped his chubby hands. "Let's go," he said. *R.M.*

HOW ABOUT YOU?

Do you enjoy finding a Sunday school when you move or are away from home? Look at it as an opportunity to meet other Christians. Whenever you can, join with other boys and girls who love Jesus.

MEMORIZE:

"I was glad when they said to me, 'Let us go into the house of the Lord.'" *Psalm 122:1, NKJV*

Attend Church and Sunday School

Courage for Christ (Read Philippians 1:27-29)

Susan and Tina sat in the school lunch room discussing the oral book reports they had given in class that morning. "I wish the reports had been written," said Susan. "I just hate standing up there and talking in front of everybody!"

"Me, too!" Tina replied.

14

MARCH

The girls were almost finished with lunch when a commotion erupted at the next table, where several older boys were sitting. Susan recognized Ken, who lived on her street. Tim, who attended her church, was there, too.

The boys were laughing and teasing Tim. One boy grabbed Tim's milk and poured it on the table. Susan heard Jesus' name mentioned mockingly. Tim fought back tears as he began to wipe up the milk.

Suddenly Ken stood up, and motioned to the others. They all rose, laughing, and joined Ken as he began to sing tauntingly "Stand Up, Stand Up for Jesus!" It was a hymn Susan had often sung, but Ken was using it to make fun of Tim and Jesus, too.

Susan hesitated just one moment. Then she got up from the table and stood quietly, looking at the boys. She didn't say anything; she just stood there.

Ken saw her and blushed. She could tell he was ashamed. He sat down quickly, and the other boys followed. He didn't look her way again.

Tina had been watching. "Why did you do that?" she asked when Susan sat down.

"Well, I guess it's because I love Jesus, and when you care about someone, you stick up for him," replied Susan. "I wanted those boys to know that I would stand up for Jesus anytime."

"You really mean it, don't you?" said Tina. "You're afraid to give a report in front of class, but you stood up in front of all those boys because of Jesus." After a short pause, she added, "You've tried to tell me about Jesus before, but it just didn't seem that important. I think I'd like to hear more about him now." *A.L.*

HOW ABOUT YOU?

Do you feel sad if someone makes fun of Jesus? He loved you enough to die for you. Do you love him enough to stand up for him? You can do that quietly without arguing or fighting.

MEMORIZE:

"Whoever confesses Me before men, him I will also confess before My Father who is in heaven." *Matthew 10:32, NKJV*

 Stand Up for Jesus

Sitting with Jesus (Read Psalm 63:1-7)

15

MARCH

It was early when Alex woke up. He could tell because it was only just a little bit light outside and the sounds were early morning sounds, like chirping birds. Alex got out of bed and looked for his mother. He looked in the kitchen, but she wasn't there. She wasn't in the living room, either. Alex peeked into his mother's bedroom. She was sitting in her rocker with her Bible on her lap. Her eyes were shut, and he knew she was praying.

Alex wanted a hug, so he crawled into his mother's lap. "Good morning," said Mother, giving him a hug. "You're up early."

"Are you praying?" asked Alex.

"Yes," said Mother.

"What about?" asked Alex.

"Oh, nothing in particular," replied Mother. "I was just sitting with Jesus."

"Sitting with Jesus?" Alex didn't understand that.

Mother nodded. "Just now you came in and got on my lap because you wanted to be with me," she told him. "I'm glad you did, because I love you, and I like to be with you, too. Well, sometimes I like to just be with the Lord. Sometimes I like to sit with him, thinking about how good he is, talking with him a little, and just enjoying him. I think he's glad I like to be with him."

"Can I sit with him, too?" asked Alex.

"Sure you can," Mother told him. "Think about him being here with us right now." Mother closed her eyes and rocked the chair. Alex closed his eyes, too, and thought about Jesus sitting with them. He liked sitting and rocking with his mom and Jesus.

M.K.N.

HOW ABOUT YOU?

Do you have a friend you just like to be with? Jesus wants to be your best friend. Try just being with him—sit and talk with him, think about him, think about what he has done for you, or think about what the Bible says. He may whisper something to your heart when you are quiet before him.

MEMORIZE:

"Be still, and know that I am God." *Psalm 46:10, NKJV*

 *Talk with Jesus*

Most-Loved Doll (Read Romans 5:6-9)

16

MARCH

Robin thoughtfully studied her doll collection. She knew they were all beautiful, and she couldn't decide which was the best one to enter in the "Most Beautiful Doll Contest." Finally she just closed her eyes, spun around a couple of times, and reached out. Her searching fingers closed around black-haired Fumiko. "This will be it," she decided.

The public library was crowded when Robin and her mother arrived. Girls accompanied by mothers—or even an occasional father—clutched large, gorgeous dolls; small baby dolls in lace and ruffles; or glamorous character dolls. Robin had never seen so many dolls in her entire life.

Suddenly Robin noticed a little girl standing alone in the registration line. In her arms she carried a straggly-haired doll whose face was chipped and faded from the hugs and kisses of many years. The doll's red dress, edged in ragged lace, was grubby and wrinkled, but the little girl gently smoothed it while she waited. Robin nudged her mother. "Mom, look! That girl over there is entering an ugly old doll," she whispered.

Mother glanced toward the child who was now speaking shyly to a lady at the registration desk. "The doll may not be beautiful, but it is certainly loved," Mother murmured. After a moment she added softly, "I think that doll must be somewhat the way we appear to God, Robin. But he loves us and accepts us even though we're not brand-new or beautiful. People come to him with scars from the wear and tear of sin, but like that little girl, he looks beyond what's unlovely. He sees a helpless soul that needs him."

They watched as the lady at the desk pinned the number forty-seven on the doll's red dress. "I really hope number forty-seven wins a prize, don't you?" said Robin thoughtfully.

"That would be nice," agreed Mother. "If there's a prize for the most loved she's sure to get it." *P.K.*

HOW ABOUT YOU?

Have you thanked Jesus for loving you just the way you are? He isn't impressed by your sharp clothes or name-brand shoes. He looks inside to see if your heart is right before him. Is it? If not, accept him today.

MEMORIZE:

"God demonstrates his own love for us in this: While we were still sinners, Christ died for us." *Romans 5:8, NIV*

 God Loves You

Ice Bags and Prayers (Read 1 Corinthians 12:12-20, 26)

17

MARCH

"Hi, Mom!" called Gerri as she pushed the kitchen door open. Mother answered from the family room, but her voice sounded funny to Gerri. "What's the matter, Mom?" Gerri asked when she saw that her mother was staring out of the window, a sad expression on her face.

Mother sighed. "Aunt Mary called. She said your cousin Jeannie ran away from home last week."

"Don't they know where she is?" asked Gerri.

"Yes, she called from some place in Texas," replied Mother. Gerri saw that Mother's eyes were filled with tears. "Jeannie is making a terrible mistake. My heart aches for her and for Aunt Mary and Uncle Tom."

"Well, Jeannie's been nothing but trouble for the last few years!" exclaimed Gerri crossly. "I have a hard time feeling sorry for her. Isn't she supposed to be a Christian? What kind of Christian does that to her family?" With these words, she strode out of the room.

Immediately a loud wail was heard. "Ooooh! Ouch!"

"Gerri! What happened?" Mother hurried to the kitchen, where her daughter crouched on the floor, clutching a foot.

"I slammed my toe into that chair," moaned Gerri. "It hurts!"

Mother hurried to fix an ice bag to place on the injured toe. "This will help ease the pain," she said. "But," she added with a frown, "such a fuss over just a toe."

Gerri blinked in surprise. "But it makes me hurt all over!" she wailed.

Mother looked at her and smiled a little. "Of course it does, honey," she comforted. Then she added softly, "Your cousin is like that toe. Jeannie's trouble pains all the members of her family—or at least it should."

Gerri looked thoughtful. "I suppose you're right, Mom," she admitted. "I just don't like to see you upset when we can't do anything about Jeannie's problems."

"Oh, but we can, Gerri!" exclaimed Mother. "As Christians, we can pray for each other, whether it's for broken hearts or sore toes."

P.K.

HOW ABOUT YOU?

Are you sensitive to the troubles of others, or do you feel like it's "their problem"? A true friend is one who shares the burdens others have and prays for them.

MEMORIZE:

"Rejoice with those who rejoice, and weep with those who weep." *Romans 12:15, NKJV*

 Share and Care

The Sacrifice (Read Hebrews 13:10-16)

Carol sighed as she looked at her memory verse. "Grandma, in Bible times people had to sacrifice an animal as payment for sins, didn't they?" she asked. "Didn't they have to be placed on an altar and killed?"

Grandma nodded as she looked up from her knitting. "That's right," she agreed, "but when Jesus died for our sins, he became the perfect sacrifice, and animal sacrifices were no longer needed."

18

MARCH

"Then what does this verse mean?" asked Carol. "It says we're to present our bodies 'as living sacrifices.' How can I be a living sacrifice when a sacrifice is something that's killed? I can't do much if I'm dead."

"To be a living sacrifice means to give your all—your whole life—to God so he can use it," replied Grandma, reaching down for a piece of yarn. "Pretend this yarn is my life," she continued. "It's my love, my family, my time, my actions. Here, I give it to you." She handed one end of the yarn to Carol while she held the other end. "There—it's all yours now, right? I'm sacrificing it to you."

"Well, if it's all mine, why are you still holding on to it?" Carol asked with a giggle.

"Good point," approved Grandma. "You see, sometimes people say they give everything into God's control—that they've made their life a living sacrifice to serve him. But they leave a 'string' attached to an area like music, friends, recreation, or something else. Then," Grandma slid the string out of Carol's grasp, "they pull it back out of God's hands. That's not a sacrifice. When an Israelite took a sacrifice to the priest, he left it there."

"So being a living sacrifice means giving your whole life to God and leaving it there, without any strings to pull it back," said Carol.

"That's right," agreed Grandma. "Once a sacrifice is given, there's no taking it back." *J.B.*

HOW ABOUT YOU?

Have you given God control of every part of your life? Does your choice of friends please him? Do your school activities and study habits please the Lord? Would he approve of the music you listen to? Sacrifice every area of your life to God—no strings attached. Be willing to do whatever he wants you to do.

MEMORIZE:

"I urge you, brothers, in view of God's mercy, to offer your bodies as living sacrifices, holy and pleasing to God."

Romans 12:1, NIV

 Give Your All to God

Spiritual Milk (Read 1 Peter 1:22–2:3)

19

MARCH

"The baby is crying again," complained Sheila.

Mother walked to the cradle and picked up the fussy little bundle. "The baby has a name. This is Michael, and you need to be a little more patient with your brother, young lady," she said. "He's only three weeks old."

"I know, Mom. But he's so demanding," grumbled Sheila. "All he ever does is eat, cry, and sleep."

Mother settled into a big wooden rocker. "You're right about that," she agreed. "I just fed him a few hours ago, but I think he's hungry again." The fussing stopped as soon as she started to feed him.

Sheila watched resentfully. "I thought a baby would be more fun," she said angrily, "but what good is a dumb baby brother!"

"Watch your tongue now," warned Mother. "You can learn a lot from Michael."

"How can *I* learn from *him?*" objected Sheila.

"Get your Bible," Mother directed, "and turn to 1 Peter 2:2. Read the verse out loud."

Sheila found the verse quickly. "'As newborn babes, desire the pure milk of the word, that you may grow thereby,'" she read.

Her mother continued to rock and feed the baby. "What is Michael doing now?" she asked Sheila.

"Eating, but he looks like he's just about to fall asleep again," replied Sheila. "I guess he's eating and resting at the same time."

"What if I had just rocked Michael or tried to give him his pacifier without feeding him? What would he have done then?" asked Mother.

"Cried and fussed, I guess," said Sheila. "He sure knows when he needs to eat."

"That's right," her mother said. "That's the example God gave us to follow in desiring his Word. We should hunger after it so much that nothing else can satisfy us. Then, as we read his Word, we should rest in it and find comfort, just as Michael does after he eats. That's one of the things you can learn from watching him."

S.P.Z.

HOW ABOUT YOU?

Are you hungry for God's Word? Do you want to read and study it on a regular basis? Do you find your comfort in it? As the psalmist said, "O taste and see that the Lord is good!"

MEMORIZE:

"As newborn babes, desire the pure milk of the word, that you may grow thereby."

1 Peter 2:2, NKJV

 Desire God's Word

Moving Molecules (Read Ecclesiastes 3:9-15)

Joey and his friend Steven stayed after school to work on their molecule model. "We need to think of a way to show that molecules move around," Joey said, leaning against the lab table. "Then our project will have a better chance of placing at the science fair."

"But we can't even see the molecules that supposedly move and bang into each other," Steven argued. "I wonder if they really do move all the time. I think this is good enough." The boys discussed it a bit more and then agreed to think about it for a day or two.

20

MARCH

During dinner that evening, Joey's dad mentioned that they should be praying faithfully for their neighbors, the Greenes, who were going through some very difficult personal problems. Joey sighed. "It seems like we've prayed for the Greenes a million times, and I haven't seen a single change in them yet," he observed.

"That doesn't mean God isn't changing things," Dad said. "Perhaps we just can't see the changes yet."

As they ate, Joey told his parents about his science project and his frustration with Steven. "We've learned that everything is made up of tiny little particles, or molecules, that are always in motion. Just because we can't actually see them, Steven isn't so sure they really are moving all the time, so he won't cooperate," Joey complained. "He ought to know that just because you can't see something, it doesn't mean it's not happening."

"Don't be too annoyed with Steven. After all, in a way you two are a lot alike," challenged Mother. Joey frowned as he looked at her. "Steven can't see the molecules move, so he's not sure they do. You can't see God work in the lives of the Greenes, so you're not sure he's working," she explained.

Dad nodded. "Good point," he agreed. "We need to trust God and believe he's active even when we don't see what's happening."

N.E.K.

HOW ABOUT YOU?

Even when you don't see action, are you sure that God is with you, taking care of things? He works in quiet ways, but he's always working. Trust him even when you can't see changes from day to day.

MEMORIZE:

"He [God] changes the times and the seasons; He removes kings and raises up kings; He gives wisdom to the wise and knowledge to those who have understanding." *Daniel 2:21, NKJV*

 God Is Working

A Home for Kitty (Read Acts 4:13-22)

Betsy had been very sad ever since the doctor said her little brother's allergies were caused by her kitten. The family prayed all week long about a new home for Betsy's pet. "I'm worried about Shadow. We still haven't found her a new home," Betsy told her friends one day. "If we can't find a home for her soon, Dad plans to take her to the humane society."

21
MARCH

That evening there was a special family night at Betsy's church. One of the new members told about years of a very troubled life. Then he shared how he had accepted Jesus as his Savior and how the Lord had really changed his life and turned it around. The entire congregation was encouraged by his testimony.

When Betsy's family returned home, they found a note on the door. The elderly woman next door had changed her mind and was now offering to take Betsy's kitten. "What an answer to prayer!" Mother exclaimed. Together they thanked God for providing a home for the kitten where Betsy could see it every day.

"Were your friends excited to hear about how God worked out a new home for your kitty?" Mother asked when Betsy came home from school the next day.

Betsy hesitated. "Well, they were glad Shadow had a new home," she said.

"Did you tell them it was an answer to prayer?" asked Mother. Betsy shook her head. "Remember how it made us all happy to hear the testimony in church last night?" asked Mother. "It's good to share the things God does for us. Christians are encouraged when they see an example of God's loving power, and it's a testimony to unbelievers. I believe God is glorified when we tell others how he has answered prayer." *N.E.K.*

HOW ABOUT YOU?

Do you tell others when God answers your prayers or when something in his Word, the Bible, helps you with a problem? Don't hide God's blessings. Share them with others for God's glory.

MEMORIZE:

"All of us can praise the Lord together with one voice, giving glory to God, the Father of our Lord Jesus Christ."

Romans 15:6, TLB

 Share Answers to Prayer

Not My Friend (Read Matthew 10:24-25, 32-34, 38-39)

22
MARCH

Danielle grabbed the backpack and lunch box from her locker and slammed the door shut. Her soft brown eyes searched the crowded hallway for her friend Elise. The two girls had been friends since their first day in kindergarten, and they usually walked home together. When Danielle saw Elise, her face lit up with a broad smile, and she skipped down the hallway toward her. Elise was surrounded by several girls that Danielle recognized as the more popular kids in her class. She didn't know them very well, and she felt a little out of place as she walked up. "Hi, Elise!" she said with a smile as she stepped closer to the group.

Someone giggled, and another girl moved away from Danielle. "Come on, Elise. Walk home with us," invited the girl. She glanced at Danielle. "You don't hang around her, do you?" she added in a loud whisper. Elise looked very uncomfortable. "Don't tell me she's your friend," someone else whispered loudly.

Elise bit her lip and turned away from Danielle. She wanted so badly to be a part of the popular crowd. "She's not my friend," Elise said quickly. She grabbed her books and coat and ran off with the girls.

Danielle stood still and silent; her heart felt empty and very heavy. As she trudged wearily home, Danielle recalled a sermon her pastor had once preached. He had read some Scripture about denying Jesus, and he talked about how Christians should never do that. Danielle thought about how much it hurt when Elise said she was not her friend. "This must be how Jesus feels when we deny him," she said to herself. She knew that Elise's denial would hurt for a long time, but she had learned an important lesson: Jesus wants his friends to stick up for him and to not be afraid to tell others he is their friend. *L.S.R.*

HOW ABOUT YOU?

Have you ever felt the hurt of having someone act as if he didn't know you? Have you hurt someone else in that way? How about Jesus—have you ever pretended you didn't know him so people wouldn't laugh at you? Remember that Jesus is proud to be your friend. And he wants you to be proud to be his friend, too.

MEMORIZE:

"**Therefore whoever confesses Me before men, him I will also confess before My Father who is in heaven.**" *Matthew 10:32, NKJV*

 Speak Up for Jesus

Blah-Blah-Blah! (Read Galatians 6:1-5)

Teresa didn't want to go to the family reunion. "I can't stand to listen to Jill's bragging for two days!" she declared. "All she can talk about is their new house, their new car, their new this, their new that."

23

MARCH

But Mother insisted Teresa should go, so Teresa went, determined to stay out of Jill's way. Surprisingly, it wasn't too hard. In fact, Jill seemed to be avoiding her.

It was late afternoon before they met in the kitchen.

As they worked in cold silence, Grandmother frowned. "This won't do, girls," she said. "What's wrong?"

"Wrong?" echoed the girls. "Is something wrong?"

Grandmother nodded. "Sit down." The girls obeyed. "Why aren't you speaking to one another?" Neither replied. Grandmother looked at Jill. "We'll start with you, Jill. Why are you mad at Teresa?"

Jill's face turned red. "I . . . I . . . well, I'm not mad at her. I'm sick of her bragging."

Teresa sat up with a start. *"My* bragging?"

"Yes, *your* bragging," Jill said. "'I made the honor roll. . . . I'm class secretary. . . . I sang lead in the choir. Blah-blah-blah!'"

Teresa sat open-mouthed. Then she started giggling and couldn't stop. Grandmother and Jill stared at her. "Would you please tell us what is so funny?" Jill asked icily.

Teresa caught her breath. "I didn't want to come because I'm sick of *your* bragging," she confessed. "It's always, 'We got a new house, a new car, a new swimming pool. Blah-blah-blah!'" Grandmother and Jill joined her in the hearty round of giggles.

When they had quieted down a bit, Teresa said, "Let's declare a truce, Jill. When one of us starts to brag, the other one says, 'Blah-blah-blah.'"

Jill nodded. "Sounds good to me," she agreed. "But what's a truce?"

Teresa raised her eyebrows. "You mean you don't know what a truce is? I learned that in third grade."

Jill grinned at her cousin. "Blah-blah-blah!" *B.W.*

HOW ABOUT YOU?

Have you noticed that sometimes the thing you dislike about someone else is a trait in your own life? God says to look at yourself before you point your finger at someone else.

MEMORIZE:

"**Do not judge, or you too will be judged.**" *Matthew 7:1, NIV*

Correct Your Own Faults

Ornamental Fruit (Read John 15:1-6)

When Bryan woke up, the strange surroundings surprised him at first. Then he remembered the plane ride that had brought him to Arizona to visit Grandma and Grandpa. He hopped out of bed at once. On his first trip here, he didn't want to waste time.

The sun streaming through the window promised a nice day. Bryan looked out and saw that the landscape was much different from that in New Jersey. When he saw the orange tree, he knew what he wanted to do first.

24

MARCH

Grandma was cooking oatmeal when Bryan went to find her. "Grandma, may I go out and pick an orange?" he asked after they had greeted one another.

"You may pick one, Bryan," said Grandma, "but they aren't good to eat." Bryan went out into the yard and picked the biggest orange he could find. It looked so good that he wondered if Grandma could be mistaken. "Grandma, are you sure it isn't good to eat?" he asked as he placed the orange on the kitchen counter.

"I'll let you be the judge," Grandma said. She cut a wedge of the orange for Bryan to taste.

As soon as his tongue touched the orange, Bryan made a face. "Ugh! Bitter," he said. "How could anything that looks so good taste so terrible?"

"That's the kind of tree it is, Bryan," said Grandma. "It looks pretty, but it can produce only poor fruit. I've often thought how much that reminds me of people."

"People?" asked Bryan.

"Yes, people who try to act like Christians without accepting Jesus," explained Grandma. "Their own efforts turn out just like the fruit of the ornamental orange tree. They may look good, but they're really not worth anything. They're actually no good at all."

E.M.B.

HOW ABOUT YOU?

Are you just trying to act like a Christian? Maybe your friends can't tell the difference, but God can. He sees your heart. He knows if you've accepted Jesus as Savior. If you've never done that, wouldn't you like to accept him now?

MEMORIZE:

"A branch can't produce fruit when severed from the vine. Nor can you be fruitful apart from me." *John 15:4, TLB*

 *Accept Christ*

Ornamental Fruit (continued from yesterday)

(Read Galatians 5:18-25)

25

MARCH

"This has been a fruitful day," Grandpa said at the close of Bryan's first day in Arizona. Bryan grinned. He and Grandpa had taken a trip to an orange grove, and they brought back lots of oranges. "Enough to have fresh fruit all week," said Grandma.

"Since our minds are already on fruit, let's examine the fruit, or spiritual qualities, that comes from following Jesus," suggested Grandpa. Opening the Bible, he found the Scripture he was looking for and handed the Bible to Bryan, pointing out the verses he should read.

"Galatians 5:18-24," said Bryan. Then in a strong voice he read the passage aloud. "That seems like a lot of fruit for one person," he added when he had finished reading.

Grandpa smiled. "Don't let the list scare you," he said. "All Christians have this fruit in their life. At the same time, we all need to work on letting more and more of it show. We aren't perfect, but we need to keep working toward that goal. That's one reason we study the Bible." He then suggested that Bryan look over the fruit listed in the passage and pick out one quality he needed to develop.

"I don't see it here," Bryan said after a moment, "but Mom says I need more patience."

"That's described here as 'longsuffering,'" Grandma told him. "Would you like us to pray with you that God will help you be more patient?" Bryan nodded, and Grandma smiled. "All right, and you can pray with me that God will continue to develop the quality of peace in my life," she said. "I still tend to worry sometimes—like when you're late getting back from the orange grove."

"And I still have trouble with self-control," admitted Grandpa. "Occasionally I get angry for some silly reason." He closed the Bible. "Let's pray daily for one another," he said. "Let's ask God to help us develop fruit to please him." *E.M.B.*

HOW ABOUT YOU?

Do you need special help with "fruit" in your life? Are you working to develop that quality? You will need the Holy Spirit's help. It's good to discuss it with your parents or pastor. They'll pray with you about it.

MEMORIZE:

"The fruit of the Spirit is love, joy, peace, longsuffering [patience], kindness, goodness, faithfulness, gentleness, self-control." *Galatians 5:22-23, NKJV*

 Produce Spiritual Fruit

Trustworthy (Read Titus 2:6-8)

Joey ran from the store with tears running down his cheeks, his feet barely touching the pavement. He felt like his heart was about to explode. When he reached home, he collapsed on the sofa. Mother gathered the little boy into her arms. "Whatever is the matter?" she asked.

26

MARCH

"Hank . . . at the s-s-store said . . . said, . . ." Joey trembled as he tried to speak. "He said, . . ." His eyes widened as he remembered. "But I didn't! I didn't!" he choked.

Mother held him tightly and asked calmly, "You didn't what, Joey?"

Joey took a deep breath. "I didn't steal candy from the store yesterday after school . . . or any time! Hank, the new clerk, said I did. He said if I'd give him five dollars, he wouldn't tell anyone. You do believe me, don't you?"

His mother stood up. "I'm going to the store."

When she returned later, Joey asked, "What happened?"

Mother smiled grimly. "When I talked to Hank, he smirked and asked how I knew you hadn't stolen the candy. I told him, 'Because I know my son.' Then Mr. Johnson, your teacher, came in. When he heard what had happened, he said, 'Joey didn't take that candy. He was with me after school. But even if he hadn't been, I'd never believe you, Hank, because Joey is one of the most honest boys I know.'"

Joey's mouth fell open. "I was so scared I forgot about going with Mr. Johnson to the library."

Mother squeezed Joey's shoulders. "Hank was mighty embarrassed. He's been getting money from little kids by threatening them. But he picked the wrong one this time."

Joey hugged his mother. "Thanks, Mom, for believing me," he said.

Mother ruffled Joey's hair. "Thanks, Son, for being trustworthy." *B.W.*

HOW ABOUT YOU?

If something like this happened to you, could your parents believe you? Are you worthy of their trust? It's important to build a good reputation—for your own sake, for your parents' sake, and also for the Lord's sake. Your reputation reflects on him.

MEMORIZE:

"**We are taking pains to do what is right, not only in the eyes of the Lord but also in the eyes of men.**" *2 Corinthians 8:21, NIV*

 *Honesty Pays*

Privilege or Punishment (Read Psalm 90:14-17)

27

MARCH

When Bill and Jane got home from school, they each found a note from their mother. She was shopping, but she had left special instructions for them. Jane's note mentioned that she was to be rewarded for being helpful lately; Bill's said he had to complete an extra task for failing to do his work earlier.

"Make a salad for supper!" exclaimed Bill as he looked at his note. "I don't think I should have to cook! It's not fair!"

"Yes, it is," replied Jane smugly. "It's your own fault for disobeying. My note said I get to wash the living room windows! I just love using the spray bottle." She went off happily, while Bill grudgingly began his tasks.

When Mother returned, Bill was in the kitchen, frowning as he chopped lettuce and tomatoes. "What on earth are you doing?" asked Mother.

"I'm doing the extra job you gave me, remember?" grumbled Bill. "And I'll be happy if I don't see another leaf of lettuce for a month."

"Oh, no!" moaned Mother. "That's the task I thought Jane would really enjoy. I must have gotten the notes mixed up. Don't tell me Jane's been washing the windows!" At that moment, Jane walked in, smiling and telling about the "fun" she had using the window spray.

As Mother explained the mistake, Jane began to giggle, and soon Bill joined in. "Isn't that funny," he said. "Jane did the hard job, but she actually liked it."

Mother nodded. "I think that's because I told Jane I was going to reward her. She believed me, and that made the dull, difficult job seem special." After a moment she added, "You know, we Christians often complain about the tasks the Lord gives us, as though he were punishing us. But if we really believe that he loves us, we'll accept those tasks as privileges instead of punishments." She turned to Bill. "And now, Son," she added, "you will have the privilege of carrying in the groceries!" *S.K.*

HOW ABOUT YOU?

Do you grumble about having to make your bed, wash dishes, or watch your younger brother or sister? The Bible says God loves you and wants to give you good things. If you really believe that, it will help you learn to enjoy the jobs you are given. Thank God for "special assignments"!

MEMORIZE:

"Trust in the Lord, and do good." *Psalm 37:3, NKJV*

 **Enjoy Serving**

When I Grow Up (Read Colossians 1:9-12)

28
MARCH

Ben frowned as he crumpled up another piece of paper. "What's wrong?" his mother asked.

"I'm supposed to write about three things I'd like to be when I grow up," replied Ben. "But the chances of me playing pro baseball aren't that good, and I don't really want to be a photographer, like Dad. I hope Dad doesn't mind."

"Ben, Dad doesn't expect you to do what he does," Mother assured him. "God has given you talents of your own to use for him."

"That's another thing. Wouldn't God want me to be a preacher or a missionary?" Ben asked.

Mother got up and walked to the window. Ben followed. "What kind of tree is that?" asked Mother.

"An apple tree," answered Ben.

"What kind of fruit does it produce?" asked Mother.

"Apples, Mom." Ben rolled his eyes.

"Apples trees don't grow grapes because they're not grape vines," said Mother. "But apple trees don't struggle to grow apples; they just produce them because God made them to do that."

"I don't get it," said Ben.

"God made you special, Ben," said Mother. "He didn't call you to be somebody you're not. Whatever you end up doing for a career should be an outgrowth of who you are. God wants you to feel good about that."

Ben thought about it. "Yeah," he said at last. "But I still don't know what to write for my paper."

"Well, think about things you're good at doing and like to do," suggested Mother. "Those can help you begin to understand God's plans for you."

Ben made two lists. One he entitled "Stuff I'm Good At." The other he named "Stuff I Like to Do." When he found that baseball, building things, and playing with little children were on both lists, he wrote his paper in no time. *M.K.N.*

HOW ABOUT YOU?

What are you good at? What do you like to do? Your interests may change as you grow up, but keep praying about these things. Be willing to let God use your special abilities in any way he sees fit, both now and in the future.

MEMORIZE:

"Commit everything you do to the Lord. Trust him to help you do it, and he will." *Psalm 37:5, TLB*

 Let God Use Your Talents

More than a Ring (Read Proverbs 3:1-10)

29

MARCH

"Now hold still, Maribeth," instructed Mrs. Dalman, who was fitting Maribeth for a junior bridesmaid dress.

"Sally showed me the wedding ring last night," confided Maribeth. She was going to take part in her cousin Sally's wedding. "I like jewelry."

"A wedding ring isn't just jewelry," Mrs. Dalman said. "Engagement and wedding rings have special meaning."

Maribeth nodded. "Everyone knows an engagement ring means a guy promises to marry a girl. I know one girl who got china instead of a ring, though."

"Rings aren't necessary," agreed Mrs. Dalman, "but they're a nice tradition. Can you guess the special meaning of the wedding ring?"

"I've heard the circle stands for unending love, and that it means 'married forever,'" replied Maribeth, "but I think that's dumb. It didn't keep my parents married."

Mrs. Dalman sighed. "I know," she said, "and that's too bad." As she helped Maribeth out of the dress, she noticed the gold cross Maribeth was wearing on a chain around her neck. "That's very pretty," Mrs. Dalman observed. "Are you a Christian, dear?" Maribeth nodded. "That's wonderful!" exclaimed Mrs. Dalman. "What church do you attend?"

Maribeth hesitated. "Actually, I can't remember the last time I've been to church," she said. "I accepted Jesus as my Savior in Bible club, but we sleep in on Sundays."

"Oh, I'm sorry to hear that," replied Mrs. Dalman. "You know, Maribeth, a couple can go through all the wedding traditions, but they also need to work at their relationship to make it grow. In a similar way, Christians can wear a cross and follow some of the Christian traditions, but if they don't want to work at their relationship with God, they don't grow spiritually. When you accepted Jesus as Savior, that was a forever heart-commitment. Attending church on Sunday is one way you can work at your relationship. Would you like me to ask your mom if you could go to church with me this Sunday?" *N.E.K.*

HOW ABOUT YOU?

Have you accepted Jesus as your Savior? If you have, the best way to grow in your relationship with him is to read the Bible, pray, and go to church and Sunday school. Even if your family doesn't attend church, maybe another relative or adult would like to take you, with your parents' permission.

MEMORIZE:

"Commit to the Lord whatever you do, and your plans will succeed." *Proverbs 16:3, NIV*

 **Be Committed to God**

Someone Is Watching You

(Read Matthew 18:6-7, 10-14)

30

MARCH

Todd pushed away the bowl of oatmeal. "I hate oatmeal, Mom. Can't I have Corn Flakes?"

"Hate oatmeal! Want Corn Flakes!" Todd's little brother screamed from his high chair and pushed his little bowl off the tray. Mother caught it just before it hit the floor.

"Todd, see what you caused?" said Mother with a sigh. "Now I'll have trouble getting Daniel to eat his oatmeal."

"Why does he always copy me?" grumbled Todd.

"Because he loves you," replied Mother. "You're his hero. He watches everything you do."

Later that day, Mother asked Todd to take out the trash. He thought she always asked him to do things at the worst possible time. "Can't I do it after I finish watching this program?" he grumbled.

"Do it now, Todd," Mother said firmly, "or you may forget."

As Todd reluctantly got to his feet, he swore under his breath. He glanced uneasily at his mother, but the commercial came on just then, and she didn't hear him.

A little later Mother called Danny. "Come and put away your toys, Son," she said.

"Watching TV," Danny replied, not moving from his cozy position beside Todd.

"Daniel," said Mother sternly, "don't make me come get you."

Mimicking Todd's words and tone, Danny swore softly.

Todd was horrified. He hadn't realized what an influence he had on his brother. "Don't say that, Danny!" he scolded. "That's a no-no. Go and do what Mom says and don't ever use that word again!"

"OK," agreed Danny. As Todd watched him leave, he couldn't help feeling guilty. Danny looked up to him, and he had set a bad example for his little brother. He resolved then and there never to use a swear word again. In fact, he didn't want to do anything in front of Danny that could be harmful to him—or to anyone else who might be watching. *E.M.V.*

HOW ABOUT YOU?

Do you do things that could be a bad example to those who are watching you? Be careful in what you do and say. Someone is always watching you. Ask God to help you be a good example to others.

MEMORIZE:

"Remember always to live as Christians should."

Philippians 1:27, TLB

 Be a Good Example

Redeeming Rosie (Read Hebrews 9:11-15)

31

MARCH

"Mom, where's Rosie?" asked Joel as he came in from school. "She's not in the yard." Rosie was their old dog.

"I'm sorry, honey," replied Mother, "but this morning I noticed the gate was open and Rosie was gone." Joel groaned. He felt terrible. "I drove all around the neighborhood, but I didn't see her," his mother continued. "Rosie's name and address are on her tags. Maybe someone will find her and call us."

The next two hours crept by as Joel waited for the phone to ring. He was upstairs when a call finally came. Mother's voice sounded excited, and Joel bounded down the steps. "Did someone find her?" he asked anxiously.

"Yes," answered Mother as she grabbed her purse and keys. "She's at the Animal Control Center, and we can go pick her up." As they drove to the center, Mother explained what had happened. "Rosie was running around in the bank parking lot, and somebody called the Animal Control Center, and they sent someone out to take her to the center. Now we have to pay the redemption fee for their services."

"Pay the redemption fee?" asked Joel. "Does that mean we have to buy our own dog back before we can take her?"

"That's what redemption means—to buy back," said Mother. She smiled at Joel's look of disbelief. "Our buying our own dog back gives us a good picture of what Jesus did for us," she said. "God made us, so we belong to him. But sin separated us from him, so he had to redeem us—to buy us back to himself."

Joel nodded. "He didn't do that with money, though, did he?" he asked.

Mother shook her head. "Not with money," she said, "but with Jesus' blood. He died for us so we could be forgiven." She turned into the driveway at the center.

Soon they were on their way home again. Rosie was so excited she could hardly sit still. "Rosie's glad to be redeemed," observed Joel, "and I am, too." *P.Y.*

HOW ABOUT YOU?

Have you been redeemed? Jesus paid a big redemption fee—his own blood—so that your sins can be forgiven. Won't you accept what he did for you?

MEMORIZE:

"It was not with perishable things such as silver or gold that you were redeemed from the empty way of life handed down to you from your forefathers, but with the precious blood of Christ." *1 Peter 1:18-19, NIV*

 Jesus Paid to Redeem You

Hard Biscuits (Read Revelation 22:17-21)

As Mike and his friend Todd Brady sat in the kitchen at Todd's house, Mike told about the joke he had played on his sister the night before. "Mom left Karen a note with directions for supper," Mike told Todd and Mrs. Brady. "I saw the note first, and I added on the bottom, 'Bake biscuits.' Karen hadn't done that before, and they were hard as rocks." He laughed as he remembered. "She was going to make me eat all the biscuits, but it didn't work. Mom wasn't really happy about it, though."

1
APRIL

The boys laughed, and Mrs. Brady shook her head. "That wasn't very nice," she scolded mildly.

"Hey, Mike," said Todd a little later, "show Mom the book about the Bible that man gave you. Some of that stuff in there sounds real weird to me."

Mike handed Mrs. Brady the book. She looked at it a few moments, then she gave it back to Mike. "I hope you throw this out without reading any more," she said. "This book is from a false cult. They deny parts of the Bible, and they also add to it."

Mike turned the book over thoughtfully. "But what if I read the book, just so I'll know what they believe?" he asked. "Then maybe I can witness to them."

"You don't know enough about the Bible yet to handle that," replied Mrs. Brady. "You might not know which part of this book is God's Word and which part is the word of a man—just as Karen didn't know which were her mother's words and which were yours."

"Yeah," admitted Mike. "Well, I don't want to do something stupid by following wrong directions. But how can I know which books are good?"

"Ask your parents and your pastor," suggested Mrs. Brady. "I'd be glad to help you, too."

Mike nodded. "OK," he agreed. "Hey, Todd," he added, "wanna play some hockey? I've got some biscuits that will make great pucks." *M.R.P.*

HOW ABOUT YOU?

Have you ever been curious about false cults or been fascinated by some strange ideas about the Bible? Be careful. You can be easily led astray. Stick with the Bible itself and with books about the Bible that can be trusted. Beware of any writings that add to or take from God's Word.

MEMORIZE:

"Don't always believe everything you hear just because someone says it is a message from God: test it first to see if it really is. For there are many false teachers." *1 John 4:1, TLB*

 Beware of False Teachings

Something Is Rotten (Read Ephesians 4:25-29)

2
APRIL

"Hi, Dad," said Melinda as she entered her father's workshop. "Can you help me build a birdhouse now?"

Dad looked up. "Hi, Melinda," he said. "I'm ready if you are. Let's pick out some wood."

Melinda and Dad went over to the bin of scrap wood. "I thought you were playing with Angie," he said as they picked out pieces they could use.

"I was," replied Melinda, "but I wanted to do this instead, so I told her I had homework to do."

Dad took several pieces of wood and put them on the workbench. "We need one more piece," he said. Then he frowned as he added, "You mean you lied to your friend?"

"Not really." Melinda shook her head. "I do have homework to do. I'll do it after we finish the birdhouse."

"But you made her think you were going to do it now, and that's a form of lying, too," Dad told her.

Melinda shrugged. "Well, it was just a little lie," she said, picking up one last piece of wood. "It won't hurt Angie's feelings or anything. She'll never know."

"Lies—even so-called little ones—hurt the people who tell them, too," Dad told her, holding a piece of wood Melinda had just handed him. Using both hands, he easily split the wood in half.

"How did you do that?" Melinda asked, wide-eyed.

"It was easy," Dad said. "Look at the wood."

Melinda looked closely and saw a crisscross of tunnels running through it. "What made that?" she asked.

"Probably termites or carpenter ants," Dad said. "They ate away at the wood until it was soft and easy for me to break apart." He looked serious. "They're not very big, but they do a lot of damage. Like lies. Lies 'eat away' at your strength as a Christian. They weaken your testimony for the Lord." *D.K.*

HOW ABOUT YOU?

Is your Christian testimony strong? Or do you weaken it with fibs and so-called little white lies to your friends, to your parents, to yourself? Telling the truth is sometimes hard, but it's always the best thing to do.

MEMORIZE:

"Do not lie to each other."

Colossians 3:9, NIV

 *Don't Lie*

Kellie's Party (Read Luke 14:15-23)

3

APRIL

When Kellie returned home from school one day, her face was glum. "I can't believe it," she said. "Sally decided to take a baby-sitting job on the day of my party. You'd think she could turn down one job! And Ann isn't coming because her favorite movie is on TV." Kellie crossed Sally's and Ann's names off her guest list.

The next day Kellie was again unhappy. "Sandra wants to hit a big sale at the mall on the day of my party," she reported to her mother. "And Liz says she has to take care of her little sister." Kellie slumped into a chair. "What's a party with no guests? I'm calling the whole thing off. Why throw a party for one or two people?"

"Well, now wait a minute!" said Mother. "Some of your friends are making other plans, but perhaps others are canceling or avoiding commitments in order to attend your party. Besides, if you want more people, there's still time to invite other classmates. You don't have to have just your closest friends."

"Oh, Mother!" wailed Kellie. "Just forget it."

Mother said nothing for a few minutes. Then she spoke quietly. "I'm reminded of another invitation," she said, "one that is given by God. He offers an invitation for salvation, but many people make other plans. They'd rather live for themselves here on earth than accept eternity in heaven." Mother smiled at Kellie. "I'm glad God hasn't chosen to forget his plan because of those who reject it. He leaves the invitation open to anyone who will accept him. God also remains willing to receive those who change their mind and decide to follow him after all. Still, it must hurt him when people refuse to accept his invitation."

Kellie knew she had never accepted God's invitation. She had heard it often, but she'd never thought much about applying it to herself personally. She thought about her own pain over a few friends and a simple party, and she wondered if God felt that way when his invitation was rejected. "I want to accept his offer of salvation," she decided. *L.B.M.*

HOW ABOUT YOU?

Have you been hurt by others who have let you down or rejected something you've offered them? Can you understand how sad God is when people refuse what he offers them? If you haven't accepted his "invitation" to have eternal life, why not do it today? He's eager to have you join his family!

MEMORIZE:

"Blessed are those who are called to the marriage supper of the Lamb!" *Revelation 19:9, NKJV*

 Accept God's Invitation

Names and Labels (Read 1 Peter 2:19-21; 3:14-17)

4

APRIL

Marcy marched into the house and headed for the kitchen, where Mom was preparing dinner. "I'm never going back to school again!" she announced, slamming her books on the table. "I hate it there."

"Why, Marcy," said Mom, looking very surprised, "what's wrong?"

"The kids call me names," complained Marcy. "Today, some of them were acting up and misbehaving, and they wanted me to join them. I wouldn't, and they chanted, 'Chicken, chicken! Marcy is a chicken!'"

Mom got out a pan and opened a can of food. "Why, look at that!" she exclaimed. "The label on this can says green beans, but there are peaches inside!"

"Good! I like peaches better than green beans," said Marcy with a grin. "But what am I going to do about being called a chicken?"

"When I was a girl, we used to say a little rhyme," said Mom. "It went like this: 'Sticks and stones may break my bones, but words can never hurt me.'"

"But words *do* hurt sometimes, Mom," said Marcy. "They hurt inside a person."

"Yes, they do—if you let them," replied Mom. "What do they mean when they call you a chicken?"

"That I'm scared—chickens are easily scared," replied Marcy.

"If that's what chicken means, I think some of those children are the real chickens," Mom said. "They're afraid they'll be laughed at if they stand up for what's right."

"Hey, that's true," said Marcy.

"But you're not a chicken," added Mom. "You weren't scared to obey your parents in spite of what the crowd did or said. You weren't afraid to do what you knew was right." She picked up the can of peaches. "No matter what label was put on this can, these are still peaches, and that's what counts. It's also what you really are that counts—not what you're called. So next time they call you names, say, 'No, I'm not a chicken. I'm a Christian, and I'm not scared to act like one.'" *M.R.P.*

HOW ABOUT YOU?

Have you ever been called names because you wouldn't do something that was wrong? Stay true to Christ. Be proud of what you really are—a faithful Christian—and never mind what label others put on you.

MEMORIZE:

"It is better, if it is God's will, to suffer for doing good than for doing evil." *1 Peter 3:17, NIV*

 Stand True to God

A New Friend (Read 1 John 5:11-13, 20)

5
APRIL

Kevin listened politely as his elderly neighbor chattered on. "I just know you and my grandson, Allen, would like each other," Mrs. Crane was saying. "He really enjoys skating. And I believe I told you that he plays football?"

Kevin nodded. "And that he's in my grade in school," he said. "And that he has a baseball card collection."

Mrs. Crane nodded happily as she left.

Kevin turned to his mother. "I don't know how often Mrs. Crane has told me about her grandson," he said. "I must know just about all there is to know about him. He sounds like a nice guy, but to tell you the truth, I'm tired of hearing about him. I wish she'd introduce us."

The next Saturday, it happened! The doorbell rang, and there was Mrs. Crane and a boy about Kevin's age. "Hi, Kevin," said Mrs. Crane. "This is Allen, my grandson." She smiled at Allen. "And this is Kevin."

Allen was visiting his grandmother for a week, so the boys played together often. Both had a great time.

"I'm glad Mrs. Crane finally introduced Allen and me," Kevin told his parents one day. "I knew all about him for a long time, but now I actually know him."

Dad nodded. "You can 'know about,' or you can 'know.' The elimination of one small word makes a lot of difference, doesn't it?" he asked. "It's that way when it comes to Jesus, too. Some people know all about him, yet they don't know him personally."

"I always think of that at this time of year," added Mother. "Many have heard the Easter story over and over. But 'knowing about' Jesus isn't enough. It's as useless as 'knowing about' Allen."

Kevin nodded. "That was really getting boring," he said. "Knowing him personally is so much better. I'm glad I know both Allen and Jesus." *H.M.*

HOW ABOUT YOU?

Have you heard over and over about how Jesus came to earth as a baby or how he died on the cross to save us. Is it getting boring to hear the same stories again and again? Maybe that's because you only know *about* him. Accept him as your Savior and friend today and begin to get to *know* him.

MEMORIZE:

"I know whom I have believed." *2 Timothy 1:12, NKJV*

 Know Jesus as a Friend

Don't Miss the Ride (Read Matthew 25:1-13)

6

Once again Allison stayed in bed after Mother had called her several times. "One of these days you'll miss that bus," Mother warned when Allison finally got up and rushed to get ready. "If you do, you know you'll be punished." Allison just shrugged as she stuffed books, pencils, and homework into her bag. Then she raced out the door and down to the bus stop. She made it! The bus hadn't come yet.

"Where are your gym clothes?" her friend Marge asked. "You know Mr. Martin's motto about being prepared."

Allison was still out of breath, but she decided to dash back home and risk missing the bus. She ran faster than ever, tore into the house, and grabbed her gym bag from the closet. Then she flew back out the door toward the bus stop. But this time the children were gone! Allison dreaded going home. "Mom," she called as she stepped cautiously into the house.

When Mother saw her, she shook her head. "How often have I warned you?" scolded Mother. "But you continue to refuse to get up in time. You know this means you're grounded and have to go to bed early for an entire week."

Allison sighed. "I'm sorry," she said as they went out to the car. "I wish being sorry would bring that bus back."

"But it won't," said Mother as she backed the car out of the drive. After a moment she added, "This makes me think of another trip that's going to take place some day. Many people don't see the need to get ready for it, and they won't be ready when it's time to go. They'll be left behind, and being sorry won't bring back the transportation for that trip, either."

"What trip is that?" asked Allison.

"The trip to heaven," said Mother. "If people aren't ready when Jesus comes for his church, they won't go with him."

"That's scary," murmured Allison.

"It doesn't have to be," replied Mother. "Since you accepted Jesus into your heart, you'll be ready for his return, and it will be exciting." *N.E.K.*

HOW ABOUT YOU?

Are you ready for the moment Jesus returns? If you haven't accepted Jesus as your Savior, ask him into your life and begin to live for him.

MEMORIZE:

"Stay awake and be prepared, for you do not know the date or moment of my [Jesus'] return."

Matthew 25:13, TLB

 Be Ready for Jesus

Four Corners (Read James 4:6-10)

Rhonda's class gathered in a big circle around the four-square game drawn on the playground. They were curious to see why their teacher, Mrs. Clint, had brought them out there. "Out west there's a place where four states meet, just like these four squares do," said Mrs. Clint, pointing to the center of the drawing where the four squares met. She used a big piece of chalk and wrote *Utah* in one square, *Colorado* in another, *New Mexico* in the third, and *Arizona* in the last. "Many tourists visit this site and enjoy walking from state to state," she told the class. "They also enjoy being in more than one state at a time. Rhonda, would you like to come and demonstrate how that can be done?"

7
APRIL

Rhonda grinned and knelt on the pavement. She put her right knee in the square marked Arizona, and her left knee in Utah, her right hand in New Mexico, and her left hand in Colorado. "I can be in all four states at one time!" she said. The other students laughed.

"Many people who visit Four Corners, USA, do the same thing," Mrs. Clint said as the students took turns trying it.

That evening Rhonda told her parents about the class. "It was fun to pretend to be in four states at one time," she said as she explained about Four Corners, USA. "I'd like to go there for real sometime."

Mother smiled. "Maybe you will," she said. "This makes me think of the discussion we had in my Bible study group today," she added. "We talked about how we, as Christians, sometimes try to stand in more than one 'state' spiritually. We say we stand on God's principles, but we want to have one foot tip-toeing in worldly activities."

"The Bible calls that being double-minded," observed Dad, "and it doesn't please God. He wants us to be sold out for him in every area of our life—not in just some areas. Just like you can't say you're actually in Colorado if one of your feet is in New Mexico, you can't say you're really living for God if one of your activities is out of his plan." *N.E.K.*

HOW ABOUT YOU?

Do you say you're living for God, but at the same time choose to do things that aren't pleasing to him? Then you're being double-minded. Living for God means living for him completely, with every part of your being.

MEMORIZE:

"A double-minded man [is] unstable in all his ways."

James 1:8, NKJV

 Don't Be Double-Minded

Accept It (Read Isaiah 55:6-9)

8

APRIL

"That dog is getting on my nerves," grumbled Linda before leaving for school. "I wish we had never agreed to watch the Carlsons' pet. He does what he wants. He never listens. And he barks, barks, barks!"

"Be glad you go to school and don't have to listen to him all day," replied Mom with a grin. "I don't think Fido is used to being tied up. The Carlsons have several acres of fenced-in land where their dog can run free, and I don't think he likes doing things our way."

"Well, we're just protecting him from traffic," grumbled Linda. "He should be grateful, but all he does is bark!"

"Fido is a dog, honey," said Mom. "He can't think like humans."

"Then he should just accept his situation," replied Linda crossly. She opened the door. "Trust us!" she hollered at the barking animal as she left for school.

That evening, Linda was so unhappy about her day that she didn't even notice Fido's barking. "I didn't get selected for the All-State Chorus," she said, almost in tears. "I think I have a good voice—and I even prayed about this. I think I should have been chosen to go."

"You do have a good voice, and I'm sorry you weren't chosen," sympathized her father. He gave her a hug. "Try to remember that God is directing your life even though you may not understand his reasons for what happens," he added.

"Well, I sure don't like what he let happen this time," complained Linda.

"That's because you're thinking like a human and not like our perfect God," replied Dad.

Mom nodded. "We're a lot like Fido," she said. "Since he's a dog and can't reason, he doesn't understand that tying him up is what's best for him. But you yourself said he needs to accept our decision and trust us even though he doesn't understand our motives. We, on the other hand, are able to reason, but not the way God does. So we need to accept his plan and trust him. Whatever he does is for our best. Accept it." *N.E.K.*

HOW ABOUT YOU?

Do you get frustrated when things don't go your way? Remember that humans don't think the way God does, so we can't always understand his perfect reasoning. He simply wants us to accept his best for our life and trust him.

MEMORIZE:

"As the heavens are higher than the earth, so are My ways higher than your ways, and My thoughts than your thoughts."

Isaiah 55:9, NKJV

 Trust God's Plan

Save the Planet (Read Ezekiel 3:18-21)

9

APRIL

Nathan carefully hung the poster up on his bedroom wall. "Extinction Is Forever . . . Save Your Planet . . . Now!" he read. Then he ran down the stairs two at a time.

"Whoa, Nathan!" said his mother. "Slow down! And what do you have in that box, Son?"

"Bumper stickers! I'm selling them for three dollars each, and the money I raise is going to help with research on ways to keep people from destroying the earth. Want to buy one of these?" Nathan asked eagerly.

"Sure," replied Mother. "I'll be glad to help in any way I can. What you're doing is very good—I'm proud of you."

Dad looked up from his newspaper. "I am, too," he agreed. Then he frowned slightly. "But isn't it too bad," he added, "that we tend to forget the thing that's in the greatest danger of all?"

"Like what?" asked Nathan. "Certain whales?"

Dad shook his head. "No, Son, I don't mean animals or the environment. I'm talking about men's souls," he said. "All those who reject Jesus are facing something worse than extinction. We should be even more interested and excited about saving souls than we are about saving the earth."

"That's right," agreed Mother. "People can save all the animals on the planet and yet lose their own souls. Now that's sad."

"I never thought about that," said Nathan. "I guess you're saying I should witness more, and invite my friends to church."

"I'm saying we all should do that," said Dad. "Now why don't I help you sell some of those bumper stickers? Maybe we'll even be able to use them as a tool for witnessing. We could hand out tracts to the people we talk to. That way we can warn them about the danger to their souls as well as the danger to the earth." *L.E.K.*

HOW ABOUT YOU?

Are you concerned about our planet? That's good—God is pleased when you do your part to stop pollution and to create an awareness of the possible extinction of some of his creation. But his greatest creation is man. People are even more important to him than the earth is—and they should be to you, too.

MEMORIZE:

"He who wins souls is wise."

Proverbs 11:30, NKJV

Work to Win Souls

Heavenly Wages (Read Hebrews 10:32-36)

10
APRIL

"Christie," said Mother, "Mrs. Jamison called, and she wondered if you could watch Matt and Stevie tonight while she's at her class." Christie gladly agreed.

That evening, Christie discovered that baby-sitting the Jamison boys was quite a challenge. All evening, they drove her crazy. She was glad when she finally saw the boys' mother pull into the driveway. Soon they all piled into the car to take Christie home.

All the way home Christie kept wondering how much she would get paid. But when they arrived at her house, Mrs. Jamison said, "Since Rick died, our budget has been really tight—I'm sorry I can't pay you now. I hope I'll have a little extra next week."

"That's OK," Christie heard herself say, but she walked into the house feeling cheated. "Mom, Mrs. Jamison didn't even pay me!" she complained loudly. "And the boys were terrible!"

Mother looked up from her sewing. "I'm sorry, dear, but I'm sure they don't have much money." Then she added, "Maybe you could do this for Jesus. If you're really doing it for him, you'll get your reward in heaven. Isn't that enough?" Christie couldn't believe what she heard! But as she went to her room, her mother's words kept ringing in her ears, and she knew God was speaking to her. Soon she returned to the sewing room. "I guess I could baby-sit as a love gift to the Jamisons and Jesus," she said quietly.

During the following weeks Mrs. Jamison often asked Christie to baby-sit. And although it meant she was in for an eventful evening, Christie chose to continue helping. She discovered that it became easier each time for her to walk away empty-handed. One day Mrs. Jamison said as she held out a check, "I appreciate your patience in waiting for this."

Christie shook her head. "There's no charge," she told Mrs. Jamison. "I just wanted to do this for you." Christie could hardly believe she had said that, but she found that it was true. She really did want to do this as to the Lord. *A.H.*

HOW ABOUT YOU?

Do you always expect people to pay you when you help them? It's nice to be paid, but any pay you may receive now cannot compare with what the Lord will give you when you serve him through serving others. Don't always expect to be paid for being helpful. Be willing to wait for the reward God will give.

MEMORIZE:

"My soul, wait silently for God alone, for my expectation is from Him." *Psalm 62:5, NKJV*

Expect Rewards Only from God

All Shook Up (Read 1 Peter 2:4-9)

Don's father picked him up after Bible club one day, and they offered Jason, a neighbor, a ride home. As they drove, they listened to a report on the cleanup efforts in an area where an earthquake had recently occurred.

"What made the earthquake start?" Jason asked.

11
APRIL

"Well, there are some places in the earth's crust that have a certain type of split, called a fault," explained Don's father. "Sometimes the sides of the fault shift, and that causes trembling, or vibrations. When they shift a great deal, even great buildings may cave in."

"Can that happen here?" Don asked fearfully. He imagined his own house tumbling down.

"According to the most recent geological maps, we're not living near any major faults in the earth's crust," Dad said. "Since we're living on a more solid foundation, chances are we won't experience an earthquake."

"I'm glad we're living on solid ground," said Jason.

Don's father nodded. "So am I," he agreed. He smiled at Jason. "But do you know," he added, "that there's a solid foundation more important than a firm spot in the earth's crust? I hope you're living on that, too."

"You mean living a life that's based on the Lord, don't you?" asked Don.

"That's right," agreed Dad. "The Lord is a firm, strong foundation, and God can hold us sure and steady even when things in life seem all shook up."

"My mom thinks her life has caved in," offered Jason.

"That's too bad," sympathized Dad. "Perhaps you can talk to her and let her know that the Lord can put her trembling life on solid ground. Or if she'd like, Don's mother and I would be glad to talk with her, too." *N.E.K.*

HOW ABOUT YOU?

Have you chosen the Lord as your life's foundation? If not, avoid a personal "earthquake" and build your life on solid ground—the Rock, Christ Jesus.

MEMORIZE:

"No one can ever lay any other real foundation than that one we already have—Jesus Christ." *1 Corinthians 3:11, TLB*

 Build Your Life on Jesus

Peggy's Rescue (Read Luke 15:11-17)

12

APRIL

Something wonderful had happened in the pig pen behind the barn. Mrs. Piggyback had given birth to ten tiny, squirming, hungry piglets! Angela was fascinated by them. She enjoyed watching Mother Piggyback gently care for her babies, keeping them close to her side, warm and cozy. Soon a delicate little reddish piglet with several spots and one black eye became Angela's favorite. "She's my little Miss Peggy Sue," said Angela proudly. "She's so cute! I love the way she trots off to explore things all by herself!"

A few days later something terrible happened. It was a cool spring morning, and Angela spotted Dad coming in with something cradled in his arms. "I need soft rags and a hair dryer," he said as he stepped into the house.

Angela's heart sank as she saw the limp form of her beloved Miss Peggy Sue tucked against his chest. "What happened?" Angela asked anxiously.

"This little piggy wandered off during the night and couldn't find her way back to the warmth of her mother and the other piglets," Dad explained. "She's very cold and weak right now."

Angela took the tiny pig and wiped off wet sand while Mother gently blew warm air around the unconscious little body. "Why? Why did she go off by herself?" Angela asked. "Piggyback was taking good care of her, and if she had stayed close to her, this never would have happened."

"I know how bad you feel," sympathized Dad as Mother looked for a box for the piglet. He put an arm around Angela's shoulders. "This reminds me of how much we, as God's children, need his love and the warmth and care of other Christians," he added. "Yet sometimes we foolishly wander away, forgetting to keep close to God's will for us." *L.P.*

HOW ABOUT YOU?

Do you become bored with church activities and think about wandering off to explore other things? Don't do it. You need the warmth and love offered by God and his people.

MEMORIZE:

"Come near to God and he will come near to you." *James 4:8, NIV*

 Enjoy Christian Fellowship

Peggy's Rescue (continued from yesterday) (Read Luke 15:18-24)

13
APRIL

Tiny Miss Peggy Sue lay propped in a box, her faint, wheezing breath the only clue that she was still alive. As Angela hung a heat bulb over the box, her cousin Jamie came in. Jamie peered at the still little form as Angela explained what had happened. Jamie shook her head. "How terrible! I'm really sorry," she said. "It's hopeless, isn't it?" She watched while Angela took an eye dropper and trickled warm milk down the piglet's throat. Jamie sighed. "It's hopeless," she repeated sadly.

All day Angela went to the box every couple of hours, feeding and stroking her pet, looking for signs of life. Finally, even her parents began to doubt the piglet would recover, but Angela refused to give up. Although they told her it probably wouldn't help, her parents allowed her to get up several times during the night to take care of Miss Peggy Sue. And even though Dad said she should be prepared for the worst, Angela kept hoping for a miracle. She prayed that Jesus would let Peggy Sue recover.

The next morning Jamie came over before school. "Come in. I have a surprise," Angela greeted her.

Jamie stared. There stood Miss Peggy Sue, wiggling and squalling for Angela to hurry with the warm milk. "If I didn't see this myself, I'd never believe it!" said Jamie. "She looked so hopeless!"

As the girls hurried to catch their bus, they chatted about things that happened over the weekend. Jamie sighed as she told Angela about the trouble she had getting along with Mike, her little foster brother. "He's so gross!" Jamie rolled her eyes. "He chews with his mouth open, steals things, and swears all the time. He even lied to Dad last night. I want my parents to take him back. We can't help him; he's hopeless!"

Angela looked at her cousin. "Didn't you say those same words about Miss Peggy Sue?" she asked.

Jamie was startled. "You're right, I did," she admitted. As she thought about it, she knew she needed to help Mike and pray for him, like Angela did for the piggy. After all, a little boy was much more important than a little pig. *L.P.*

HOW ABOUT YOU?

Do you know someone who seems hopeless? Keep praying for him or her, helping in any way you can. God's love can change that person's heart. With God all things are possible.

MEMORIZE:

"Happy is he who has the God of Jacob for his help, whose hope is in the Lord his God."

Psalm 146:5, NKJV

With God, All Is Possible

Always Shining (Read Luke 11:1-13)

14

APRIL

"What a miserable day!" grumbled Adam as he and his friend Steve trudged home from school. They walked carefully, trying to sidestep the puddles an unexpected cloudburst had produced.

"Duck weather, I call it," agreed Steve. "It's hard to believe the sun is hanging up above those clouds."

Adam looked up doubtfully at the gray skies. When a raindrop hit him in the eye, he blinked and quickly looked down again. "How do you know the sun's shining up there?" he asked.

"Remember when my mom and I flew to Houston?" asked Steve. Adam nodded. "It was a day just like this when we left," continued Steve, "but the plane got way up high—higher than the clouds. Then we could see the sun shining, and the clouds looked white and soft, like piles of cotton or something."

Adam thought about that as they reached his driveway. From below, the clouds looked more like the hard, sharp-edged sheet metal his dad had used to repair the roof of the tool shed. Could the sun really be shining up above the clouds? He decided to check with Mom.

After telling Steve good-bye, Adam raced up the walk. "Mom," he called as he went inside, "is it true that the sun is still shining?" Mother looked up from her work, puzzled at the question, so Adam explained what Steve had said.

Mother smiled and nodded. "Yes," she said. "Isn't that wonderful? If we could rise above the clouds, we could see the sun." She paused for a moment. "Even though we can't rise above the clouds in the sky today, we can rise above the clouds in our life," she added. "God's light—his understanding and help—is always there for us. As we bring our problems to him in prayer, they no longer need to weigh us down like a rainy day. We can rise above them as we trust God to deal with them." *N.E.K.*

HOW ABOUT YOU?

Do you let problems get you down, or do you quickly give them to the Lord? When you pray, do you expect an answer? You should! God is eager to bless your life and give you peace and joy. Pray every day!

MEMORIZE:

"You can get anything—*anything* you ask for in prayer—if you believe." *Matthew 21:22, TLB*

 *Pray Always*

Reminders (Read 1 Corinthians 11:23-26)

15
APRIL

"Look what my teacher gave me!" exclaimed Luke as he burst into the house waving a small flag over his head.

Mother came into the kitchen. "That's a nice flag," she said. "Do you know what it stands for?"

Luke nodded proudly. "The flag is a symbol, or a reminder, of our freedom."

"I wish I had a flag," said Natalie, Luke's little sister.

"Maybe you'll get one when you're in the second grade," Luke consoled her.

"Where's your sweater, Natalie?" asked Mother.

"At school," replied Natalie. "I keep forgetting it."

Mother frowned. "Tomorrow, I'm going to tie a string around your finger to remind you to bring it home."

Natalie giggled. "Are you really?"

"I certainly am," Mother assured her.

The next morning Mother stopped Natalie at the door. "Hold out your finger," said Mother. She tied a string around the little girl's finger. "Don't tighten it," warned Mother. "I don't want it to stop the circulation. But I do want you to remember your sweater."

Luke grinned. "The string is a symbol," he told his sister. "It's to remind you of something important."

Natalie blew Mother a kiss. "I won't forget," she said. "I promise." And she didn't.

On Sunday morning, Luke listened as the pastor explained the meaning of the Communion they were about to observe. "I know what the Communion service is for," announced Luke on the way home. "The juice and the bread are symbols—just like the flag."

"Or like the string on my finger," added Natalie. Then she looked puzzled. "But what do they remind us of?"

"Of Jesus!" stated Luke. "Right, Dad?"

"That's right," agreed Dad. "The juice is a symbol, or reminder, of Jesus' blood, and the bread is a reminder of Jesus' body. They remind us of his death on the cross."

Mother nodded. "They also remind us to thank him for what he did for us," she added. *B.W.*

HOW ABOUT YOU?

The Communion service is an important reminder of Jesus' death on Calvary. Don't ever forget the price he paid so your sins could be forgiven. Why not stop right now and thank him?

MEMORIZE:

"Do this in remembrance of me [Jesus]." *1 Corinthians 11:24, NIV*

 Remember What Jesus Did for You

The Changeable Lizard (Read Psalm 1)

Tyler took a few small bites of his dinner, but mostly he just pushed the food around on his plate. "You're being awfully quiet tonight, Tyler, and you've hardly touched your dinner," said his mother. "Did something happen at school today?"

"Rex Cofield brought a chameleon to class," Tyler said quietly. "Chameleons are lizards that change their color to blend in with their surroundings. My teacher says that protects them from their enemies."

"That sounds interesting," said Mother, "but why so quiet? Did something else happen at school?"

Tyler kept his eyes on his plate as he nodded slowly. "Rex took his chameleon out of the cage and handed it to me. We were playing with it when we were supposed to be working. Miss Evans caught us, and now we have to stay after school for a week."

Mother frowned. "That's the second time you've gotten into trouble at school this month," she said. "Rex was involved last time, too."

"Well, he always dares me to do stuff," said Tyler.

"Hmmmmm. I guess you're like that chameleon—you change to match your surroundings," observed Dad. "When you're around Rex, it's apparently a change for the worse, because that's when you get into trouble."

"You're right, Dad," agreed Tyler. "Rex always gets me into trouble."

"No, you get yourself into trouble," corrected Dad. "Perhaps you should spend more time with other friends and less time with Rex, but in any case, the way you behave is your own responsibility."

Mother nodded. "When you're tempted to do wrong," she said, "don't forget to ask the Lord to help you say no." *D.K.*

HOW ABOUT YOU?

Do you feel tempted to do the things your friends are doing, whether they're right or not? Don't be changeable, like a chameleon. Stand firmly for Jesus, and do the things that please him, no matter whom you're with. Jesus is ready to help you resist temptation. Ask him for that help.

MEMORIZE:

"**Blessed is the man that walks not in the counsel of the ungodly . . . but his delight is in the law of the Lord.**"

Psalm 1:1-2, NKJV

 **Stand Firm for Jesus**

Elephant Rides

(Read Jeremiah 31:18-20, Hebrews 12:11)

17
APRIL

"You're always scolding and punishing me," Alicia complained to her mother as she sat on the "time-out" chair. "You never get mad at Seth."

"Oh, yeah?" Seth had come into the room and overheard the remark. "I used to get punished a lot—still do sometimes. So quit poutin' and learn your lesson, Sis."

That afternoon, the whole family attended the spring festival held on the outskirts of their town. One of the main attractions for the children was the elephant rides. Dad focused his camera on Alicia and Seth as they rode first the smaller elephant, and then the bigger one. They held on tightly as a friendly trainer led them around the circle.

"Here are some pictures to help you remember this day," said Dad, holding out several pictures he had just taken with his camera. They all gathered around to see them.

"Why did that trainer hit that poor little elephant so often?" asked Mom as she looked at one of the pictures. "He didn't hit the bigger one."

"That's because the smaller elephant wouldn't go the right way. The trainer had to make it obey," explained Alicia. "He wasn't being mean."

"Oh, I see," said Mother. She nodded, then added, "Do you know that, in a way, Dad and I are 'trainers,' too? We sometimes need to correct, or discipline, you so you'll learn a lesson—like with the 'time-out' chair this morning, remember? I imagine the older elephant gets disciplined from time to time, too. But apparently it has learned from its earlier training, just like your older brother has learned from more years of training than you've had."

Dad nodded. "The Bible instructs parents to correct their children," he said.

"Hey, Mom, maybe you should hang these elephant ride photos near the 'time-out' chair at home," suggested Seth.

"Yeah—and I hope I'll never have to see them again!" exclaimed Alicia. *N.E.K.*

HOW ABOUT YOU?

Do you think your parents are mean because they correct you? Does it seem like you get punished more than your brother or sister? Remember that God uses your parents to train you to go the right way. Be thankful for them—and even for the discipline they give.

MEMORIZE:

"Train a child in the way he should go, and when he is old he will not turn from it."

Proverbs 22:6, NIV

 Accept Discipline

The Finished Table (Read Romans 4:1-8)

18

APRIL

"I'm going to Mr. Harvey's shop to pick up the table I made for Dad," Ted told his little brother. "Want to come along? We'll take the wagon. You can help pull it."

Marty clapped his hands. "Goody!" he exclaimed. "You'll tell Daddy the present's from me, too, won't you?" he asked. "Because I'm helping." Ted smiled and agreed.

At the shop, Ted showed Marty the table. Then he walked over to Mr. Harvey in a back corner of the shop and handed him some money for the supplies he had used. "Thanks for showing me how to make the table," said Ted. He waited while Mr. Harvey wrote out a receipt, and then they both turned to the bench where the table stood.

Ted gasped. Marty stood over the table with a saw in his hand. "What are you doing, Marty?" Ted yelled, running over to grab the saw. "You'll ruin the table!"

"I want to help make Daddy's table, too," said Marty, a big tear rolling down his cheek. "You said I could help."

"Yes, but you can't help make it," Ted replied, "because it's absolutely, completely finished now. You can help give it, OK?" Sniffling, Marty nodded.

"Ted, before you go, let's talk a minute," said Mr. Harvey. "What happened just now reminds me of something we talked about while you were working on the table. You told me how you hope to get to heaven. Do you remember what you said?"

"Well . . . I said that I try hard to be good," replied Ted. "I obey my parents, and I go to church. I think I'll get to heaven all right."

"Ted," Mr. Harvey said, "when Jesus died on the cross for you, he said, 'It is finished.' He did everything necessary for you to have the gift of salvation. But just as Marty tried to help you with your finished table, you're trying to help God with his completed work. Do you understand what I'm saying?"

Ted nodded as he slowly ran his fingers over the glossy table top. *M.R.P.*

HOW ABOUT YOU?

Do you think you must do good works to earn salvation? Trusting in your own good works is like saying God's plan isn't good enough by itself. Believe in Jesus, who is the "author and finisher" of your salvation.

MEMORIZE:

"Looking unto Jesus, the author and finisher of our faith."

Hebrews 12:2, NKJV

 Trust Jesus Alone for Salvation

Personal Messages (Read Ephesians 1:13-23)

19
APRIL

"You got a lot of birthday cards, Mom!" exclaimed Cal, picking one up. "This one has a note that says, 'Remember the old shoe and feeling young!' What does that mean?"

"That's from my friend Eleanor," said Mom, chuckling. "It's an old joke we have about birthdays."

Before she could explain, Cal held up another card. "This says, 'Don't forget to count to three!' I don't get it."

"That's from Uncle Dan and Aunt Betsy," replied Mom, taking the card. "It's another old joke we share with each other." She looked at a third card. "This one's from my cousin Martha, but I'm not sure what she means by the message she wrote. I guess I'll have to call and ask her."

Cal was tired of the cards. "None of them make any sense to me," he said. "I think I'll go outside."

When Mom tucked Cal into bed that evening, she noticed his Bible on the nightstand. "Did you read your Bible today?" she asked.

"A little," Cal replied, "but I didn't really understand what it was talking about, so I didn't read very long."

"Hmmm," murmured Mom. "Remember the messages on my cards? You couldn't understand them, but I could because I was familiar with the people who wrote them. That's true of the Bible, too. People who have known the Lord longer than you have can understand God's Word more easily. They can often explain it to you."

"You didn't know what the message on one card meant, though," Cal reminded his mother.

"That's a good point," agreed Mother. "I had to check with Martha to find out what she meant. In a similar way, we need to ask the Holy Spirit—the writer of God's Word—to show us the message he wants us to learn. Without his guidance, reading the Bible would be just as frustrating as trying to read the messages on someone else's mail. You wouldn't get anything out of it at all."

N.E.K.

HOW ABOUT YOU?

Do you read quickly through the Bible, ending up confused and unsure of what God wants to teach you? Ask the Holy Spirit to help you understand what he is saying. If you still don't understand, seek help from a mature Christian he has placed in your life.

MEMORIZE:

"Open my eyes that I may see wonderful things in your law."

Psalm 119:18, NIV

 *Get Help Understanding God's Word*

The Relay Race (Read Hebrews 12:1-3)

20

APRIL

Aaron stood in place on the race track, alert and ready to spring into action. He knew the other Eagles were counting on him to do his best in the relay. This year they were determined to take the trophy away from the Panthers, who had been unbeaten for four years.

When it was Aaron's turn to run, the race between the two teams was tied. Sprinting along the track at full speed and pushing himself to his limit, Aaron streaked ahead of his opponent. They were a full yard apart by the end of his run. The Panthers never made up the difference, and the Eagles won the race. Aaron was so excited!

Two weeks later, Aaron and his mother sadly arrived home from his grandfather's funeral. "I'm sure going to miss Grandpa," said Aaron, tears filling his eyes. "He was the best grandfather a guy could have. He almost seemed like my father to me, since Dad died before I can remember."

"Yes," agreed Mother as Aaron picked up a picture of his grandfather and gazed at it. "And most importantly, he set a good example for you as a Christian. He witnessed for Christ everywhere he went, and he always gave his time and his money to help others, too."

Aaron nodded. "I don't know of anyone who can take Grandpa's place," he said with a sigh.

His mother smiled. "You can," she said. Aaron looked up, startled. "You see, the Bible says that living the Christian life is like running a race. In a way, it's like a relay race," Mother explained. "The Christians who've died and gone to heaven ran in their appointed place and time—some running well, and some not so well."

"Grandpa sure ran well," said Aaron. "I think he was one of the best runners. And now I'm next in the relay!"

"Yes," replied Mother. "Grandpa has run his race. He held up the Word of God like a flaming torch as he ran. Now he's passed that torch on to you. With God's help, take the torch and run the very best you can." *M.R.P.*

HOW ABOUT YOU?

Do you know that you, too, are a runner in life's race? Many heroes of the faith have run ahead of you. But now they're gone, and the torch is passed on to you. What kind of race are you running?

MEMORIZE:

"Holding fast the word of life, so that I may rejoice in the day of Christ that I have not run in vain or labored in vain."

Philippians 2:16, NKJV

 Run Life's Race Well

The Relay Race (continued from yesterday)

(Read 1 Corinthians 9:24-27)

21

APRIL

Aaron burst into the kitchen after school one day. "Look what I've got," he exclaimed, holding up the golden figure of a runner. "Each of us Eagles got a trophy like this for winning the relay race." He held it out to his mother.

"It's beautiful, Aaron, and I'm very proud of you," said Mother, giving him a squeeze. Aaron beamed proudly as she placed the prize on a shelf. "I hope you'll have even more trophies from running life's race," she added.

"I didn't know I'd get trophies for that," said Aaron, looking surprised.

"Trophies, or rewards, will be given for faithful service to the Lord," Mother replied.

"I bet Grandpa will get lots of rewards," said Aaron. He was silent for a few moments. "It's so much harder to live a good Christian life now than it was when Grandpa was young," he added. "We kids have temptations his generation didn't have—like drugs and alcohol everywhere, and bad shows on TV, and rock music."

"That's true," agreed Mother, "but be careful not to make excuses. Each generation has its own temptations." She looked at Aaron's trophy on the shelf. "Does a good athlete face any temptations?" she asked.

"Oh, sure," replied Aaron. "Lots of times I'm tempted to eat the wrong foods, or to stay in bed when I should be up early to exercise. Sometimes I want to goof off with my friends instead of practicing my running."

"But you control your body instead of letting it control you?" Mother asked. Aaron nodded. "In your Christian race you must also deny self and resist temptations," Mother went on. "And you must run according to God's rules—his Word. If you run well, you'll receive rewards." *M.R.P.*

HOW ABOUT YOU?

Do you like trophies? Even though salvation is a free gift, the Bible says that God will give extra rewards to Christians for faithful service to him. You may have to make some sacrifices to earn them, but when you see Jesus, you'll be glad you did.

MEMORIZE:

"Behold, I am coming quickly, and My reward is with Me, to give to everyone according to his work." *Revelation 22:12, NKJV*

 Earn a Full Reward

The Growing Boy (Read Hebrews 5:12-14)

22
APRIL

"God is great; God is good," prayed Dennis, "and we thank him for our food. Amen."

Mother frowned as Dennis poured milk on his cereal. "You've been reciting that same prayer for an awfully long time," said Mother. "Maybe it's time you speak your own words when you talk to God." Dennis just shrugged.

"It's supposed to be very warm today," said Mother as Dennis put his bowl in the dishwasher a little later. "You may dig out some of your lighter-weight clothes if you like." With a grin, Dennis went to get ready for school.

Soon he returned. "Mom," he said, "my shirt shrunk!"

Mother looked at him. "That shirt is certainly too small for you," she said with a laugh, "but it didn't shrink. You're a growing boy—you're bigger." She went to help him find a different shirt, but they were all too small. Mother left the room for a moment. "Try this one," she said when she returned. She handed Dennis one of his father's shirts.

"Mom, that's way too big!" said Dennis. "I haven't grown that much." He pulled a winter shirt over his head.

"We'd better go shopping after school," decided Mother, "and get you some clothes that fit." As they returned to the kitchen, she looked thoughtful. "This reminds me of what I was saying at breakfast," she said. "Every morning you recite the same prayer. That was fine a year or two ago, just like these shirts were fine then. But you've grown. And now you're old enough to express more of your own words to God when you pray."

"But I wouldn't know what to say in a prayer," protested Dennis. "I couldn't pray like Dad and you do."

"You don't need to pray the same way your dad does, just like you don't wear his shirts yet," said Mother. "But you aren't a baby Christian anymore, either. You can just talk to God like you talk to Dad and me. And if you like, we'd be happy to help you." *N.E.K.*

HOW ABOUT YOU?

Are you satisfied just saying the same prayers that you learned when you were little? It's fun to grow and get new clothes that fit. And it's fun to grow spiritually. Try to read God's Word more, memorize more verses, and pray in your own words as you grow up in the Lord.

MEMORIZE:

"Anyone who lives on milk, being still an infant, is not acquainted with the teaching about righteousness."

Hebrews 5:13, NIV

Pray in Your Own Words

For a Good Cause (Read Genesis 45:4-8; 50:18-20)

Rodney hated riding the late bus home, but since he stayed after school for track practice, it was necessary. "Those guys are so mean to me—just because they know I go to church," he complained when he arrived home one day. "I feel like punching them out!"

"And what would that do for your Christian testimony?" asked Mom. "Be patient, Son. Be true to God, and he'll turn this around for his purpose."

Rodney wasn't so sure. "It's been a couple of weeks already," he said with a sigh.

After the evening meal, Rodney got up stiffly from the table. "You're walking around like you feel awfully sore and tired," Dad observed. "Are you sure being on the team isn't too much for you, Son?"

"I feel pretty sore," Rodney agreed. He stretched his body, then slowly collapsed on the couch. "But I don't mind aching," he added. "It's for a good cause. Coach says we're strengthening our bodies so we'll be ready when we go against tough competition."

"So I guess what seems bad now will be turned around for good?" asked Dad.

Rodney grinned. "Now you sound like Mom," he said. "That's what she tells me when I complain about the problem I'm having on the late bus. But I don't see anything good about that."

"I heard that!" Mom called from the kitchen.

Rod and Dad grinned. "Mom's right," said Dad. "Just as the hard workouts work for good to prepare your track team for success later, difficult situations we face as Christians build us up for whatever the future holds. So when circumstances seem unbearable, think of them as being for a good cause, too. God will eventually turn those negative experiences into something for his good." *N.E.K.*

23

APRIL

HOW ABOUT YOU?

Do you get discouraged and angry when you're treated badly or when seemingly bad things happen? Ask God to turn these difficult experiences into something good.

MEMORIZE:

"God turned into good what you meant for evil."

Genesis 50:20, TLB

 God Uses Difficulties

Powerful Words (Read Ephesians 4:29-32)

24

APRIL

Bang! The door slammed behind Holly. Dad looked up from his newspaper. "It seems like Holly is always angry these days," Mother told him. "It's so peaceful until she comes home. In five minutes she has Jeremy crying and me upset. Nothing and no one pleases her."

Dad folded the paper. "Part of being a teenager?"

Mother shrugged. "Maybe," she said, "but we can't live with this another seven years. Holly has to get control of her temper and her tongue."

Five-year-old Jeremy burst into the kitchen. "Holly threw my markers on the floor and called me a brat!" he said with a sob.

Mother gave a tired sigh. "I'll talk with her, Jeremy," she promised. "Would you like to watch for Grandpa Nels? He should be here any minute for dinner."

"Grandpa Nels is coming! Whoopee!" His problems forgotten, Jeremy went jumping down the hall.

During dinner, everyone—even Holly—laughed and talked and listened. "I'm glad you're here, Grandpa," Holly said with a smile. "You make us all feel so good."

"That's 'cause he says funny, happy things," stated Jeremy.

The elderly gentleman winked at the little boy. "Let's have a little quiz. Holly, how did God create the world?"

Holly thought for a moment. "He just spoke, and it was there," she said.

Gramps nodded. "Right. Hebrews 11:3 says the worlds were formed by the word of God. Now here's something interesting—God has given us the ability to create things with our words, too. We can create happiness or gloom."

"Holly makes storms with her words," Jeremy declared. Mother gave him a warning look. "But you make sunshine, Gramps," Jeremy continued. "That's why we like you to come to our house."

And for once, Holly did not argue. *B.W.*

HOW ABOUT YOU?

What do you create with your words? Are people glad to see you come? Or are they glad to see you go? Words are powerful. Be careful how you use them.

MEMORIZE:

"May my spoken words and unspoken thoughts be pleasing even to you, O Lord my Rock and my Redeemer."

Psalm 19:14, TLB

 Use Words Wisely

Green Thumb (Read Romans 12:3-11)

Plink! Plink! Plink! Marcy slowly picked out the notes of her new piano recital piece. "This piece is too hard, Mom," she complained. "I'll never get it." She struggled on for a few minutes—*plink, plink, plink.* Suddenly she slammed the music book shut and tossed it on the floor. Then she began to play a song she knew from memory. *Oh, this was much more fun!* she thought as she played.

25

APRIL

Later that day, Marcy helped her mother plant seeds in the flower garden. "You had the prettiest flowers in the neighborhood last year, Mom," she said. "Grandma says you have a green thumb, whatever that means."

Mother laughed. "She means I have a talent for growing things," she replied. "That may be true, but I have to put in a lot of work, too. Thomas Edison, the great inventor, said, 'Genius is one percent inspiration and 99 percent perspiration,' and I think he was right."

Marcy grinned. "You do work hard in the yard," she agreed. "What's worse," she added teasingly, "you make me work hard, too. I don't mind gardening, but I don't have a green thumb like you do."

"What do you like to do best of all?" asked Mother.

"Play the piano," said Marcy promptly.

Mother nodded. "Good," she approved. "The Lord definitely did give you the talent for it. But, like having a green thumb, having musical ability is not enough. If you want to develop it into something worthwhile, you'll have to really work at it. I believe God wants us to use our talents for him, and he deserves the very best we can do, doesn't he?"

"I guess so," agreed Marcy. "I guess I ought to practice my recital piece. But it's not fair! I can help you in the garden, but you can't help me play the piano!"

"That's true," said Mother, "but I'll tell you what. When we're finished here, I'll use another one of my talents while you practice the recital piece. I'll work on your new dress. How's that?" Smiling, Marcy agreed. *M.R.P.*

HOW ABOUT YOU?

What talents has God given you? Perhaps the Lord will want you in his service full-time. If not, there are many other ways you can serve God. Begin now to work hard at developing your talents for his service. Make your possibilities become realities!

MEMORIZE:

"Whatever you do, work at it with all your heart, as working for the Lord, not for men."

Colossians 3:23, NIV

 Do Your Best for God

Color-Blind (Read Acts 17:24-28)

26
APRIL

Bernie struggled with the color chart. *Why is Mrs. Lebo making such a big deal about primary and secondary colors before letting anyone paint?* he wondered.

"Bernie, please come up front and take the red color card," Mrs. Lebo said. Bernie rose from his seat slowly. He looked at the cards resting in the chalk ledge against the board. Then he lifted a card. Everyone laughed. "You're not funny," Mrs. Lebo said sternly. "Put down that green card and pick up the red one."

Bernie frowned. "I'm color-blind," he said softly. "It's hard for me to tell red from green."

"Oh, I'm sorry, Bernie. I didn't know that," apologized Mrs. Lebo. "You're excused." Bernie returned to his seat, feeling like everyone was looking at him.

At recess time, Bernie played with a boy of a different nationality from his own. "Hey, Bernie," one of their classmates called to him, "no wonder Ray is your best friend. You can't tell that he's a different color!"

"Ignore him," Bernie told Ray. "He's so dumb!" Bernie could never understand people who decided not to like a person based on the color of his skin.

During science class, the subject of color blindness came up again. Bernie was asked several questions about it. "You mean a lot of times you don't know what color things are?" asked one girl. "Like spinach or strawberries?"

Bernie grinned. "What does it matter what color they are?" he asked. "They taste good, and Mom says they're good for me." Bernie paused. Then, taking a deep breath, he added, "Color isn't what makes something good or bad. God made everything and everybody, and he gives them their value." He looked at the boys who had teased him at recess. "Especially people," he added. "I think everybody should be 'color-blind' when it comes to seeing people."

N.E.K.

HOW ABOUT YOU?

Do you develop opinions about others based on their color? Remember that God made everyone special. Love people for who God made them to be—his children.

MEMORIZE:

"And [God] has made from one blood every nation of men to dwell on all the face of the earth." *Acts 17:26, NKJV*

 Don't Be Prejudiced

How Many Legs on a Sheep? (Read Psalm 32:1-7)

27

APRIL

"Come on, Greg. Try your luck," called Chuck. "It's just a nickel a throw, and the winner takes all." He and several classmates stood in a group on the playground. "Just stand on this chalk mark and throw your nickel as close to that other mark as you can," instructed Chuck. "The one who gets closest wins all the nickels."

Greg hesitated. This sounded a little bit like gambling. Then he shrugged his shoulders, telling himself it was just a game of skill. He joined the others and played three games, losing each time. "This is fun," Greg said. "I'll get my nickels back tomorrow and win a few more besides!"

Each day the boys played. Sometimes Greg won, but usually he lost all he put in. One day he took his lunch money, changed it to nickels, and lost every one of them. He went home very hungry.

As he raided the refrigerator, Mom asked, "Why are you so hungry, Greg? Didn't you eat lunch?" As Greg fumbled for words, Mom went on. "Your sister tells me you changed your lunch money into nickels at the store this morning. What's going on?" Knowing he couldn't hide much from his mother, Greg told her about the game. "Why, that's gambling," said Mom. "Don't you know that?"

"It's a game of skill," protested Greg. "The trouble is I'm not very good at it—but I'm getting better."

"Greg, how many legs would a sheep have if you called his tail a leg?" asked Mother.

Greg laughed. "What a funny question! If you called his tail a leg, a sheep would have five legs."

Mom shook her head. "No. It would still have four legs. Calling his tail a leg wouldn't make it one. And calling gambling by some other name doesn't change it. You've not been playing a game of skill, but of chance—taking a risk. And gambling is wrong." *M.R.P.*

HOW ABOUT YOU?

Have you been trying to cover up some wrongdoing by calling it a habit, a mistake, an imperfection, or some other such thing? If you have, admit your sin, confess it to God, and ask him to help you never to do it again. He'll gladly forgive you.

MEMORIZE:

"I finally admitted all my sins to you and stopped trying to hide them. I said to myself, 'I will confess them to the Lord.' And you forgave me! All my guilt is gone." *Psalm 32:5, TLB*

 Call Wrongdoing Sin

Lavender Green (Read Romans 15:1-7)

28 APRIL

"Whatever happened to your friend Matt?" asked Laura as she worked with her brother in the garden. "How come he doesn't go to youth group with you anymore?"

"I don't know," replied Peter. He settled back on his heels and looked up. "He seemed to fall apart when his parents got divorced. He started hanging around with the wrong crowd and didn't seem to have time for church."

"He is a Christian, isn't he?" asked Laura.

"Yeah, I think so, but you sure can't tell it now." Peter went back to weeding. "Kinda disgusting, isn't it? Sometimes I feel like telling him a thing or two!"

"Watch what you're doing!" exclaimed Laura. "That's one of Mom's lavender plants you're trying to pull up." Laura knelt beside him. "Look, it's not really dead. There's a little green on it down here." She showed him what she meant. "And it's stuck because lavender plants put their roots down really deep."

"Well, if it's not dead, why does it look like it is?" Peter wanted to know.

Laura shrugged. "It just had a hard winter, I guess. Some of Mom's plants weathered the winter just fine, but that one had a tougher time for some reason. We'll just have to take special care of it now."

Peter sat and stared at the lavender plant for a long time. Finally Laura nudged him. "Hey, get back to work."

"I was just thinking," said Peter slowly, "that maybe Matt is like the lavender. He's had a rough time lately, so maybe I should be taking special care of him."

"I think you're right," agreed Laura. "Instead of judging him, you should pray for him, and I should, too."

"And I'll be sure to include him in things at church," Peter said. He jumped up. "In fact, I'm going to call him right now and invite him to youth group this week." *S.P.Z.*

HOW ABOUT YOU?

Do you have a friend who seems to have forgotten the Lord? Are you praying for that person? Are you encouraging him to come to church activities? Are you loving him like Jesus would?

MEMORIZE:

"We urge you, brothers, warn those who are idle, encourage the timid, help the weak, be patient with everyone."

1 Thessalonians 5:14, NIV

 Encourage One Another

Gone Fishin' (Read John 6:32-35)

29

APRIL

Don sighed. He wished a fish would take his bait. When the line finally jiggled, he jerked it up quickly, but there was no fish, and part of the worm was gone. "That's one that got away," said Grandpa with a chuckle. "Try again." Grandpa helped Don bait the hook.

After a little while, Don pulled up a fine-looking fish. "I got one this time," he yelled.

After Don and Grandpa caught several more fish, Grandpa stuck the oars in the water and rowed for shore.

"Jesus talked to his disciples about fishing," said Grandpa as he rowed. "Some of them had fished for a living, so they understood fish talk. Jesus told them they should be fishers of men."

Don wrinkled up his nose. "I know," he said. "We sing that song in Sunday school, but I don't get it. How do you fish for people?"

"You offer them food—spiritual food—just like you offered worms to the fish," replied Grandpa. "Jesus called himself the Bread of Life, so telling others about their need of him is like offering them food."

Don thought about that. "Sometimes they don't bite, though, do they?" he said.

Grandpa shook his head. "Nope," he said. "Some don't want to hear about Jesus at all. And others are like the fish that only nibble. They're sort of interested, but not too much, and they leave after hearing only a little about Jesus. But," Grandpa's eyes sparkled like the water around the boat as he spoke, "other people are like the fish we caught. They want to know all they can, and they receive Jesus as Savior."

Don grinned as he admired the fish in the bucket. "So we have to keep fishin', don't we?" he said. "Even when it seems like they're not bitin', we have to keep telling people about Jesus." *C.Y.*

HOW ABOUT YOU?

Would you like to be a fisher of men? Then watch for opportunities Be patient and faithful, and maybe someone will come to the Lord because of your witness.

MEMORIZE:

"Follow Me, and I will make you become fishers of men."

Mark 1:17, NKJV

 Fish for People

It's Not Really Free (Read Ephesians 2:4-9)

30

APRIL

As Brandon sat down to eat lunch at the kitchen table, an advertisement on the bread wrapper caught his attention. "Free gift!" he read. "Skipper Sam Raceboat! See details on bottom of package." Brandon flipped over the loaf of bread. "Mom, look!" he exclaimed. "A Skipper Sam Raceboat for absolutely nothing! This costs $12 if you buy it at the store."

"Let me see," said Mom, wiping her hands on a towel. She studied the information. "Brandon, did you notice what you need to send in with this order form?" she asked, handing him the loaf of bread.

"I think three proof-of-purchase tags from Skipper Sam Raceboats—hey!" Brandon interrupted himself. "That means I'd have to buy three boats just to get one free. That's $36!" He pushed the bread away. "It's not really free," he said, disappointed.

"Very often when something is offered for free, there is something to buy first, or there's some other requirement to meet," said Mom as she sat down at the table. "There's only one offer I've found that is truly free."

"What's that?" asked Brandon eagerly.

"It's the gift of salvation," Mom replied with a smile. "God's gift of eternal life is free to anyone. The only special requirement is that you accept the offer."

Brandon grinned. "Yeah, and that's a requirement I can meet!" he said. "In fact, I already met it."

"It's a requirement everyone can meet," Mom said, as they bowed their heads to thank the Lord for their meal. *D.E.M.*

HOW ABOUT YOU?

Have you heard about God's free gift? You can't earn it or buy it. But you do need to accept it. Jesus has paid the price for your salvation. Why not tell him you'll accept his offer of eternal life?

MEMORIZE:

"For the wages of sin is death, but the gift of God is eternal life in Christ Jesus our Lord."

Romans 6:23, NIV

 Salvation Is Free

Grounded (Read Numbers 12:5-15)

Ben was in trouble. He had come home late again. He explained that the guys wanted to play just one more inning. "The game was tied up, and no one wants to quit then, do they?" Ben asked logically.

"Your mother and I understand what you're saying," said Dad, "but you were given a special warning to be home right on time today. So we have decided to ground you for the rest of the week, including Saturday. Is that clear?"

1

MAY

"Grounded!" Ben was horrified. "Oh, please—I promise to come straight home from now on. Just don't ground me on Saturday," he pleaded. But his parents remained firm.

Ben was grumpy as he turned away. "Whoever invented grounding, anyhow?" he muttered to himself, but loud enough to be sure his dad could hear. "I don't think it's right to keep a person from his friends."

After dinner Dad picked up the family Bible. "Listen to this, Ben," he said, leafing through it. "I think you'll find it interesting." Dad began to read about Moses and the children of Israel. Moses' sister, Miriam, who had been a great help to Moses, later rebelled against him, and God had to discipline her. Dad read, "'The Lord replied to Moses, . . . "Confine her outside the camp for seven days; after that she can be brought back"'" (*NIV*). Dad closed the Bible and looked at Ben, whose downcast expression showed that he realized the idea of keeping a person from being with his friends hadn't been invented by his parents.

"The Lord knew the kind of discipline Miriam needed at that point, didn't he?" said Dad. "She had to accept the punishment he ordered and learn from it. We trust you will accept and learn from your grounding, too." Dad smiled and put his arm around Ben's shoulder. "It's OK, Son. It won't be so bad. At least we're not shutting you out in the backyard for seven days, right?"

With a sigh, Ben nodded. *P.K.*

HOW ABOUT YOU?

Do you feel picked on when your parents punish you—especially if you feel you had a good reason for breaking a family rule? God has given your parents authority, and because of this, you are to honor and obey them. Accept the discipline they give. Learn from it.

MEMORIZE:

"No discipline seems pleasant at the time, but painful. Later on, however, it produces a harvest of righteousness and peace for those who have been trained by it." *Hebrews 12:11, NIV*

 **Be Obedient**

The Brick House (Read Luke 6:47-49)

2
MAY

"Here's where I'll be laying bricks soon," Dad told Billy as he stopped his car. "Want to take a look?"

"Sure, Dad," answered Billy, getting out of the car. "What are you going to build here?"

"A beautiful brick house," answered Dad. "I came to check on the foundation." He walked all around, viewing the groundwork from every angle. "This is excellent," he said as they returned to the car. "I'm satisfied that I'll be laying bricks on a good foundation. Do you remember the news report about the beautiful house that was destroyed in the storm we had the other day? It fell because it was built on a poorly-constructed foundation. I'd hate for that to happen to a house I build."

"Me, too," agreed Billy.

"So, are you building on a solid foundation then?" asked Dad.

"Me?" Billy was surprised. "I want to be a builder like you someday, but I'm not building anything now."

"Yes, you are," insisted Dad. "Oh, you're not building a house of bricks or wood, but you're building your 'life-house' day by day. Jesus talked about the importance of building it upon the proper foundation. Do you know what that is?"

"Sure," replied Billy. "It's Jesus. I trusted him as Savior, so I'm building my life on him."

"Good," approved Dad. "When the Rock, Jesus Christ, is the foundation for your life-house, you can stand in the storms of life—during the times when troubles come. And when life is over, you'll go to heaven and won't have to face the greatest storm of all, Judgment Day. But what do you think would happen if your life-house were built on 'sand'—on anything or anyone but Jesus?"

"And the house on the sand went smash!" sang Billy. Dad joined him, and together they sang the last verse. "So build your life on the Lord Jesus Christ. . . . Build your life on the Lord."

M.R.P.

HOW ABOUT YOU?

On what foundation are you building your life-house? Are you hoping to get to heaven because you behave well and go to church? If so, you're building on shifting sand. The Rock, Jesus Christ, is the only sure foundation. Believe in him now.

MEMORIZE:

"For no other foundation can anyone lay than that which is laid, which is Jesus Christ."

1 Corinthians 3:11, NKJV

 Build on the Rock, Jesus Christ

The Brick House (continued from yesterday)

(Read 1 Corinthians 3:9-15)

"The bricks have arrived for that house I'm building, Billy," said Dad. "I'm going over there. Come along and see how many bricks it takes for one house."

Soon they arrived at the building site. "Wow, that sure is a big pile of bricks!" exclaimed Billy. "I guess that means you've got a whole lot of work to do."

Dad nodded. "If I do my work right, these bricks will become the walls of a beautiful, sturdy house." He smiled at his son. "We talked the other day about building a life-house," he said. "Billy, since you're still young, I think we can say that you have a great pile of bricks to work with, too. All your thoughts, words, and deeds are like bricks with which you're building your life-house day by day, as long as you live."

"Oh, neat," said Billy with a grin.

His father motioned toward the bricks. "Can you think of any other buildings I might be able to build with these bricks?" he asked.

"Oh, you could build a church or a hospital or a shopping mall—most any kind of building," said Billy.

Dad nodded. "That's right. These bricks could even be built into a bar—although I would never be the builder. Billy," he said, "it's up to you, the builder, to decide what kind of building your life will be. Day by day you can lay the bricks of glorifying God and witnessing for him, or you can build selfishly, living to please yourself."

"I really do want to build a good life-house, Dad," Billy said seriously. "I'm going to be very careful how I build." *M.R.P.*

3

MAY

HOW ABOUT YOU?

What kind of life-house are you building? Think of each thought, word, and deed as a brick to be used in building your life-house. With God's help, build wisely.

MEMORIZE:

"Through wisdom a house is built, and by understanding it is established." *Proverbs 24:3, NKJV*

 Build Your Life-House Wisely

The Brick House (continued from yesterday)

(Read Psalm 119:9-16)

4
MAY

"There it is, Billy—all completed. What do you think of the brick house now?" asked Dad.

"Wow! It's super!" exclaimed Billy. "Look how straight and even those bricks are! I've been telling everyone that my dad's the best bricklayer in town."

"Well, how nice! Thank you," said Dad. "I did have a problem one day, though—I laid some bricks out of line. I didn't realize it until I used the plumb line."

"The plumb line? What's that?" asked Billy.

"It's a line that's fastened to a narrow board on one end and to a piece of lead on the other. I'll show you when we get home," promised Dad. "When a plumb line is hung alongside a wall, the weight of the lead keeps the line straight. As I build, I often use one to see if my bricks are in line."

"What did you do with the crooked bricks?" asked Billy.

"I knocked them out and started again from that point," answered Dad. After a pause, he added, "Did you know that we sometimes get the bricks of our life-houses out of line? It happens when we sin. Sins, even though they seem small to us, keep our life from being straight and true."

Billy was silent for a few moments. "But I can't undo things I've done wrong and start over again, can I?"

Dad put his arm around Billy. "Well, you can confess your sin to God," he said. "That's something like knocking out the crooked bricks, because God will forgive you. Then every day use God's plumb line, the Bible, to help you stay in line with what's right."

M.R.P.

HOW ABOUT YOU?

Have you been letting God's Word be the plumbline for the building of your life-house? Read the Bible often and apply its teachings to your life. Use it to check your thoughts, your words, your actions, your companions, and your desires. Keep the walls of your life-house straight and true.

MEMORIZE:

"Every law of God is right, whatever it concerns. I hate every other way."

Psalm 119:128, TLB

Stay in Line with God's Word

Wade's Secret Project (Read Luke 17:11-19)

5
MAY

Wade took the glue his mother handed him and ran out to the shed. He worked for a while on his special project. Then he ran back to the house. "Can I use a hammer and some nails?" he asked his father. Soon he ran back to the shed carrying the hammer. "Paint! I need paint," Wade said later, and he went to find his sister, Margie. "Can I use some of your paint?" he asked. While Margie was still giving him special orders not to use it all, Wade took the paint and darted out the door.

After school the following day, Wade brought his friend Bob home to play. Mother set out glasses of cold milk and shiny red apples. "Thank you, ma'am," said Bob as he helped himself. When he had finished eating, he again thanked her for the food. Before leaving for home later, Bob politely thanked Wade's mother for letting him come. Mother was impressed. "Bless his heart," she said after Bob had left. "Bob seems to be very polite."

"Yeah, he's like that," agreed Wade. "He even says thank you when the teacher hands papers back to him."

"Well, that's good," approved Mother. "After all, God says we are to be thankful for everything. That means little things, too. We should give thanks to God and to other people as well."

After dinner, Wade brought out his secret project. He had made something for everybody. "We learned how to make these things in shop class at school," he explained. For Mother, there was a recipe holder; for Dad, a tie rack; and for his sister, a jewelry box.

Wade beamed as his family exclaimed over the gifts and thanked him warmly. He was happy that his family appreciated his hard work and the special big surprise. *Thank-yous really are nice,* Wade thought. Aloud he said, "Now I'm going to start on another secret project. And thank you for the paint, the glue, and the hammer." He decided not to tell anybody, but from now on Wade's secret project was going to be taking time to say thank you—even for little things. *N.E.K.*

HOW ABOUT YOU?

Do you sometimes forget to say thank you? Do you get things and just assume the giver knows you appreciate it? Remember to express your thanks to people and to God for all things, no matter what the size.

MEMORIZE:

"Giving thanks always for all things to God." *Ephesians 5:20, NKJV*

 **Say Thank You**

Trusty (Read Isaiah 55:6-9)

6
MAY

Aaron and his mother were cleaning his closet. "Here," said Mom as she handed him a box, "you sort through this."

Aaron sat down with the box. He found an old pair of ice skates that were too small now and a perfectly good yo-yo. He put the yo-yo in his pocket. Then he found an old, red rubber ball. "Look, Mom! Trusty's ball," he said.

"Yes," said Mom quietly.

"Can I keep it? To remember him by?" Aaron asked.

"If you want to," said Mom.

Aaron sighed. "I wish God made dogs so they live as long as people do," he said. "I miss Trusty."

"I know. I do, too," said Mom. "But you know, he was an old dog. He lived a good, long life."

"Yeah, but I loved him," replied Aaron. "I still don't see why he couldn't have lived a little longer."

Mother gave Aaron a hug. "Remember how Trusty hated it when we had to go away and he had to stay home?" she asked. "He had to stay in the basement because he'd tear things up if he were left alone in the house."

Aaron nodded. "I always hated to make him go down there. I tried to tell him we'd be back soon, but he didn't understand."

"Sometimes it's like that with God and us," said Mom. "I think there are things he can't explain to us because we can't understand them. We just have to trust him anyway, like our dog always trusted us. He always went into the basement, even though he didn't like it, remember?"

"Yeah," said Aaron. "I guess we should all be like Trusty, huh?"

"We really should," agreed Mom. *M.K.N.*

HOW ABOUT YOU?

Do you sometimes wonder why God lets certain things happen? Can you trust him even when you don't know why? The Bible tells us that God is faithful and true and that he loves us. Trust him even when you can't understand.

MEMORIZE:

"Trust in the Lord with all your heart, and lean not on your own understanding."

Proverbs 3:5, NKJV

 Trust God in Everything

Just like the Kings (Read Luke 6:40-46)

As Josh and Jennifer walked home, Jennifer told a joke she'd heard at school that day. Josh laughed heartily.

Just then an old man standing in the yard they were passing spoke to the children. "Excuse me," he said, "do you kids belong to the Joshua King family?"

Surprised, Josh and Jennifer stopped. "Yes, sir," answered Josh. "Joshua King is our father."

The white-haired old man smiled. "I used to live next door to your grandpa when your pa was a little boy," he said. "The two of you look like he did then, with your blonde hair, freckles, and turned-up noses. And that laugh of yours, young fella—why, your pa used to chuckle like that when he was tickled. Yep, I just knew you belonged to the Kings."

That evening the children told their father about their conversation. "That must have been our old neighbor, Mr. Tidewell," decided Dad. "You'll have to show me where he lives, and I'll stop by to see him." Looking thoughtful, Dad went on, "You know, Josh, there's one trait of the Kings I've seen in you lately that bothers me."

Josh looked surprised. "Really?" he asked. "What is it?"

"I'm afraid many of us Kings have been known for our bad tempers," answered Dad. "This is something I've had to work on in my own life. With God's help, I've learned to control my temper. Like me, you tend to fly off the handle too easily, Son."

"It's OK to be just like the Kings in the good stuff, but not the bad, right?" said Jennifer. "I'm glad I don't have a temper like that."

Dad frowned. "The Kings tend to be a little proud and boastful, too," he told her. "That's not good, either."

Josh grinned. "Looks like we both need to ask Jesus to help us be more like him," he said. "Hey! Wouldn't it be great to have someone ask us if we're in God's family because we look and sound like Jesus?" *M.R.P.*

7
MAY

HOW ABOUT YOU?

Are you in God's family? If so, can people tell it by watching you? Make it easy for everyone to tell you're a Christian because you act like a child of God.

MEMORIZE:

"Whoever is living a life of sin and doesn't love his brother shows that he is not in God's family." *1 John 3:10, TLB*

 Act like God's Child

The Safety Pin (Read Psalm 101:1-8)

8
MAY

"Mary, please play ball with me," pleaded little Amy.

Mary frowned. She didn't want to play ball. "I can't," she said. "I have to do my homework."

As Amy walked sadly away, the phone rang. "I'll get it, Mom," called out Mary. She picked up the phone. "Hi, Andrea," she said. "What? No, I don't have anything else to do. Making cookies sounds fun. I'll ask Mom if I can come over. I'll call you back. Bye."

As Mary turned from the phone, she saw her mother shaking her head. "How could you tell Andrea you were free when you just told Amy you had to do your homework?" asked Mother.

Mary looked uncomfortable. "Well, I do have homework, but it can wait a while," she said. "I needed an excuse to keep from having to play Amy's childish games."

Mother shook her head. "That was more than an excuse, Mary," she said. "It was a lie."

"But it was just a little white lie," protested Mary.

Mother sighed. "Mary," she said, "lately you've been acting as though a little lying or a little disobeying isn't very bad. But all our sins—whether we consider them little or big—are why Jesus died for us. We should hate them." After a moment she added, "We've told you about our scary experience when you were a baby, remember?"

"You mean when I swallowed an open safety pin and almost died," replied Mary.

Mother nodded. "When the doctor removed the pin from your throat, he asked me if I wanted to keep it for a souvenir. I shuddered and said, 'No! Please take it away. It almost killed my baby, and I never want to see it again.' It was just a little pin, but it almost killed you. And, Mary, our sins—big and small—killed Jesus. Do you think we should want to hold on to any of them?"

Mary slowly shook her head. "I'll tell Andrea I can't come, and then I'll play with Amy," she said. "I never thought about it that way before." *M.R.P.*

HOW ABOUT YOU?

Do you excuse some of your sins, calling them little or not very bad? Since even "little" sins are part of the reason Jesus died, you should never want anything to do with any of them.

MEMORIZE:

"For whoever keeps the whole law and yet stumbles at just one point is guilty of breaking all of it." *James 2:10, NIV*

 Don't Excuse Sin

Trapped (Read Philippians 4:11-13)

Dave watched as his grandfather tightened the final screw on the birdhouse they had made. Then they mounted the complete birdhouse on the trunk of a maple tree in Grandpa's back yard.

9

MAY

Later that afternoon, Grandpa grinned at Dave. "If you keep pacing back and forth to that window, you'll wear holes in your tennis shoes," he teased.

"I want to see what kind of birds come," replied Dave. "Hey!" He pointed out the window. "A squirrel is trying to get into the birdhouse!"

"Don't worry. The bird book says the hole is too small for that furry fellow," Grandpa reassured Dave. "He can't chew the entrance larger, either, because we put a piece of metal around the hole."

Grandpa and Dave laughed as they watched the squirrel wiggle, squirm, and turn circles, trying to get into the birdhouse. Suddenly, to their amazement, the squirrel squeezed through the hole! He disappeared for a few minutes. Then he stuck his head back out. Once again they watched as he struggled and squirmed and stretched, trying to get back out, but he couldn't escape.

"Well," said Grandpa, "if that squirrel could talk, I imagine he'd say, 'What I thought I wanted became my trap.' And if he knew the Bible, he'd probably quote the verse we memorized this morning."

Dave wrinkled his brow. "This morning?" he asked. "Oh, yeah." He grinned. "God gave them their request, but sent leanness into their soul."

Grandpa nodded. "Let's go rescue Mr. Squirrel," he said. They went out to the yard, and Grandpa blocked the hole in the birdhouse and took it down. After releasing the squirrel, they decided they had better make the hole in the birdhouse a little smaller.

"You know, Dave, sometimes we're like that squirrel—we squirm and struggle to get what we want, too, whether it's what God wants or not," said Grandpa as he worked. "Then sometimes God will let us have what we think we want. When we get it, though, we find it doesn't make us happy after all." *D.S.B.*

HOW ABOUT YOU?

Do you beg your parents to let you take part in questionable activities or to go places that would not please God? Do you plead with God for more and more things rather than thanking him for what you already have? Be careful. Learn the following verse to remind you to be content with what God provides.

MEMORIZE:

"[God] gave them their request, but sent leanness into their soul." *Psalm 106:15, NKJV*

 Want What God Wants

In the Dark (Read Psalm 119:105-112)

10
MAY

Chip was sitting next to his grandma in her big armchair as she read aloud from her Bible. The thunderstorm made him glad to be safe and warm in the house, but Chip would have preferred to hear Grandma read something from his new story book.

All of a sudden, there was a flash of lightning followed by a big crack of thunder. All the lights went out. "Grandma!" Chip cried out. "What happened?"

"It's nothing to worry about," Grandma assured him. "Sometimes the lightning hits a power pole. Often the electricity is just out for a few minutes."

"I don't like the dark," Chip said. "It's scary."

"There's a flashlight in the drawer next to the stove," said Grandma. "Do you want to go find it?"

Chip jumped up and started toward the kitchen, but he bumped his knee on an end table. "Ouch!" he yelped. He took a couple more steps and bumped into the couch. Then he had an idea. He dropped down onto his hands and knees and crawled the rest of the way to the kitchen.

Chip opened the drawer, found the flashlight, and switched it on. The way back to Grandma's chair was easy, now that he could see where he was going. Just as he reached the chair, the lights came back on.

Chip rubbed his sore knee. "It sure was hard trying to find my way in the dark," he said.

Grandma smiled. "People who live without reading the Bible live in the dark all the time," she told him. "Do you know why?"

"I guess because the Bible is like a flashlight, showing us the way to love God and be more like Jesus," Chip decided, and Grandma nodded. Chip set the flashlight on the table. "Grandma, let's keep this close by, just in case the lights go out again," he suggested.

"OK," agreed Grandma with a smile. "And let's keep God's Word close by, too. Let's keep it in our heart for times of spiritual need."

G.L.A.

HOW ABOUT YOU?

Do you read the Scriptures daily? Do you memorize portions of it each week so that you are never without the light of God's Word? When reading the Old Testament, we learn from the lives of godly men and women. In the New Testament, Jesus is our example. Reading your Bible each day lights up your life!

MEMORIZE:

"Your word is a lamp to my feet and a light to my path."

Psalm 119:105, NKJV

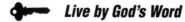
Live by God's Word

The Bottom Line (Read Genesis 9:8-17)

Lisa watched as Mr. Harmon, the salesman, pushed a long paper across the desk. "Sign here, Mr. Baker, on the bottom line," he said. After Dad signed it, the men shook hands. "Thank you. You've made a good choice," said Mr. Harmon. He winked at Lisa. "Enjoy your new car."

As they drove home later, Lisa peered at the black sky. "I hope it doesn't hail on our new car," she said.

Dad slowed the time-controlled wipers. "I think the rain is about over," he replied.

Lisa leaned back against the leather upholstery. "This is a beautiful car," she said. "Can we take a trip back home in it soon? I mean . . . back to Stockton?" Lisa was referring to the town where they had lived before Dad got a promotion and they had to move.

"Do you still miss your friends?" asked Dad.

Lisa blinked back the tears. "Yes. I've prayed and prayed for a new friend, but God doesn't seem to care."

Dad set the cruise control and leaned back. "Oh, yes, he does, honey," Dad assured her. "God has promised to supply all our needs, and he knows you need a friend soon."

At that moment the sun peeked out. "Oh, look, Dad!" Lisa pointed toward the east. "Look at the gorgeous rainbow!"

Dad nodded. "That's God's 'signature' on the contract he made with Noah thousands of years ago," he said. Dad smiled at Lisa. "I signed a contract today and promised to make payments to pay for this car. You can be sure I'll keep my word," he told her. "You can be even more sure that God will keep his word, whether it's his promise to never destroy the earth with a flood or his promise to supply our needs, like your need for a friend."

As Dad turned the car onto their street, Lisa squealed. "Ohhhh, someone is moving in next door. And look! That girl must be about my age. Maybe she's my new friend."

"Maybe," agreed Dad. "The bottom line is . . . God always keeps his word." *B.W.*

11
MAY

HOW ABOUT YOU?

Have you been asking God to meet a special need? Be patient. Not one of God's promises has ever failed. The next time you see a rainbow, remember that fact. It's a reminder that God keeps his word. It's God's "signature" on the bottom line!

MEMORIZE:

"And my God will meet all your needs according to his glorious riches in Christ Jesus."

Philippians 4:19, NIV

 God Keeps His Word

The World's Best Baby-Sitter (Read 1 John 4:7-11)

12

MAY

Jennie and her twin brother, James, skipped along happily. It was going to be a fun morning; Grandma was taking them to the park. They were nearly there when a lady stopped them on the street. "Well, Helen, I declare!" she said in a shrill voice. "You've got those grandkids again! Wasn't it enough that you raised six of your own?" Narrowing her eyes she squinted at Jennie and James.

"Oh, Dorothy, I enjoy the children," said Grandma. She chuckled softly.

"Mommy went to see the doctor, so we're going to the park to swing," Jennie piped up.

"Doctor!" the lady exploded. "Don't tell me there's going to be another baby?"

"Wouldn't that be nice?" Grandma answered sweetly. "Now we must hurry, or all the swings will be taken."

As they went on their way, James said, "Grandma, that lady was crabby. Doesn't she like kids?"

"I'm sure she does, honey," replied Grandma. "She just would rather not take care of them, I suppose. She doesn't know what fun she's missing." Grandma's voice was quietly reassuring.

"Do you like taking care of kids?" Jennie asked.

"I like taking care of you!" Grandma answered.

James squeezed Grandma's hand. "You're the best baby-sitter in the world," he told her.

Grandma squeezed back. "I feel the ability to care for children is something Jesus has given me—something of real value," she said. "You know, Jesus told us that we show our love for him when we show love for one another."

"I guess that lady doesn't love Jesus then?" asked James.

"We don't know that, but I hope we've shown her today that we love him," Grandma said with a smile. She released their hands as they approached the swings. "Let's see how many ways we can find today to show that we love Jesus, OK?"

James nodded and turned to his sister. "Want me to give you a push?" he asked her. *P.K.*

HOW ABOUT YOU?

Sometimes it's the little things you do that show your love for Jesus best, things like being nice to a sister or brother, obeying your parents, running errands, or helping a neighbor. Try it . . . and be sure to smile.

MEMORIZE:

"By this all will know that you are My disciples, if you have love for one another."

John 13:35, NKJV

 Show Love in Small Ways

Jonathan's Bath (Read Psalm 51:1-12)

Jonathan took out his Dad's aftershave lotion and splashed it on his face before leaving the bathroom.

"What do I smell?" Mother asked a little later when she stepped into Jonathan's room.

"He used Dad's aftershave," Sophie hollered from her own room. "He didn't take a bath again."

Mother checked the bathroom. "The towels are damp."

"But he forgot to wet the soap," tattled Sophie. "He's so disgusting!" Sophie just couldn't understand why her brother hated to take a bath. He often just wet his wash cloth and towel and pretended to have taken a shower.

13 MAY

Mother sat on the edge of Jonathan's bed. "Sophie, come join us," she called. Mother held a bar of soap in one hand and the aftershave in the other hand.

"I hate baths," Jonathan said defensively.

"You're so gross," sputtered Sophie.

"Shhhh." Mother held up a finger. "You know, when we splash on perfume or lotion instead of washing ourselves, we smell nice but the dirt remains," she said.

"Like Jonathan," accused Sophie, wrinkling her nose. "He covers up the smell while the dirt and odor builds."

"Yes, and Jonathan is still going to take his bath," said Mother, looking sternly at her son. "It's important to keep our bodies clean, but it occurs to me that we should also think about something even more important. Just as our skin gets dirty, our life and heart also get dirty—only this dirt is sin. Such things as pride or an accusing, unloving attitude fall into that category. So does deceiving your mother." Sophie and Jonathan both squirmed guiltily. "Just as Jonathan likes to cover up dirt by putting on something that smells good, we all sometimes like to cover up, or hide, the wrong things we do," continued Mother. "We need to learn to confess our sin to God. Then he'll forgive us and wash us white as snow." *N.E.K.*

HOW ABOUT YOU?

Do you try to cover up your sins? God can see through any cover-up. You need to confess your sins to God. Trust him to wash your heart and life and make you clean in his sight.

MEMORIZE:

"**Oh, wash me, cleanse me from this guilt. Let me be pure again.**" *Psalm 51:2, TLB*

 Confess Sin

A Dead Stick or a Living Tree (Read John 15:1-7)

14

MAY

As David got close to Mr. Gordon's house, he saw his Sunday School teacher planting fruit trees in his backyard. "Good morning, David," said Mr. Gordon. "How are you doing?"

"OK, I guess," muttered David. He shuffled his toe in the dirt. "But I'm always gettin' in trouble at school," he added with a sigh. "Since I've been coming to your Sunday school class, I've been trying to change and be good, but I just can't seem to do it. What's wrong with me?"

Mr. Gordon leaned on his spade. "Have you trusted the Lord Jesus as your personal Savior, David?" he asked.

"Well . . . no, sir. I guess not," admitted David. "I've heard you talk about it in class, but I didn't really understand it. I thought if I'd just go to church and read the Bible and start living better, I'd be all right."

Mr. Gordon picked up a small, dead branch that had fallen from a tree. "I'm planting fruit trees," he said. "I'm going to water them and put fertilizer around them. One day they'll bear juicy peaches and nectarines for me to eat. Why don't you help me plant this stick. I'll treat it just like all the other trees I'm planting, and then when I get fruit from it, I'll share it with you."

David laughed. "You're kidding," he said. "That stick will never have any fruit. It's dead."

Mr. Gordon looked at the stick. "That's true. This stick has no life," he agreed. "And do you know what, David? You don't have real life, either. You can read the Bible and go to church and even pray, but you can't produce the fruit of a Christian life until you have Christ within you. He gives you life, for he is the Life."

Slowly David nodded. "Will you show me how to accept Jesus?" he asked with a smile.

Mr. Gordon went to get his Bible. *M.R.P.*

HOW ABOUT YOU?

Do you try to be good, only to fail? You can't live the Christian life when you don't have Life—the Lord Jesus—within you. Ask him to save you now.

MEMORIZE:

"Through Christ Jesus the law of the Spirit of life set me free from the law of sin and death."

Romans 8:2, NIV

 Receive Christ's Life

Sweeter than Chocolate (Read Psalm 119:97-104)

Angela read Mom's grocery list as she pushed her cart down the familiar aisles at the store. Out of the corner of her eye she saw the shelves with chocolate cream-filled snack cakes. *Yummy!* she thought. *I wish Mom had put Choco-Cakes on this list.*

15
MAY

All the way home Angela thought about how good those Choco-Cakes would have tasted. Walking into the house, she set the sack of groceries on the table just as Mom came in from working in the garden. "Why are you wearing such a scowl?" asked Mom.

"I didn't know I was," Angela answered. "I was just wishing I could have bought Choco-Cakes at the store instead of these things. I love Choco-Cakes! Sometimes when I walk past them in the store, I can almost hear them call out my name: 'Angela, We're over here! Buy us! Eat us!'" Mom and Angela giggled together.

"And what do the jars of honey say when you walk past them?" Mom asked with a grin as she took honey from the bag and put it in the cupboard. "I read a verse about honey in Psalms this morning," she added thoughtfully. "David said God's words were sweeter to him than honey."

"I've read that verse before, but I don't understand it," said Angela with a shrug. "Maybe it would make more sense if I liked honey better."

"Why not think of it this way," suggested Mother with a smile. "God wants you to hunger for his Word—even more than you crave Choco-Cakes." *J.V.*

HOW ABOUT YOU?

Do you hunger for God? Taste the sweetness of God's Word every day by taking time to read it. His Word is a spiritual treat.

MEMORIZE:

"How sweet are your words to my taste, sweeter than honey to my mouth!" *Psalm 119:103, NIV*

 Hunger for God

Like Grandpa (Read 1 John 3:1-3)

16

MAY

Alex peered sadly through the fogged-up window. His grandfather had said, "See you at eight Saturday morning, Alex—that is, if it doesn't rain." But it was raining, so now he faced a whole boring day with nothing to do.

A man's voice coming from the radio caught Alex's attention. "We know that when Jesus appears, we shall be like him, for we shall see him as he is."

Alex's thoughts lingered on that last phrase. What did it mean to see Jesus 'as he is'? *I wonder what Jesus looks like,* Alex thought. *I wish somebody who knew him had described him. Was he tall? Or short? Did he really have long brown hair like the pictures in Bible story books? I bet he probably smiled a lot, and maybe his eyes twinkled like Grandpa's. . . .*

The sound of the phone caused Alex to jump. "It's for you," his mother called from the other room.

Lifting the phone, Alex heard, "Hi, what do you think of the weather?" It was his grandfather's cheerful voice, and Alex knew Grandpa was smiling. He was calling from miles away, but Alex could easily imagine how he looked, just as if he were right there. Grandpa still had mostly dark hair and blue eyes that twinkled when he and Alex talked together. Alex liked it that everybody said he looked like his grandfather.

"I wish it wasn't raining," Alex answered.

"Well, don't worry. I've got another idea. Can you be ready soon?" his grandfather asked.

"I'm ready now!" exclaimed Alex. A few minutes later he hung up the phone. *Oh boy! It's going to be an OK rainy day after all,* he thought.

The radio voice caught his attention again. "Our hope lies in the glorious appearing of Jesus Christ, when we shall not only see him, but we shall be like him. . . ."

"I know Grandpa will have a big smile on his face when he comes," Alex said happily. "And when Jesus comes some day, I think he'll be smiling too. It's nice to be like Grandpa, but it will be even better to be like Jesus." *P.K.*

HOW ABOUT YOU?

Does it make you happy when people say you look like someone else in your family? It's nice when people think we're like someone we love. It's even better when people see we're like Jesus. And when Jesus comes back, he says he'll make us just like he is!

MEMORIZE:

"**Dear friends, now we are children of God, and . . . we know that when he appears, we shall be like him, for we shall see him as he is.**" *1 John 3:2, NIV*

Be Ready for Jesus' Return

Lessons from the Garden (Read Psalm 71:15-18)

Keith, Heather, and Kevin had enjoyed watching the spring flowers unfold their pretty petals. The children had learned the names of the different flowers in Mother's garden, and each had a favorite. "I love the hyacinths, Mom," said Heather as they looked at the flowers one day. "They're the best!"

17
MAY

Four-year-old Kevin had a different opinion. "I like the yellow daffodils," he said.

"My favorites are the tulips," declared Keith. "They have so many different colors—they're not all the same."

Mother smiled. "How about the crocuses?" she asked. "I always think they look so brave peeking out of the early morning frost."

"But some of the flowers are dying! What happens to them when they die, Mommy?" asked Kevin with a sad look on his face. "Will they come up again sometime?"

Mother nodded. "They'll be back next year," she assured him, "and they will have multiplied."

"Mulipied?" asked Kevin. "What's that mean?"

"Its 'multiplied,' not 'mulipied,'" corrected big brother Keith. "That means the bulb in the ground will produce more of its kind of flowers for you to see next spring, doesn't it, Mother?"

"That's right," replied Mother. "And I was just thinking that the pretty spring flowers are an example of how Christians should be. We should 'bloom' for Jesus—our life should be beautiful. And just as the flowers multiply, Christians should multiply. By our example and by our words, we should be bringing others to Jesus so they, too, can start new lives that are beautiful."

Kevin bent over to look more closely at one of his favorite daffodils. "I wonder how many new flowers there will be next spring," he said.

"Yeah." Heather nodded thoughtfully. "And how many new Christians." *S.J.*

HOW ABOUT YOU?

Have you asked Jesus to forgive your sins and give you a beautiful new life to live for him? Then let your new life be an example to others so they will want to start a new life with Jesus, too.

MEMORIZE:

"Whoever lives in me and I in him shall produce a large crop of fruit." *John 15:5, TLB*

 Jesus Gives New Life

Junior Bridesmaid (Read Matthew 25:1-13)

18
MAY

"I'm so glad I get to be a junior bridesmaid," said Bethany as she twirled around in her long pink dress. "I'm so excited about Sharon's wedding—like I'm getting married myself."

"If you don't hold still, honey, I'll never get this hem pinned," cautioned Mother. "Besides, you're a little young to be a bride."

"Sharon knows exactly when her wedding's going to be, doesn't she?" asked Bethany.

"That's a funny question," said Mom, taking more pins from the pin cushion. "Of course your sister knows when her wedding will be. She's been planning it for months."

"But in our Sunday school lesson, the bridesmaid didn't know when the bridegroom would come or when the wedding would be," said Bethany.

Mother nodded. "That seems very strange to us, doesn't it?" she replied. "Wedding customs have changed a lot."

Bethany looked dreamily around the room. "Not knowing when the bridegroom was coming would be thrilling," she declared. "I wish we still had that custom. Then I'd keep this dress and a flashlight beside my bed every night."

"Turn, please." Mother continued pinning. "Speaking as the mother of the bride, I'm glad Sharon has a definite wedding day set. As for you, Bethany, since you like mystery and suspense, there's another Bridegroom who will come suddenly."

"I know who you mean," said Bethany. "In Sunday school we learned that Jesus is the Bridegroom and that he's coming for us. But we don't know when. My teacher says the important thing to know is that you're ready to return to heaven with him."

"That's right," agreed Mother. "I'm so glad everyone in our family has accepted Christ as Savior. Some day we'll all be together in heaven—part of the Bride of Christ, along with all those who have been saved throughout the ages."

"Wow!" Bethany said after a moment. "What a wedding! What a big, exciting, fabulous wedding that will be!" *R.M.*

HOW ABOUT YOU?

Are you ready for Jesus to return? Don't miss out on the most exciting wedding in history. Accept Jesus as your Savior so you can be with the Bridegroom in heaven.

MEMORIZE:

"So you also must be ready, because the Son of Man will come at an hour when you do not expect him." *Matthew 24:44, NIV*

 Jesus May Come Any Time

What Do You See? (Read Matthew 7:1-5)

19
MAY

Quentin leaned over the front seat of the car. "Mom and Dad expect too much from me," he told his grandparents. "Nothing I do pleases them."

"Really?" asked Grandpa. "That's odd. Just yesterday your dad was bragging about what a good worker you are."

"Really?" Quentin echoed. "But he—"

"Look!" Grandma pointed out the car window. "See that gorgeous bush? God is a marvelous artist!"

Quentin and Grandpa looked blank. "Where?"

"Back there." Grandma laughed. "Too late."

"Cindi is a real pain in the neck." Quentin continued complaining, hoping for sympathy. "She's always bugging me. Mom makes me take her everywhere I go."

Grandma looked around. "Cindi?" she called. "Where are you?"

Quentin grinned. "Well, almost everywhere," he said.

"Cindi told me that you're the 'bestest biggest brother in the world,'" Grandma quoted.

Quentin looked ashamed. "Well, I mean she . . . she—"

"Look!" Grandpa slowed down. "See that deer."

"Where?" Grandma and Quentin asked.

Grandpa pointed. "Over there . . . in those trees." Quentin squinted. He and Grandma didn't see it. "Well, it's too late now," said Grandpa as they rounded a curve.

"Isn't it strange how we see what we're looking for?" Grandma asked. "I like flowers, so I watch for them, and I saw a beautiful bush. Grandpa likes animals, so he saw a deer."

Grandpa's eyes met Quentin's in the rearview mirror. "When we look for bad things, we find them," he said. "When we look for good, we find that."

"The Lord has given you a wonderful family, Quentin," Grandma said softly. "You should look for good in them. When you do, you'll find it. They—"

"Look!" Grandpa cried. "See those quail in the grass along the highway?"

"I see!" Quentin exclaimed. "I see." *B.W.*

HOW ABOUT YOU?

Do you look for good, or bad, in others? Are your remarks positive or negative? God wants his children to be gentle and kind, not harsh and judgmental. So start looking for good and then talk about it. Your day will be brighter, you'll be better company for others, and you'll be a better testimony for the Lord.

MEMORIZE:

"Speak evil of no one."

Titus 3:2, NKJV

 **Look for Good**

The Sad Night (Read Luke 12:16-21)

20
MAY

"La Noche Triste," murmured Scott as his sister Carrie entered the living room.

"What's that?" Carrie asked.

"It's Spanish for 'The Sad Night.' You'll learn about it next year," said Scott, as he closed his social studies book.

"Why was it sad?" asked Carrie.

"Well, over four hundred years ago, the Aztec Indians had a great city on an island," Scott began. "A Spanish leader, Cortes, was able to take his army into the city because the Indian ruler thought Cortes was a god." In her mind, Carrie pictured the Spanish troops visiting the Indian settlement. "When the Indian ruler died, Cortes and his men had to leave," continued Scott. "But before they left, they loaded up all the gold they could carry. As they tried to escape, the Indians attacked. Many Spanish soldiers tried to swim to the mainland, but they drowned because the weight of the gold pulled them down. Over half of the Spanish army was lost that night, so they called it 'The Sad Night.'"

"Why didn't they get rid of the gold before they tried to swim?" asked Carrie. "Then they might have made it."

Scott shrugged. "Too greedy, I guess."

"Apparently they were a lot like people today," observed Dad, who was listening. "Often people load up on earthly treasures, thinking money can buy anything they want."

"But it can't, can it?" murmured Carrie. "Our Sunday school lesson last week was about that. Money can't buy forgiveness of sins."

"Exactly," agreed Dad, "and it will be a sad night for those who stand before God, empty of the one treasure that could give them eternal life." *J.B.*

HOW ABOUT YOU?

Do you think money can buy friends and happiness? Even eternal life? The only way to true happiness and eternal life is through Jesus Christ. Accept him today.

MEMORIZE:

"For where your treasure is, there your heart will be also."

Matthew 6:21, NIV

 Christ Is True Treasure

The Memory Box (Read Revelation 21:1-4)

Becky rocked slowly in her grandmother's favorite chair. Usually when Becky visited her grandparents' home, Grandma called her to help prepare a snack. Grandma didn't call her today.

"How's school?" asked Grandpa.

"OK," said Becky. She looked at the picture of her grandparents that hung on the wall. She closed her eyes tightly and hoped Grandma would be standing there when she opened them. But, of course, that couldn't happen.

21
MAY

"You miss Grandma, don't you?" Grandpa asked quietly. A tear slid down Becky's cheek. "I miss her, too," Grandpa said sadly. "Sometimes I want to call out to her in the kitchen. It's hard to believe she isn't here anymore." He opened a desk drawer and pulled out a box. "But look," he said, taking out a picture Becky had drawn for Grandma. "Whenever I feel especially sad, I look through this memory box. For each memory, I say a prayer, thanking God that I could share that time with Grandma."

Becky looked through the special box. "Here's a picture of Grandma planting flowers out front!" Becky exclaimed. "She always planted the prettiest garden."

"Shall we thank God for that?" asked Grandpa. Becky nodded. "Father," Grandpa prayed, "thank you so much for her. Thank you for the memory we have of those beautiful gardens. We know Grandma is with you now, and we thank you for that, too. Help us look to you for strength when we miss her so much." A few tears wet Grandpa's face. He hugged Becky tightly.

"I have an idea," Becky said. She got up and went into the kitchen. Grandpa followed. He smiled as Becky began putting crackers and cheese on a plate. "Grandma used to tell me funny stories when we were in the kitchen together," Becky said. "The funniest one was about how she met you," she added, giggling. She gave Grandpa a hug. "Let's thank God again," she suggested, "and then I'll tell you what she said." *N.E.K.*

HOW ABOUT YOU?

Has someone you love died? Talk to God about the way you feel. He understands your tears and will help you deal with the pain. Then enjoy the good memories you have of that person, and thank God for happy times you shared.

MEMORIZE:

"The Lord gave, and the Lord has taken away; blessed be the name of the Lord." *Job 1:21, NKJV*

 Thank God for Happy Memories

Riding on Clouds (Read Proverbs 4:13-27)

22

MAY

Rose and her brother, Chad, lay in the grass looking up at the clouds. Rose pointed. "That one looks like a ship."

"Neat! And there's an elephant," replied Chad. "But its trunk is gone."

"I'd love to walk on a cloud, or ride on one," said Rose as they went in to eat a little later.

"Me, too," Chad agreed. The phone rang, and he raced to answer it. "Mom, it's Bruce," he called. "Can I go to the arcade to play video games after supper?"

"I don't think that's a good idea," replied Mom. "There are a lot of drugs circulating through that arcade at night."

"But, Mom," protested Chad. "I won't do anything wrong. I'll even take Rose along."

"The answer is no," said Dad firmly as he came into the room. "That's no place for a Christian to be."

Chad moped around most of the evening. "Parents never want kids to have fun," he complained to his sister. "You'd think they'd remember what it was like to be kids."

As the family was returning from a visit to the children's grandparents the next day, the car crept along slowly through an unusually thick fog. Rose shivered. "Are we on the road?" she asked. "I don't like this."

"I thought I heard you kids wishing you could walk on clouds yesterday," Mom said, "and that's sort of what we're doing. Fog is like a cloud in contact with the ground."

"Well, this cloud is no fun at all," said Chad, watching his father concentrate on driving. "It's dangerous."

"It reminds me of what happened last night," said Dad. "The idea of playing at the arcade sounded like fun to you, but being in that atmosphere would have been much more dangerous than being in this cloud. You would have had to fight off a lot of temptations. I know. I was a kid once, too." *N.E.K.*

HOW ABOUT YOU?

Do you get angry when you aren't allowed to do things you think would be fun? Things that would lead you to sin often look like fun. Ask God to keep you alert to such dangers and to help you avoid them. Be thankful for those who watch out for you.

MEMORIZE:

"Do not set foot on the path of the wicked or walk in the way of evil men. Avoid it . . . turn from it and go on your way."

Proverbs 4:14-15, NIV

Be Alert to Spiritual Danger

Puzzle Pieces (Read Romans 8:28-32)

23
MAY

"Hi, Mom," said Brooke. Then she frowned. It seemed strange to see Mom in a hospital bed. "You feel OK?"

"Sure." Mom nodded. "They only did tests today. The surgery isn't until tomorrow." She noticed a box under Brooke's arm. "What did you bring?"

"You said to bring something we could do together," Brooke reminded her. She dumped the pieces of a puzzle onto Mom's bedside table, and they began searching for the pieces that went around the edge of the picture.

Brooke frowned as she worked. So many questions filled her mind. Would Mom's surgery hurt her? Would it make her well? And the question that bothered Brooke the most—could Mom die during the surgery? But she didn't want to worry Mom with her questions at a time like this.

"I can't figure out where this piece goes," Brooke said, still frowning.

Mom smiled at her. "I'm glad you brought a puzzle," she said. "It's kind of like my life right now. Being ill and needing surgery is like that piece of the puzzle—I don't know where it fits into the picture of my life. But I've seen how God has put many other pieces of my life together already. That helps me trust him to work this piece in, too."

"What do you mean?" asked Brooke.

"Remember how worried we were when Dad lost his job?" Brooke nodded. "God provided Dad with a job in this city where Dr. Campbell practices," Mom continued. "He's the best doctor in the country to perform my surgery. Do you think that happened by accident?"

"No. God was taking care of you," Brooke answered slowly. "And he'll take care of you tomorrow, won't he?"

Mom nodded. "I don't understand how this fits into my life, but he does," she said. "I trust him to work it into the best possible picture for me. Will you trust him, too, honey?"

Brooke nodded. She was finally smiling. *K.R.A.*

HOW ABOUT YOU?

Are there things in your life that you don't understand? Take comfort; God sees the total picture of your life, and he's fitting the pieces into just the right places. You can trust him to work everything out for your good, even though you may not see it now.

MEMORIZE:

"And we know that in all things God works for the good of those who love him, who have been called according to his purpose." *Romans 8:28, NIV*

 Trust God to Work

Do You Hear? (Read James 1:22-25)

24

MAY

Ben unlocked the garage door, swung it open, and plopped his school books under the clip on his bike. He had just adjusted his mirrors when he heard, "Ben! Oh Be-e-n!"

I suppose Mom wants me to do something before I go to school, thought Ben. *I'll just pretend I don't hear her—I want time to play.* As Ben quietly glided out of the garage, he could hear his mother still talking.

It seemed that school was such a drag that day, but finally Ben closed his locker for the last time and headed home. *I suppose Mom will be sure to have a job waiting for me,* he thought, sighing. *I just don't feel like working on a hot day like this!*

When Ben opened the kitchen door, Mother looked up in surprise. "Ben, I thought you had gone fishing with Grandpa," she said. "He called just after you left the house. You were still in the garage when I called to you, and I was sure you could hear me. I took your overnight bag and fishing gear to his house at noon, and you were to go there directly after school."

As Ben looked at Mother, he remembered that he had deliberately not listened when he heard Mother calling to him. "I guess I missed a good time, didn't I, Mom? It's my own fault; I wasn't listening," was all Ben said.

Ben turned and stumbled up the stairs to his room. Big sobs were smothered in the bed covers as he pictured Grandpa and his boat on the river at that moment. *I'm going to listen when I'm spoken to after this,* he thought. *And I'm going to quit trying to get out of work.* With a determined look, he got up and ran down to the kitchen. "Mom," he said, "is there anything you want me to do?"

Mother looked at Ben, saw his red, tear-filled eyes, and gave him a hug. "Sure, Ben," she said. "Let's go find Grandpa!" *R.M.*

HOW ABOUT YOU?

Do you really listen to your parents? It's important that you do. It's even more important to listen to God. He uses parents, teachers, and the Bible to talk to those who will listen. When you listen as you should, it will affect your actions. So listen to God today. He may be trying to tell you something really great!

MEMORIZE:

"Be careful how you listen."

Luke 8:18, TLB

 **Listen to God**

God's People (Read Colossians 1:21-25)

"Look how hard it's raining!" said Robert as his family pulled out of the driveway one Sunday morning. The wind was driving big raindrops against the car windows, and the streets were flooded. In the back seat, Robert could hear the windshield wipers *slap-slapping* as they pushed sheets of water out of the way. A flash of lightning flared across the sky, and a rumble of thunder shook the car.

25
MAY

As they approached their church, Mother gasped. Part of the church roof had been torn off by the wind, and men in raincoats were scurrying around in the rain. Dad dashed inside. Soon he returned. "We're meeting at the school gym today," he reported.

At the school, the children were assigned to classes. "We can go to Sunday school class today, but we can't go to church," Robert told one of his classmates.

The teacher, Mrs. Brown, disagreed. "We'll have our church service after Sunday school as usual," she said.

"But we can't go to church," repeated Robert, "because our church is damaged."

"Our church building is damaged," replied Mrs. Brown, "but the building isn't really the church." She thought for a moment. "Suppose a gym class were scheduled to take place in this gym. You tell your friends you're going to gym. But suppose, when you get here, there's no one here but you."

"There wouldn't be a class then," said Robert. "You can't have a gym class without people."

Mrs. Brown nodded. "The building isn't the gym class, is it?" she said. "Now, when we speak of going to church, we sometimes mean we're going to the church building. Other times, we mean we're going to worship with God's people, with other believers. So you see, the storm may have damaged our church building, but it didn't hurt the real church—the people. So we're still 'going to church.'" *S.L.S.*

HOW ABOUT YOU?

What do you think of when you hear the word *church?* God speaks of Christians as his church. Live for Jesus every day of the week, no matter where you are or what you're doing. You may be the only "church" some of your friends ever see.

MEMORIZE:

"**For where two or three come together in my name, there am I with them.**" *Matthew 18:20, NIV*

 The Church Is God's People

The Needy Baby (Read Philippians 4:18-20)

26

MAY

"The baby is crying again," Bonita told her aunt. "What does she want this time?"

"She's probably hungry," replied Aunt Susan with a smile. "She usually lets me know when it's time to eat." Bonita watched as Aunt Susan picked up five-week-old Marcie.

"She can't do anything for herself, can she?" asked Bonita. "You have to pick her up to move her. You dress her. You feed her. You rock her. And you bathe her."

"That's right," agreed Aunt Susan. "Right now your little cousin depends on me for almost everything. I have to be right there to meet her needs, day and night."

When Bonita returned to her own home, she told her parents all about baby Marcie. "No wonder Aunt Susan is so tired," said Bonita. "She has a lot of work to do—she does everything but breathe for that baby!"

"That's right," said Dad. He smiled at Bonita. "You were a baby like that once, and Mom and I did the same things for you," he added.

"I'm not like that anymore," Bonita boasted, standing tall. "I take care of myself."

"In a way, I'm still like a baby," said Mom. Bonita giggled, looking at her grown-up Mom. "I am," insisted Mom. "I depend on my Father for everything. Sometimes I fuss because he doesn't meet my needs right at the time I think he should. But most of the time I know that he is holding me in his loving arms."

"But Grandpa lives in California," protested Bonita. "You don't depend on him to take care of you. Dad takes care of us."

"I don't think Mom means her earthly father. She means her heavenly Father—God," explained Dad.

Mom nodded. "I need my heavenly Father to be with me day and night," she agreed.

"We all do," said Dad. "When we think of all the time, love, and care that Aunt Susan is giving baby Marcie, it seems like a lot to us. But just think—God gives more to us all the time!" *N.E.K.*

HOW ABOUT YOU?

Think about the way a baby depends on his parents for everything. You need to depend even more on your heavenly Father to meet all your needs. The wonderful part is that he will!

MEMORIZE:

"In Him [God] we live and move and have our being."

Acts 17:28, NKJV

 **God Takes Care of You**

Grandma's Coming (Read Mark 13:27-37)

27
MAY

"Mommy, when will Grandma be here?" asked Lisa as she stared out the window. "She's going to give me a great big hug and bring me a present. I just know it! I'm going to watch for her!"

"Lisa," said Mother, "watching for Grandma is fine, but are you ready for her to come? She'll sleep in your room, you know. Why don't you clean it up so it looks nice for her? Maybe you could draw a picture for her, too."

Lisa clapped her hands at the idea and skipped off to her room. She picked up all her clothes and cleaned up the closet, placing her shoes neatly in a row under the hanging clothes. Each time she heard a car, she ran to look out the window, hoping it was Grandma. As she sat at her desk drawing a picture, Mother called her for lunch.

"Mommy," said Lisa as she took a bite of her boloney sandwich, "I've been waiting so long for Grandma, and she's still not here!"

"I know, but she'll come sooner or later," said Mother. "Let's just keep busy until she gets here. You can help me do the dishes. Then we'll make her favorite dessert for tonight."

The dessert was made and Lisa was helping her mother set the table when they heard a car turn in their driveway. Lisa ran to the window. "She's here! She's here!" shouted Lisa, jumping up and down.

Lisa gave Grandma a big hug, and Grandma handed her a flat, square package. Lisa was right! Grandma did bring her a present— a Bible story book.

That night Grandma sat on Lisa's bed and read about Jesus coming back. "We don't know when Jesus will come," said Grandma, "but we know for sure that he is coming."

"Just like you, Grandma," said Lisa. "I knew you were coming today, but I didn't know when!"

"That's right, Lisa," answered Grandma. "Your mother told me how you kept busy while you waited—how you did the things I would appreciate. While we wait for Jesus, it's important that we keep busy, too—busy doing the things he wants us to do." *S.E.F.*

HOW ABOUT YOU?

Are you ready for Jesus' return? What are you doing to "keep busy" until he comes? Are you doing the things he wants you to do—things like witnessing for him, cheerfully doing your tasks each day, being helpful and obedient? He is coming—keep busy while you wait.

MEMORIZE:

"Watch . . . lest, coming suddenly, he find you sleeping."
Mark 13:35-36, NKJV

 *Jesus Is Coming!*

A Different Beat (Read Ephesians 2:1-10)

28

MAY

"Look at that guy, Mom," said Tricia as she and her mother waited at a red light. "Is there something wrong with him? He's sure walking funny."

Mom smiled when she looked in the direction Tricia indicated. "Hmmm," she said, "I think he's listening to his radio. See his headphones?"

"Oh, I see," said Tricia. "And he's walking to the beat of the music, isn't he?"

"That's how it looks to me," agreed Mother, "and that could be dangerous. He sure doesn't seem to notice much about what's going on around him." The traffic light changed, and the car moved forward. "That fellow reminds me of our walk as Christians in this world," added Mother.

Tricia gave her mother a puzzled glance. Then she grinned mischievously. "You mean because when we listen to God and to his Word even though no one else is, we're in danger of being teased for being odd?" she suggested.

"Well, I didn't mean it was dangerous," said Mother, "but you're right, actually. Sometimes we do feel like we're walking around looking pretty strange compared with the rest of the world."

"That happened to me just last week," said Tricia. "Even my very best friend made fun of me because I wasn't allowed to watch a TV show that everyone in class was talking about."

"Did that bother you?" asked Mother.

Tricia nodded. "Yeah," she said, "but I guess we just have to be like that guy back there and not worry about what other people think about us."

"You're right, Tricia," replied Mother. "What God thinks is much more important than what people think. I pray you'll always choose to listen to Jesus instead of marching to the beat of the world."

L.W.

HOW ABOUT YOU?

Are you marching—or walking—to a different beat than most of your classmates? Perhaps that's as it should be. You can't expect the world to hear God's beat, to have the same high standards that you do. Don't worry about what others think. Walk the way Jesus wants you to walk.

MEMORIZE:

"Set your mind on things above, not on things on the earth." *Colossians 3:2, NKJV*

 **Live for God**

Cobwebs and Cables (Read Proverbs 3:1-6)

"My Sunday school teacher told us we should read the Bible by ourselves every day—not just in family devotions," Nancy told her parents on the way home from church. "I signed a card to say I'd try to do that from now on."

"That's great," said Dad. "Since you're reading well now, you ought to have your own personal daily devotions."

That afternoon Nancy read two chapters. For a couple of days after that, she managed to find time to read a few verses before going to school. But as time went by, she read less and less.

As Nancy and her mother sat on the front porch one evening a few weeks later, Nancy gave a little sigh. "Mom," she said, "I'm so mad at myself. When I signed the card to say I'd read the Bible every day, I really meant it. But I forget to do it half the time. How can I remember to do better?"

"I used to forget to read my Bible, too," Mom told her, "but then I made it a habit to read at a certain time every day. For me, mornings are best. I try to not let anything interfere with my Bible-reading time. By doing this, I've developed a habit, and I seldom forget now."

Suddenly Nancy pointed upward. "Oh, look!" she exclaimed. "There's a huge spider web between the post and the telephone cable."

Mom laughed. "Why, that's odd!" she said. "I was just thinking of an old Spanish proverb: 'Habits are first like cobwebs—then like cables.' What do you think that means?"

Nancy was quiet for a minute. "I think I know," she said. "At first habits are easy to break—like cobwebs. But if you keep on doing something, your habit will become strong and hard to break—like a cable."

Mother nodded and smiled. "Make Bible reading a real strong habit," she encouraged. "Shall I wake you up fifteen minutes earlier every morning so you can read the Bible first thing each day?"

Nancy nodded. "Let's try that," she agreed. *M.R.P.*

29
MAY

HOW ABOUT YOU?

Do you take time to read the Bible alone each day? If not, why not? Do you forget? Or do you think it's not important? Begin now to make daily Bible reading a "cable" in your life—make it a lifetime habit.

MEMORIZE:

"I delight in your decrees; I will not neglect your word."

Psalm 119:16, NIV

 Read the Bible Daily

Carmel and David (Read Romans 15:1-7)

30

MAY

Eric and Sean were walking home from school. "Oh, no," groaned Sean. "Here comes David. Let's cut between these houses so we can get away. Hurry!"

Sean quickly dodged across the lawn, but Eric lagged behind. He didn't want to irritate Sean, but he didn't think it was right to run away from David, either. "Eric, come on!" Sean hissed, and Eric reluctantly followed him.

"That David is so dumb. And he's no good at sports. He's no good at anything!" Sean declared as he led the way to his house. "Hey, want to see our new puppies?"

"Yeah, sure," replied Eric, and soon they were bending over a box in the family room. Daisy, the mother collie, was surrounded by four little balls of fur.

Sean pointed to one that was smaller and weaker than the others. "That's Carmel. She's the tiniest one," he said. "Mom calls her the runt of the litter. She can't move around as well as the others. Dad says if Daisy didn't help her and protect her more, she wouldn't have much of a chance to make it."

As Eric walked home later, he was thinking about Carmel and how she was weaker and different from the others. It occurred to him that David was something like Carmel. David wasn't as smart or coordinated as his classmates. Still, he was part of their class, and Eric didn't feel right about shutting him out.

As he approached David's house, Eric saw that David was outside. Eric walked toward him and called, "Hi, David. Can I play catch with you?" A smile broke out on David's face, and he tossed the ball to Eric. Eric was glad he had made the right choice this time. He knew he'd have to talk to Sean about what he decided.

J.B.

HOW ABOUT YOU?

Do you accept those who aren't quite like you? God wants us to accept all the people he made, so that we can show how his love is different from the world's love. Think of something you can do to show you accept someone who may not be well liked by others—someone who needs extra help.

MEMORIZE:

"**Receive one another, just as Christ also received us, to the glory of God.**" *Romans 15:7, NKJV*

 *Accept One Another*

God's Flower Garden (Read Leviticus 19:33-37)

31
MAY

"Tim! I'm here in the garden," called Mother as she saw Tim coming home from kindergarten.

Tim raced around to the side of the house, laughing excitedly. He found his mother on her knees, pulling weeds from a bed of brightly colored flowers. "Want to hear a joke Tommy told me on the way home?" he asked.

Mother smiled as she stood up and walked a few feet to a stone bench. "Come sit with me, Tim," she invited. "Let's hear that joke. I bet it's a good one."

Tim sat on the ground beside the bench and started to tell his mother a story that made fun of Hollanders. She laughed at the silly joke. Then she said, "I have a surprise for you, Tim. You're a Hollander. Your great-grandparents came from Holland. So when you make fun of Hollanders, you're making fun of yourself." Tim's mouth dropped open in surprise. "Laughing at yourself is one thing," continued Mother, "but laughing at others is something else. You need to be very careful about telling jokes that poke fun at different nationalities or races."

"Do you think they might get mad?" asked Tim.

"Well, lots of people don't mind," replied Mother, "but others might feel hurt or angry. So unless you know such a joke won't hurt anyone's feelings, it's better not to tell it at all. Always remember that people are different from each other because that's the way God meant them to be." She waved a hand toward the flower bed. "What do you notice about the flowers?" she asked.

Tim considered them for a minute. "Well, they're all different colors," he said. "I like 'em that way."

"So do I," agreed Mother. "Some are red, and some are yellow and some are purple. God didn't make all flowers the same color, and he didn't give all people the same color skin or hair. God likes variety, and we should, too." She smiled at Tim as she added, "I hope, Son, that you'll be a person who appreciates everyone God has created." *A.L.*

HOW ABOUT YOU?

Are you considerate of people who are different from you? It's interesting to learn about different races and cultures. God created each one for his own pleasure and in his own image. Learn to see others as God sees them.

MEMORIZE:

"When an alien lives with you in your land, do not mistreat him." *Leviticus 19:33, NIV*

 *Accept All People*

A Special Poem (Read Ephesians 2:4-10)

1

"Sometimes when I get home from school, all I want is food that's cool." Mandy made up a rhyme as she opened the freezer and took out a Popsicle. She grinned at her brother, Michael.

Michael rolled his eyes and made up a rhyme of his own. "Your poems are all rather quaint, telling me a poet you ain't," he said.

Mandy laughed and went outside. Her mother was working in the garden. "Hello, Mother with a thumb that's green. You have the nicest vegetables I've ever seen."

Mother smiled. "Still working on a poem for school, Mandy?" she asked.

"Trying, but I'm about ready to give up. We read such neat poems in class, but all I can think of are silly things," complained Mandy.

When Dad arrived home from work, Mandy greeted him with another of her rhymes. "Dad, you've had to work all day. Sit down and relax now while you may."

"You're getting worse, Mandy," teased Michael. "How about this. Mom, that chicken looks so fine. It's time that we sat down to dine."

Dad laughed and joined in the fun. "My family is always such a delight. It's a joy to be home this Monday night." He sat down at the table. "Actually, I know a very special poem," he added. "It's mentioned in the Bible, in Ephesians 2:10."

"I just memorized that verse for Sunday school!" exclaimed Mandy. "Let's see . . . it says, 'For we are His [God's] workmanship, created in Christ Jesus for good works.' It doesn't say anything about a poem!"

"Yes, it does!" declared Dad. "The word *workmanship* comes from the Greek word *poema*. That's the same word our English word *poem* comes from. So to say we are his workmanship is like saying we are his poem."

"Wow, that's neat!" Mandy said. "Then I guess we should be careful to be the kind of poem he can be proud of." *L.W.*

HOW ABOUT YOU?

What is your favorite poem? Maybe it's a serious poem about trees or flowers. Maybe it's a silly poem about cats or peanut butter! Did you know that, as a Christian, you are God's poem? You're his special creation, his workmanship, his special poetry. What kind of poem are you?

MEMORIZE:

"For we are His [God's] workmanship, created in Christ Jesus for good works."

Ephesians 2:10, NKJV

━━ ***Christians Are God's Poems***

The Woodpecker (Read Matthew 4:1-11)

As Jasmine's youth group walked through a park, Pastor Jim, the group leader, pointed out various kinds of wildflowers and animals. Suddenly Jasmine gasped. "Is that a snake?" she asked in horror, looking up at a tree. "I didn't know they could climb."

2
JUNE

"That kind can," replied Pastor Jim. "Let's watch for a bit." All the kids watched as the snake got closer and closer to a hole in the tree where a woodpecker had its nest. As the snake neared the hole, it began to squirm around. Then to the group's surprise, the snake began to retreat down the tree.

"He's leaving," Jasmine observed. "Why?"

"Well," said Pastor Jim, "that's a red cockaded woodpecker's nest—he builds it in trees with a thick resin, like sap, in them. The sap comes out around the woodpecker's hole, and the snake doesn't like to get that resin on its skin, so it leaves."

"Well, I'm leaving, too, before that snake gets down here," declared Jasmine, and they all continued on their walk.

"Whenever I see one of those birds' nests," said Pastor Jim, "I think of the Scripture, 'Resist the devil, and he will flee from you.' The devil is like that snake. When he comes to tempt us, we can use the word of God to resist him, just as Jesus did." *S.N.*

HOW ABOUT YOU?

Do you know that you can have victory over temptation? When you're tempted to sin, quote verses that remind you of what you should not do. Also, quote verses that remind you of the good things you should do instead. The devil will have to flee from you when you use God's Word!

MEMORIZE:

"Submit yourselves, then, to God. Resist the devil, and he will flee from you." *James 4:7, NIV*

 Resist the Devil

Keep Knocking (Read Luke 18:1-8)

3

JUNE

"Amen." As the Anderson family ended their nightly devotions, Beth stretched. "Every night we pray for Mrs. Gerard, but she just gets meaner," she observed. "I'm tired of praying for her."

"Me, too," agreed Zach. "Yesterday she swore at me because my ball bounced into her yard. I think she likes being mean."

"All the more reason to pray for her," said Dad. "God says we are to pray for those who 'despitefully use' us. Besides, Mrs. Gerard may be closer to being saved than you realize." He reached for his coat. "Would anyone like to ride down to the post office with me to mail a letter?"

"Zach might," Mother said. "I have to shampoo Beth's hair."

"We won't be gone long," Dad promised.

Soon Beth was in the bathtub, and her hair was covered with a mountain of suds. She squeezed her eyes shut. "I think I hear the doorbell," she murmured.

Mother stopped scrubbing Beth's scalp and listened. "Oh, dear," she said. She reached for a towel and knocked over the shampoo. "Grab it . . . too late! What a mess!" She dried her hands. "I'm coming! I'm coming!" she called as the bell rang again.

Beth peeked up at her mother. A drop of sudsy water rolled into her eye. "Ohhh, I got soap in my eye."

Mother handed her the towel. "Just sit still," said Mother. "I'll be back in a minute."

Beth rubbed her eye gently as she waited. In a few seconds Mother returned. "Who was it?" Beth asked.

Mother shrugged as she turned on the faucet to rinse Beth's hair. "I don't know," she said. "They drove off just as I got to the door. I wish they hadn't been so impatient."

As Mother cleaned up the shampoo, Beth wrapped a towel around her head. Her mother smiled at her. "This reminds me of our earlier conversation," added Mother. "Wouldn't it be too bad if we quit praying for Mrs. Gerard just before God answers?"

Thoughtfully, Beth nodded. *B.W.*

HOW ABOUT YOU?

Have you been praying for someone for a long time? Are you getting discouraged? Don't quit. Keep asking. The next knock on heaven's door may be the one that gets the answer you've been waiting for.

MEMORIZE:

"Men always ought to pray and not lose heart." *Luke 18:1, NKJV*

Keep Praying

Picking up the Pieces (Read Isaiah 54:4-5; Psalm 10:14-18)

4
JUNE

Amy curled up on the sofa, watching her green parakeet, who perched sadly in his little brass cage. Dad had given him to her just a few weeks before he had died and gone to be with Jesus, and she remembered Dad saying, "This little guy will keep you company." That was why Amy had named him Little Guy.

Now Dad had been gone six months. Although Amy had almost become accustomed to the emptiness of the house, she still missed little things—Dad in his place at the table, the sound of his laugh, the way he used to tap a good night signal on her bedroom door. There was a sadness in Mom's eyes, too, and Amy knew she missed Dad a lot. But Mom had said something about 'picking up the pieces' and going on. They had discovered some wonderful promises for widows and children as they read the Bible together each evening.

"Mom, what's wrong with Little Guy?" asked Amy. "His cage is clean and he has fresh water and seed, but he acts sick or something." Amy sounded worried. "I haven't heard him chirp lately, either," she added.

Mom came in from the kitchen and studied the little bird huddled in the sunshine. "Oh, he's just molting, Amy," she said. "Haven't you noticed all the feathers he's lost? Sometimes birds become droopy and often stop singing during this period, but he'll be all right. He just needs a little time." Mom smiled encouragingly. Then she said, "You and I are a little like that, honey. We've lost our desire to sing, too, but God knows how we feel and he has promised to take care of us. He knows we both miss Daddy very much, but he wants us to trust him and be happy again."

"Like I want Little Guy to be happy?" Amy's words were more of a statement than a question. She gently poked a finger into the cage, touching the soft green feathers. Little Guy cocked his head and ruffled his feathers. "Chirp," he responded softly, almost as if he understood. *P.K.*

HOW ABOUT YOU?

Is there some big problem in your life? Do you feel sad and lonely? Remember, God loves and cares for you even when you can't see him. Pray about your problems and trust him to help you through.

MEMORIZE:

"[God] is a father to the fatherless; he gives justice to the widows, for he is holy."

Psalm 68:5, TLB

 God Understands

The Dirty Socks (Read 2 Timothy 3:14-17)

5
JUNE

"Dad! I don't have any clean socks!" called Steven. A few moments later, Dad walked into the bedroom, lifted up the edge of Steven's comforter, and pointed under the bed. There, in crumpled heaps, were several pairs of socks. All dirty! "Oh, no," moaned Steven. "I forgot all about them when I got stuff together for the laundry."

"Son," Dad said, "you'll have to wash these yourself. I showed you how to use the washer."

"I know, but I don't like to wash clothes," said Steven. "I never used to have to do stuff like that."

"You're older now, Steven," said Dad, "and it's time you assumed a little more responsibility around here, especially now that Mother has gone to take care of Grandma."

After supper that evening, Steven went to the laundry room. He piled the socks and some of his shirts into the washer, added detergent, and pushed the button. As water poured into the washer, he lowered the lid and stepped back, feeling rather proud of himself.

When Steven took the clothes to the family room, where he began folding them, Dad was at the desk, studying his Bible. He looked up and smiled. "Good job, Son," he said. "By the way, are you entering the Bible memory contest at church next week?"

Steven shook his head. "Those verses are too hard," he replied, "and Mom's not here to help me."

"Well, I'll help you when I can," said Dad. He watched as Steven finished folding his clothes. "But you can learn by yourself, too," Dad added. "You know, I wanted you to take more responsibility, and you have."

"What do you mean?" asked Steven.

"Well," said Dad, "you accepted Christ as Savior nearly three years ago. Maybe the Lord thinks it's time for you to work a little harder at memorizing. Maybe he wants you to learn some more difficult verses—even on your own."

Steven gathered up his clothes. "I guess I could try," he said slowly. "I'll start as soon as I put this stuff away." *C.B.*

HOW ABOUT YOU?

Do you take the responsibility of reading God's Word, praying, and learning Bible verses? Or do you wait for an adult to make you do those things? Why not talk to God today—tell him you're ready to become a responsible Christian.

MEMORIZE:

"**Now the most important thing about a servant is that he does just what his master tells him to.**" *1 Corinthians 4:2, TLB*

🔑 *Be a Responsible Christian*

Flying Is for Birds (Read Psalm 19:7-11)

"Hello there, Jim. I hear you forgot that flying is for birds," joked Uncle Jon, as he surveyed the chalky white cast plastered around Jim's ankle. "Your mother tells me you jumped off the edge of the garage. Good thing you landed in the shrubs, or you might have broken both ankles."

"It was higher than I thought," replied Jim, embarrassed.

6

JUNE

"Well, I'm sure you have a new respect for the law of gravity now," said Uncle Jon, sitting down on the edge of the bed. "I've certainly come to appreciate all of God's laws."

"You mean like the Ten Commandments?" asked Jim.

Uncle Jon nodded. "Yes, but those are only some of God's laws," he said. "When God created the world, he invented every scientific law there is." Jim looked puzzled. "For example," continued Uncle Jon, "he made botanical laws that say certain seeds produce certain fruit, and biological laws that say people require food and water to stay alive. There are chemical laws that say certain mixed gases will create explosions, and reproductive laws that say chickens hatch chicks, never ducks. There are mathematical laws that say two plus two equals four."

"Don't forget the law of gravity," Jim added with a grin.

Uncle Jon laughed. "Right!" he said. "God holds the universe together, and his laws never change. It pays to respect God's laws if you want to stay alive." Uncle Jon took a small New Testament from his shirt pocket. "Now," he added, "we need to talk about God's most important laws—his spiritual laws."

"Like the things Pastor Harris preaches about in his sermons?" asked Jim.

"Yes," answered Uncle Jon. "Some people refuse to believe there are spiritual laws, but these laws are as real as the physical ones. You either respect them and do what they say, or you go your own way and lose in the end."

"And that's even worse than forgetting the law of gravity, isn't it?" said Jim with a smile. *J.R.G.*

HOW ABOUT YOU?

Do you respect the laws God has established? Even the spiritual ones? Those laws say you must trust in Jesus alone as Savior and Lord to become his child. Will you trust Jesus today?

MEMORIZE:

"For the wages of sin is death, but the gift of God is eternal life in Christ Jesus our Lord."

Romans 6:23, NKJV

 Trust Christ Today

The Bald Eagle (Read 1 Peter 2:11-25)

7

JUNE

Jeremy and his dad were enjoying a vacation together; they were camping out, "roughing it." They saw a lot of beautiful scenery and many wild animals in the woods and along the lakes and streams. One day they even spotted a bald eagle. Jeremy was thrilled. "I never saw one of those before," he said excitedly. "I bet my friends never did, either. They'll be surprised when I tell them about it." He grabbed his camera to take a picture. "I'll take back some proof," he added with a grin.

Dad nodded. "You know the bald eagle is a symbol of our country, don't you?" he asked.

"Of course!" replied Jeremy. "We learned that in school, and I think it's cool. Eagles are strong and graceful, and they do a lot of neat things." As they watched the eagle soaring high above, Jeremy went on to tell Dad some of the things he had learned.

"That's a magnificent bird, all right," murmured Dad. "A good representative of our country, I think." After a moment he added, "You know, Son, in a way, the bald eagle is like Christians." Jeremy looked puzzled at that idea. "What I mean is that just like the bald eagle represents the United States, Christians represent Jesus Christ," explained Dad. "You've thought of some good things about the eagle, some things that make you glad to have him as a representative for you and your country. I hope the Lord sees things in us that make him happy to have us as his representatives, too." *K.L.*

HOW ABOUT YOU?

Are you a Christian? If so, are you a faithful representative of Christ? What does he see in your life? He wants to see love, honesty, obedience, joy, peace, patience, kindness—and all of the good traits that were in his life. Jesus, himself, is the example for you to follow.

MEMORIZE:

"Let no one despise your youth, but be an example to the believers in word, in conduct, in love, in spirit, in faith, in purity." *1 Timothy 4:12, NKJV*

 Christians Represent Jesus

Breakthrough (Read John 1:14-18)

8

JUNE

Brian turned away from the television news program. "What does it mean when they say they've made a medical breakthrough?" he asked.

"It usually means they think they've finally found the answer to a medical problem, or at least they're going the right direction toward solving it," explained Dad.

"There are other kinds of breakthroughs, too," declared Mom with a smile. "You might say I had a 'culinary breakthrough' the other day. I finally figured out what was missing in that candy recipe I've been experimenting with."

"All right!" exclaimed Brian. He grinned at his mother. "They ought to put that on TV, too," he teased.

"There was another breakthrough that changed the world forever," said Dad thoughtfully. "It happened very quietly one night. The news wasn't reported on TV or radio—or even in the newspapers."

"Then how did anyone know there was a breakthrough?" Brian asked, leaning forward eagerly. "Where did it happen? And how did you find out about it?"

Dad's eyes sparkled. "Well, Brian, the big breakthrough took place about 2,000 years ago," he replied. "God came to earth."

"Oh, Dad," Brian sank back in his chair.

"Think about it," urged Dad. "God had tried to reach the hearts of men on earth for thousands of years. He spoke through nature, through man's conscience, and through prophets. But the biggest breakthrough to the hardness of men's hearts came about when God took the form of a baby—Jesus. He came to earth to help people understand how they could have a right relationship with God."

"Right." Mother nodded. "Jesus is the only way to God. He breaks down barriers so we may be saved. So when someone asks Jesus to forgive his sins and be his Savior, you might consider that a breakthrough, too." *V.L.C.*

HOW ABOUT YOU?

Has God made a "breakthrough" into your life? Have you trusted Jesus as your Lord and Savior? If not, don't wait. Trust him right now.

MEMORIZE:

"The Word became flesh and dwelt among us . . . full of grace and truth." *John 1:14, NKJV*

 Let God Save You

Hidden Dirt (Read Matthew 23:25-28)

9

Jeanine answered the door. "I'm sorry I can't play with you now," she said in her most pleasant voice. She was glad to be doing the dishes so she could send Chad, the little neighbor boy, home. She ruffled his hair and waved to his mother across the street. "Come another time," added Jeanine. Closing the door, she turned to her mother. "He's such a bratty pest," she complained. "I wish he'd stay away."

"He likes you," said Mother as she left the room. "He doesn't have an older sister of his own."

Jeanine began to wash dishes. But before she finished she was tired of her job. She carelessly ran the dishcloth around the outside of a pan. After a feeble attempt to remove some burned-on food, she set the pan in the drainer, cleanest side up.

"Let me help you dry some of these," offered Mother, coming into the kitchen. She lifted the saucepan from the rack and dried the outside. Then she looked at the inside. "Jeanine," she said, "the inside of this pan is still dirty!"

Jeanine shrugged. "It's burned on, but at least the outside is sparkling," she said.

"That seems to be the way you do things lately," observed Mom, putting the pan down to be washed again.

"Things?" asked Jeanine. "Like what else?"

"I was thinking of how nice you acted with the neighbors earlier," replied Mom. "I'm not saying you should play with Chad, but if you don't want him coming over, don't encourage him. Be kind, but let him know firmly that he should play with kids his own age. As it was, from the outside you appeared to be a very loving girl. But what was going on inside your heart was anything but kind and loving." Jeanine blushed as she began to scrub the pan.

"The Bible says people who put on an act to impress others while having ungodly thoughts are hypocrites," continued Mom. "After you clean the inside of this pan, perhaps you should spend some time in prayer, asking Jesus to clean your heart and mind."

N.E.K.

HOW ABOUT YOU?

Do you put on a nice act in front of people and then grumble behind their backs? If you're letting Jesus make you more like him, you won't have to be two-faced.

MEMORIZE:

"First clean the inside of the cup and dish, and then the outside also will be clean."

Matthew 23:26, NIV

 Don't Be a Hypocrite

Sea Lion Ears (Read Philippians 4:4-9)

10
JUNE

"Sea Lion Caves," read David, pointing to a sign. "We're there!" His family had been driving along the sandy beaches and rocky headlands of the Oregon coast.

Dad turned into the parking lot. Soon they stood in the underground viewing area, close enough to see, smell, and hear the roaring creatures without disturbing them. A torpedo-shaped body with a whiskered, catlike face, brown eyes, and spiky teeth slid through the water outside the grotto and clambered up onto the cave floor. Dad stood beside David with the guide book he'd bought. "This seal is a stellar sea lion," said Dad. "If you look closely, you can see what looks like dimples on the side of the seal's head. Those are tiny ears. Most seals just have openings, but the stellar sea lion is an eared seal. When he dives, those tiny earflaps cover the ear openings. When he surfaces, the ears open up again."

"Wow! That's cool!" said David.

Back in the car and on their way again, they talked about the animals they had seen. "Hey! Why didn't God give me closable ears?" David asked, chuckling at the thought of his ears flopping down. "I'd like to be able to shut out some things I hear."

"I thought you already could," said Mother, pretending to be surprised. "For example, sometimes you appear to be unable to hear when you're told to pick up your room!" David looked at her and grinned. He knew she was teasing, but he figured she was half-serious, too.

"That's a good point," observed Dad. "God didn't give you earflaps, but he did give you the ability to close your ears by not paying attention and not letting certain things stay in your mind. On the other hand, you can open them by paying attention to what is being said."

"Yes, and you need to be very careful in choosing what to keep in your mind and what to let go," added Mother. "It might be a good idea to close your ears to some things you hear on TV or on the playground. But keep them open to your parents and teachers, and especially to God." *B.K.*

HOW ABOUT YOU?

Do you close your ears when you hear bad language, dirty jokes, or suggestions to do something wrong? Do you open them when your parents or teachers ask you to do something? Please God in the way you use your ears.

MEMORIZE:

"The ear tests words as the tongue tastes food." *Job 34:3, NIV*

 Screen What You Hear

Minced Oaths (Read Matthew 12:35-37)

11

JUNE

Karen was at Sue's house, and the girls were working on their Sunday school lesson, which included looking up some Bible words in the dictionary. "I found *gospel*," said Sue. "It means 'good story' or 'good news.'" Karen wrote the definition on a sheet of paper.

Then Sue pointed to another word in the dictionary. "Hey, look at this. Here's the word *gosh*, and I don't like what I'm reading."

Karen moved closer so that she could read from the dictionary. "It says *gosh* is a form of the name God," she said in surprise. "I didn't know that."

"Me, neither," said Sue. "I've said that word lots of times. I never even thought about what it meant." The girls decided to look up the words *golly* and *gee*. They were surprised to find that these were also derived from the names of God and Jesus. "Does it really matter if we use those words?" asked Sue. "Everybody does, and we don't mean anything by them."

"I don't know," said Karen slowly. "My mom always says just because everybody does it, it doesn't make it right."

Sue shook her head. "I guess not. But what can you and I do about it? We can't change the whole world."

"No," said Karen, "but we can change. I sure don't want to be guilty of using God's name in the wrong way."

Sue nodded. She made a copy of the information they had found and tucked the paper into her Bible. The girls decided they should share this with the whole class. *S.L.S.*

HOW ABOUT YOU?

Do you avoid using swear words? Good! But how about words like *golly, gosh, gee,* or *darn?* You could let your friends know that not everyone uses these words—you don't.

MEMORIZE:

"For by your words you will be justified, and by your words will you be condemned."

Matthew 12:37, NKJV

 Keep Your Speech Pure

The Abscessed Tooth (Read 1 John 1:8-10; 2:1-2)

12
JUNE

Robbie carefully felt the funny little hole with his tongue. "My mouth feels better," he told his mother, "but my tongue won't stay away from the empty spot. What did you say was wrong with my tooth? I want to tell Grandma when she comes this afternoon."

"There was an abscess at the root of your tooth—that's kind of like an infected sore," explained Mother. "Since it was just a baby tooth, the dentist pulled it so the poisons could be cleaned out."

When Grandma came that afternoon, Robbie told her all about his tooth. He felt the empty spaces in the front of his mouth where some of his other teeth were missing. "Pretty soon I won't have any more teeth than Missy," he said, pointing to his baby sister, who was bouncing in her high chair.

Grandma laughed. "Your permanent teeth are almost through," she said, "so it's good that the dentist pulled the bad one. If he hadn't taken care of it, it would have gotten worse. The poison from the abscess could have made you sick." She gently rubbed the side of Robbie's face. "You know," she said thoughtfully, "I think I'll use your tooth as an illustration for my Sunday school class, OK?"

"OK," agreed Robbie.

"You see," Grandma continued, "sin—things like lying or disobeying—is like an abscessed tooth. We have to get rid of sin in our life, or it gets worse. We need someone to clean it out and replace our bad thoughts with good ones, just like your bad tooth will be replaced with a new, good one."

"Jesus takes our sin away, doesn't he?" asked Robbie.

"He surely does," replied Grandma. "We can't do it ourselves. We need to confess our sin to God and ask him to forgive us. Then he gets rid of it for us." She smiled at Robbie. "The dentist cleans out the abscess, and Jesus cleans out the sin."

Robbie smiled, too. "I'm sure glad someone's around to clean out both of them," he said. *D.R.O.*

HOW ABOUT YOU?

Do you have sin that needs to be cleaned away? Take care of it right away before it gets worse. Confess to God that you have lied, cheated, been unkind, gossiped—whatever it is, tell him all about it. Ask him to forgive you. He promises that he will.

MEMORIZE:

"If we confess our sins, He is faithful and just to forgive us our sins and to cleanse us from all unrighteousness."

1 John 1:9, NKJV

 Confess Sin to God

Audible Repetitions (Read 1 Thessalonians 1:4-10)

13

JUNE

"Yummmm! Those smell good!" exclaimed Wendy as Mother turned the hamburgers on the grill. "I'll call Dad and Jason." The family was camping in a mountain canyon, and Wendy's father and brother were out hiking. Wendy faced the high cliffs opposite the campsite, took a deep breath, and shouted loudly, "Yoo-hoo!"

"Yoo-hoo!" came back to her, as clear as a bell.

"Come for supper!" yelled Wendy.

"Come for supper!" was the immediate response.

Wendy looked puzzled, and then she grinned at her mother. "When I heard 'Yoo-hoo!' coming back from across the canyon, I thought Jason answered me." She giggled. "But I'm sure that wasn't him inviting me to supper! That was my own echo!"

Just then Dad and Jason walked up. "What's going on?" Jason asked, not too happily. He was as hungry as a bear.

"When Wendy called you for supper, she got acquainted with a friendly echo who lives on the canyon wall," Mother told him.

"That's ridiculous," grumbled Jason. "Friendly echoes don't live on canyon walls. Echoes are made by sound waves bouncing back to us so that we hear the sound again. Now, may I please have a hamburger? I'm starved."

After supper, a more civil Jason joined Wendy in talking with the canyon echo. Finally, Wendy called, "Good night," and then listened while the echo repeated the message.

"Echoes are fun," declared Wendy.

Dad smiled. "Did you know that we should be echoes, too?"

"What do you mean?" asked Jason. "How can we be echoes?"

"Well," said Dad, "God's words are found in the Bible, but many people don't read the Bible. Those folks will hear of God's love only as we who know God's Word echo it back to them."

"I get it," Wendy said. "It's like we're God's echo."

"People hear what he says by listening to us," added Jason.

"Amen!" said Dad loudly, and they all listened quietly as the answering "Amen!" returned from the canyon wall. *T.V.*

HOW ABOUT YOU?

Is anyone hearing about Jesus as you echo God's Word and his love? It's your privilege and responsibility to be God's echo.

MEMORIZE:

"How can they hear without someone preaching to them?"

Romans 10:14, NIV

 Echo God's Love

Try It! You Might Like It! (Read Psalm 34:3-8)

14

JUNE

"Would you go with me to church, Derek?" asked Jacob. Before Derek answered, Jacob already knew what he was going to say.

"No, I won't. I don't like Sunday school."

"But how do you know you don't like it?" Jacob argued with his cousin. "You've never been there."

"I just know—that's all," Derek snapped. "Let's go see what's for dinner." He led the way to the kitchen, where he peered over his mother's shoulder. "Yummmm!" he said, rubbing his stomach. "Shrimp!"

Jacob frowned. Then he was embarrassed when he realized Aunt Betty noticed. "Don't you like shrimp?" she asked. Jacob shook his head. "Have you ever eaten any?" asked Aunt Betty. Again Jacob shook his head.

"Then how do you know you don't like it?" asked Derek, jumping into the conversation.

Jacob shrugged. "I just know, that's all."

"That's stupid!" Derek argued. "Fried shrimp is so good! But if you don't want any, I'll eat your share."

Aunt Betty smiled. "Before you do that, I think Jacob really should try it," she said.

"Yeah," agreed Derek. "Try it. You might like it."

Jacob grinned. "I'll try shrimp," he said, "if you'll try Sunday school."

Derek frowned for a minute. Then he chuckled. "You got me. OK," he agreed. "It's a deal. You try shrimp. I try Sunday school."

Later, at dinner, Jacob took his first bite of shrimp. "Hummmmm, not bad," he said. "Pass the shrimp, please."

And next Sunday on the way home from church, Derek said, "Hummmmm, not bad. Think I'll try it again next Sunday." *B.W.*

HOW ABOUT YOU?

Do you think you won't like church or Sunday school? Then you're missing so much! Try Sunday school or church or Bible club. Listen to what God says in his Word. You may want to know more and more.

MEMORIZE:

"Oh, taste and see that the Lord is good; blessed is the man who trusts in Him!"

Psalm 34:8, NKJV

 Attend Sunday School

Obedient Rex (Read Exodus 1:15-17, 20-21)

"Sit, Rex! Sit." Rex sat, and Jenny gave the big black dog a pat on his head. "Good boy! Here's a treat for obeying." She gave Rex a dog biscuit.

"Rex is getting good at obeying you," Dad called to Jenny. He was watching from the porch as Jenny worked with Rex in the backyard.

Jenny grinned and nodded. "Stay," she said firmly to Rex. "Stay." Jenny walked a few steps away just as her cousin Brian came up the walk.

"Hi, Rex!" called Brian. "Come here, Boy. C'mon, Rex. Come here."

Rex perked up his ears and looked at Brian. Then he looked back at Jenny and whined, but he stayed where he was. "Good boy!" Jenny gave him another dog treat.

"Rex reminds me of the Hebrew midwives we read about during devotions last night," said Dad.

Brian laughed. "What on earth do you mean by that?"

"We read about some women named Shiphrah and Puah," explained Dad. (See today's Scripture.) "The Hebrew midwives were told by the king to kill all the boy babies born to the Israelites. But they knew it was better to obey God than man, so they decided not to do it. Because of that God blessed them. Even though they disobeyed the king, they still were blessed by God."

"I know what you're getting at." Jenny put her arm around Rex as he lay beside her on the floor. "Rex had to disobey Brian in order to obey me, but he did it."

"Yes, he did." Dad gave Rex a pat on the head. "We must always obey our master. In Rex's case, his master—or mistress—is Jenny. Our Master is God. If we obey God, he will bless us." *A.L.*

HOW ABOUT YOU?

Would you steal if your friends encouraged you to do so? Would you cheat on a test because your friend wanted the answers? Or do you obey God rather than people? When you're tempted to sin, ask God to give you strength to obey him. Then do it; he'll bless you for it.

MEMORIZE:

"We must obey God rather than men!" *Acts 5:29, NIV*

 *Obey God*

Baby Birds (Read John 10:1-5)

"Sara, I have a surprise to show you," Daddy announced one morning. "Come with me." Sara ran to her father and together they went out to the patio. "Some finches made a nest out here," Daddy said, pointing to a large plant that hung outside the kitchen window. "The mother bird laid five eggs in the nest, and they've all hatched."

Sara's eyes grew wide as her father lifted her onto his shoulder so she could peek into the nest. "I just see a pile of fuzz in there," said Sara. "Where are the baby birds?"

16

JUNE

"Watch," said Daddy. He made clicking noises with his tongue, and suddenly five tiny heads popped out of the fuzz.

"Oh," squealed Sara. "I see them! I see them! They have their eyes closed." Gradually the heads sank back into the fuzz. "Do it again, Daddy," begged Sara. Daddy made the clicking noise again, and up popped the heads.

For the next several weeks, Sara and Daddy visited the birds every day. Sara watched the baby birds grow. Their eyes opened and they got new, larger feathers, but it became harder to get them to respond to Daddy's clicking noise. "They're learning that I'm not really their mother bringing their dinner," said Daddy when Sara asked him about that. "They know I'm just fooling them." He smiled at his little daughter as he added, "We're kind of like those baby birds. We have to learn to recognize who it is that is telling us to do things. We have to be able to tell when it's God's voice."

"We do?" asked Sara. "How do we do that?"

"By learning about God in church and Sunday school and by listening to his Word and memorizing it," said Daddy.

"Satan is the one who tries to fool us. I know Jesus tells us to do good things," said Sara, "and Satan tries to get us to do bad things."

"It sounds like you're learning to recognize God's voice already," said Daddy with a smile. *P.Y.*

HOW ABOUT YOU?

Have you learned to recognize God's voice? The more you study the Bible, the easier it becomes to tell the difference between what is true and what is false. The more you learn of God, the easier it is to know when he wants you to do something.

MEMORIZE:

"Faith comes from hearing the message, and the message is heard through the word of Christ." *Romans 10:17, NIV*

 Listen to God's Voice

Sand Castles (Read Luke 6:47-49)

17

JUNE

"Hurry up with that!" Scott warned. "The tide is coming in. One big wave, and your castle will be washed out!"

"Help me," said Michelle, handing her brother a pail and shovel. Water washed around her feet and pulled back toward the ocean, just missing the castle.

"I told you to build it farther from the water," Scott said, adding a pail full of damp sand to the castle. "Maybe we should build a moat around it, or a wall—"

"Oh no!" exclaimed Michelle as the water came up fast. There was no time to protect the castle. A big chunk of the front side washed back with the sea. "My shovel," Michelle called, chasing after it into the water.

"Wash out!" Scott declared. Michelle's lip trembled as she stood looking at her masterpiece, now destroyed. "That always happens to sand castles close to the water, no matter how good they're made," Scott told her.

The next day Mother received a letter from her sister. "Aunt Betsy needs our prayers," she told Michelle and Scott when she finished reading it. "She's going through stormy times in her life, and she's finding she can't stand up against them." Mother sighed. "She does have some big problems, and since she's not a Christian, her life isn't built on a solid foundation. When things go wrong, she tends to fall apart."

"Just like Michelle's sand castle yesterday," Scott said. "It looked awesome, but it was built in a place where it couldn't stand up against the flood. That castle is history."

Mother nodded. "Jesus gave an example like that to show that we can't depend on our own strength or our own ideas to make us strong," she said. "We need to build our life according to God's Word and depend on him for our strength. If Aunt Betsy had Jesus in her heart and was building her life on his word, she could depend on God for strength to deal with all the problems she faces."

N.E.K.

HOW ABOUT YOU?

Do you ever feel overwhelmed by problems? The first thing you need to do is make sure you're building your life on Jesus Christ, the solid Rock. Accept him as your Savior. Trust him so you will be able to be strong when troubles come.

MEMORIZE:

"No one can ever lay any other real foundation than . . . Jesus Christ." *1 Corinthians 3:11, TLB*

 Jesus Is the Solid Foundation

Big Sister (Read Matthew 7:1-5)

"Oh, no!" cried Nicole as her little brother pushed the magazines off the coffee table. "What an awful day! Scotty threw his food during breakfast, tried to drown my Bible in the bathtub, and now this."

"Some people call this age the terrible twos," said Mother, "but I prefer to think of it as the curious twos. It's an age when children are learning so much."

Nicole helped her mother rearrange the magazines. "It must be hard having such a bad boy after having had a perfect child like me," she said with a grin.

18
JUNE

Mother laughed. "You'll get a chance to see yourself at that age when Aunt Gina comes," she said. "She's going to bring a videotape she made the summer when we went out to her wedding."

"Good." Nicole smiled. "I'll make sure Scotty watches and sees how a two-year-old should act."

The next week Nicole and her family all gathered in the living room to see the videotape made several years before. "Oh, look," Nicole cried as the screen showed the family seated around a table. "There I am in my high chair saying grace. How sweet."

"Look again," said Aunt Gina.

"I can't believe it!" Nicole gasped. "I'm pouring milk on the floor." More scenes passed. "Why is that dog under the chair?" asked Nicole.

"You pulled his tail," replied Dad. Nicole was shocked.

"Here you are dressed for the wedding," said Mother.

"How cute." Nicole smiled. "Such a pretty white dress with blue bows." But a moment later Nicole again saw herself on the screen—this time the white dress was covered with brown streaks.

"Just before we were to leave for church you got outside and stomped through a mud puddle," explained Aunt Gina.

Nicole grinned as Scotty climbed up on her lap. "Hey, little brother," she said, "from now on I'm going to be more patient with you—I promise!" *R.M.*

HOW ABOUT YOU?

Do you judge little brothers and sisters too harshly? How about your brothers and sisters in the Lord—other Christians? You need to be patient with them, too. God wants his children to help each other become better Christians. You can't do that if you spend all your time complaining about each other's faults.

MEMORIZE:

"Judge not, that you be not judged." Matthew 7:1, NKJV

 Be Patient with Others

Scars to Remember (Read Hebrews 12:5-11)

19
JUNE

Adam hesitated as his friend Stephen held up a video he and some other boys were going to watch. "Come on, Adam," urged Stephen. "Are you a wimp or something?"

Adam was curious about the popular horror movie. However, he wasn't anxious to break his parents' rule about not watching horror movies. He'd recently broken a lamp when he disobeyed the rule about not playing ball in the house. Although the lamp was fixed, it still had a crack in its base.

"Wimpy! Wimpy!" the boys chanted. Adam gave in.

When he got home, a wave of guilt overcame him. "How did it happen, Lord?" he prayed. "I really didn't mean to disobey. I should have said no. Please forgive me." He felt better then.

Adam went to bed with a clear conscience and fell right to sleep. But then the dream came—a terrible dream in which the monster from the movie was after him.

"Adam, wake up." Adam heard Dad's voice over his own cries. Dad's words were comforting, but the terror was still with Adam, and he couldn't stop crying. Through his tears, he told Dad about the movie and how it had brought on the dream. "I asked God to forgive me. Why didn't he? Why did he let me have that dream?" Adam asked.

"Remember the lamp?" asked Dad. Adam nodded. "We forgave you for breaking it, but the lamp will always have a scar—the crack in its base," Dad said. "Tonight, you asked God to forgive you for watching that movie you shouldn't have watched. He has forgiven you, too, but that doesn't mean there will be no scars."

"The dream was a scar, wasn't it?" asked Adam.

"I think so," said Dad. "Even though God forgives us, we still have to live with the consequences of our sin. They help us remember not to do that sin again. And they help us to not commit sins that have even worse consequences."

Adam thought about the lamp and the nightmare—two scars to help him remember not to disobey. *K.R.A.*

HOW ABOUT YOU?
Have you tried something wrong because you were curious or because others pressured you into it? Accept God's ready forgiveness when you confess your sin, but also remember that you will still experience the consequences of that sin. Sin is dangerous and not something to be played with.

MEMORIZE:
"**Those whom I love I rebuke and discipline. So be earnest, and repent.**" *Revelation 3:19, NIV*

 *Accept the Consequences of Sin*

Adjustments (Read 1 Timothy 6:6-8)

20
JUNE

"Hi, Grandpa," Alex said as he came out on the terrace. His grandfather was watering pink and white impatiens in a flower box.

"Hi, yourself," replied the elderly man. "Have you adjusted yet to being back in your father's old hometown?"

Alex put his Bible down before he answered. "No," he said. "My Sunday school class is fine, and school was OK, but I'm still praying every night that Dad will get transferred back to Oceanview. I miss swimming in the ocean and playing tennis every day."

"We do have swimming and tennis here, you know," said Grandpa as he watered the plants in a large terrace urn.

"That's what Sean said—he's in my Sunday school class," replied Alex. "We went to the only place to swim around here—the city pool. It was so crowded, it was no fun at all. Then we went over to the tennis courts. Would you believe only girls play tennis in this town? Sean says the boys play baseball and basketball."

"Sounds like you need to adjust," observed Grandpa.

Alex frowned. "I don't want to," he said.

"I didn't either," sympathized Grandpa. Alex looked at him in surprise. "Do you remember the garden I had before I had to move to this apartment?" Grandpa asked. Alex nodded. "Well," Grandpa continued, "when I first moved here, I tried to grow the same flowers on this north side terrace as I had in my big, sunny garden. Most of them either died or grew spindly and didn't bloom."

"Your flowers look OK to me." Alex pointed to the flower boxes and urn.

"That's because I adjusted and planted flowers that bloom in the shade," explained Grandpa as he sat down on a metal chair. "I learned that God has more than one kind of beautiful flower."

"Are you saying I should adjust to this town by taking up baseball and basketball?" Alex asked.

"I've learned to like different flowers," said Grandpa. "I think you should continue with your swimming and tennis, but God supplies other forms of enjoyable recreation, too." *R.M.*

HOW ABOUT YOU?

Do you have to adjust to a new Sunday school class, home, school, or family member? If you see only the bad things about your new situation, you'll miss out on the good things God has for you. Don't sit back and pout. Instead, ask God to help you adjust.

MEMORIZE:

"I have learned to be content whatever the circumstances."

Philippians 4:11, NIV

 **Learn to Adjust**

What's in the Well (Read Psalm 138:1-5)

21

"I'll pray," said Robbie as the family sat down for dinner. He bowed his head and thanked the Lord for the food. Then, looking up, he groaned. "I hate broccoli! And I don't like chicken fixed that way!" But because he knew he had to eat some, he took a little from each dish. "This weather is way too hot," he complained between bites.

His father frowned. "Robbie, do you suppose God heard your prayer tonight?" he asked.

"Sure," replied Robbie confidently.

Dad helped himself to the chicken. "And did he hear your grumbling, too?"

Robbie looked down at his plate. "Yes," he admitted.

"Then which did God believe?" asked Dad. Not waiting for a reply, he went on, "After dinner, we're going out to the old well."

Once at the well, Robbie asked, "Are we going to water the garden?" He knew the water in the old well wasn't fit to drink, but sometimes they used it on the plants.

Dad shook his head. "Let down the bucket and haul up some drinking water for yourself," he said.

Robbie looked surprised. "The water in this well is no good," he protested.

"True. The water in this well is no good," agreed Dad, "but you'll drink the water in your bucket."

Robbie made a face. "If the water in the well isn't good, the water in the bucket won't be good either," he said.

Dad nodded. "That's true," he agreed. "What's in the well will come up in the bucket. It reminds me of the words of Jesus when he said, 'Out of the abundance of the heart the mouth speaketh.' Robbie, I've often noticed that you thank God when you're asked to pray, but then you gripe about many of the good things God has given you. If you ask me, those complaining words of yours must come out of a very unthankful heart."

Robbie drew up the bucket and looked at the garbage that was floating in it. If that represented the condition of his heart, he knew he'd better see what he could do to change it. *M.R.P.*

HOW ABOUT YOU?

What's in your heart? Try to be aware of all the good things God does for you each day. Then instead of complaining, continually thank him. This will give you a truly thankful heart.

MEMORIZE:

"Giving thanks always for all things to God the Father in the name of our Lord Jesus Christ."

Ephesians 5:20, NKJV

➤ *Have a Thankful Heart*

Run (Read 1 Corinthians 10:6-7, 12-14)

As Michelle carefully counted out the money she had taken from her drawer, her sister, Rachel, watched from a comfortable spot on the bed. "If we go around the neighborhood and ask if there are any odd jobs we can do, we just might make enough money to get Mom that Bible we looked at!" Michelle explained. The girls had decided to pool their money and get Mom a special birthday gift.

"Mrs. Stowe is always looking for someone to mow her lawn. Let's try her house," suggested Rachel eagerly.

22
JUNE

Soon the girls were busily mowing and raking Mrs. Stowe's yard. It was a very hot day, and they were wet with sweat by the time they were finished. Wiping her forehead, Michelle gratefully took the money Mrs. Stowe gave them and put it in her pocket. "I'd give anything for some ice cream right now!" she said as they started down the street.

"A Fudgsicle sure would taste great!" agreed Rachel.

Just then the girls heard the music from the ice cream truck—it was coming around the corner.

Michelle and Rachel looked at each other. "Oh, this is so tempting, Rachel. What should we do?" asked Michelle.

"Run!" shouted Rachel.

And that's exactly what they did! They ran straight home to get a nice cold glass of water before looking for more work.

Later, Michelle turned to Rachel as she counted out their earnings. "Now we have just enough to get that Bible," she said happily. "Good thing we didn't spend any on ice cream."

Rachel nodded. "My Sunday school teacher says the best way to keep from giving in to temptation is to run from it," she said. "I'm glad we did that. It really works!" *L.E.K.*

HOW ABOUT YOU?

Do you sometimes find it hard to say no to temptation? When you're tempted to commit any sin, remember that God always provides a way for you to escape. But you have to do your part, too. Often that involves getting out of situations that could bring about defeat. In fact, you should run from them.

MEMORIZE:

"Flee the evil desires."

2 Timothy 2:22, NIV

 Run from Temptation

Fresh Air (Read Psalm 141:1-4)

23

JUNE

"Do I have to go to family camp this year?" Tom asked, scowling. "All the guys say it's kids' stuff."

"Exactly who says that?" asked Dad. "Dan and Bob, those new boys you've been hanging around with lately?" Tom nodded and lowered his eyes. "Well, I think a week at family camp away from those boys will be good for you," Dad said firmly, and Tom knew there was no use arguing.

At camp the next week, Tom did have a good time. He even enjoyed the devotional times around the campfire, but he'd never admit that to Dan or Bob!

When they got home, Tom was the first one in the house. "P-U!" he exclaimed. "What died in here?"

His father trudged in with three suitcases and a sleeping bag. He sniffed the air, then frowned. "You're right," he agreed, "something does smell bad. But it doesn't smell like something died. It smells more like stale smoke."

"The washing machine repairman came the morning we left, remember?" asked Mother. "We left just after he did. I noticed that he smoked a cigar in the utility room, and I guess with the house closed up all the time, the odor had a chance to take over." She opened the kitchen window. "This house needs fresh air," she declared.

"This reminds me of sin," mused Dad. "It has a 'bad odor,' too—it's an offense to God. While we live in this world, we naturally rub shoulders with those who don't love the Lord. But we need 'fresh air,' too. We need to study God's Word and spend time with believers so that our association with sinners doesn't pollute us."

Tom thought of Dan and Bob. He knew that he had started picking up some of their bad attitudes and habits. Perhaps being around them had caused him to "smell bad." It probably was a good thing his folks had made him go along to family camp. That had been like the fresh air he needed—and it had been fun, too.

A.K.D.

HOW ABOUT YOU?

Are you spending too much time with non-Christians? Do you see yourself sharing their attitudes and copying their actions? God wants you to keep yourself pure, and that includes staying away from people who will have a bad influence on you.

MEMORIZE:

"Be with wise men and become wise. Be with evil men and become evil."

Proverbs 13:20, TLB

 Beware of Bad Influences

A Torn Sail (Read Psalm 32:1-7)

24

JUNE

The little blue-and-green sailboat was running free when suddenly there was a loud tearing sound. The sail had ripped, and the boom swung backwards, nearly hitting Dave's head. As the boat capsized, Dave was thrown into the water. He came up next to the sailboat, gasping for breath. The boat was turned over in the water, its hull sticking up like the shell of a turtle. Dave grabbed the rudder and held onto it. "Help!" he cried. "Help me!"

Dave's dad, who was fishing nearby, heard Dave's voice. He sped across the lake in his motorboat and hauled Dave to safety. Then they turned the sailboat over, tied a rope to it, and towed it to shore. "What happened, Dave?" Dad asked as they examined the shredded sail.

"I don't know," Dave replied. "Just before I started out, I saw a tiny hole in the sail up near the top. I was going to tell you about the hole when I got back, but I didn't think it would hurt anything. I guess the wind caught that hole and ripped the whole sail. I'm sorry, Dad." Dave tried to choke back his tears.

Dad put his arm around Dave's shoulders and hugged him. "It's not your fault," said Dad. "Accidents happen. It's no sin, Dave." Dad was thoughtful for a moment, then he added, "You know, it occurs to me that this accident does have something in common with sin, though. Sin is like a hole in a sail. If it's allowed to remain in a person's life, it will grow bigger. That person's life may eventually be all torn up. Many people have shipwrecked their faith by allowing seemingly small sins to remain in their lives."

"Well, I'm sure glad you rescued me—I was so scared out there," replied Dave. "I'll remember that holes in a sail need to be fixed right away—and that sin does, too!" *A.L.*

HOW ABOUT YOU?

Is there a sin in your life that you think no one knows about? Don't allow it to grow or become a habit; confess it now. Tell Jesus about it and ask him to forgive you. He'll help you overcome it.

MEMORIZE:

"What happiness for those whose guilt has been forgiven! What joys when sins are covered over!" *Psalm 32:1, TLB*

 **Don't Ignore Sin**

Catch Me, Daddy! (Read Hebrews 11:1-6)

25

JUNE

Little Kelsey climbed from the pool. Then she eagerly walked along the edge to the side where her father was standing in waist-deep water. "Catch me again, Daddy!" she called. She leaped toward her father almost before he could get his arms up to catch her.

"Wheee!" called Daddy, as he pulled her around in the water and then took her to the shallow end, where she could touch bottom. Soon Kelsey was back up the steps and heading toward her jumping spot.

"Kelsey sure does trust Dad to catch her," observed her older sister, Linda. "And I can't believe how many times Dad keeps doing it. You'd think he'd get tired of it."

Mother smiled. "You know," she said, "I think this is a good picture of our faith in God. It makes your father happy that Kelsey trusts him enough to jump into his arms again and again. And because he caught her the first few times, she learned to trust him more and more—she jumped almost before he was ready the last time."

Linda was perplexed. "How is that like us and God?" she wanted to know.

"Well, I think God is pleased, too, when his children trust him," explained Mother. "And the more we trust him, the easier it is to trust him."

Linda nodded. "I think I'm starting to find that out for myself," she said.

"Good," said Mother. "The more we use our faith, the more it grows. When Kelsey jumps into the pool, she doesn't think, *Maybe Dad will catch me*. She knows he will. That's the kind of faith that pleases God." *L.W.*

HOW ABOUT YOU?

Do you have enough faith to trust God to help you with your problems? Trust him to help you walk calmly past that yard where a dog barks fiercely. Trust him to care for you in the middle of a thunderstorm. Trust God to take care of each problem you have. Then watch your faith grow.

MEMORIZE:

"Without faith it is impossible to please Him [God]."

Hebrews 11:6, NKJV

 **Faith Pleases God**

Press On (Read Philippians 3:12-14)

Halfway though her piano piece, Carla couldn't remember the notes. She ran off the stage in tears. Her first piano recital, and this had happened!

Backstage, her teacher said, "Don't be too discouraged. Developing a talent takes a lot of time." And just as she expected, Carla's family praised her for doing her best. But Carla never wanted to touch a piano again.

26
JUNE

The next day, Carla discovered that her bike had a flat. She asked her mother to help fix it. Mom agreed, and she gathered the tools as Carla fetched her bike. "Remember when you were learning to ride?" Mom asked.

Carla nodded. "I fell down a lot," she said with a giggle.

Mom smiled. "Yes, you did," she agreed. "I remember that once you hurt your knee and you said you would never get back on the bike again." Carla remembered, too. She had climbed back on the bike, though, that same afternoon.

"Carla," said Mom, "I know you were discouraged by what happened at your piano recital, but in some ways, learning to play the piano is a lot like learning to ride a bike. They both take practice." Carla said nothing, so Mom continued. "I was just thinking of how the apostle Paul suffered as he traveled around spreading the gospel of Jesus Christ. Maybe there were times when he felt like giving up. But he didn't. He said, 'Forgetting those things which are behind and reaching forward to those things which are ahead, I press toward the goal for the prize of the upward call of God' [Philippians 3:13-14, NKJV]." Mom smiled at Carla. "I think the Lord is pleased when we work hard at developing our talents—especially when we go on to use them for him," she added.

As Carla thought about it, she really knew Mom was right. And she wasn't surprised when, after tightening the last screw, Mom said, "Come in and practice your lesson before you play any more this afternoon."

Carla sighed. She could practice cheerfully and enjoy it, or practice against her will. Quickly, she made up her mind.

"OK," she said quietly. "I will." *D.R.K.*

HOW ABOUT YOU?

Does the task you are working on seem too hard? Are you thinking of giving up? Ask God for strength and keep working. Do it cheerfully. He will help you succeed.

MEMORIZE:

"I can do all things through Christ who strengthens me."

Philippians 4:13, NKJV

 ***Keep Trying***

A Bit of Beauty (Read Isaiah 43:1-5a)

27

JUNE

As Nicole stood near the Visitor Center on Trail Ridge Road, she could see patches of snow on the mountainsides. The few trees in the alpine area just below the timberline had been dwarfed and twisted by the icy winds of winter. But summer had come, and miniature white and yellow flowers were waving their bright heads as if dancing to music. The tundra was in bloom. "Look, Nicole," said Dad. He was kneeling by the flowers, cupping one of the fragile white blossoms gently in his large, rough hand. "See how very tiny it is! But isn't it beautiful? There must be a million of them!"

"That one has a torn petal, though," noticed Nicole.

"I know," Dad answered, "yet here it is, adding its own little bit to the beauty of this place. Though tiny and imperfect, it has a purpose for being here, just like all the other things in God's world!"

Though Nicole wondered what her father was getting at, she didn't ask. But as they drove back down the mountain a little later, Dad said, "That little flower reminded me of you, Nicole. You've lived through some cold and blustery times in your life."

Nicole knew what he meant. She had been sick many of her early childhood years, and as a result she had to wear hearing aids. She was also a grade behind in school. "I know you feel very small and insignificant," continued Dad, "but I want you to remember that your heavenly Father doesn't reject you because of your disabilities. You have a purpose for being just where you are and just as you are."

Nicole thought about the little flower adding its small bit of beauty, and she decided that she too would add whatever bit of beauty she could in the place where God had put her. *T.V.*

HOW ABOUT YOU?

Do you compare yourself with others and feel you don't measure up? Do you have some disability or scar that makes you feel self-conscious? Do you think God must love the prettier and more talented kids more than you? Remember—God doesn't make junk! He sees you as precious and valuable.

MEMORIZE:

"I have called you by your name; you are Mine. . . . Since you were precious in My sight, you have been honored."

Isaiah 43:1, 4, NKJV

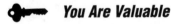 *You Are Valuable*

A Very Special Day (Read 1 Corinthians 12:18-27)

Carmen and Amanda were planning their last day together at their grandmother's house. "Can we do something extra-special today, Grandma?" asked Carmen.

"Yeah! Let's make this the best day ever," agreed Amanda, "even better than the zoo."

"Well, I do have an idea for today," replied Grandma, "but you'll never guess what it is."

28

JUNE

"Tell us! Tell us!" the girls shouted.

"All week we've been doing fun things for ourselves," said Grandma, "so today let's do something for the Lord by doing something for someone else." She paused. "Do you remember Uncle Bob, the playground supervisor at the park? Well, he's a shut-in now, so let's take a nice lunch over to his house and see if we can help him in some way."

Carmen and Amanda tried to be polite. This was not the kind of day they had in mind. But Grandma was already packing a box of goodies, and before they knew it, they were turning into Uncle Bob's driveway.

Their hearts sank as they walked in and saw their old friend in a wheelchair. But as they began to talk with him, they saw a familiar twinkle in his eye and his same warm smile. "I'm so pleased you came," he said, his eyes shining with tears of joy. "Would you like to see how I keep busy now that I can't walk?"

Carmen and Amanda watched as Uncle Bob opened a box and took out the most beautiful little carved animals they had ever seen. Two by two, Uncle Bob lined them up—a pair of every animal, from elephants to tiny birds. "Animals for Noah's ark!" exclaimed Carmen.

Uncle Bob nodded. "You can each choose a zebra and a tiger to take home," he said, "and I'll carve another one to replace it."

The girls gave him a hug and picked a zebra and a tiger to take back to their home. The animals would remind them that doing something to please others could also bring a very special joy to themselves. They agreed that this was indeed the very best day of all. *L.P.*

HOW ABOUT YOU?

Do you try to help others be happy? Could you visit a shut-in or lonely person? Could you take someone a flower, read him a psalm, or share a snack? God is pleased when you take time and make the effort to be helpful to others.

MEMORIZE:

"[Christians] should no longer live for themselves but for him who died for them and was raised again." *2 Corinthians 5:15, NIV*

 **Help Others**

Building Bridges (Read Luke 10:29-37)

29

JUNE

Frank and his friend Marc looked at the creek that ran through the field near their homes. They were trying to figure out how to build a bridge over it. "I bet my dad has a board we could use," said Marc.

The two boys ran to the shed in Marc's back yard and found a wide board. They carried it to the creek, lifted it high, and gave it a heave, hoping it would land with both ends on dry ground. *Splash!* One end missed.

"I don't think this board will work," said Frank. "Look how it sags in the middle." He looked at his watch and said, "Mom expects me home soon. Let's work on this some more tomorrow. I'll ask my parents for suggestions on bridge building." The boys set the board against the outside of the shed to dry, and Frank headed home.

Mother greeted Frank at the door. "I'm glad you're home a little early," she said. "We're having the Habibs for dinner tonight."

"Not them!" groaned Frank. He didn't like these new neighbors. They didn't speak English very well, and the boy his age didn't act like the other boys. Frank still couldn't pronounce his name. "Maybe I can eat at Marc's," he said. "We're building a bridge."

"You're eating here," Mother said firmly, disappointed with her son's attitude. "It will be good for you to learn more about a different culture."

"I don't think the Habibs believe in God," said Frank. He thought for sure he had one up on Mom with that comment.

"Perhaps not," said Mother, "but they'll have a better chance to get to know him if we share his love with them tonight."

"They're so weird, Mom," Frank complained.

"They aren't weird," said Mother. "They seem different to us, just like we're different to them." She looked at Frank thoughtfully. "I thought you were interested in building bridges," she added.

"I am." Frank nodded. "It's a real challenge."

"Then let's build one here tonight by using whatever means we can to reach out to other people," suggested Mother. "Now go wash up for dinner." *N.E.K.*

HOW ABOUT YOU?

When you see people who are different from you, do you stay away or do you "build a bridge" with Jesus' love? He loves all the people of the world. He wants to show that love through you.

MEMORIZE:

"Therefore receive one another, just as Christ also received us, to the glory of God." *Romans 15:7, NKJV*

 Reach Out with Jesus' Love

Firmly in Place (Read Ecclesiastes 11:9-10; 12:1, 13)

30
JUNE

"Mom, why is Dad frowning?" asked Daniel. "I think the patio looks great!"

Mother put her arm around Daniel's shoulder as they watched his father trying to put an edge on the new concrete patio he had poured. "The concrete set up faster than Dad had counted on," she answered.

"'Set up'? What does that mean?" asked Daniel.

"That means the concrete hardened," replied Mother. "Remember when Dad first poured it? He could tap it down and level it and smooth it. You have to work pretty fast to get it the way you want it because once it sets up, you can't work with it anymore."

Daniel nodded sympathetically. Then, turning, he grabbed his baseball and glove off the table. "Sean and I are practicing this morning," he said, "and his mom said she'd drive us to the game at noon."

"Have you brushed your teeth and done your Bible study?" Mother asked. "It's important to practice good habits."

Daniel grinned. "I know," he said with a nod, "so they harden in place like the concrete."

"Very good," agreed Mother with a laugh. Then she added, "Good or bad habits can become hardened into a person's life. That's why you need to practice the good ones while you're young— before your life 'sets up.'" *P.Y.*

HOW ABOUT YOU?

Do you take time every day to read God's word (2 Timothy 2:15) and pray (1 Thessalonians 5:17)? Do you practice gratitude by thanking God for food, family, and friends (1 Thessalonians 5:18)? Do you go to church each week (Hebrews 10:25)? These are habits you should form now.

MEMORIZE:

"Remember your Creator in the days of your youth."

Ecclesiastes 12:1, NIV

 Practice Good Habits

Blind Bats (Read Psalm 27:1-6)

1

JULY

Bonnie only half listened to the conversation at the dinner table, but then, something caught her attention—bats in the attic! She stopped eating. "Bats!" she exclaimed. What if they get in the house?"

Her brother Scott spoke up. "We learned in school that they can't see in the light and become very defenseless," he said. He grinned at his sister. "I know!" he added. "We can put a bright light in the attic, and they'll all leave. Of course, they might take refuge in Bonnie's nice dark room."

Bonnie turned to her father. "You'll get them out of here, won't you?" she asked, her voice trembling.

"Don't worry," said Dad. "We'll take care of them. But bats aren't as harmful as you may think."

"Nah," agreed Scott. Girls are just scaredy-cats."

Dad smiled. "Quit teasing your sister," he said. "After all, boys can be scaredy-cats, too. In fact, we all are sometimes scared of things that we could control simply by turning the right kind of light on them."

"Such as?" asked Scott.

"Such as being afraid of having kids tease us for going to church and Sunday school," said Dad. Scott remembered complaining about that problem the week before.

"Or being afraid of being laughed at for saying no when we're asked to do something wrong," added Mother.

Scott frowned. "You said we should turn the right kind of light on such problems," he reminded dad. "What do you mean by that?"

"I'm talking about the light of God's love and power," replied Dad. "Turn that on obstacles you face in your Christian walk, and they'll become as defenseless as the bats in the light."

"Sounds good," said Bonnie, "but how do we actually do that?"

"A good place to start is by knowing God's Word and then praying about the situation," suggested Mother.

"Yes," agreed Dad. "Really trust God to help you do what he wants you to do." *N.E.K.*

HOW ABOUT YOU?

Do you have Jesus, the Light of the world, within you? Then remember that and trust him. He will take care of you.

MEMORIZE:

"The Lord is my light and my salvation; whom shall I fear?"

Psalm 27:1, NKJV

 Walk in God's Light

No More Dust (Read Genesis 1:31–2:3)

"I wish there were was no such thing as dust!" grumbled Pam as she dusted the furniture.

"Well, you'll soon be finished, and then you may go for a swim at Marcie's," said Mother.

Soon Pam was on her way, eager to jump into the refreshing water. When she got there she saw Marcie and Amanda, another neighbor, already splashing around. *Oh, no*, thought Pam. *Why did Marcie invite her?*

2
JULY

"Watch this," Amanda called out as Pam stepped slowly into the pool. Amanda dove down into the water and did a handstand. "Watch this," Amanda said again. She plunged under, this time spinning into a somersault. Water splashed into Pam's eyes. "I can do more," Amanda boasted, back on her feet and smoothing the hair from her face.

Pam swam and played with the other girls for a little while, but Amanda splashed and showed off too much for her. So Pam went home. "I wish there were no such thing as Amanda," she told her mother after explaining why she was back home so soon.

"First it was dust, now it's Amanda," said Mother, shaking her head. "They appear to be your two worst enemies today."

"I'd be a lot happier without them," Pam agreed.

"Don't be so sure," Mother warned. "Remember the beautiful sunset we watched last night? If the dust in the air wasn't reflecting the sun's rays, we wouldn't have seen those beautiful colors." Pam looked surprised. "It's hard to believe a nuisance like dust could perform such a special purpose," Mother added.

"I know you're going to say something about Amanda's purpose, too," guessed Pam, not really wanting to hear it.

Mother nodded. "For one thing, she helps teach a swimming class for disabled children," she said. "Amanda has good points, and you need to look for those. You see, God didn't intend for the people and things he created to get on our nerves. We need to look past the things we don't like and find the more positive, special reasons God created them. Then we can be thankful, rather than angry, that they exist." *N.E.K.*

HOW ABOUT YOU?

Do you look for the good in both people and things? Learn to be thankful for all that God has created.

MEMORIZE:

"To every thing there is a season, a time for every purpose under heaven."

Ecclesiastes 3:1, NKJV

⚷ *Look for Good in All Things*

The Beautiful Apple (Read Psalm 139:1-5, 13-24)

3
JULY

Aaron woke up early, dressed quickly, and hurried down to eat breakfast. This was the day he'd been looking forward to—his family was planning a trip to the fair.

When they finally arrived there, Aaron went to look at all the horses, cows, and other show animals. He rode the Scrambler, and he threw darts at balloons and won a prize. As he and his family walked through the fairgrounds all afternoon, he searched for a place to buy the biggest and best caramel apple. Then when it was almost time to go home, he quickly ran to a booth at the far corner of the fair. "I came to buy a caramel apple," he told the lady. "May I pick out a big one?"

"Sure," she replied. "Help yourself."

Aaron carefully studied the apples on display. He found a huge one loaded with nuts and caramel, and he asked for a box to take the apple home in.

Later that evening, Aaron settled down to read a book and eat his prized apple. He took a big bite. "Oh, yuk!" he groaned as he looked at the apple. He ran to the kitchen for a paper towel.

"What's wrong, Aaron?" asked Dad.

"This apple was the biggest, most beautiful caramel apple in the whole fair, but when I bit into it, I found a worm hole," moaned Aaron. "It's soft and mushy inside, too." He looked sadly at the apple. "It was such a pretty one," he added, "but it's no good."

Dad nodded sympathetically. "It's the inside that counts, isn't it? That's what God says about people, too."

"People?" Aaron looked at Dad in surprise.

"That's right," said Dad. "We can look neat and clean, and we may even act nice, but God looks at our heart. He knows all our secret thoughts and feelings. It's important to keep ourselves clean on the inside." *L.P.*

HOW ABOUT YOU?

Have you carefully combed your hair, brushed your teeth, and put on clean clothes? That's good. But are your thoughts what they should be? Ask God to help you keep your heart pure and clean. When you sin, ask him to forgive you and make you beautiful and good inside. He will!

MEMORIZE:

"The Lord does not look at the things man looks at. Man looks at the outward appearance, but the Lord looks at the heart."

1 Samuel 16:7, NIV

 *God Sees Your Heart*

A Reason to Celebrate (Read John 8:31-36)

"Grandpa, look at that one!" exclaimed Danny. "It's the best one yet!" The fireworks display was spectacular. Reds, greens, yellows, blues, and blazing whites lit up the sky in all their thundering glory.

After the grand finale, Grandpa Wright and Danny began folding up their lawn chairs. "Do you know why we celebrate the Fourth of July?" Grandpa asked as they began the walk back to the car.

"Sure," replied Danny. "It's a special day that's set aside to celebrate our freedom and liberty."

Grandpa nodded. "We live in a country where we can choose our own occupation, travel where we want to, say what we think, vote for those we want to be elected, and meet for public worship. Not everyone can do that."

"I'm glad I live in America, Grandpa," declared Danny.

"I am too, Danny," agreed Grandpa, "but did you know that the greatest freedom anyone can ever enjoy is available to people in every country of the world?"

"It is?" asked Danny.

Grandpa nodded. "Yep," he said. "I'm talking about the freedom that Jesus Christ offers. When we ask him to forgive us and save us from sin, he does. The liberty and cleansing that his forgiveness brings is the most spectacular freedom anyone will ever experience."

"Then I think we should celebrate that, too," said Danny with a grin. "Can we have fireworks again tomorrow?"

Grandpa laughed. "That might not be a bad idea," he said. "Certainly we should joyfully declare to the world that we have this great freedom—and let others know they can enjoy it, too. Let's think about it, Danny. Let's decide what would be the best way for us to celebrate our freedom in Christ. Then let's do it!" *L.E.K.*

4
JULY

HOW ABOUT YOU?

Do you know Jesus as your Savior? Then you are truly free—free from the penalty of sin. Do you joyfully let others know that you belong to Jesus and that they can find peace and freedom in him, too? Be as noisy about your freedom in Christ as you are about other freedoms you enjoy. You have a reason to celebrate!

MEMORIZE:

"So if the Son sets you free, you will indeed be free."

John 8:36, TLB

Celebrate Freedom in Christ

Proper Care (Read Psalm 24:1-5)

5

"I hope we don't have to have the Cookes over here again for a few years," grumbled Katie. "Those little kids messed up my whole room this afternoon." She began putting things in order again.

"Just remember you used to be little yourself," Mom reminded her. "I'll give you a hand so we can get going to pick up Dad at the airport." Soon the job was finished.

After meeting Dad, they had some soda pop while they waited for his luggage. Katie finished her pop just as they left the building. When they reached the car, she looked around the parking lot and then casually dropped the can on a clump of grass near a light post. She also unwrapped a stick of gum and left the wrapper beside the pop can.

"You can't leave your trash out here on the ground!" Dad exclaimed.

Katie shrugged. "Everybody does it," she said.

"Pick that up right now and put it in the car," ordered Dad. "You know we return the cans for recycling, and you can put the paper in the waste basket at home." Katie frowned, but she did as she was told and climbed into the car without a word.

"The Cookes visited this afternoon," Mom told Dad as he started the engine.

"And their kids terrorized my room," Katie blurted out.

"Toddlers really can trash something in a hurry," agreed Mom. "They don't take proper care of others' property."

"Yes, but it's even worse when older kids or adults do that kind of thing. They ought to know better," said Dad, looking back at Katie through his rearview mirror. "God created this beautiful earth, but we sometimes don't take proper care of his property. We mess it up by polluting." Katie got the point. *N.E.K.*

HOW ABOUT YOU?

Do you take time to find a wastebasket—even for small things like candy wrappers? Respect God's earth the way you would want others to respect your property.

MEMORIZE:

"The earth belongs to God! Everything in all the world is his!" *Psalm 24:1, TLB*

 Care for God's Earth

It Takes Two (Read Luke 6:27-35)

"Keith Gordon really makes me mad!" said Joe as he sat in the living room one evening. "He's always picking on me. No matter what I say or do, he won't leave me alone."

Just then, four-year-old Ted came into the room. "Play catch with me, Joey," he begged.

"Not now," replied Joe. He continued telling his parents about his problem. "No matter how mad I get at Keith, he just won't quit bugging me."

"Catch this, Joey!" interrupted Ted as he threw a soft foam ball into Joe's lap.

Joe looked at Ted angrily. "I told you, I don't want to play," he said, and he tossed the ball back. Ted threw it right back again. Now Joe was really annoyed. *Cut it out!* he shouted, throwing the ball to the other side of the room. With a happy grin, Ted ran to retrieve it from under a table. He tossed it to Joe.

"Make him stop!" whined Joe in disgust. "He's driving me crazy!" He kicked the ball in Ted's direction.

"That's obvious," said Mother dryly. "But it's your fault, too."

"My fault?" objected Joe. "He keeps throwing the ball!"

"But you keep throwing it back," said Dad. "It takes two to keep it going."

"Next time he throws it," Mother said, "put the ball down on the floor and ignore him."

Joe looked doubtful, but he tried it. Sure enough, Ted soon went off to do something else.

"Now, about your problem with Keith," said Dad. "I think you're part of the problem there, too. It sounds like Keith enjoys upsetting you, so as long as you keep responding to his remarks in anger, he's not going to quit."

"Oh! I get it," said Joe. "I should just ignore him next time."

"You could even respond to his insult with a sincere compliment," suggested Mother. "That would certainly be a better testimony for the Lord."

"And as we used to say, that should really take the wind out of his sails," added Dad. Joe grinned and nodded. *S.K.*

HOW ABOUT YOU?

Do you remember that it takes two to make a quarrel? When someone irritates you, why not try saying something nice instead of something nasty? You'll be surprised at the difference it makes, and you'll be pleasing the Lord by following his example.

MEMORIZE:

"A soft answer turns away wrath, but a harsh word stirs up anger." *Proverbs 15:1, NKJV*

 Don't Return Insults

The Prison Breakout (Read Isaiah 61:1-2; John 8:31-36)

7

JULY

Mike joined his father in his workshop one afternoon. "I've got a riddle for you, Dad," he said. "Suppose you were in a prison with solid-rock walls—no doors or windows. How could you break out?"

Dad thought a moment. "You didn't mention a roof. Maybe there is none. I could escape by climbing out."

Mike shook his head. "No," he said. "The roof is solid rock, too. The room is like a box with no openings."

Dad picked up his sledgehammer and swung it playfully. "OK," he said, "since you're supposing a prison, I'll suppose I have a sledgehammer. I'll knock a hole in the wall and escape."

"Not in my prison!" declared Mike. "The walls are too thick. Give up?"

"I guess so," said Dad. "There seems to be no way out."

Mike grinned mischievously. "Oh, yes there is!" he exclaimed. "You could break out with the measles!"

Dad chuckled. Then looking serious, he said, "Did you know that many people are in a sort of 'prison' they can't break out of? I'm afraid you may be, too, Mike."

Mike's mouth flew open. "Me? In a prison? You're joking! I'm here in your workshop. I can walk out any time I want."

"I'm talking about a spiritual prison," said Dad. "It's the prison of sin. We need to be rescued from it—we can't escape from it by ourselves, no matter what we do. Even 'breaking out with the measles' won't help," he added with a smile.

Mike looked thoughtful as he ran his fingers over Dad's sledgehammer. "I have to let Jesus rescue me, don't I?" he asked. "I've been thinking a lot about that since last Sunday, when the pastor talked about how good works can't save a person. I know that Jesus died and rose again for me." He looked at his father. "I'd like to ask Jesus to break me out of the prison of sin right now," he added softly.

Dad slipped his arm around Mike's shoulders, and together they dropped to their knees to talk to the Lord. *M.R.P.*

HOW ABOUT YOU?

What are you counting on for salvation? Your good works? Your baptism? Your church membership? None of these can break us out of our prison of sin. We would have no escape if Jesus hadn't come to die on the cross. He'll break us out of our prison the moment we trust him to do it.

MEMORIZE:

"Bring my soul out of prison, that I may praise Your name."

Psalm 142:7, NKJV

 **Jesus Delivers from Sin**

In God's Care (Read Matthew 6:26-34)

The buildings seemed to whiz by as Morgan looked out the car window. Mother had just picked up Morgan and her little sister, Lisa, from the baby-sitter's on her way back from a job interview—one of many in recent days. Morgan wondered if Mother would get the job. More importantly, she wondered what they would do if she didn't.

"Mom, when is Daddy coming back?" Lisa asked this question almost daily.

"He isn't," Morgan snapped before Mother had a chance to answer. "Mother's told you a hundred times." Morgan wanted Dad to come back, too. She missed him, and she felt scared, but Lisa's question just reminded her that it wasn't going to happen. How would they ever manage with Dad gone?

8
JULY

Mother seemed to sense her thoughts. She smiled at Morgan. "Don't worry," she said. "The Lord will take care of us as he's promised." Morgan wanted to believe her mother, but how could God do it?

Suddenly the car began to slow down. Morgan couldn't hear the motor running any longer. Mother steered the car off the road just before it stopped completely. Mother turned the key, but the engine wouldn't start. "Well," she said, "look where we stopped—right at a service station." An attendant came up, and soon he was looking under the hood as Mother stood by watching.

As the children waited in the car, Lisa began crying. "I'm scared," she sobbed. "How will we get home? What if they can't fix the car? What will we do?"

"I don't know, but Mother will take care of everything," Morgan told Lisa. "She'll know what to do even though we don't. There's no need to worry." As Morgan tried to comfort Lisa, she realized that her mother had been giving her similar advice. Suddenly she knew that, even though none of them knew what to do about Dad's leaving, God did. He really would take care of them. There was no need to worry. "Everything will be all right," Morgan assured Lisa again. And now Morgan knew it was true. *K.R.A.*

HOW ABOUT YOU?

Is there a situation in your life that you worry about? Is there something about your future that scares you? Trust God for his care. He has promised to take care of you when you put him first in your life. Rest in that promise, knowing there is no need to worry.

MEMORIZE:

"**Don't worry about anything; instead, pray about everything; tell God your needs, and don't forget to thank him for his answers.**" *Philippians 4:6, TLB*

 **Don't Worry**

The Christian Bouquet (Read Romans 14:1-2)

9
JULY

The sounds of the lawn mower next door cut through the silence of the lazy Sunday afternoon as Andrea and her mother worked on a fresh flower arrangement. Andrea peered out the window and caught a glimpse of Cindy's bright red shirt between the hedges as she pushed the mower. "I sure am glad the Andersons moved in next door," observed Mother. "It's nice having Christians for neighbors, isn't it?"

Andrea nodded as she handed Mother a couple of red roses, being careful not to prick herself on the thorns.

"Yeah," she agreed, "but . . ." She hesitated. "Cindy mows the lawn almost every Sunday," she added. "How can she be much of a Christian if she doesn't even care about keeping the Lord's day holy?"

Mother smiled as she arranged the flowers in a bouquet. "Does Cindy love Jesus?" she asked.

"She says she does," began Andrea, "but—"

"Then how can you judge her?" asked Mother.

"But we always mow our lawn on Saturday so we don't have to work on Sunday," protested Andrea.

"Yes," said Mother, "your father and I both believe that's right for our family. But there may be things we do on Sunday that Cindy's family would never do." She held up the bouquet. "Look at these flowers—each one is different." She pointed to a yellow one. "This one doesn't have much scent, but I love its color. This one next to it isn't quite as brilliant, but it makes the whole bouquet smell good." Mother took out a rose. "Then there's the rose—my favorite. This one has thorns, but we don't throw it out and call it a thorn bush. It's still a beautiful flower."

Mother replaced the rose. "It's the same with Christians," she added. "We may do things a little differently, but we still accept one another as Christians."

Andrea smiled; she felt better. "Can I go play with Cindy?" she asked. "And may I take a rose for her?" Smiling, Mother nodded.

A.J.S.

HOW ABOUT YOU?

Are you able to accept Christians who do things a little differently from the way you do them? You may look at things in a different way, but you need to be careful not to judge others. Leave that to God.

MEMORIZE:

"Why do you judge your brother? . . . For we shall all stand before the judgment seat of Christ." *Romans 14:10, NKJV*

 ***Accept Other Christians***

TLC For Tippy (Read Hebrews 12:5-11)

"Hold still, Tippy," Kurt commanded. "I know you don't like this, but you have to be on a leash when we take a walk." The impatient little dog wriggled and squirmed, but at last Kurt said, "OK, fella, now we can go."

As they walked along, Tippy kept pulling on his leash, wanting to dash off after a butterfly or to investigate a rustling in the bushes. "You've got a lively dog there," called Mr. Bell from his yard.

"Yeah," agreed Kurt, walking over to Mr. Bell. "You know what?" he asked with a sigh. "We might have to move, because Dad's lost his job. And last night my bicycle was stolen. It seems like everything is going wrong for me. I'm so mixed up!" He paused, then added, "Mr. Bell, you're a Christian. Tell me . . . if God really cares for me, why has he let all these bad things happen?"

As Kurt spoke, Tippy tugged hard on his leash. Kurt picked him up and held him in his arms. "Tippy doesn't like that leash, does he?" observed Mr. Bell. "Why don't you just let him roam free?"

Kurt gave his puppy a squeeze. "If he ran free, he might get run over or attacked by a big dog or something."

"I suppose he doesn't like some other things you do, either—like giving him a bath or taking him to the vet for shots," suggested Mr. Bell. "Or punishing him when he's naughty."

Kurt managed a little smile. "Sometimes Tippy thinks I'm being mean to him, but I'm really just giving him TLC—tender, loving care."

"Kurt," said Mr. Bell, "God is giving you TLC, too. He loves you far more than you love Tippy, and he knows what's best for you. He allows trials in your life as a way to train you and to develop your Christian character. Learn from them, and trust the Lord to take care of you." Just then Tippy reached up and nuzzled Kurt's cheek. "See how much Tippy loves you, even though you discipline him?" Mr. Bell asked. "Shouldn't you give the same response to God?" *M.R.P.*

HOW ABOUT YOU?

Are you wondering why God allows some trial or problem in your life? God may be using that problem to get your attention or to discipline you. If you know of a sin you need to confess, do it. But otherwise, trust God to use your troubles to teach you and to make you the person he wants you to be.

MEMORIZE:

"Blessed is the man whom God corrects; so do not despise the discipline of the Almighty."

Job 5:17, NIV

 Learn from God's Discipline

Night Vision (Read Psalm 139:1-12)

11

Tim stretched and yawned, lazily watching the campfire. He was on a camping trip with his Sunday school class, and he was tired. His head started to nod, and his eyes grew heavy. But suddenly he sat up, wide awake at the eerie sound coming from the dark, forbidding woods nearby. "Whooo, hoo-hoo, whooo," came the cry. Everyone peered into the darkness, and Tim and a few other boys scooted a little closer in the bright, comforting fire.

"That's my friend the owl—probably ready to do a little hunting for his dinner," came the teacher's reassuring voice. "Let's see what you boys know about owls. What kind of beaks to they have?"

"Hooked beaks!" Tim blurted quickly.

"Right," said Mr. Atkins. "What are their claws like?"

Another boy volunteered the answer. "They're short."

"Hey, you're pretty good," approved Mr. Atkins. "Who can tell me something about their eyes?"

"They can see in the dark," offered one of the boys.

Mr. Atkins nodded. "They have night vision," he said, "so they sleep during the day and hunt at night. Owls have very sensitive eyes, and when they fly overhead they can see even very small animals on the ground below."

From the woods came another *Whooo, hoo-hoo, whooo,* but this time no one seemed afraid.

Mr. Atkins stretched his legs. "God gave owls wonderful vision," he said, "but as well as owls can see, it's nothing compared to the way God can see. The Bible says 'the eyes of the Lord are in every place.' Now that's great eyesight—to be able to see everywhere at one time, isn't it?"

"Yeah, but it's kinda scary, too," someone suggested.

Mr. Atkins smiled. "Well, it could be," he agreed, "because God sees whenever you do something wrong. But it's important to remember that God also sees you when you do what's right. He also looks right into your heart and sees the love you have for him."

C.Y.

HOW ABOUT YOU?

Are you glad that God can see over the whole world all at one time—even into the heart of each person? Every time you have a feeling of love for him or have a desire to do something to please him, he knows about it. What will he see today?

MEMORIZE:

"The eyes of the Lord are in every place, keeping watch on the evil and the good."

Proverbs 15:3, NKJV

 **God Sees You**

An Unkind Prank (Read Proverbs 23:22-26)

12
JULY

Gregory was hiding in the bushes with his friends Tom and Alan, but he knew he shouldn't be there. "Let's get out of here before someone sees us," he urged.

"We're just gonna have some fun with old Mrs. Wilson," said Tom. "You chicken?"

"I'm not chicken," protested Gregory, "but it's just not right to mistreat old folks."

"Oh, c'mon," coaxed Alan as he and Tom moved toward the porch steps. "What's it gonna hurt if we just ring the bell and then hide in these bushes and listen to Mrs. Wilson complain? She'll never know who did it. Even if she sees us, she can't see well enough to tell who we are." He tiptoed up to the door, with Tom close behind.

As Gregory hesitated, Alan punched the bell. Alan and Tom headed for the bushes, but Gregory bent down and picked up a newspaper from the sidewalk. Then he planted himself at the top of the steps and waited for Mrs. Wilson to open the door.

A moment later, the door swung open, and there stood Mrs. Wilson, squinting out of the dark hallway.

"Excuse me, Mrs. Wilson," said Gregory, holding out the paper. "You didn't pick up your newspaper this morning, so I brought it to you."

"Why, thank you," said Mrs. Wilson. "Aren't you kind! Do I know you?"

"I'm Gregory Smith, and this is Tom Newton and Alan Welch." Gregory motioned to his friends, and they stepped hesitantly forward. "We all live on this street."

"Why yes, I know all of your parents," replied Mrs. Wilson. "I'm going to have to tell them what nice boys they have. Some children aren't nice to old women anymore, you know."

"Yes ma'am," said Gregory. "We know." As he turned to go, he flashed a triumphant grin at his friends. *S.L.S.*

HOW ABOUT YOU?

Do you treat elderly people with the respect God wants them to have? God loves old people just as much as he loves younger ones, and he is very specific about the way he wants us to treat the elderly. He wants you to show them the same kindness you will expect when you are old.

MEMORIZE:

"Rise in the presence of the aged, show respect for the elderly and revere your God. I am the Lord." *Leviticus 19:32, NIV*

 Respect Your Elders

Baseball (Read Psalm 119:1-6)

13
JULY

"Well, that was a great game," declared Dad as he drove Patrick and Howard home after their baseball game. "It reminded me of a Christian's walk with Jesus. Can you figure out why?"

The boys looked at each other. "Maybe it's because we were on the winning team?" suggested Patrick.

Dad smiled. "That's a good thought," he said. "With Jesus you're always on the winning team. But I had some specific plays in mind. Let's start with you, Patrick. Remember the home run you hit?"

"Sure, Dad. Who could forget a hit like that?" asked Patrick with a grin.

"It was quite a blow all right," said Dad. "But when you reached third base, you did something that could have cost you a run. Do you know what it was?"

"No." Patrick shook his head.

"The third base coach motioned for you to keep going, but you slowed way down and looked around for the ball," explained Dad. "You didn't trust your coach. You wanted to see for yourself and then decide whether you should run home or stay on third."

"Oh, yeah. I guess I did," said Patrick slowly.

"Sometimes we do that with Jesus," continued Dad. "We don't trust him enough to immediately act on his directions. Sometimes we want to think it over and decide if it looks like the best thing for us to do or not. Unfortunately, by the time we look around and make the decision, we may miss the Lord's timing. The Lord wants us to be obedient to him as soon as we know what it is he wants us to do. When you listen to your coach, you'll do better in baseball—and in the game of life." *C.G.*

HOW ABOUT YOU?

Are there times when you know the Lord wants you to do a certain thing, but you hesitate? Perhaps you know he wants you to speak to someone about him, to be kind to a new student, or to help someone with some job. Ask the Lord to help you obey immediately, no matter what he asks you to do.

MEMORIZE:

"My sheep listen to my voice; I know them, and they follow me." *John 10:27, NIV*

 **Obey God Immediately**

Baseball (continued from yesterday) (Read Acts 4:13-20)

Howard and Patrick listened quietly as Dad talked about some things that happened in their baseball game that reminded him of the Christian's walk with Jesus. "Now, Howard, let's talk about something I saw you do at the game," Dad was saying. Patrick was relieved to have the attention turned off himself and onto his brother. "Sometimes when your coach was talking to you, you were listening to your friends instead of listening to him," continued Dad.

14
JULY

Howard looked surprised. "I was?" he asked. "When?"

"I noticed it several times between innings," replied Dad. "The boys were joking around and being silly, and you were distracted. Now it's not necessarily bad to have fun with your friends, but maybe you missed something important by not paying attention to your coach."

"Well . . . maybe," said Howard reluctantly, "but I don't get it, Dad. How is that like being a Christian?"

"I think the Lord is talking to us a lot more than we're listening to him, too," explained Dad. "Many times we're just too busy or too distracted to listen. Other times the voices of the 'world'—our friends, our family, or just society in general—are what we listen to rather than to Jesus. Just as you need to learn to listen to your coach, Christians need to learn to hear what God says and not be distracted by other voices." *C.G.*

HOW ABOUT YOU?

Is it easier to listen to the "world" than to the Lord? He speaks to you through his Word, through pastors and teachers, and even through your own conscience. Be alert to what he is saying. When it's different from what your friends or classmates are saying, be ready to say no to them and yes to the Lord.

MEMORIZE:

"We must obey God rather than men!" *Acts 5:29, NIV*

 Say No to the World

The Sleeping Flamingo (Read James 5:13-18)

15

JULY

"Ay-vee-air-ee," read Paul, looking at the name above the door of one of the buildings at the zoo. "What does that mean?" He was visiting the zoo with Uncle Mike.

"That's a building with all kinds of birds," his uncle answered. "Lets go see it." As they opened the door they heard a lot of chirping and squawking. Walking through the building, they saw many different kinds of birds.

"Look over there," Uncle Mike said, pointing to a flamingo standing on one leg with his head on his back. "That one's asleep."

"What a funny way to sleep," said Paul. "How can that skinny leg hold up that big bird?"

"God made it that way," answered Uncle Mike. "Isn't it amazing?" Paul nodded in agreement.

After leaving the aviary, Uncle Mike bought them each a snack, and they sat on a bench to eat. As they munched on their chips, Paul was very quiet. "Thinking about your parents again?" asked Uncle Mike finally.

"Yeah," Paul answered. "I just know they're going to get a divorce."

"Now, you don't know for sure, Paul," Uncle Mike said comfortingly. "They had you come stay with me this weekend so that they could go to that marriage seminar. I think they'll try to work things out."

"Yeah, I know," Paul said. "I just wish I could do something to help."

"You can pray," his uncle answered.

"Oh, I do that," said Paul. "All the time! But that's such a little thing."

"That's what you said about that flamingo's leg," Uncle Mike reminded him, "but that little leg held that bird up, didn't it? And your 'little' prayers can do great things too. God made it that way."

S.N.

HOW ABOUT YOU?

Do you have problems you can do nothing about? Nothing, that is, except pray? You need to remember that God made prayer very powerful. It's the best thing you can do for your problems.

MEMORIZE:

"The earnest prayer of a righteous man has great power and wonderful results." *James 5:16, TLB*

 Pray about Your Problems

Sandspurs (Read Romans 13:12-14)

"Guess what?" said Mike one evening. "Pete Blackborn invited a bunch of us to spend the weekend at his ranch. There'll be horseback riding and a barbecue and everything. Please, may I go?"

"Tell us more," Dad said. "Are these boys Christians? Will you be going to church Sunday morning?"

16
JULY

Mike shuffled his feet uneasily. "I don't know, but I'd get back in time for church Sunday night." However, after more discussion, Mike admitted that after the barbecue, the boys planned to go into town with Pete's dad. While he took care of some business, they were going to play video games at a place where there would be a lot of rough kids hanging out. "But I won't do anything I shouldn't," pleaded Mike.

"Don't be too sure about that," Mom told him. "You'd be putting yourself in a position where there could be strong peer pressure. It might be harder than you think to resist doing something wrong."

"But, Mom," protested Mike, "there are temptations everywhere I go. I can't help that."

"You're right, Mike," replied Mom, "but you don't have to hang around places where temptation might be especially hard to resist. When I was a girl . . ."

Mike sighed. "Here goes one of your stories," he said.

"But it fits the occasion," Mom insisted. "When I was young, a barefoot girl walked to our house across a field where there were many sandspurs. My mother asked, 'Clara, how did you keep from getting those sandspurs on your feet?' 'Oh,' said Clara, 'I gits where they don't be.' That's the way a Christian should walk in this world, Mike. The temptations to sin are there, but as much as possible you should stay where they are not."

"I tell you what, Mike," Dad said. "You may go with the boys, but I'll pick you up right after the barbecue Saturday evening. How's that?"

"OK, Dad!" agreed Mike. "I'll have a good time, but as for the temptations, well, I'll git where they don't be!" *M.R.P.*

HOW ABOUT YOU?

Is there strong peer pressure for you to do wrong? It's hard enough to resist evil in everyday life, but in some situations the temptation can be much stronger. Avoid such situations. Spend time with your Christian friends and join in wholesome, Christ-honoring activities.

MEMORIZE:

"Clothe yourselves with the Lord Jesus Christ, and do not think about how to gratify the desires of the sinful nature."

Romans 13:14, NIV

 Avoid Places of Temptation

Different Weather (Read Ecclesiastes 3:1-8, 11a)

17

JULY

Being a teenager is rough, Missi thought moodily as she gazed at the lashing rain. *You're treated like a kid, but expected to act like an adult!*

"It's raining! It's pouring," sang five-year-old Josie as she ran into the room. She slid to a stop beside Missi's chair. "I love rain. It makes puddles to wade in."

"Yeah," Missi snapped, "and it cancels picnics."

"Were you going on a picnic?" Josie asked.

Missi scowled. "No, I'm grounded."

Josie patted Missi's hand. "I hope it storms. Storms are exciting! The lights go out, and we use candles."

Missi shuddered. "I hate storms! You're a strange kid. You love storms and rain and snow and cold weather—and hot weather, too."

Mother laughed as she came into the room. "To Josie there is no such thing as bad weather," she agreed, "just different kinds."

Josie wrinkled her brow. "Do you know the seasons, Missi?" Josie counted on her fingers. "There's spring and fall and winter and . . . uhhh . . ."

"Summer," Missi filled in.

Josie threw her arms open wide. "And I love them all!"

Mother sat down beside Missi. "There are different seasons in life, too," she said. "There's childhood and adolescence. Then, before we know it, we are adults, parents, and even grandparents."

"And the teen years are the worst!" Missi exploded.

Mother shook her head. "No, honey," she said. "God has planned for every age to have its special blessings as well as its problems. It's true there are stormy times in teen years, but people of every age experience storms."

"Is it going to storm?" Josie asked. "I'll get the candles." She ran from the room, and Missi gave a half-smile.

Mother smiled, too. "Even storms have a purpose. For example, lightning puts nitrogen into the air to help plants grow," she said. "As we trust the Lord to teach us, he'll help us grow in all kinds of life's weather, too, Missi." *B.W.*

HOW ABOUT YOU?

Are you going through some stormy times? Remember, there are no bad days, just different ones. Make a list of things that are happening to you. Then thank God for everything. It'll help you grow. God will teach you something as you trust him through all the experiences he allows to come your way.

MEMORIZE:

"This is the day the Lord has made; we will rejoice and be glad in it." *Psalm 118:24, NKJV*

⚷ Thank God for Everything

Eric's Echo (Read Psalm 119:1-8)

Eric was enjoying a Saturday hike with his father. As they approached a tunnel that went under the road, Eric called out, "Hello in there!"

"Hello in there . . . hello in there," repeated an echo.

"I'm Eric," Eric hollered.

"I'm Eric . . . I'm Eric . . . I'm Eric," his voice echoed back.

18
JULY

Soon they were through the tunnel and heading across the next open field. "Hello there!" Eric yelled again. There was no answering echo. "Why was there an echo in the tunnel but not out here?" Eric asked.

"When sound waves hit the walls of the tunnel, they bounce back—or are reflected—in an echo," his father explained. "Out here in this open space, there aren't any obstacles like that, so the sound keeps going."

After a good hike, Eric and Dad headed home. "I hope Lisa and Ellen are gone somewhere when we get home," Eric told Dad. "All they ever do is giggle and scream."

"I recall that they have complaints about you, too. They claim you pick on them all the time," observed Dad. "I think you should all try harder to get along."

"C'mon, Dad," protested Eric, "you had sisters. You know what a pain they can be."

Dad smiled. "I don't think it's any easier for girls to get along with brothers," he said. "Besides, God says we're to love others and live at peace with them—sisters included."

"I've heard that enough," Eric said, "at home, in Sunday school, in Bible club. Love others and be kind."

"What do you do with those instructions after you hear them?" asked Dad. "Remember how everything you said in the tunnel was echoed, or repeated? Well, when you hear what God says about the way he wants you to live, it's important that your actions echo, or reflect, those words. Don't be like an open field where the message just goes off into space." He ruffled Eric's hair. "Apply those words to how you get along with your sisters," added Dad. *N.E.K.*

HOW ABOUT YOU?

Does your life reflect, or echo, the Scripture lessons you hear? Don't let those important words drift into space. Apply them in your everyday relationships with others.

MEMORIZE:

"You have given us your laws to obey." *Psalm 119:4, TLB*

 Reflect God's Commands

God's Helping Hands (Read 2 Corinthians 4:1-7)

19
JULY

"Why do we have to pick up Mr. Adams?" asked Bobby. "The nursing home isn't by our house."

"If we don't pick him up, he won't get to come to the church picnic," answered Dad as he drove. "Besides, it makes him happy to be with a family from time to time. This is a small job we can do for the Lord."

Bobby thought about that. "It seems like a funny way of helping God," he decided. He grinned as he added, "God could take Mr. Adams to the picnic on a flying carpet if he wanted to. God doesn't really need us, does he?"

Just then they drove up to the nursing home. Mr. Adams was standing outside, waiting—just as he did each Sunday when they picked him up for church. But today he had a small brown bag he waved in the air. "I remembered it was a picnic," he said. "I brought some lunch."

At the park, Bobby's family spread their lunch on a picnic table. They had brought fried chicken, potato salad, rolls, pickles, celery, carrots, a giant chocolate cake with cherries on top, lemonade, and a watermelon. Bobby saw Mr. Adams open his bag at the next table. He took out half of a bologna sandwich.

Bobby's mother walked over to Mr. Adams. "Please don't eat by yourself, Mr. Adams," she said. "Come on! Bring your lunch and put it with ours. There'll be plenty."

Mr. Adams grinned and came to Bobby's table. He carefully placed his sandwich next to the basket of golden rolls. They prayed and began to eat. To Bobby's surprise, his little sister, Susie, immediately reached for the bologna sandwich.

Bobby's father leaned toward his son. "Bobby," he whispered, "we 'help' God in the same way Mr. Adams is 'helping' us. God has all the power and all the resources, but he allows us to put in our effort, too. We bring almost nothing to God, yet he uses what we bring, and we receive great blessings from him." *C.R.*

HOW ABOUT YOU?

Do you feel the Lord doesn't need you to help him perform his will on earth? He is all-powerful, yet he has chosen to use your small efforts to bring about large blessings. Thank him for the privilege of serving him. Be a "helping hand" for him.

MEMORIZE:

"We have this treasure in jars of clay to show that this all-surpassing power is from God and not from us." *2 Corinthians 4:7, NIV*

 *You Can Serve God*

Adopted by God (Read Romans 8:14-17)

As Jennifer tried to fix her hair, she wondered what her cousin was like now. Melissa and her family had moved away nearly two years earlier, but now they were coming for dinner. Melissa, who was a year older than Jennifer, had never had much time for her younger cousin.

At dinner, the two girls got along quite well. Then Jennifer invited Melissa to her room. She found that two years apart hadn't made Melissa more friendly, but Jennifer went all out to be nice.

20
JULY

"For my birthday, Grandma gave me this doll," Jennifer said as she carefully took a porcelain doll from the shelf. "It was hers when she was a little girl."

Melissa gasped. "Grandma gave that to you?" she asked. "That should be mine! You don't even belong to this family—you're adopted!" With that, Melissa walked out of the room, leaving Jennifer to cry in private.

Later Jennifer told her mother about it. "I always thought it made me special to be adopted," she said between sobs.

"You are special," Mother assured her. "Melissa was just being unkind."

"Am I really part of the family?" Jennifer asked.

"Indeed you are," insisted Mother. "Adoption makes you just as much a part of the family as if you were born to us." Mother held Jennifer close. "You know, Jennifer," she continued, "adoption is the only way to get into the most important family of all."

"Which family is that?" asked Jennifer.

"The family of God," said Mother. "Listen." Mother picked up a Bible, turned to Romans 8:14-17 (see today's Scripture), and read the passage to Jennifer.

"What does 'joint heirs with Christ' mean?" asked Jennifer.

"When we accept Jesus as Savior, God adopts us as his children—we become just as much God's child as Jesus is," explained Mother. "Let's pray that Melissa will come to know Jesus, too," she added. "Then she'll see how wonderful it is to be adopted."

E.M.B.

HOW ABOUT YOU?

Have you been adopted by God? You can be. God is always looking for more children, and Jesus died on the cross to make it possible for you to join God's family. Accept him today.

MEMORIZE:

"You received the Spirit of adoption by whom we cry out, 'Abba, Father.'" *Romans 8:15, NKJV*

 Become God's Child

Two Different Directions

(Read Proverbs 15:24; Matthew 7:13-14)

21

JULY

The Moores had many more miles to go before reaching home. It had been a great vacation trip, but now they looked forward to hot baths and their own beds. "This is our last pit stop," Dad told the children, as he pulled into a service station.

When everyone was aboard again, Dad drove back onto the interstate. It was a cloudy day, but finally the sun broke through the clouds. Suddenly Mother exclaimed, "Look! The sun's in our faces. That's not right. Aren't we going west instead of east?"

Startled, Dad slowed down. "I must have turned the wrong way on the interstate!" he said. "I can't believe I did that! We'll turn around at the next exit." But they didn't come to an exit very quickly. Groans came from the children in the back seat as they went farther and farther in the wrong direction. Finally they were able to turn around.

"Well," said Dad as they once again headed toward home, "we might just as well learn a lesson from this. I'm reminded that the Bible talks about two roads people travel. One road leads to heaven, and the other to hell. Sadly, many people who are on the road to hell don't realize it. They think they're headed the right way, just as we rode along for many miles thinking we were headed in the right direction."

Mother nodded. "We have the responsibility of showing them what is really at the end of their road," she said, "and of showing them the real road to heaven."

"Then maybe they'll turn around, like we did," put in Matthew. "I'm glad we're going in the right direction now." *M.R.P.*

HOW ABOUT YOU?

Are you going in the right direction—spiritually, that is? That's the most important thing in life, because the wrong road leads to hell. Jesus died and rose again to become the only way to heaven. Won't you trust him today?

MEMORIZE:

"There is a way that seems right to a man, but in the end it leads to death." *Proverbs 14:12, NIV*

 Jesus Is the Way to Heaven

Fuzzy No More (Read Romans 8:5-11)

22
JULY

"Mom! Mom!" cried Joey one morning. "Something just awful has happened to Fuzzy! Come look quick!" Joey was clutching a glass jar. It had holes punched in the lid, and a long twig with some leaves was on the inside.

Mom gently took the jar from Joey and peered through the glass. "Oh, good," she said. "This is wonderful!"

"Wonderful?" wailed Joey. "How can you say that? Fuzzy's dead! Look at him! He's all closed up in that dead piece of skin. He's not moving or anything."

"It's OK, Joey," said Mom. "You're going to learn a lesson in nature. We can learn a lesson about Jesus through this, too. It's all about new life."

"What do you mean, Mom?" asked Joey. "Is Jesus going to give Fuzzy new life?"

"In a way he is, Joey," replied Mom. "This is all part of God's plan for caterpillars, and it's a picture of God's plan for us, too. I know you like Fuzzy as a caterpillar, but he can stay a caterpillar for only so long. When the time is right, caterpillars weave a cocoon around themselves. That's what you see around Fuzzy now. While Fuzzy is in the cocoon, he dies as a caterpillar, but in a few weeks, you'll get to see him as a new creature. He won't be a caterpillar anymore—he'll be something even better. He'll be a butterfly. We talked about that before, remember?"

"I forgot," said Joey. Then he added with a grin, "But we don't get to be butterflies some day."

Mom laughed. "No, Joey, not butterflies," she replied. "But like Fuzzy died to his old caterpillar nature, we also die to our old nature—that is, our sin nature—when we accept Jesus as Savior. Then we become alive in Christ, and that new life is much more beautiful and free than the old one."

"I can't wait till Fuzzy comes out all new and beautiful," said Joey. "Do you think I should give him a new name?"

"That might be a good idea, Joey," said Mother with a smile. "I don't think I've seen any fuzzy butterflies." *L.W.*

HOW ABOUT YOU?

Have you received new life in Christ? If not, why wait? The new life Jesus gives is better in every way than the old sinful life. Accept Jesus today.

MEMORIZE:

"Therefore, if anyone is in Christ, he is a new creation; the old has gone, the new has come!" *2 Corinthians 5:17, NIV*

 Jesus Brings New Life

Soap Bubbles (Read 1 Peter 5:5-11)

23
JULY

"I hope I'm good enough to play in an All-Star game some day," said Jerry as they drove away from the ball park.

"I'd rather sing 'The Star-Spangled Banner' before the game," declared his sister Christy.

"I'll bet baseball players have more fans than singers do," retorted Jerry. "Besides, if you're good enough, you get to be in the Baseball Hall of Fame." All the way home, the children debated the question of whether singers or athletes were more popular and famous.

"Why is it so important to be famous?" asked their father, turning into their driveway.

"So everybody will like you and talk about how good you are," replied Jerry.

"And so they'll know your name, and nobody will say 'Christy who?'" added his sister, jumping out of the car.

In the back yard, Mother was blowing soap bubbles for two-year-old Sherry. What fun the others had watching Sherry's puzzled expression whenever she got one in her hands, only to find it had totally disappeared.

"Those bubbles have a shimmering beauty that is very attractive as they bounce about just out of reach," said Dad. "Even if you manage to catch one and briefly hold it in the palm of your hand, the bubble soon bursts. Fame is like that. The adoration a popular figure receives looks good, but the few people who ever succeed in reaching stardom often find that their popularity lasts only a short time, and *poof!* It's gone, and someone else is the star."

Mother nodded. "You should try hard to become the very best person you can be, of course," she said, "but you should do it so that the Lord will receive glory from your life—not so that you get the applause of people."

"Living that kind of life may never give you recognition from people," added Dad, "but the Lord will give you honor and rewards in heaven that will never fade away." *M.R.P.*

HOW ABOUT YOU?

Do you want to be famous when you grow up? The praise of people seldom lasts long. As God's child, determine to bring glory and honor to him all your life. Then, at the judgment seat of Christ, you'll receive eternal rewards and be praised by God himself.

MEMORIZE:

"And whatever you do, do it heartily, as to the Lord and not to men, knowing that from the Lord you will receive the reward." *Colossians 3:23-24, NKJV*

 Honor God, Not Yourself

Redemption Policy (Read Galatians 3:10-13; 4:4-7)

Joey was sitting at the kitchen table, helping his mother sort coupons. "Mom, what does *redeem* mean?" he asked.

"Redeem?" repeated Mother. "Well, it means to buy back. Why?"

"Well, it says here that this cereal coupon will be redeemed in accordance with company policy," replied Joey.

24
JULY

"Oh," said Mom. "In that case it means that after we use the coupon to get the cereal, the company will redeem it—or buy it back—from the store. But it has to be by the rules, according to their redemption policy." She smiled at Joey. "The Bible talks about redemption, too," she added.

"You mean people in the Bible used coupons?" asked Joey with a grin.

Mother laughed. "No. No, they didn't have coupons back then," she said. "But when Jesus died on the cross, he paid the price for us to be redeemed. We've all strayed away from God, but Jesus' blood was shed to buy us back."

"So does God have a redemption policy like this cereal company does?" asked Joey, pointing to the coupon he held in his hand.

Mother nodded. "Actually, he does, Joey," she said. "It's a pretty simple policy, but a lot of people don't seem to want to follow it. God asks that we admit our sins and our need for him to redeem us. Of course, we must believe that he really did die to save us. We need to accept him as our Redeemer, or Savior."

Joey nodded. "And that's God's redemption policy?"

"That's right," said Mother, "and no one can make his own rules or set his own policy. No one can pay the price of redemption by doing good works. Only Christ's blood can pay for our sins." *L.W.*

HOW ABOUT YOU?

Have you taken advantage of God's redemption offer? You can be redeemed only according to God's redemption policy—only by receiving Jesus as your Savior. Accept him today.

MEMORIZE:

"In whom [Jesus] we have redemption through His blood, the forgiveness of sins."

Colossians 1:14, NKJV

 Receive Jesus and Be Redeemed

Transplanted for Strength

(Read Deuteronomy 31:6-8)

25
JULY

"I wish I was a plant," grumbled Billy as he helped his grandfather water the garden. "These plants are lucky. They get to stay here in the same place their whole lives."

"Not looking forward to moving, are you, Billy?" said Grandpa sympathetically. Billy's father had taken a new job in another state.

Billy poked his toe at a weed. "I'll have to make all new friends. Plus I'll have to get used to a new school." He sighed as he emptied the watering can.

"Let me show you something," said Grandpa. He led the way to some shelves beside the garage. "See these plants?" he said, pointing to some pots on the shelves.

Billy nodded. "They're all tomato plants," he observed. "But why are they all in different sized pots?"

"As they grow, I move them into larger containers," explained Grandpa. "A lot of people don't know that the tomato plant is one of the few—if not the only—plant that is improved by transplanting. I transplant them two or three times, and it makes them stronger. The roots are better, and the whole plant is more fruitful." Grandpa paused, then he added, "Maybe the Lord is transplanting you to make you stronger, too."

"I'm not a plant!" protested Billy.

Grandpa chucked. "No," he agreed, "but the Lord knows that we often grow stronger in different situations. They cause us to sink our 'roots' deeper in him, and then we can be more fruitful for him." Grandpa squeezed Billy's shoulder. "Don't walk away from transplanting," he encouraged. "Let God strengthen you through it." *D.E.M.*

HOW ABOUT YOU?

Do you allow tough situations to make you stronger? Do you sink your 'roots' deeper in the Lord? Or do you wilt? No matter where God has planted you, he'll make you strong if you'll let him. Why not thank God right now for the strength he has made available to you, and determine to do good things for him.

MEMORIZE:

"Be strong and take heart, all you who hope in the Lord."

Psalm 31:24, NIV

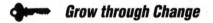 *Grow through Change*

Randy's Giant (Read 1 Samuel 17:45-50)

26
JULY

"I can't do this," Randy said, wadding up another sheet of paper. "I can't draw. And I don't know what to write, either."

"I've got my cards all finished," said his big sister, Ella. "They were fun to make. I can't wait to go with the youth group to take them to the nursing home."

Randy rested his head on the table. "You're older," he said, "so you can draw better, and you know what to say to old people. I'm just a kid." He stood up. "I'm not going!"

Randy went outdoors and sat on the steps. He watched his little sister playing with a neighbor girl. "You come to me with a sword, with a spear and a javelin, but I'm not scared," his little sister called to the other girl, who was standing tall on a stump.

"What are you playing?" Randy asked.

"We're playing David and Goliath," his little sister said. "I'm little David, and she's the big giant."

Randy wandered back into the house. The paper and art materials were still lying on the table. "Why would those old people listen when we tell them about God anyway?" he said to himself. "We're just kids." He sat down at the table. "Forget it," he added with a sigh.

His little sister danced in through the door singing a song about David. "Just think, David was just a kid, but he conquered that huge giant!" she said. "All he had was a sling and a stone."

"He had more than that," argued her playmate, chasing in behind her. "He had the power of God. David could do anything God wanted him to do. Anyone can when they ask God for help."

Randy's little sister looked at him. "What are you doing?" she asked, reaching for a crayon.

Randy shrugged. "Drawing a card for our youth project."

"You?" both girls giggled.

At first Randy felt angry. "Sure," he said, after a quick thought. He reached for a sheet of paper and folded it into a card. "And I can do this because I'm going to ask God to help me. He helped David, and he'll help me, too." *N.E.K.*

HOW ABOUT YOU?

Do you have trouble witnessing to others or serving the Lord in some way? The next time you feel like you can't do something for the Lord because you're "just a kid," remember David, and ask for the Lord's strength.

MEMORIZE:

"I can do all things through Christ who strengthens me."

Philippians 4:13, NKJV

 Kids Can Serve God

The Filter System (Read 1 Corinthians 6:9-11)

27

JULY

"Dad, what does 'die-alices' mean?" asked Tim. "I heard you and Mom talking about Uncle Jim, and you said he was going to have die-alices." Tim's voice trembled as he finished. "Does that mean Uncle Jim's going to die?"

Tim's father looked up from his newspaper to see his son's troubled face. "That's not what the word means," replied Dad, "but Uncle Jim does have a serious health problem. God says in his Word that our bodies are wonderfully made. Each organ, or part, has a job to do, and if it doesn't work right, doctors often have to repair it so that we can be healthy again."

"Does Uncle Jim have a part that doesn't work right?" Tim asked.

Dad nodded. "All of us have two kidneys that act as filters to remove poisons and impurities from the blood, but Uncle Jim's kidneys have quit working," explained Dad. "When that happens to someone, he may have to be connected to a dialysis machine. It takes over and does the filter work for the kidney. It's a complicated procedure, but necessary if the blood is going to be cleaned. We can't live very long without removing the poison in our bloodstream, so dialysis is like receiving a gift of life."

Tim sat quietly thinking while his father talked. Then he said, "When I accepted Jesus as my Savior, you told me he took all my sins away and made my heart clean on the inside. That sounds something like dialysis, doesn't it?"

"Why, yes, Son, that's right!" exclaimed Dad in surprise. "Sin makes our spiritual 'bloodstream' impure. But when we accept Jesus as Savior, he takes away all the sin and gives us the gift of eternal life. Dialysis is a wonderful thing, Tim, but salvation through Jesus Christ is even better, don't you think?"

Tim nodded. "Yeah, but I'm glad, too, that there's a machine that can help Uncle Jim," he said in a relieved voice. *P.K.*

HOW ABOUT YOU?

Are you thankful for all the wonderful things doctors and hospitals can do? That's good, but you can be even more thankful for what Jesus did for you on the cross. Have you been made clean by his blood? If not, accept his cleaning and forgiveness today.

MEMORIZE:

"If we confess our sins, he [God] is faithful and just and will forgive us our sins and purify us from all unrighteousness." *1 John 1:9, NIV*

 *Believe in Jesus*

The New Neighbor (Read Leviticus 19:33-34)

"I don't see why I have to invite Kim to my party just because he moved in next door," grumbled Chris. "He's got funny eyes and he talks like Tarzan."

"Kim is Oriental, and he's working hard to learn English," said Mom. "Instead of making fun of him, you should be helping him fit in with the other boys."

"I suppose," murmured Chris, "but he's so weird! He even has a girl's name."

28
JULY

"Chris is a girl's name, too, but it's also a boy's name, just like Kim," Mother reminded him. "I'm sure Kim won't seem so strange to you once you get to know him." With a sigh, Chris addressed an invitation to Kim.

The day of the party arrived and all the boys on the street came with birthday presents. Kim looked very happy as he came in and handed Chris a big package. "For birthday," Kim said haltingly. "You have much happy."

"Thank you," said Chris.

The boys played several games, and Kim often won. When they played a word game, Chris was glad to find himself on Kim's team. He thought for sure his team would win. But they lost!

After the game, Kim came up to Chris. "I sorry, Chris," he said sadly. "I not good yet at English words."

Chris was disappointed at losing, but he remembered how hard Kim had tried to win. "That's OK," said Chris. "You did your best. Would you like me to help you learn English?"

Kim nodded. "OK. I teach you Korean. You like?"

"I like!" said Chris. He decided that it was good having a friend like Kim, who always tried his best. And Kim didn't sound so funny to him anymore. *G.L.A.*

HOW ABOUT YOU?

Are you kind and friendly with everyone, or do you save your friendship for people who look like you? Instead of making fun of people who are different, try making friends with them. Remember, God made all people in his own image. He loves them and wants you to love them, too.

MEMORIZE:

"**How good and pleasant it is when brothers live together in unity!**" *Psalm 133:1, NIV*

 Love Your Neighbor

Paper Grandpa (Read Psalm 16:1-11)

29
JULY

Janie plopped down in the porch swing. It was a beautiful day with sunshine and singing birds—a day when she should have been happy, but she wasn't. Her friend, Karen, had just left for Disneyland.

"Hi, Janie," greeted Uncle Tim as he pushed his way through the screen door. "What are you doing? Counting butterflies?"

"No, just wishing," muttered Janie. "Karen's rich grandpa paid for a neat vacation in Florida for her whole family. He's going to meet them there, and I heard all the details at least a hundred times. Karen says she feels sorry for me because I don't have a grandpa with money and everything." Janie paused, then added, "Why can't I have a rich grandpa, too, instead of a paper one?"

"A paper one! What do you mean?" asked Uncle Tim.

"Well, Grandpa's picture has been sitting on the desk for as long as I can remember," explained Janie, "and I don't know anything about him. What good is a paper grandpa anyhow?"

"Now look here, Janie, your grandfather was a great Christian," said Uncle Tim. "True, he's been in heaven a long time, but he made sure his family knew what the Bible teaches about sin and salvation. He wanted to meet us all in heaven someday." Janie watched Uncle Tim's expression as she listened to his words. "Maybe someday you'll go to Disneyland," Uncle Tim continued, "but remember, Janie, that's only a temporary trip. The trip to heaven is a forever one. Your grandpa may not have been rich, but his greatest hope was that you and I, plus a lot of other people, would love and accept Jesus as Savior."

Janie gave a little smile. "When Karen comes back, maybe I should tell her about the trip Grandpa planned for us," she said.

"Good idea." Uncle Tim grinned. "Grandpa would be pleased. Maybe he's just a picture to you now, but when you meet him in heaven, he won't be a paper grandpa anymore." *P.K.*

HOW ABOUT YOU?

Does doing fun things like other people you know sometimes seem like the most important thing in the world? Try to remember that for Christians the "best is yet to come." Thank God for giving you people who help you learn about God and his Word. Thank God for letting you live where you can be a Christian.

MEMORIZE:

"The lines have fallen to me in pleasant places; yes, I have a good inheritance."

Psalm 16:6, NKJV

 *Thank God for Your Heritage*

Swimming Upstream (Read 2 Corinthians 6:14–7:1)

30
JULY

Brian watched as the big plane from Tokyo taxied up to the ramp. Moments later, he and his father were greeting Mr. Sato, who had come from Japan to visit them.

When they arrived home, Mr. Sato gave each family member a present. Their Japanese friend put Brian's present together in their backyard. When it was finished, three plastic fish billowed in the wind at the end of a long aluminum pole.

"In Japan we have a special day for boys," Mr. Sato told them. "We set up a pole like this, with carp waving from it. The carp is a determined fish. He swims upstream and overcomes obstacles. We try to teach our boys to be brave and strong like that." He paused, then added sadly, "They can't do it by themselves, though. And many of them do not know that they need to trust Jesus to make them strong enough to 'swim upstream.'"

Brian couldn't forget about the carp when he went to bed. He had accepted Jesus as his Savior, but was he trusting him for the strength to "swim upstream"? Just the day before, he and several other boys had tried smoking marijuana. Brian didn't really want to do it, but how could he refuse in front of all the guys? They probably would've called him a baby. So he told himself that smoking marijuana was a manly thing to do, but he really knew it was cowardly. He was afraid of being laughed at by the other boys, so he had done it even though he knew it was wrong.

"Dear Lord, forgive me," Brian prayed. He made up his mind that, with Jesus' help, he would never smoke again.

As Brian walked into the school building the next day, his friend Gary approached him. "Come over after school," Gary said. "I got some more grass from my brother."

Brian took a deep breath and shook his head. "No, I'm not going to do that anymore." There, he had said it! The boys might tease him, but Brian had never felt so grown up before—so much like a man. In his heart he thanked Jesus for helping him "swim upstream." *M.N.*

HOW ABOUT YOU?

Do you go along with what the other kids do because you're afraid to be different? Any dead fish can float downstream, but it takes a strong one to swim against the current. Jesus will help you to "swim upstream." Ask him to make you strong.

MEMORIZE:

"Be strong in the Lord and in the power of His might."

Ephesians 6:10, NKJV

 Say No to Wrong Things

The Auction (Read Joshua 24:14-18)

31
JULY

"Well, kids, what did you think of the auction?" asked Dad as he and Mother, with Erica and Andrew, left the auction hall and headed for home. Now that one of their elderly neighbors was with the Lord, her belongings had been sold at the weekly community auction.

"Awesome!" That was Andrew's favorite word for everything. "But now I wish I hadn't spent my money on that sausage stuffer. What will I do with it?"

"I wanted the music box," said Erica wistfully, "but after I bought some candy and a soda, my money was gone."

"One thing we learn at auctions," observed Dad, "is to think before we bid. That's a lesson we need to learn about life in general, to think before we act. We need to have the right priorities."

"Pri-or-what?" asked Erica.

"Prior means before," explained Dad, "so our priorities are the things we put first."

"Candy was a priority for you at the auction; a better one would have been the music box," said Mother. "The sausage stuffer was a priority for Andrew, but now he sees that wasn't a wise one, either."

"I didn't really want that sausage stuffer," Andrew said, "but when someone else started bidding, I got excited and didn't think."

Dad nodded. "As I said, priorities are important, especially in life. Each day we choose between good and bad, better and best, pleasing God and letting people persuade us. If we listen to others or make decisions too hastily, we sometimes make mistakes, and then we can spend years paying for them . . . not with money, but with unhappiness and guilt."

"Think about it carefully, kids," added Mother. "What do you put first in life?" *J.R.*

HOW ABOUT YOU?

Do you make speedy decisions or act without thinking? Check your priorities. Ask God to help you put the important things—the things that please him—first in your life. God promises to give wisdom if you ask.

MEMORIZE:

"Seek first the kingdom of God and His righteousness, and all these things shall be added to you." *Matthew 6:33, NKJV*

 Put First Things First

Old Unreliable (Read Proverbs 25:11-15, 19)

1

"Jenny," said Mother one Saturday morning, "isn't your youth group doing a community service project this afternoon?"

Jenny shrugged. "Yeah, but I don't want to go," she said. "It's too hot to mow lawns and hoe gardens today."

"I heard you tell Pastor Jim you'd be there," said Mother with a frown. "I think you should go."

"Well, I go to lots of things," replied Jenny. "I can't see how it would hurt to miss once."

Later Jenny decided to go along with her mother to the supermarket. "It's too bad we have to take the small car," said Mother as they went out to the garage. "I really could use more room for groceries."

"Let's take the other car then," suggested Jenny.

"You mean 'Old Unreliable'?" asked Mother with a smile. "I haven't dared to drive it since it broke down on the expressway. I'll wait till it's fixed."

"It's lots prettier than this car," observed Jenny.

"Well, that doesn't mean much if it's not dependable," said Mother. Then she added, "I hope you won't be offended, honey, but in a way, you remind me of that car."

"Huh?" Jenny was surprised. "How come?"

"You're a wonderful person in lots of ways, and you have talents that could be used for the Lord," Mother told her. "However, lately you've made commitments to your youth leaders, your teachers, and your father and me, but you often haven't followed through on them. Very soon, I'm afraid, people will feel they can't count on you." Jenny was silent as they rode along. "I'm going to insist that you go to help with the service project this afternoon," added Mother.

Jenny nodded. "I guess that's just as well," she said with a sigh. "After all, I don't want anybody calling me 'Old Unreliable.'" *S.K.*

HOW ABOUT YOU?

Do you keep the commitments you make? Faithfulness is important to the Lord as well as to people. Determine now to always keep your promises and to be a reliable Christian.

MEMORIZE:

"Confidence in an unfaithful man in time of trouble is like a bad tooth and a foot out of joint." *Proverbs 25:19, NKJV*

 Keep Your Commitments

Flying Lessons (Read Deuteronomy 32:9-12)

2
AUGUST

Matt and his father were fishing when Matt made a discovery—an eagle's nest way up near the top of a tall tree. And high in the sky, they saw a large bird soaring high over the river. "Wow!" Matt exclaimed. "I wish I could fly like that!" Eagles were his favorite bird, but he had never seen one before, except in a zoo.

"Well, that eagle didn't always have such great flying skills," Dad told him. "Baby eagles are afraid of flying. In fact, it takes a great deal of their mother's prodding to get them out of their soft, warm nest."

"I know. I read about that," said Matt. "The mother eagle pushes them right out over the side of the nest. That must be scary." Matt looked again at the nest so high in the tree.

Dad nodded. "They probably think they'll fall to the ground," he said. "But after the mother lets the little eaglet flutter and fall for a time, she soars underneath it and lets it land on her wings. Then she takes it back to the nest. Over and over she helps each eaglet practice flying until they are all brave enough and strong enough to fly on their own."

A few days later, Matt was asked to do something he had never done before—to give his testimony at the youth group meeting. He agreed to do it, but he felt so scared! "If only they hadn't asked me!" he groaned on the afternoon of the meeting.

His father overheard him. "Of course it's scary, Matt," he said, "but you haven't forgotten how eagles learn to fly, have you?"

"What does that have to do with giving a testimony?" Matt asked.

"God is like the mother eagle," explained Dad. "Sometimes he has to prod you to try new things, things that make you feel helpless or afraid. But he'll be there to teach you and catch you!"

T.V.

HOW ABOUT YOU?

Do you hang back when there are challenges to face? God will not let you crash as you "try out your wings." Even when you feel as if you are falling—or failing—you will discover that "the eternal God is your refuge, and underneath are the everlasting arms" (Deuteronomy 33:27, *NKJV*). As a Christian, you can "fly"!

MEMORIZE:

"Those who wait on the Lord shall renew their strength; they shall mount up with wings like eagles, they shall run and not be weary, they shall walk and not faint." *Isaiah 40:31, NKJV*

 *Dare to Do Things for God*

Harvest Time (Read Matthew 9:36-38)

Joel put five plump tomatoes and two cucumbers in a paper sack. "Thanks so much, and come again," he said, giving his customer the sack in exchange for some money.

He'd been busy at his roadside stand all morning, and now he noticed his supply of corn was getting low. Just then he heard the hearty voice of his grandpa, who was visiting from Florida. "Well, well, nearly out of corn, I see. How would you like me to watch your stand while you pick more?" Grandpa offered.

3

AUGUST

"That'd be great, Grandpa," Joel said. "I'll hurry." When Joel came back with a wheelbarrow full of corn, he saw Grandpa putting a white piece of paper into the sack with a customer's vegetables. "What was that paper you put in the sack?" Joel asked.

"Well, Joel, while you've been out harvesting more corn, I've been doing a little planting of seeds," explained Grandpa. "Along with the produce, I've been putting a tract in the sack, one that tells about Jesus."

As Grandpa talked, he helped Joel restock the pile of corn. He motioned toward the colorful array of vegetables. "Your harvest here is very nice," observed Grandpa, "but I'm looking forward to a harvest of people instead of produce. Jesus said the harvest is plenteous—meaning there are many people wanting to hear the good news of salvation. Sad thing is, there aren't many who will do the work of sowing the seed of the gospel or of harvesting, of bringing people to the Lord."

Joel grinned at his grandfather. "I guess it's time I do some planting and harvesting for the Lord," he said. "Got any of those tracts left? I see some more people are stopping." *C.Y.*

HOW ABOUT YOU?

Will you be a worker for the Lord? There are many different ways to join in planting and harvesting for the Lord. Ask those who don't know Jesus to come to church or Sunday school; do kind deeds in the Lord's name; explain how to come to Jesus; give a tract. How will you help?

MEMORIZE:

"The harvest is plentiful but the workers are few." *Matthew 9:37, NIV*

 Witness to Unbelievers

Learning to Forgive

(Read Matthew 18:21-22, Luke 6:31-38)

4

AUGUST

At the first jingle of the telephone, Kevin rushed to answer. He figured it would be Grandma calling to wish him a happy birthday. "Kevin?" said a man's voice. Kevin wondered who it could be. "This is your father," the man continued. Kevin fingered the cord of the telephone, uncertain how to respond. "I called to wish you a happy birthday," his father added when Kevin didn't answer.

"You said you didn't want any more to do with me," said Kevin finally, "so I don't want to talk to you." With that, he hung up the phone.

Kevin went to tell his mother about the call. He thought she would be pleased with the way he had handled it. After all, during the time of the divorce nearly two years before, she had often had harsh words for his father. So he was surprised when she said, "Kevin, we need to talk about this." Then Mother did something very strange. She called Kevin's dog, Splash, to join them. Kevin laughed when Splash ran in, jumped up on his lap, and tried to lick his face. "See how much Splash loves you," said Mother.

"I love him, too." Kevin gave Splash a pat on the head.

"I know you do," said Mother, "but do you remember what you said when you got mad at him last week?" Kevin thought for moment. Then he nodded. "I said, 'Bad dog. I don't want you anymore,' didn't I, old boy?" He hugged his pet. "I'm sorry, Splash; I didn't mean it."

"Your father may feel the way you do," Mother said gently. "Two years ago, we all said many things out of anger. Now we need to learn to forgive one another, just as God forgives us."

Kevin buried his cheek in Splash's fur as he thought about what Mother was saying. "Mom, do you know Dad's phone number?" he asked at last.

"Yes. I'll get it for you," said Mother as her arm circled Kevin's shoulder. *E.M.B.*

HOW ABOUT YOU?

Do you have trouble forgiving someone? Most people do. Would it help to remember how often you have been forgiven? By your parents? By your friends? By an enemy? It's most important to remember that God forgives.

MEMORIZE:

"If you do not forgive, neither will your Father in heaven forgive your trespasses."

Mark 11:26, NKJV

 *Forgive Others*

God's Helper (Read Matthew 25:34-40)

5

Jesse sat in church with his mother. He was seven and had never been away from home, but now they were listening to a missionary talk about a faraway land. The man, who wore a long, white robe and a scarf wrapped around his head, turned so everyone could see his clothes. "This loose scarf keeps the sun off my head," he said.

Jesse leaned against his mother as the missionary continued. "The people are difficult to reach, but I'm happy to be there, because I know God sent me to this land." Jesse's eyes opened wide. He hoped God wouldn't send him to a strange land. He didn't want to leave home.

The next evening Jesse sat on the front porch. He listened to his mother in the kitchen. He could hear the hum of his father's lawn mower in the backyard. He liked these sounds. Jesse looked down the street and saw old Mrs. Quarry, his neighbor, walking home with a heavy bag of groceries. She stopped in front of Jesse's house and leaned against the fence. As her groceries slipped from her arms, an orange rolled across the lawn and a can of tomatoes clattered into the street.

Jesse ran to help her. "I'll get your groceries, Mrs. Quarry," he said.

The old woman gave a deep sigh. "First, Jesse," she said, "please help me up my front steps. I'm so tired." She put a hand on the fence and the other on Jesse's shoulder. He hoped she wouldn't fall.

When they reached Mrs. Quarry's steps, Jesse walked beside her and held her arm. At the top of the stairs, she sat down in a porch chair. She looked up at Jesse and smiled. "God sent you, Jesse," she said. "He knew I needed help, and he sent you."

Jesse ran to pick up the groceries. He felt good. There were many ways he could serve God, and he didn't even have to leave home. At least not yet. *R.H.*

HOW ABOUT YOU?

Are you serving God in your family? In your neighborhood? With your friends? You don't need to wait until you're older to go to a faraway land and serve God. Ask God where he wants you to serve now. Tell him, "Here am I. Send me."

MEMORIZE:

"Then I heard the voice of the Lord saying, 'Whom shall I send? And who will go for us?' And I said, 'Here am I. Send me!'" *Isaiah 6:8, NIV*

 Serve God Where You Are

Following Instructions (Read 2 Timothy 3:14-17)

6

AUGUST

The contents of David's model airplane kit lay scattered on the desk top in front of him. A frown creased his forehead as he looked at the part he had already assembled. He was so engrossed in what he was doing that he didn't hear Mom come into the room until she spoke. "Thought you came up here to study your Sunday school lesson," she said.

"I did, Mom, but it's a hard one, and I'm tired," replied David. "Besides, I want to get this airplane together. I'm having trouble with the wing assembly. I just can't get it right!"

"Maybe I can help you," offered Mom. She began reading the instructions, step by step.

At step number four, David stopped her. "I see what's wrong!" he said. "This piece is upside down." He quickly changed it. "This isn't so hard when you follow the instructions," he added with a grin.

"That's the secret to living the Christian life, too," Mom said. "The Bible is God's instruction manual. In one place there's a set of instructions listed in much the same way as the steps on your airplane instructions."

"There is?" David was really getting interested now.

Mom smiled and nodded. "We call that list the Ten Commandments," she said, "but they're just part of God's instructions. You need to study all of his Word. You just saw what happens when you goof up on any part of the instructions."

"Yeah," said David, "but there's an awful lot to learn."

"True," agreed Mom. "I guess we never stop learning. One good way to study is by doing your Sunday school lesson each week."

"I thought you'd be getting to that," said David with a grin. "I'll do it right now." *J.U.*

HOW ABOUT YOU?

God has given you a complete set of instructions—the Bible. In order to follow them, you have to be familiar with them. Are you reading his Word and studying your Sunday school lessons? Be sure to do that faithfully.

MEMORIZE:

"Do your best to present yourself to God as one approved, a workman who does not need to be ashamed and who correctly handles the word of truth."

2 Timothy 2:15, NIV

 The Bible Is God's Instruction Manual

A Growing Boy (Read Hebrews 5:11–6:1)

Jason stepped away from the door frame in the kitchen, and Dad measured from the floor to the mark where Jason's head reached. "You're as tall as I am," Mom said with amazement as Dad announced Jason's height. "You're growing up so quickly." Jason's face glowed.

"All that good food and exercise you've had lately has helped you grow right up," Dad said proudly.

"All that exercise I had today made me tired," said Jason, yawning. "I'm going to bed."

7
AUGUST

"Another sign that you're growing up! We don't have to make you go to bed," said Dad, patting Jason on the back.

In his room, Jason glanced at the Bible next to his bed, but he didn't pick it up. He'd been putting off devotions for several nights, and the more often he put it off, the less guilty he felt.

There was a knock on the door, and Mom came in. "Are you too grown up to be tucked in?" she asked.

Jason shook his head and grinned as Mom sat on the edge of his bed. They talked about Jason's busy day for a few moments. "Mom, I played awfully hard, and I'm beat. May I skip Sunday school once and sleep in tomorrow?" asked Jason. "A growing boy needs his rest, you know."

"About that growing—I think you've grown enough for a while," declared Mother. "I bet if we'd cut out the healthy food you've been eating—maybe give you milk like a baby—you'd stop growing."

Jason laughed. He knew Mom was kidding. "I want to keep growing," he said.

Mom smiled. "Well, OK," she agreed. Jason saw her glance at his Bible, which had remained unopened so long it had gathered dust. "How about spiritually?" she asked. "Don't you want to grow in the Lord, too?"

Jason's guilty feelings returned in full force. He knew his spiritual growth was far more important than his physical growth. He'd have to quit "starving" himself spiritually. "I'll be up for Sunday school," Jason assured Mom as she left, and he reached for his Bible. *K.R.A.*

HOW ABOUT YOU?

Do you get as excited about growing in the Lord as you do about your physical growth? Do you read your Bible daily? Do you attend church each Sunday and study the Bible regularly with other Christians? Make sure you tend your spiritual growth.

MEMORIZE:

"But grow in the grace and knowledge of our Lord and Savior Jesus Christ." *2 Peter 3:18, NIV*

 Grow Spiritually

What Color? (Read Acts 17:22-28)

"What are those for?" Jason asked, pointing to the bouquet of flowers Lisa was arranging.

"For the dinner table," Lisa replied. "Aren't they pretty?"

"Yeah, I guess so." Jason walked to the window. "Some new people moved in across the street today."

Lisa added a stem of daisies to the centerpiece. "I hope they have a girl my age."

"They do," Jason informed her. "And a boy my age. His name's Joey."

As Lisa placed the flowers on the table, Dad came into the dining room. "That is certainly a pretty bouquet, Lisa," he observed.

"Thank you," Lisa replied. "I love to work with flowers. There are so many pretty kinds and colors. They make me feel beautiful."

"Boy, that would take a lot of doing," teased Jason. Lisa gave her grinning brother a gentle shove.

Mother came in and set the salad on the table. "I'm glad God painted our world with color," she remarked. "And not just flowers are colorful. Look at this salad—green lettuce, red tomatoes, white mushrooms—"

Lisa gasped. She pointed out the dining room window. "Is that the new family getting in the car across the street?" Everyone looked.

Jason nodded. "Yep, that's them."

"But . . . but . . . ," Lisa stammered, "they're . . . they're not like us."

"You mean they're a different color?" Mother looked Lisa straight in the eye. Lisa nodded.

"So what?" Jason demanded. "What difference does that make? All roses aren't red."

Dad nodded appreciatively. "Right. And all vegetables aren't green. Remember, God used color to make this a beautiful world."

"I think Joey's cool," Jason declared. "I like white people."

B.W.

HOW ABOUT YOU?

Do you judge people by the color of their skin? If you do, you may miss some beautiful friendships. God says all races are made "of one blood." We all belong to the family of man. God doesn't favor one race or color over another. Don't sin by doing that.

MEMORIZE:

"If you show favoritism, you sin." *James 2:9, NIV*

 Don't Be Prejudiced

The Book Pass (Read Acts 1:6-9)

Paul and his parents joined the long line of people standing side by side for the community "book pass." The line began inside the old library and extended down the street and into the new library. "This is going to be fun," said Paul, waving to some friends.

After the mayor gave a speech, the book pass began. Someone inside the old library removed books from the shelves and handed them to the first person in line. Then the people passed the books down the line from the old library right into the new one.

9

AUGUST

"I'm getting tired," Paul said after a while. "My arms are sore." A little later, he spoke again. "I'm dropping out. I can't pass one more book. Let the people with longer, stronger arms do it." He stepped out of line, leaving a gap between his parents. Mom stretched toward Dad as she passed the books. Dad reached out to get them. It was much more difficult without Paul in his place. Soon he stepped back in line. "I'll finish my part," he mumbled. "You're slowing things down with all that reaching."

That evening, Paul was studying his Sunday school lesson about witnessing. "It's hard to tell people about Jesus," he said. "I tried to talk to my friend Pete, but I'm no good at it."

Dad looked up from his newspaper. "It can be hard," he agreed, "but it's our responsibility—and it *is* a command."

"I know," Paul said, "but since some people can do it better than others, why not just let them do it?"

"The gospel message needs to be passed on from one person to the next, just like those books we passed today," said Dad. "When you got tired and dropped out of the book line, the work was much more difficult for your mother and me. That principle is true when it comes to giving out the gospel, too. When someone fails to do his part, it puts more work on other people and slows down the spread of the Word."

"That's right," agreed Mother. She ruffled Paul's hair. "I hope you'll decide to 'stay in line' and do what you can to win your friends to Jesus." *N.E.K.*

HOW ABOUT YOU?

Do you tell others about Jesus or do you think it's someone else's job? It is your responsibility to help spread the gospel message. Get in line and do your share.

MEMORIZE:

"You are to go into all the world and preach the Good News to everyone, everywhere." *Mark 16:15, TLB*

 Spread the Gospel

Spooked (Read Psalm 91:1-10)

10

AUGUST

Deborah was excited when she returned home from her horseback riding lesson. "It was so great!" she told her family. "My whole class went on a trail ride through the woods. My horse was spooked once, but I didn't even get off balance!"

"What's 'spooked'?" asked Deborah's little brother, Dave. "Did you see a ghost?"

Deborah laughed. "No, silly," she said. "Some horses get scared easy. When they see something they don't expect—like a piece of paper blowing—they might jump sideways or try to run away. We call that spooking. If you're not a good rider, you might fall off when they do that."

"Horses are so big," said Dave. "Why are they scared?"

Deborah shrugged. "It's just the way they are," she said. "If the horse gets to know you and trust you, he calms down a lot, though. Then he'll go places he's scared to go because he knows you won't let him get hurt."

"You've learned a lot about horses—and about riding them," said Dad with a smile. "You know, I was just thinking that the way a horse and rider develop a trusting friendship is a good picture of how we should develop a trusting relationship with God."

Deborah looked at Dad. "You mean like we shouldn't be afraid to go wherever God wants us to, because we know he won't let us get hurt?" she asked.

"That's part of it," agreed Dad. "We need to trust him in every situation. Sometimes we get spooked when something unexpected happens in our life and things aren't the way we thought they would be. We need to trust God to take us through even the scary places."

Mother smiled at Deborah. "Next time your horse is spooked," she said, "let it remind you that a close, loving relationship with God can keep you from being spooked. He can take away all of your fears." *D.M.*

HOW ABOUT YOU?

Are you ever afraid? Sometimes you have to do things that make you nervous or scared, but there's a cure for that. Walk close to God; read and think about what's in his Word; talk to him in prayer; be aware of his promise to never leave you and to protect you. God loves you and he wants you to trust him.

MEMORIZE:

"Fear not, for I am with you; be not dismayed, for I am your God. I will strengthen you, yes, I will help you, I will uphold you with My righteous right hand." *Isaiah 41:10, NKJV*

 ***You Don't Need to Fear***

The Full Cup

(Read Proverbs 11:24-28, 2 Corinthians 9:6-8)

As Jill and her mother left the grocery store, they met their pastor. "I'm here to buy some food for that family whose house burned yesterday," Pastor Holt told them after they had exchanged greetings.

At once Jill's mother reached into her purse, pulled out ten dollars, and handed it to the pastor. "Here's a little bit to help out," she said.

11

AUGUST

As Jill and her mother went on their way, Jill frowned. "Mom, I wanted to buy those special cookies I like so much, and you said we couldn't afford them," she complained. "I thought I understood about that, since Dad is out of work. But then you gave away ten dollars. That doesn't make any sense. How can you afford to give away money when we don't have enough for ourselves?"

"The Lord has marvelously blessed us during this time, and we've been able to get everything we really need," answered Mother. "Your dad and I believe we should share the good things God has given us and not just keep them for ourselves. He always repays us in one way or another." Jill didn't really looked convinced, but she didn't say any more about it.

That afternoon as Jill helped prepare dinner, Mother asked her to measure out one and one-fourth cups of milk for a casserole. "Fill the cup and pour it into the bowl; then just fill it to the one-fourth line the second time," she instructed. Then she added, "You know, Jill, emptying the measuring cup so you could add more is a little like what I was trying to tell you about giving. If we hoard God's blessings, keeping them all for ourselves, we may have no more room to receive anything else because our 'cup' may be full. But if we generously share what we have with others, God will see to it that our needs continue to be met." *M.R.P.*

HOW ABOUT YOU?

Are you saving for something you need or want? It's good to do that, but don't selfishly hoard your money and possessions. By holding tightly to everything, refusing to give for God's work or the needs of others, you might be missing more blessings from God. He loves a cheerful giver!

MEMORIZE:

"Freely you have received, freely give." *Matthew 10:8, NIV*

 Share God's Blessing

Batting Champion (Read Ephesians 4:30-32; 5:1-2)

12
AUGUST

"Look at this trophy, Dad!" exclaimed Christopher. "I still can't believe it—I won the batting championship!"

"I'm very proud of you, Son," said Dad. "All those long, persistent hours of practice paid off."

At home, Mother had a celebration dinner waiting, but after dinner Christopher left the table without a word of thanks. And when his sister picked up his trophy, he grabbed it from her, saying, "Don't touch it! You'll get fingerprints on it."

"Christopher," said Dad sternly, "I don't like what I'm hearing. The Lord commands us to treat others as we would like to be treated, but how about the way you treated your sister just now? And I didn't hear so much as a thank-you to Mom for preparing a special meal for you, either."

Christopher looked ashamed. "I'm sorry," he said. "I forgot." He sighed. "I always forget," he added in a defeated tone.

"Well, Son, tell me something," said Dad. "You really wanted to win the batting championship, didn't you?"

Christopher nodded. "Sure," he said. "That's why I practiced so hard."

"That's my point," said Dad. "It took a lot of practice, and I think we can all learn a lesson from that. We all know we should put others ahead of ourselves. If we really want to learn to do that, what should we do?"

Christopher looked puzzled a moment. Then he grinned and said, "Oh . . . you mean we should practice doing that?"

"Right!" said Dad. "We don't become mature Christians the moment we're saved—we have to grow in Christ. That takes practice, and lots of it. Just as you were determined to be batting champion, you need to set your mind on treating others as Christ would have you treat them. Then work hard at it every day. We all need to do that."

"That would be sort of like becoming a champion for Jesus," added Mother. "It's something worth working for." *M.R.P.*

HOW ABOUT YOU?

Are you practicing being Christlike in your treatment of others? Being kind and loving isn't easy. It takes practice. Each morning ask the Lord to help you show love and kindness to others on that day. And then work hard at doing it.

MEMORIZE:

"Let brotherly love continue."
Hebrews 13:1, NKJV

 Practice Being Kind

The Pesky Kitten (Read John 10:7-10)

13

AUGUST

Judy's black-and-white kitten dug his claws into the leg of Judy's blue jeans. She shook him off and started loading the dishwasher. "Meow!" protested the kitten.

"What do you want, Buster?" asked Judy. Buster bounced to the closed door of the kitchen and scratched at it. "Are you ready to go outside?" asked Judy. The kitten made a sound and—according to Judy—smiled. "You said, 'Uh-huh,' didn't you?" she asked. "I'll open the door for you as soon as I finish putting the dishes in the dishwasher." But Buster didn't like to wait. He attached himself to the leg of Judy's jeans again. "Ouch!" exclaimed Judy. "You quit that!"

Buster trotted back and forth between Judy and the door. Finally, he stationed himself at the door and looked at Judy with enormous green eyes. "You're my person," he seemed to say. "Why don't you tend to me—right now?"

Once more, the kitten started toward Judy's blue jeans. "You win, Buster," said Judy. "I'll open the door for you." She dried her hands and walked to the door with Buster at her heels. When she opened the door, he bounded outside and made a beeline for his favorite spot in the sunshine. He rolled over and over, cleaning his fur with sand.

As Judy finished loading the dishwasher, her mother came into the kitchen. "Buster is pretty smart," Judy told Mother. "He knows the door won't open until he comes to me to open it for him."

Mother smiled. "So in a way, you're the 'door' for him," she said. "In other words, the way outside is through you. That's an illustration of how Jesus is the door to God the Father for us. As we trust in him, it's as though he opens the door to heaven for us."

Mother and Judy smiled as they watched Buster jumping around on the grass, having the time of his life. "Buster's a lot of fun, and now he's been your teacher, too," observed Mother. "Be sure to thank the Lord for that pesky little kitten."

Judy nodded. *G.R.*

HOW ABOUT YOU?

Have you learned that you can come to God the Father only through God the Son, the Lord Jesus Christ? Jesus "opens the door" for you to receive salvation. If you haven't come to God through Jesus, do so today.

MEMORIZE:

"I [Jesus] am the door. If anyone enters by Me, he will be saved, and will go in and out and find pasture." *John 10:9, NKJV*

 Jesus Is the Way to God

Come into My Parlor (Read Matthew 6:22-24)

14

AUGUST

Tim sat on the back steps, deep in thought. He didn't know what to do about Jim's birthday party. The other kids got all excited when Jim announced, "We're going to have a horror video to watch tonight!" "Wow!" "Great!" and "Oh, boy" were the exclamations that followed. Tim had just sat and said nothing. He knew they'd all call him a wimp if they knew what he was thinking, but he really didn't want to see the film.

Pastor Jed, the youth director at Tim's church, had recently talked about such things. "Horror movies may sound like fun in a scary sort of way," he said, "but there's a real danger in watching them. They could cause nervousness or nightmares for some kids. Worse still, they could harden you and make you insensitive to suffering and fear. They could even lead to something much worse. They appear to be a factor in some of the horrible crimes that are committed." He looked at the group. "I know you don't think such things could happen to you," he added, "but it isn't worth the risk."

As Tim thought about these things, he noticed his mom's rose trellis. There hung a large and glistening spiderweb—a masterpiece of construction. As Tim watched, it suddenly began moving; a housefly was caught by a sticky strand at the very edge. The motion of the trapped insect set up a tiny vibration across the connecting network, and Tim watched in fascination as a fat, brown spider picked up the signal and came scurrying out. In no time, the fly was snugly imprisoned in a cocoon of sticky bands.

The words of the nursery rhyme popped into Tim's head: "'Will you come into my parlor?' said the spider to the fly." Tim shuddered as he thought of the fly's ignorance of the danger. Or was it plain stupidity?

"Well, it's a sure thing, I'm not ignorant of the dangers at Jim's party." Tim addressed the spider, who was waiting for her next victim. "In fact, I'm not going to be stupid either! Wimp or no wimp, I'm not going." Feeling better after having made his decision, Tim went into the house and dialed Jim's number. *P.K.*

HOW ABOUT YOU?

Your eyes are like an open doorway to your mind, so be careful what you allow to go through that doorway. Ask God to help you keep your mind clean and pure.

MEMORIZE:

"The lamp of the body is the eye. If therefore your eye is good, your whole body will be full of light." *Matthew 6:22, NKJV*

 Look at Good Things

Busy Signal (Read Romans 8:24-32)

15

AUGUST

Just as Lindsey finished dialing, her mother walked into the living room. "Are you still on the phone?" asked Mother. "Hang up now, please. I have to make a call to the dentist's office."

Lindsey shook her head. "Just a second, Mom!" she said. "I might get it this time!" As Mother was about to reply, Lindsey frowned and hung up the phone. "Awww—busy again," she muttered.

Mother folded her arms crossly. "What's going on, anyway?" she asked.

"I thought you knew," said Lindsey. "Radio station WHUM is having a contest this week. Every now and then they play a certain song, and whoever is the third person to call wins fifty dollars." She sighed. "They've played it four times today, and every time I call I get a busy signal."

"Well, I need to make a dental appointment," said Mother. "Don't you have anything more constructive to do? How about studying your Sunday school lesson?"

Lindsey frowned. "Oh, Mom, that stuff's boring," she said with a sigh. "What's the use of doing it if I don't get anything out of it?"

Mother looked concerned. "Well," she said, "What's the use of continuing to call that radio station number? You don't get anything out of that, either."

"But one of these times, I'm going to get through!" exclaimed Lindsey. "Then my calling will pay off. I'll have some more money for my bicycle fund."

Mother gave Lindsey a hug. "Persistence is a good quality, honey," she agreed, "and if you apply it to studying God's Word, you'll find it pays off there as well. Keep reading your Bible. Keep on doing your Sunday school lesson. One of these times you'll 'get through.' You'll get something important out of it. Be as persistent in your spiritual life as you are with that contest. You'll find that a close relationship with God is worth much more than a bike."

S.K.

HOW ABOUT YOU?

What should you do when the Bible seems boring and your prayers "bounce back"? First, make sure you know Christ as your Savior. Then ask God to show you any of sin in your life and deal with it. If you still feel out of fellowship, just keep trusting and obeying him. You'll be rewarded if you don't give up!

MEMORIZE:

"Let us not become weary in doing good, for at the proper time we will reap a harvest if we do not give up."

Galatians 6:9, NIV

 Don't Give Up on God

Reserved Seats (Read 1 Peter 1:2-9)

16

AUGUST

"Hurry, Dad!" urged Daniel excitedly as the car sped down the freeway toward the baseball stadium.

"Don't worry, Son," said Dad with a smile. "They won't give our seats away."

"What if they do?" Daniel's eyes grew wide with concern. "What if we can't find a place to sit?"

"The tickets are right here," Dad answered, tapping his left jacket pocket. "Bought and paid for. Our places are reserved for us."

"What does reserved mean?" asked Daniel.

"It means they're saved, or set aside," replied Dad, as he turned into the stadium parking lot. "People make reservations all the time—for airplane tickets, hotel rooms, fancy restaurants." Dad glanced at Daniel. "When you trusted Jesus as Savior and Lord last Sunday, you may not have known it, but you were making a reservation, too."

"I was?" Daniel was surprised.

"Yes, you were," said Dad. "You made a reservation in heaven. And that place will always be there for you."

They parked the car, and Daniel followed his father through the stadium gate, up and down stairs, and into a sea of squirming spectators. Every seat looked full. "Oh!" Daniel moaned. "I bet we'll have to stand up the entire game!"

Dad smiled as he studied the stubs of his two tickets. Then he lifted Daniel above the crowd to view the area. "Look down there," said Dad, "and tell me what you see."

Daniel gazed into the mass of people. Suddenly his eyes rested on two empty, shiny seats. "There they are, Dad!" he exclaimed. "Waiting just for us!"

"No one else," agreed Dad. He set Daniel down, and they made their way through the crowd. As they settled down into their reserved seats, Dad grinned at Daniel. "Always remember," said Dad, "there's a place in heaven just for you." Then they watched the game together. *J.R.G.*

HOW ABOUT YOU?

Do you sometimes wonder if you'll ever really get to heaven? Don't let doubts bother you. If you trusted God to save you, he guarantees that your place in heaven is reserved for you. Trust him to keep his promise.

MEMORIZE:

"In his [God's] great mercy he has given us new birth into a living hope through the resurrection of Jesus Christ from the dead, and into an inheritance that can never perish, spoil or fade." *1 Peter 1:3-4, NIV*

 Heaven Is Reserved for Believers

The Form Letter (Read Hebrews 4:14-16)

"Guess what, Mom!" yelled Jimmy when he and his father got home from the baseball game. "I got to meet Ted Brewer, and he even gave me his autograph. Imagine meeting a real, live baseball star! I'm going to take his autograph to school tomorrow. The guys won't believe I'm friends with him!"

17

AUGUST

"I'd hardly call him your friend, Son," said Dad. "After all, you just met him once. And he meets a lot of people. He probably doesn't even remember your name."

"I'll bet he does," insisted Jimmy. "I'm going to write him a letter tomorrow and see if he writes back."

A few weeks later, Jimmy came home from school and found a letter waiting for him. "It's from Ted Brewer!" he exclaimed. He smiled broadly as he tore the letter open. A moment later, however, his smile faded. "Aw, it's just a form letter," he grumbled. "Ted didn't even sign it. There's just a stamped-on signature."

When the family sat down for dinner, Dad asked Jimmy to thank God for their food. Jimmy bowed his head. "Thank you, Father, for this delicious food," he mumbled quickly. "Thank you for all your many blessings. Help us do your will. In Jesus' name. Amen. Hey, Dad, I got a stupid form letter from Ted Brewer today."

Dad looked over the letter. "Why, this is very nice," said Dad. "It's written quite well, the typing is good, and it's almost a page long."

Jimmy looked at Dad in surprise. "So what?" he asked. "I'd much rather have two lines scribbled by Ted himself. At least I'd know he really meant it."

"I see," said Dad. Then he added, "Jimmy, don't you think God might feel the same way about your prayers?"

"My prayers?" asked Jimmy in surprise.

Dad nodded. "Lately it seems that you often just mumble the same phrases without really meaning them," he said. "Don't you think God would rather hear a simple, sincere prayer than a lot of empty, impersonal words? Think about what you're saying when you pray. God deserves better than a 'form letter' prayer." *S.K.*

HOW ABOUT YOU?

Do you pray without much meaning? Do you tend to repeat the same words and phrases every time? God does not want 'form letter' prayers! Come before God in reverence and humility. Tell him what you really feel. God is not just a name or an idea—he's a real person. Make your prayers personal!

MEMORIZE:

"When you pray, do not use vain repetitions as the heathen do." *Matthew 6:7, NKJV*

 Pray with Sincerity

Caught in the Current (Read Psalm 119:1-12)

18
AUGUST

Tom and his brother, Andy, picked up their fishing poles. "The sun is too hot for the fish to bite today," said Tom. He moved under the shade of a cottonwood on the riverbank and kicked a thick grapevine out of his way.

"Yeah," agreed Andy. "Let's take a swim before we go home." He put down his pole and stripped off his shirt.

Tom looked at the cool, sparkling river. "We can't swim here." He pointed to a sign. "See that? It says, 'No swimming. Dangerous current."

Andy laughed. "I'll be careful. Just don't tell Mom and Dad." He waded into the river.

Tom rubbed his sweaty hands over his jeans. His chest felt tight as he watched his brother. "You've cooled off," he called. "Now let's go home."

Suddenly Andy disappeared. Tom watched breathlessly until Andy's head bobbed to the surface. "Tom," gasped Andy, "help me!"

Tom jumped up. He saw the current carrying Andy farther from shore. If he swam to his brother, he would be caught, too. "Help!" he shouted. He stumbled over the long grapevine. Suddenly he had an idea. "Andy! Catch this!" he called. He hurled the vine at his brother, who was struggling against the current. Andy reached out and grasped the vine. "Hold on!" Tom cried. He pulled and tugged as the river battled him. His arms ached.

"Let me help," someone called. Tom looked up to see Ranger Connors running toward him. Together, Tom and the ranger hauled Andy to the riverbank.

Ranger Connors helped Andy into his truck, and Tom climbed in beside him. "I'll take you home," said Ranger Connors. "I hope you have learned a lesson about obeying warning signs, Andy."

"I thought I would step in just a little ways," said Andy, "but the current caught me before I knew it."

"Wrong things are like that," warned Ranger Connors. "You can't go in just a little way. Before you know it, you're in too deep. Getting out can be very hard."

"I'll remember," said Andy. *B.M.*

HOW ABOUT YOU?

Do you think it's all right to tell just one lie or to cheat on a test now and then? Everyone who gets caught in sin probably thought the same thing. God warns about sin in the Bible. Ask him to help you say no to every temptation. All of them are dangerous.

MEMORIZE:

"Submit yourselves, then, to God. Resist the devil, and he will flee from you." *James 4:7, NIV*

 *Obey God's Warnings*

Made to Last (Read Matthew 6:19-24)

19
AUGUST

Sharon is so lucky, Nick thought as he plopped down on the front steps of his house. He sighed as he stretched his long legs out in front of him. Sharon's family was wealthy, and Sharon had all sorts of neat things: a phone, her own TV, and a closet bursting with clothes. She bragged a lot, though, and swished her long braided hair around all the time. And just now, Sharon had held up the special baseball card Nick had been wanting. "Look what I've got," she said smugly.

Some friend, Nick thought. She knew he'd been trying to get that card for a long time.

The clanging of dishes told Nick that his mom was setting the table for supper. He went inside. "Hi, Mom," he murmured, and she looked up. "It's not fair," complained Nick. "Sharon gets everything she wants. She even gets everything I want."

Before Mom could answer, a car pulled into the driveway. "Dad's home," said Mom.

During supper, Nick complained to his father about Sharon and how she made sure he saw her baseball card. "It's so frustrating," he said. "She has so many special things. That's OK, but she doesn't have to wave them in front of my face!"

"Sharon does seem to have a lot of special treasures," agreed Dad, "but will any of them last very long?" Nick shrugged. "Does she have any treasures in heaven that can't be taken away or stolen?" continued Dad.

Nick remembered their devotion time that morning. He knew that all the things Sharon possessed would get lost, broken, or worn out—including the baseball card. "You know, Dad," said Nick suddenly, "I don't think Sharon even knows about having treasures in heaven."

"She could," said Dad.

Nick smiled. He could hear Sharon calling him. "Yeah," he agreed, "like right now." *C.A.D.*

HOW ABOUT YOU?

Are you unhappy because of the bikes or games your friends have that you don't? Those things are nice, but the really important and lasting treasures are available to you, too. It's only what you do for Jesus that's going to last forever.

MEMORIZE:

"For where your treasure is, there your heart will be also."

Matthew 6:21, NKJV

 Serve Jesus, Not Things

The Kite (Read Psalm 8)

20
AUGUST

"Are you coming to Sunday school with me tomorrow?" Karl asked his new neighbor. As he spoke, he tied the last ribbon to the tail of a kite they were making.

"Nah, I don't think so," replied Jeff. "My dad says God is just in people's minds, and I think he's right. After all, nobody ever saw God. I'd feel funny sitting in church, listening to talk about somebody who's not there."

Karl's heart sank. How could he explain that God is everywhere, even though you can't see him? He bit his lip and silently prayed for the right time to speak and the right words to use.

"Let's see if this masterpiece will fly," said Karl, changing the subject. He held onto the string while Jeff carried the kite, and together they ran across the yard. Karl felt the string pull taut as Jeff let go of the kite. He turned to watch it soar high into the air.

"Wow!" cried Jeff. "We did it!"

After a while, Karl handed the string to his friend. "Here, you try it," he panted.

Jeff eagerly took the line and ran with it. All afternoon they passed the kite back and forth until they were too tired to run any more. At last Jeff pulled it in and collapsed on the ground. "That was great!" he exclaimed. "It was almost like someone was holding it up there."

Karl's heart leaped with hope. "Did you see anybody or anything holding it?" he asked.

"Of course not," Jeff replied, laughing. "You can't see the wind. But it's there, and you can see what it does."

"Just like you can't see God," Karl pointed out quietly, "but he's there, too. And you can see what he does. Just look at everything—the trees, birds, your dog, your family, yourself. God made them all. Could anyone else do that?"

Jeff sat silently for a long moment, studying his hand. "Maybe you're right," he admitted at last. "I'll have to think about it." *J.B.*

HOW ABOUT YOU?

Do you find it hard to believe in God because you can't see him like you can see another person? You can see what he does in all of nature. If you know some Christians, you can also see how he changes lives. He makes people become more kind, likable, and honest. He gives comfort, peace, and joy. He is real!

MEMORIZE:

"The heavens declare the glory of God; the skies proclaim the work of his hands." *Psalm 19:1, NIV*

 *God Is Real*

"Burry" Interesting (Read Proverbs 4:14-27)

21
AUGUST

"Mom, I'm home!" shouted Sandie as she came in the kitchen door. Then she noticed the note Mom had left. It said, "Gone to the store. Will be right back."

"Hey, Sandie!" called a voice at the back door. It was Kelly, a neighbor girl. "Come on out and play tag with us."

"Well . . . ," Sandie hesitated. She knew her mother didn't like her to spend time with Kelly because she used bad language. But Mother always told her to be friendly, didn't she? And she would be very careful not to repeat anything Kelly said. She decided to go.

The game of tag was in a nearby field of tall grass. The girls were running and screaming as they chased one another. When Sandie saw her mother come around the corner and pull into their driveway, she told the girls good-bye and headed home. "Hi, Mom," she said as she went into the house. "I was playing tag with some of the girls."

"Hi, honey," greeted Mother, glancing at Sandie. She gasped. "Look at you!" she exclaimed. "You didn't even change out of your school clothes before going to play. You're going to have a terrible time picking off those burrs."

Sandie looked down. She was surprised to see that her pants were covered with burrs. Without a thought, Sandie swore. Quickly she put her hand over her mouth—she was so embarrassed! She had promised herself that she would never repeat the words she had heard some of the girls using, but they had just slipped right out. She wished the floor would swallow her up.

"I see you picked up more than a few burrs while you were playing," Mom said. "Who were you playing with?" When she heard who Sandie's friends were, she nodded. "It's easy to pick up habits without even knowing it," she said. "And bad habits, like burrs, are hard to remove."

"I see what you mean," groaned Sandie as she began pulling the sticky burrs from her jeans. "I think I better watch where I play and who I play with!" *D.E.M.*

HOW ABOUT YOU?

Do your friends have bad habits? Do they curse or smoke? Do they gossip or tell lies? Although you should be kind and friendly toward everyone, don't choose as close friends those with habits you know are wrong. Don't give bad habits a chance to get "stuck" on you. They are hard to shake!

MEMORIZE:

"Do not enter the path of the wicked, and do not walk in the way of evil." *Proverbs 4:14, NKJV*

 Choose Friends Carefully

The Ant Farm (Read Psalm 139:1-12)

22
AUGUST

Sally and her little brother, Joey, watched the ants in her ant farm. Joey asked, pointing at one of the ants, "Why is that one digging a new tunnel? Oh! Is that one cleaning up? Ants are neat. Did God make ants, too?"

"So many questions from such a little boy," teased Sally. "Yes, God made ants, too."

"Are these ants like the ones outside?" asked Joey.

"Well, yeah, I guess so. I'd say they're cousins anyway," replied Sally with a grin. "But my ant farm isn't like the anthills outside. There you can only see ants when they come out, but here you can see everything they do." She stood up. "I have to go study now. But if you're careful, you can watch my ants some more."

Sally was in her room when she heard Joey run outside. Minutes later, she heard him run into his room. When she went to check on him, he had his head under the sheets, and his legs were sticking out. Sally knew Joey was hiding when he did this. "Joey, I see you," she said. "What happened?"

Slowly Joey pulled his head from under the sheets. He looked like he might cry. "I wanted to show your ants to their ant cousins outside. But I dropped the ant farm," he confessed. "It broke open, and all the ants ran away."

"Oh, Joey!" cried Sally.

Joey hid his face in his hands. "I didn't want you or God to see what I did."

"Well, you might have hidden it from me, but you can't hide from God," scolded Sally. "Just like you could see the ants in the ant farm, he always sees everything you do. In fact, he sees you better than you saw them."

Joey ran quickly to his sister and hugged her neck. "I'm really sorry. Really I am," he said.

Sally sighed. "I forgive you. And God will forgive you, too," she replied. "Just remember that God always sees you. And that you can never run away like the ants did."

"I'll remember," promised Joey. *D.K.*

HOW ABOUT YOU?

Do you sometimes forget that God sees everything you do? Would he be happy or sad with the way you have acted today? Ask him to help you live your life in a way that shows you are a Christian.

MEMORIZE:

"His [God's] eyes are on the ways of men; he sees their every step." *Job 34:21, NIV*

 **God Sees All**

The Homing Pigeon (Read 1 Corinthians 3:11-15; James 1:27)

23
AUGUST

Matthew stood staring up at the sky. "What are you looking for?" asked his friend Kyle, walking over to where Matthew stood. "I don't see anything unusual."

"I'm looking for Bettina," answered Matthew. "She's my homing pigeon," he added, seeing Kyle's puzzled look. "We've been training her with short flights ever since she was young. This will be her longest flight yet—three hundred miles. My aunt took Bettina home with her, and she was going to release her this morning."

"Well, you don't expect that bird to fly three hundred miles in one day, do you?" asked Kyle. "That's impossible."

Matthew shook his head. "No, it's not. Homing pigeons can fly fifty or sixty miles an hour. She'll make it today. Hey!" He pointed to the sky. "I bet that's her now!" he shouted. Sure enough, a bird was coming in closer and closer. "She's home! Hooray!"

Bettina floated down to Matthew's waiting hands. He placed her in her cage, where a big meal and some water awaited. Matthew looked her over as she ate. "Good bird!" he said. "You didn't even stop along the way."

Kyle raised his eyebrows. "How can you be sure of that?" he wanted to know. "You weren't there."

"I know because her feet are clean; there's no dirt or mud or bits of grass on them," replied Matthew.

Just then Matthew's father came home, and the boys told him about Bettina. "She's going to be a good homer," said Matthew. "She came in clean."

Dad looked thoughtful. "You know, boys," he said, "we're sort of like homing pigeons. We're on our way home to heaven. We need to come in clean, too. Do you understand what I mean?"

"I think so, Dad," replied Matthew. "If we mess around with sin, we'll get dirty. Is that it?"

Dad nodded. "When that happens, you need to quickly confess and forsake your sin, but it's better to not mess with it at all. Remember Bettina when you're tempted to do wrong," he advised.

M.R.P.

HOW ABOUT YOU?

As you're on your way to heaven, are you keeping clean and unspotted by things of the world? Even though you're saved, sin will rob you of rewards and make you ashamed. Confess your sin, turn from it, and ask the Lord to help you keep pure and clean.

MEMORIZE:

"Keep yourself pure."

1 Timothy 5:22, NKJV

 Enter Heaven Clean

A Hole in the Roof (Read Mark 2:1-12)

24

Tyler stood in the backyard looking up at the roof of the house. It was a busy place as the remodeling crew climbed up and down the ladders, working on the rectangular-shaped hole in the roof. "Having a skylight will really brighten up our dark kitchen," Dad said, coming up behind Tyler.

Tyler grinned at his father. "This is like my Sunday school lesson," Tyler said as he watched the workmen carefully lifting the window. "It was about the four men who brought their sick friend to Jesus. They cut a hole in the roof and let him down to Jesus."

Dad nodded. "I know the story," he said. "There was such a crowd around the house that they couldn't get the sick man in through the door."

"Even with power tools it's a big job to cut a hole in the roof," said Tyler, standing back to watch the men work. "I always wondered how those guys in Bible times could climb up a ladder with a stretcher and do that."

"The roof was probably flatter than ours," suggested Dad. "And there may have been outside steps going up to it."

"Maybe. Anyway, Woody and I were wishing we could take Eric on a stretcher and carry him to Jesus and let Jesus heal him," Tyler told Dad.

"You can do that in prayer, Tyler," said Dad gently.

"We have, but Eric still has cancer," replied Tyler sadly. "Doesn't Jesus heal anymore?"

"Jesus still heals," Dad assured him. "Sometimes he does it with doctors, sometimes with a miracle. But sometimes, like with your great-grandmother, he takes the person to heaven. There is no sickness there.

"Keep praying, and visit Eric whenever you can," Dad told him. "Tell him about the skylight. If I were sick, it would make me feel better just to know I had two friends who would like to put me on a stretcher, carry me up a ladder, and cut a hole in the roof to get me to Jesus." *R.M.*

HOW ABOUT YOU?

Do you have a friend or relative who's very ill? Do you feel there's nothing you can do? You can pray with and for that person. In some cases you can send cards, cheerful notes, or small gifts. Be sure the sick person knows you care and that Jesus does, too.

MEMORIZE:

"[Jesus] healed all the sick."

Matthew 8:16, NIV

 *Jesus Heals*

Fish Ears (Read Psalm 40:1-8)

Hurry up, Todd thought as he glanced at his watch. Dad was reading some Bible verses, but Todd was anxious for morning devotions to end and for the day's fishing trip to begin. To him it seemed like a long time before Dad finally closed with prayer.

"Ready to go!" Todd announced moments later. "The gear is in the car." He grinned at his mother. "We'll be back with supper, Mom," he boasted.

25

AUGUST

At the river, Todd and his father cast their fishing lines into the water. They waited and waited, but they didn't get even one nibble. "Maybe talking scares the fish away," observed Todd as he and Dad moved up the riverbank to a different spot. "I won't talk so much this time. Maybe they heard us talking about catching them." Dad grinned at him.

A few minutes later Todd felt something tugging at his line. "A fish! A fish!" he exclaimed. "I've got one." He pulled in his catch. "Supper," he said, smiling. After they had caught a few more, Todd frowned as he took one off the hook. "Here I was worried about being too loud and scaring the fish away," he said, "and fish don't even have ears!"

"Sure they do," said Dad. "You just can't see them." Todd examined the fish carefully. "Fish have ears that are internal, not external like yours and mine," explained Dad, tugging gently on Todd's ear. "But you know what?"

"What?" asked Todd.

"Well," said Dad, "even though our ears are on the outside, our most important hearing takes place on the inside. That happens when we listen carefully and take to heart the messages God has for us."

Suddenly Todd remembered the morning devotions. He had heard Dad's voice, all right, but he was too busy planning for the fishing trip to listen with his heart and hear God's message.

"Yep. It's the hearing on the inside that makes a real difference in our life," finished Dad. "And now let's get home with this fish supper." *N.E.K.*

HOW ABOUT YOU?

How well do you listen? When someone reads the Bible, do you just hear words or do you hear the message with your heart? Listen from the inside.

MEMORIZE:

"Listen to what the Lord says."

Micah 6:1, NIV

 Hear God's Word

Open Your Mouth! (Read Luke 12:22-31)

26

AUGUST

"Just a minute, Cindy. Your bottle's almost ready," called Julie from the kitchen. She was watching her baby sister so Mother could work in the garden, and now Cindy was crying. Julie tested the bottle to make sure it was just the right temperature. Then she got Cindy out of her crib and took her to the sofa. "Here, let's get comfortable," she said as the baby continued to fuss. She laughed as she saw Cindy sucking on her hands. "Take your hands out of your mouth, silly!" she said. "How can I give you your bottle when your mouth is full of your own fingers?"

Finally, she held the baby's hands down while she placed the nipple in Cindy's mouth. At last Cindy settled down and began to drink her bottle.

"What was wrong?" asked Mother when she came in. "I heard Cindy crying." Julie told her how Cindy sucked her own fingers instead of taking the bottle. Mother smiled. "Even older people sometimes act that way," she said.

"Older people refuse their food and suck their hands?" asked Julie with a laugh.

"In a way they do," replied Mother. "Christians often try to meet their own needs instead of letting God provide for them."

"Like how?" asked Julie. "Oh," she added, "I know! Like when you and Dad told me I couldn't hang around with Becky anymore because she smoked and drank and was a bad influence. For a while, I was mad. I told you I had to run around with Becky or I wouldn't have any good friends."

Mother nodded. "That was like sucking your own hand to meet your needs," she said. "But when you admitted we were right, it wasn't long before God helped you find a new best friend." She looked at baby Cindy, who was now contentedly sleeping on Julie's lap, as she added, "Sometimes we forget that God always wants what's best for us, and that he knows even better than we do what will make us happy." *S.K.*

HOW ABOUT YOU?

Is there something you think you need—clothes, money, a new friend, or maybe to feel important? God can provide you with everything you really need. Instead of trying to make yourself happy, turn to him and follow him. Trust him. He will provide.

MEMORIZE:

"And my God shall supply all your need according to His riches in glory by Christ Jesus."

Philippians 4:19, NKJV

 **God Meets All Needs**

The Smoking Wick (Read Colossians 3:8-11)

Grandmother glanced up as Jacob stomped into the house. "You look as angry as those thunderclouds in the west," she said.

"Thunderclouds?" asked Jacob.

Grandmother stood up. "Guess you were too busy storming yourself to notice them. Help me close the windows."

As Grandmother began supper, she asked, "Why are you mad this time, Jacob?"

Jacob's face flushed. "Chuck won't let me borrow his calculator. He's so selfish."

Crash! A loud roll of thunder shook the house, and lightning flashed. Jacob and Grandmother jumped. "The lights are out!" Jacob wailed.

"Sit still," Grandmother ordered as she rummaged in the cabinet. "I have an old lamp somewhere. Ahhhh, here it is. Now for a match . . . here they are." As she lit the lamp and set it on the table, she continued, "Isn't Chuck the boy who's coming to Sunday school with you next Sunday?"

Jacob nodded. "Yes—I mean, no. I doubt if he'll come now. I told him what I think of him." Jacob coughed. "What's wrong with the lamp, Grandma? It's smoking and not putting out much light."

Grandmother fanned the smoke away from the lamp with her hand and lifted the globe off with a potholder. She turned a little knob and adjusted the wick in the lamp. Then she cleaned the globe. As she worked, she explained what she was doing. "I had the wick turned up too high," she said. "When the wick is too long, it smokes up the globe so the light can't shine through." When the lamp was burning brightly again, she looked at Jacob. "The light of God's love can't shine through you when you're angry, Jacob," Grandmother told him. "Your temper has smoked up your witness."

Jacob hung his head. "I know," he admitted. "Guess I'd better tell Chuck I'm sorry." He grinned. "My temper's not too long, though—it's too short." *B.W.*

HOW ABOUT YOU?

If your friends don't seem to listen when you witness to them, take a look at your life. Are you doing something that "smokes up" your witness? If so, now is the time to clean up your act and let the light of God's love shine through.

MEMORIZE:

"Let your light shine before men, that they may see your good deeds and praise your Father in heaven."

Matthew 5:16, NIV

 Let Your Witness Shine

Am I Lost? (Read Luke 15:3-10)

28
AUGUST

Stacy started down the sidewalk. Mother was very busy, so Stacy decided she'd go to the park and play for a little while. She'd get back before Mother could miss her. Mother seemed to think she wasn't old enough to go to the park alone. That was silly!

After turning a corner, Stacy heard a dog barking behind her. She was afraid of dogs, and she began to run. She dodged through a yard and came out on the next street. She was relieved to find that the dog had not followed. She skipped merrily down the walk for a couple of blocks before realizing she didn't know where she was. *Am I lost?* she wondered with a feeling of terror.

"Hi, honey," said a man working in his yard. "Are you out for a walk?" Quickly Stacy took off in the opposite direction. She knew she mustn't talk to strangers. But where was the park? After turning another corner, she stood still. Now she knew she was lost. Her eyes filled with tears as she sat down on the curb.

After what seemed a long, long time, a familiar-looking car came around the corner. It stopped, and Mother jumped out! Stacy burst into tears, and Mother gathered her into her arms.

"I d-d-didn't think you'd come," sobbed Stacy. "I thought you were busy."

"I was busy," Mother said, "but when you were missing, I left everything and came looking for you. Nothing else was as important." She looked at Stacy. "I don't know when I've been so glad to see anybody in my life."

Stacy looked at her mother a little fearfully. "Even though I was naughty?" she asked.

"Even though you were naughty," said Mother solemnly. *H.M.*

HOW ABOUT YOU?

Have you ever suddenly discovered that you were lost? It's a terrible feeling, isn't it? Whether we realize it or not, we're all lost in sin. But there's good news! We're so important to Jesus that he left heaven and came to earth to find and save us. Trust him today.

MEMORIZE:

"For the Son of Man came to seek and to save what was lost." *Luke 19:10, NIV*

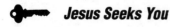 *Jesus Seeks You*

Chameleon Christians (Read Philippians 2:12-15)

"I hate being cooped up with this broken leg," Jeff complained to Uncle George. "I can't play ball or anything. I'm sick of my crutches."

"Maybe what I brought you will help," said Uncle George, handing Jeff a package. Eagerly Jeff opened it. He found a jar containing a little green creature about three inches long. "It's a chameleon," explained Uncle George. "Here, let him out of the jar. He'll enjoy running around your mother's house plants."

29

AUGUST

Jeff carefully placed his new pet on the stem of a large plant. Suddenly he looked closer. "He looks different, Uncle George!" he exclaimed. "His color is changing."

Uncle George chuckled. "He's turning a brownish color because he's on a brownish stem," he said.

"That's cool!" exclaimed Jeff.

"He can change to gray, green, brown, or a yellowish brown. He changes color, not only to blend in with his surroundings, but also according to the mood he's in or how he feels," explained Uncle George. He turned to Jeff. "But I don't want you to learn his tricks!"

"I couldn't change the color of my skin," said Jeff.

"Oh, but lots of people are like chameleons, though," replied Uncle George. "They act like Christians when everything is going their way, but when something unpleasant happens they 'change their color' fast. Nobody could tell by watching them that they have a loving Savior and a wonderful home waiting for them in heaven."

Jeff took a deep breath. He knew he hadn't been acting much like a Christian lately. Ever since he had broken his leg, he'd been pouting and feeling sorry for himself. Neither of them said anything for a few minutes. Then Uncle George stood up. "I must be going," he said. "Enjoy your pet. The feeding instructions are on the jar."

"Thanks," answered Jeff. "I'll have fun taking care of him, and I've already learned something from him." *M.N.*

HOW ABOUT YOU?

Do you act one way at church but another way at school and at home? Do you "change color" according to your mood or your circumstances? If you're willing to let him, God will help you be a consistent Christian instead of a "chameleon."

MEMORIZE:

"I will walk within my house with a perfect heart."

Psalm 101:2, NKJV

 Be a Consistent Christian

Eagles (Read Isaiah 40:28-31)

30
AUGUST

Lisa looked out the window, singing softly to herself. "They that wait upon the Lord shall renew their strength; they shall mount up with wings as eagles."

"Time to go," Dad called.

Reluctantly Lisa turned and followed her father to the car. Usually she loved going to church retreats, but this year her best friend, Julie, wouldn't be there—she died two weeks ago. A tear trickled down Lisa's cheek, and she hastily rubbed it away as she closed the door and fastened her seat belt.

"All set?" Dad asked. Lisa nodded and started humming the song again, trying to seem cheerful. "I know that song," said Dad as he started the car. "I always sing it when I feel down—it helps me feel better."

Biting her lip as another tear escaped, Lisa whispered, "It helps me, too." Dad hugged her. He began singing the song as he pulled out of the driveway. With a tearful smile, Lisa joined him.

When they finished the song, Lisa asked, "Dad, what does the part, 'They shall mount up with wings as eagles' mean? We can't really fly."

Smiling, Dad replied, "The eagle is a unique bird, Lisa. When there's a storm, other birds try to avoid it, but the eagle flies straight into it and uses the storm's own winds to lift him above the clouds."

"Where he can fly better and be safe," said Lisa.

"Yes." Dad nodded. "With God's strength, you can be like an eagle and fly straight into the storms of life, instead of running away from them. Then you can use those hurts or troubles—even the hurt and loneliness you feel from Julie's death—to grow as a Christian."

Brushing away the tears, Lisa squared her shoulders. "It still hurts, even though I know Julie's in heaven," she said, "but I do want to 'fly' the way God wants me to. Will you help me, Dad?"

"Sure, Lisa," Dad assured her. "Let's sing that song together again." *J.B.*

HOW ABOUT YOU?

Are you sad because a friend has died or moved away? Because your mom or dad is out of work? Because it seems like your world is falling apart? God loves you and wants to help you face your problems.

MEMORIZE:

"Those who wait on the Lord shall renew their strength; they shall mount up with wings like eagles, they shall run and not be weary, they shall walk and not faint." *Isaiah 40:31, NKJV*

 Get Strength from God

The Sunflower Dilemma (Read Deuteronomy 19:16-20)

31

AUGUST

"It had to be Eric," Tyler insisted.

"Now, Tyler," said Mom, "please don't accuse anyone unless you have proof." She frowned. "Don't forget God's commandment in Exodus 20:16, 'Thou shalt not bear false witness against thy neighbor.' One translation says, 'Do not accuse anyone falsely.' You need to be very careful." Tyler scowled and went back outdoors.

Early in the spring, Tyler had planted a row of sunflower seeds along the fence that separated his back yard from Eric's back yard. Both boys had been excited when the first green shoots appeared. They had watched the plants grow until they towered above the fence. At first, the flowers had looked like giant daisies, always smiling in the sun. "They smile at me in the morning and at you in the afternoon," Tyler had told Eric, and the boys made a game of playing in the yard where the sunflowers smiled. When they were tired of playing, they rested on the grass and watched the squirrels walk across the wires overhead, like daring circus performers.

As the sunflowers matured, their heads no longer followed the sun. Instead, they hung heavily downward. But now the biggest head was missing. Tyler was sure Eric must have taken it, and he was furious. "I bet he'll take others, too," muttered Tyler to himself, "but I'll catch him!" Standing on a stepladder, he looped a piece of twine around a couple of the biggest plants. He hung a small cowbell on the end of the twine and hid it as best he could under the leaves.

On his way to empty the trash a little later, Tyler heard the bell. He dashed to the backyard. There he saw a squirrel busily gnawing on a sunflower plant. The head fell to the ground. With a loud shout, Tyler chased the little animal. Then he picked up the sunflower head and ran to tell his mother about it.

Mom smiled and nodded. "Aren't you glad you didn't accuse Eric?" she asked. *J.U.*

HOW ABOUT YOU?

Have you ever accused someone and found out later you were wrong? Be very sure you know the facts before you accuse someone. If you have already broken God's commandment regarding this, apologize to the person you have wronged and try to be more careful next time.

MEMORIZE:

"Do not be a witness against your neighbor without cause."

Proverbs 24:28, NKJV

 **Don't Make Hasty Judgments**

Special Delivery (Read 2 Kings 23:1-3)

1

SEPTEMBER

"Would you sign here, please," said the postal carrier. Mother signed while Beth and Jeremy studied the envelope he brought.

"OK, kids," mother said with a grin as she closed the front door a moment later, "let's get back to work."

"Aren't you going to open your envelope?" cried Beth.

"Pretty soon," Mother answered, "but I'd like to get the rest of those beans canned first."

"You've got to be kidding!" protested Jeremy, but the children followed their mother back to the kitchen.

Time seemed to pass very slowly as they washed and snapped beans. All Beth and Jeremy could think about was the envelope stamped Special Delivery. "What do you suppose is in that letter?" they asked over and over. "Can't we just open it and see?" They couldn't believe Mother wasn't as eager as they were to open the letter.

After a little while, Mother left the room. She soon returned with the letter. She carefully placed it on the table and resumed her work. "I thought you might like to look at it while you work," she said.

"Mom," groaned Jeremy, "we don't want to see the outside of the letter. We want to know what it says. Why are you teasing us with it?"

"I decided to use it as an object lesson," Mother said, "to show you what some people do with their special letter from God."

"You mean the Bible?" asked Beth.

Mother nodded. "Many people have Bibles in their homes," she said, "but they leave them on a shelf or in a drawer. Others put a Bible out where everyone can see it instead of opening it and reading it."

"And others are like you, Mom. They have things they want to do before they read their letter," offered Jeremy.

Mother smiled. "Exactly. It's very easy to let other things get in our way." She picked up the letter. "I hope you will always make a special time to read your letter from God," she added. *J.B.*

HOW ABOUT YOU?

Are you eager to read letters that come in the mail? Are you also eager to read God's letter? Don't let things like friends, sports, or TV get in the way. Set aside a special time to read your Bible and pray each day.

MEMORIZE:

"Do your best to present yourself to God as one approved, a workman who does not need to be ashamed and who correctly handles the word of truth."

2 Timothy 2:15, NIV

 Read God's Word

Go for the Gold (Read 2 Chronicles 12:9-12)

2

SEPTEMBER

James worked faithfully all summer on his swimming techniques. How he wished he'd be good enough to compete in the Olympics some day! "Did you know that the guy who won the bronze medal one year was a graduate of our school?" he asked his parents one evening.

Dad nodded. "At one time, people believed he might win the gold," said Dad, "but he got careless and broke some of the training rules. And the bronze was the best he could do."

"Really?" asked James. He frowned as he added, "That was stupid of him."

"I imagine he'll always wonder what might have happened if only he had stuck to the rules," said Mother.

"Yes," agreed Dad thoughtfully. "This goes right along with the sermon I'll be giving tomorrow. You see, the Bible tells about some bronze—or brass—and gold, too. King Solomon made many shields of beaten gold to be held by guards at the entrance of his house. But after he died, his son Rehoboam became king, and Rehoboam quit following God's law. As a result, the Israelites were defeated in war, and many of their treasures were taken away—including the gorgeous shields of gold. Although Rehoboam later asked God's forgiveness and God turned away his anger, the beautiful treasures were gone. They were replaced with shields of brass."

"So Rehoboam gave up gold and settled for brass, too—just to indulge in his own sinful pleasures," observed Mother. She grinned at Dad. "And now why don't you tell us what practical application you're going to make in your sermon tomorrow?" she suggested.

"Well, this reminds me that Christians are God's special treasure," said Dad. "He wants us to shine as brightly as possible for his glory. However, when we fail to maintain a clean testimony, we don't do that."

"Good point," agreed Mother. "Go for the gold, James—in swimming, and especially in your spiritual life. Don't allow a few temporary pleasures to keep you from the best God has to offer."

M.R.P.

HOW ABOUT YOU?

Do you want to be your very best for God, or are you willing to settle for less? If you get careless about the things of God, sin can creep into your life. Don't be satisfied with anything less than God's best for your life. Go for the gold.

MEMORIZE:

"Set your minds on things above, not on earthly things."

Colossians 3:2, NIV

 Be Your Best for God

Quick as a Bunny (Read Psalm 121)

3

SEPTEMBER

"Are we almost there?" asked Heidi, peering out of the car window. "I'm awfully tired."

"We'll be there in about an hour," replied her father. "Aren't you getting excited about seeing our new home?"

"I guess so," answered Heidi. "But I sure wish I didn't have to change schools. What if the kids in the new school laugh at me for being on crutches? What if someone trips me and knocks me down? What if I can't find my way around? What if—"

"That's too many 'what ifs,'" said Mom, patting Heidi's hand. "Don't borrow trouble before it happens."

"Well, back home all the kids knew what kind of help I needed, and they took care of me," answered Heidi, "but there won't be anybody to help me in the new school."

"You'll have God," observed Dad. "The Bible says he's a 'very present help in trouble.'" As he spoke, Dad slammed on his brakes, barely missing a rabbit that suddenly hopped in front of the car. The next moment, a truck turned from a side road and came toward them, right in Dad's lane. Everyone gasped in fright. But the other driver pulled his truck into his own lane just in time to pass by safely.

"Oh, my!" said Mother in a shaky voice. "You know, if you hadn't braked for the rabbit when you did, we probably would have met that truck head-on."

"We're lucky the bunny came out on the road, aren't we?" asked Heidi.

"Not lucky—protected by God," replied Dad. "The rabbit caused me to slow down for the seconds we needed to avoid that truck. I'm certain God caused him to cross at just the right moment—he knew what that truck would do." After a moment Dad added, "He also knows what your new school will be like—and no matter what your needs will be, he already knows how he'll meet them."

"And he'll send help quick as a bunny, won't he?" asked Heidi with a grin. She sat up straight. "I'll try not to worry anymore!"

M.R.P.

HOW ABOUT YOU?

Are you afraid something bad will happen in the future? While you know only what's happening now, God knows all about what's out there in the future. He's ready with whatever help you need.

MEMORIZE:

"God is our refuge and strength, a very present help in trouble." *Psalm 46:1, NKJV*

 God's Help Is Never Late

Hitting the Mark (Read 1 John 1:8-10; 2:1-2)

Kevin watched as his big brother took aim with his new bow and arrow. Finally, Bill handed the bow to Kevin. Eager to take a turn, Kevin stood at the line Bill had marked, and Bill showed him how to hold the bow and align the arrow with the small dot in the center of the target. The large bow felt awkward in Kevin's hands, but he took careful aim. Anxiously he watched the arrow's flight, but it didn't even reach the target. Kevin was surprised!

4

SEPTEMBER

"I need to be closer," said Kevin. "Then I can hit the bull's eye for sure." Moving several steps nearer to the target, he again sighted down the arrow, and slowly pulled back on the string. This time the arrow went far enough but was way off course. After a few more tries, Kevin was ready to give up.

"Here, I'll help you," offered Bill. He leaned down, put his head very close to Kevin's and wrapped his arms around him to hold the bow and arrow. Together they pulled back slowly on the string. Kevin heard the solid thud as the arrow pierced the target only a half inch away from the bull's eye. He tried again, but only with Bill's help could he hit the mark.

A little later, Kevin went slowly into the house. "I missed every time," he said, sitting down at the table with his mother. "I can only hit the target when Bill helps me."

"Hmmmm," murmured Mother. "Do you know that I need someone to keep me on target, too?"

"You do?" asked Kevin, looking up.

Mother nodded. She pointed to her open Bible. "I've been a Christian a long time, but I still sin," she told Kevin. "In a way, sin is missing the mark, and as I said, I constantly need someone to keep me on target."

"You mean Jesus," said Kevin, and Mother nodded. *P.Y.*

HOW ABOUT YOU?

Do you still find it hard to always tell the truth? Do you try to be kind but sometimes lose your temper? Do you mean to obey your parents right away but sometimes fail to obey at all? Ask Jesus to help you live the way he wants you to. He will help keep you on target.

MEMORIZE:

"If anybody does sin, we have one who speaks to the Father in our defense—Jesus Christ, the Righteous One." *1 John 2:1, NIV*

 Ask Jesus to Keep You from Sin

No More Weights (Read Matthew 11:28-30)

5

Molly sighed as she read her list of spelling words. She wished her dad still lived at home. He always helped her study. "Molly!" Mother sounded angry. "This is the third time I've called you." Molly had noticed that her mother wasn't as patient as she used to be. And she always looked so tired and sad.

"I'm sorry," Molly said, taking her seat at the table. "I'm not hungry," she added, her voice trembling. "I'm worried about how we'll make it until you find a job. And I worry about doing better in school so you'll be happier. And I've been trying to clean up after myself so you won't have to yell." Tears slipped down Molly's cheeks. "I worry that Daddy won't come back."

Mother sighed. "I worry too," she admitted, hugging Molly.

"Anybody home?" interrupted a loud, cheerful voice at the kitchen door.

"Uncle John!" exclaimed Molly. Then she pointed to his wrists and ankles. "Why are you wearing those?"

"My weights?" Uncle John grinned. "I wear these when I run. It helps me build strength for the marathon," he explained. "But you can be sure I won't wear them for the race!" Uncle John left soon to continue his workout. "Chins up!" he said on his way out.

"I can't imagine wanting to weigh myself down like that," Molly told her mother. "Running is hard enough."

"It does seem silly," Mother answered. "But I think we're doing the same thing—and we're wearing weights in the race itself." Molly held up her wrists and one leg to show that she wasn't wearing any weights. "That's not what I mean, sweetheart," Mother said. "Our weights are on the inside—weights like a mind full of worries."

Molly sighed. "But we can't take our weights off," she said. "We're stuck."

"Ours can come off, too," Mother said with new hope. "The Bible tells us to cast our cares on the Lord. So why have we waited so long? Let's pray right now and really trust God to take charge of our situation. If we let him, he'll carry the weights for us." *N.E.K.*

HOW ABOUT YOU?

What do you worry about? Are there family problems or school problems that make your spirit heavy? Ask God to carry your burdens (big or small) and to fill you with his strength for living.

MEMORIZE:

"Casting all your care upon Him, for He cares for you."

1 Peter 5:7, NKJV

 **Give God Your Problems**

Disobedient Duke (Read Deuteronomy 26:16-18)

Dawn was delighted when she got a puppy for her birthday. "I'll call him Duke!" she announced as she watched him scamper around the living room.

"Well, Duke has a lot of things to learn," her father said. "You'll need to reward him when he's good and spank him when he's bad. Then he'll learn what he's not supposed to do."

6

SEPTEMBER

Dawn frowned. "He won't be bad, Daddy. I'll love him so much he'll want to be really good. You'll see— Duke's going to be the best dog in the world!"

But Duke was not a good dog. He dug up flowers and chewed on shoes. He ran away when he was called. Dawn scolded and spanked until she was tired of it, but it seemed to do no good. Duke went right on chasing the cat and getting into places he wasn't supposed to be.

One day Dawn sadly came into the living room. "Why is Duke so bad?" she burst out. "I scold him and scold him, and he acts like he's sorry. He licks my face and wags his tail, so I pet him and hug him, and then he's bad all over again. I love him so much—why does he keep on being bad?"

Dad put down his paper and pulled Dawn onto his lap. "Sometimes it takes a long time to train a puppy," he said. "I'm sure Duke will learn eventually. But you know what? The way Duke responds to you is somewhat like the way we often respond to God."

"What do you mean?" asked Dawn.

"Remember when you got Duke? You said you would love him so much that he'd want to be good to please you, but instead he's been a lot of trouble," replied Dad. "Very often we're the same way with God. He loves us so much that we should want to please him, but instead we want to do things our own way—and we keep on doing things we know we shouldn't." Dad shook his head. "You just told me about how bad you feel when Duke disobeys you," he added. "Think how bad God must feel when the people he cares about keep ignoring his teaching." *D.M.*

HOW ABOUT YOU?

Are you an obedient child of God? He loves you so much and wants only the very best for you. Stop hurting him by disobeying. Listen to his Word and do what it says. God will be pleased, and you will be happy, too.

MEMORIZE:

"If you love Me, keep My commandments." *John 14:15, NKJV*

Obey God's Commandments

Things to Remember (Read Psalm 119:9-16)

7

SEPTEMBER

After school one day, Mother waited for Frankie's bus to arrive. But when the bus came, Frankie didn't get off. Mother got in the car and drove to the school. Frankie wasn't there, either. She asked several of Frankie's friends, but no one knew where he was. She was quite worried by the time a school bus with only one child pulled up in front of the school. "Frankie!" Mother called, relieved. Poor Frankie had forgotten his bus number and had somehow slipped past the bus driver and onto the wrong bus.

Back home, Frankie told his older brother, Drew, all about his experience. "It's very important for me to remember things like my address and my phone number," he said seriously, "and the bus number, too!" He was very glad to be safely home.

As Drew grabbed his jacket to go out and play, Mother reminded him that he needed to learn his memory verse for Sunday school. "I'll do it later," Drew promised. He helped himself to an apple. "What's for dinner tonight?"

"Dinner!" exclaimed Mother. "Oh, dear! I meant to run to the store as soon as Frankie got home from school—I needed a couple of things for the meal I was planning to make. But in all the excitement I forgot all about dinner."

"It's important to remember to feed your hungry husband—and especially your hungry children," teased Drew. "It's something you should never forget."

"Well," said Mom, "while I start dinner, why don't you study your Bible verse? That's something you should not forget, either!"

Drew shrugged. "I don't see why I have to remember verses when I can open my Bible and read them any time."

"I know my verse," Frankie said. "When I was on the wrong bus, I said it to myself over and over so I wouldn't be scared."

Mother smiled at the little boy. "Frankie didn't have a Bible with him, but the Word of God was in his memory," she said. "It gave him peace of mind during a scary time. Knowing and remembering the Word of God will help you through all kinds of situations."

N.E.K.

HOW ABOUT YOU?

Is it a chore for you to memorize Bible verses? The more Scripture verses you know by heart, the more often they will be there to help you live.

MEMORIZE:

"For whatever things were written before were written for our learning, that we through the patience and comfort of the Scriptures might have hope."

Romans 15:4, NKJV

 Memorize Scripture

Camouflage (Read Matthew 26:69-75)

8

SEPTEMBER

"Why won't you buy me a camouflage outfit?" Lonnie asked his mother. "All the guys are wearing them to school."

"We already bought your school clothes," Mother reminded him, "and even if we hadn't, I'm not sure you'd get that kind." Lonnie scowled and left for school.

In English class, Lonnie's teacher introduced a unit on myths. "Myths are stories people made up to explain how certain things came to be," Mrs. Snowdon explained. "Can anyone give me an example of a myth?"

A girl raised her hand. "The Bible is a book of myths."

Mrs. Snowdon nodded. "Some people believe that," she said. "Others believe the stories in the Bible are true."

Lonnie was startled. *The Bible is the true Word of God,* he thought to himself. But he didn't say anything.

"We're going to read some Greek myths today," said Mrs. Snowdon. "Let's see what you think of them."

After reading aloud a story about how the world was made, one of the girls spoke up. "I can see why people believed this," she said. "It kinda makes sense." Several of the other students agreed.

That's ridiculous, Lonnie thought. *I know how things really came to be.* But when Mrs. Snowdon asked how many thought they could have once believed the story, Lonnie saw hands go up all around him. Slowly, he raised his, too.

That afternoon, Lonnie told his mother about the lesson.

"Did you speak up and tell the class what you know is true?" Mother asked.

"I thought about it," Lonnie said, "but I didn't want them to think I was weird."

Mother raised her eyebrows. "I don't know why you keep asking me to buy you a camouflage suit," she said. "It seems to me you're wearing one already."

"What?" asked Lonnie, looking at his blue jeans.

"You let yourself blend right in with the nonbelievers today," explained Mother. "It sounds like your true Christian identity was camouflaged rather well." *N.E.K.*

HOW ABOUT YOU?

Do you hide your Christian beliefs in order to blend with others, like the apostle Peter did? As a result, he "wept bitterly." Don't share that experience. Take off the camouflage and stand up for what you believe.

MEMORIZE:

"I will declare this forever; I will sing praise to the God of Jacob." *Psalm 75:9, NIV*

 Speak Up for Jesus

The Spark Plug (Read Psalm 37:16-23)

9

SEPTEMBER

One day the biggest, fanciest car Billy had ever seen pulled in at his dad's repair shop. Out climbed a man and a boy. "Hi, Kevin," Billy greeted the boy. "That your car?"

Kevin nodded. "Yep, it's ours," he said.

"It looks neat!" exclaimed Billy. "Is it fun to ride in?"

Kevin shrugged. "It's OK," he said. While their fathers talked about the work needed on the car, Billy tried to get Kevin to show him some of its special features, but Kevin didn't seem interested. A little later, Kevin's mother came in a different car to pick up Kevin and his father.

"Is Kevin a friend of yours?" asked Dad after they had left. "I haven't seen him around before."

"He's new at school," replied Billy, "and he's kind of different. I mean . . . he's smart and rich—his family seems to have a lot of money—but he never seems very happy about anything."

"Hmmmm." Dad stood up with a spark plug in his hand. "All that fancy equipment on this car," he said, "but Mr. Peters said it didn't have much spark. And no wonder; the spark plugs are bad." He shook his head. "Apparently Kevin has a lot going for him, but maybe he doesn't have any spark, either," he added.

Billy looked at his father suspiciously. "Oh, right! Kevin's dad should have left him here so you could give him some spark plugs, too, huh?" he asked with a grin.

Dad laughed. "Nope. I couldn't give him the spark he needs," he replied. "God is the spark that Kevin needs to be happy."

"Ohhh!" Billy began to see what Dad was getting at. "Now that you mention it, I don't think his family goes to church anywhere," said Billy thoughtfully. "I think I'll ask him to Sunday school."

"That's a great idea," approved Dad. "Perhaps at church—or perhaps through your witness—Kevin will see that he needs Jesus as his Savior. Then there will be some spark in his life, too." *D.K.*

HOW ABOUT YOU?

Have you learned that being smart or good-looking or having lots of money doesn't bring happiness? Do you have spark in your life—do you know Jesus as Savior? If not, trust him today.

MEMORIZE:

"Whoever trusts in the Lord, happy is he." *Proverbs 16:20, NKJV*

 Jesus Gives Real Joy

Granny's Helper (Read John 14:13-17, 25-27)

As Kevin looked out the window at the rain, he felt his life was just as dismal as the day. *Dad left home, and we don't know where he is,* he thought. *Now Mom is sick, and it's up to me to look after her and my two little sisters. But how can I do all that and run my paper route and go to school? I can't do it all alone.*

10

SEPTEMBER

Just then, the city bus pulled up to the corner and let off Granny Gresham, a nearby neighbor, and she had a big suitcase. The wind was so strong that Granny could scarcely take a step forward, and she bent way over as she tried to walk. Kevin hurriedly put on a raincoat and headed for the door. "I'm going to help Granny Gresham," he called to his mother.

When Kevin and Granny finally reached her door, she turned to him gratefully. "What would I have done without your help?" she said. "Would you like some cocoa?"

"No, I have to hurry home," replied Kevin. "Mom's sick."

"Oh, that's too bad," said Granny. "Now you remember—you don't ever have to face your problems alone, Kevin. I'm so grateful you came alongside to help me. And what you did is an example of what Jesus did for us. He sent the Holy Spirit to be our Comforter. The word means 'one sent alongside to help.' As a Christian, you can depend on the Holy Spirit to be right there, ready to take your burdens and give you the strength you need."

Kevin thought about that as he hurried home. "Heavenly Father," he prayed, "I turn my burdens over to you right now. Please help me take care of everything."

That night, Kevin received a phone call. It was Granny. "Will you carry my suitcase again?" she asked. "I'm coming to your house to help out until your mom is well." Kevin grinned. Why, he'd had a Helper with him all along. One who'd carry his burdens—as soon as he turned them over to him! *M.R.P.*

HOW ABOUT YOU?

Do you sometimes have so many problems you don't know how to handle them? If you're saved, you have a perfect helper—the Holy Spirit. He even understands your thoughts and has the power to solve every problem. Turn your problems over to him, and trust him to meet your needs.

MEMORIZE:

"Casting all your care upon Him, for He cares for you."

1 Peter 5:7, NKJV

 Give Your Problems to the Lord

The Nail and the Toothpick (Read Psalm 27:1-5, 14)

11

SEPTEMBER

The boys of Bay Street were at it again, cursing and telling dirty jokes. Andy stood there, hating it all, but saying nothing. "Didn't you get it?" asked one of the boys when Andy didn't laugh at his joke.

Andy swallowed hard. "I got it," he said. "It's late. I gotta go." He mumbled a good-bye and hurried away. *Why didn't I tell them to stop?* he thought. *And why did I hang around so long? It's sure hard to be the only Christian boy in the neighborhood.*

Running fast with his head down and his mind on his troubles, Andy didn't see Pastor Flint until he smacked right into him. "Oh, I'm sorry, Pastor!" he exclaimed.

"Where are you going in such a hurry?" asked the pastor.

"No place—just getting away from the guys. They're talking dirty," said Andy. "I should have said it wasn't right, but I didn't. It's really hard standing for the Lord all by yourself."

"Yes, it is," agreed Pastor Flint. He took a toothpick from his pocket. "You're like this toothpick. Here, try to break it." Andy broke the toothpick easily.

"Yeah, I'm like that," he agreed. "I'm the only Christian, and I'm not strong enough to say anything."

"But you're not alone," said the pastor, holding out a nail and another toothpick. "Now, can you break this toothpick with the nail alongside it?"

"Oh, no," answered Andy. "But who's the nail like? Dad? Or you? I'd feel much stronger with one of you around, but you're not always there."

"No," said Pastor Flint, "but Jesus is. Ask him to help. He's always there to give you strength to resist evil."

"That's my trouble—I haven't been depending on Jesus," Andy admitted, looking at the nail. "Say, Pastor, why do you have a nail in your pocket?"

"I brought it along to show this object lesson to Ralph," said Pastor Flint. "He's having trouble with those boys, too. You see, he thinks *he's* the only Christian boy in the neighborhood." *M.R.P.*

HOW ABOUT YOU?

Do you have trouble standing up for what's right? You can have the strength you need if you trust Jesus. With his help, you can find the courage to speak out against sin. And when you do, you may even discover there are other Christians around. You can encourage them to take a stand, too.

MEMORIZE:

"Strengthened with all power according to his glorious might." *Colossians 1:11, NIV*

 *Be Strong in the Lord*

Dynamite (Read 1 Corinthians 1:18-24)

Joshua and his father stood watching a tall, old building. Suddenly, with a *poof* the bricks of the huge building tumbled down like toy building blocks. They all fell right where the building had stood. "Wow!" exclaimed Joshua. "How did they make it do that?"

12
SEPTEMBER

"Well, the men who prepared the building for demolition knew how much dynamite to use and where to place it," answered Dad. He grinned at Joshua. "Seeing this reminds me of God's dynamite."

"God's dynamite?" asked Joshua. "What's that?"

"Let me explain with a story," replied Dad. "There was a boy who took his first drink of beer while in high school. Soon he was drinking regularly. In college he drank more and more and did many wicked things, until finally he was kicked out of school. Then he heard the gospel message from the Bible. He believed it and asked Jesus to save him. His life was completely changed, and he never drank again or did the other terrible things he had been doing. He graduated from college with honors." Dad stopped and looked at Joshua. "I was that young man," he added.

"You!" exclaimed Joshua. "It's hard to believe you were ever that bad."

"I'm not proud of it," said Dad, "but it's true. The wonderful part is that God changed me. The gospel is God's message about the Lord Jesus, who died on the cross for our sins and rose again. The Bible calls the gospel the 'power of God to salvation for everyone who believes.' It's the power—or dynamite—of God. When I believed it and received Jesus as my Savior, God blew to pieces all the awful sins of my old life. Then, just as they'll build a beautiful new building in the place of that old one, God gave me a new life. He's still working on me, making me what I ought to be as I yield him." *M.R.P.*

HOW ABOUT YOU?

Do you need a great change to take place in your life? If you will believe the gospel message and receive Christ as your Savior, God's dynamite—his power—will destroy the old, sinful life and build you a new life. Trust him today.

MEMORIZE:

"For I am not ashamed of the gospel of Christ, for it is the power of God to salvation for everyone who believes."

Romans 1:16, NKJV

 **Let God's Power Change You**

Chad's X Ray (Read Hebrews 4:12-16)

13

SEPTEMBER

Chad sat silently, his head pounding loudly. If only he had listened to his parents and stayed away from the construction site. "How did you say this happened?" Dr. Jones asked when he finished stitching up Chad's forehead.

"I was running home from school and tripped over a crack in the sidewalk," Chad explained, hoping his face wouldn't reveal the lie.

"Well, you'll be OK," said Dr. Jones. "But I do want you to get a skull X ray, just to be on the safe side."

Chad and his mother went to the hospital's X-ray department. Chad's head still throbbed. He rested it on Mom's lap and tried to relax. He wondered what it would be like getting an X ray of his head. Suddenly Chad sat straight up. "Will this X ray show my brain and all my thoughts?" he blurted out. As soon as he asked the question he knew it was a foolish one.

"Relax, Son," Mother said, chuckling. "Are you afraid it may show thoughts you don't want anyone to see?"

Chad put his head back down. He was glad the X ray couldn't show his thoughts. Then everyone would know how his head really got hurt. They'd find out he'd lied.

"I think you're next," Mother said, rubbing Chad's back.

"I'm sorry," Chad blurted. "I lied. I got hurt at the construction site."

"We'll talk about this later," Mother said with a firm, yet quiet voice. "Let's go with the nurse."

They did discuss Chad's problem later that night. "Never forget that God sees all our thoughts just like you imagined the X-ray machine might have shown yours, Chad," advised his Mother. "There's nothing we can hide from him." *N.E.K.*

HOW ABOUT YOU?

Do you have thoughts that you'd be afraid or ashamed for anyone else to know? Share them with God—he knows them already. Ask him to help you keep your thoughts honest and pure.

MEMORIZE:

"But Jesus, knowing their thoughts, said, 'Why do you think evil in your hearts?'"

Matthew 9:4, NKJV

 God Knows Your Thoughts

Storing Up Wisdom (Read Matthew 4:1-10)

"Can we take a break before we finish?" asked Shawn as he and his father raked leaves into a large pile.

"OK," agreed Dad. "Why don't you go get something for us to drink?"

14

SEPTEMBER

Shawn put down his rake, ran into the house, and soon came back with two cans of cola. He and Dad sat on the porch steps in the warm autumn sun, enjoying the cold sodas and talking together. They discussed the ball game they had watched on TV the night before and the Sunday school picnic to be held the next week. "By the way, have you finished memorizing your Bible verse for Sunday school tomorrow?" asked Dad.

"Well, no." Shawn sighed. "I don't see why we have to learn a verse every week. We recite them in class, and that's the end of it. Why bother when we'll probably never need them again?"

Dad sat quietly for a few moments sipping his pop. Then he pointed to a squirrel that was scurrying about and apparently burying acorns under the oak tree in a neighbor's yard. "Look, Shawn. Do you see what that squirrel is up to?" asked Dad.

Shawn nodded. "Yeah—he's storing his food for the winter, I guess."

"That's right," Dad replied. "And he's starting early. When the winter storms hit and he can't find food, those acorns will help him survive." Dad looked at Shawn. "You will also face storms in your life, Son," he added. "Sometimes you won't know what to do, and you'll need those verses you're storing up now. When Jesus lived on this earth, he faced temptations and trials, too. It was his knowledge of Scripture that protected him and helped him obey his heavenly Father. If he needed the Scriptures, we surely do, too."

A.L.

HOW ABOUT YOU?

Do you understand why memorizing Scripture is important? What if you were in trouble and didn't know what to do? Or suppose you were in a place where no Bibles were available? Would you be able to remember what the Bible says? Verses you learn now will help you in the future.

MEMORIZE:

"Your word I have hidden in my heart, that I might not sin against You." *Psalm 119:11, NKJV*

 Remember God's Word

A Big Friend (Read Judges 7:1-8, 21-22)

15

SEPTEMBER

Zac plopped down on the couch. "Oh, Dad, I'm sick of school," he complained. "You ought to hear those kids talk. They cuss and cut people down and tell filthy jokes. Then they call me a geek because I don't act like they do. I'd like to punch those guys in the nose!"

Dad had just begun to reply when they heard a loud snarl near the back door, followed by some sharp yips. *Arf-arf! Grrrowwwl! Yap-yap!* "That sounds like Cuddles," cried Zac, jumping to his feet. "It must be a dog fight." He ran out of the house, followed by his father. Cuddles, Zac's cocker, was on the bottom of the dog pile. "They're going to kill her!" Zac screamed.

Dad ran toward the garage. "I'll get the baseball bat."

Grrroowwl! An extra loud growl chilled the air as Pete, the neighbor's chow, jumped into the fight. Dogs scattered. "Look, Dad!" Zac yelled. "Pete is fighting Cuddles's battle."

The big dog stood protectively over the little one. Dad shook his head in amazement. When Zac knelt beside his whimpering puppy, Pete turned and walked proudly down the street. Zac chuckled. "You've got yourself some friend, Cuddles," he said.

Zac felt a hand on his shoulder. He looked up. "So do you, Son," said Dad. "You may be outnumbered at school—there may be a lot more unbelievers than believers, and they may pick on you. But you've got a Friend who makes up the difference, and that's Jesus."

Zac stood up with Cuddles in his arms. "Guess I do, don't' I?" he said. "Thanks, Dad, for reminding me." He started up the steps. "Sure helps to have a big friend, huh, Cuddles?" *B.W.*

 Let God Fight Your Battles

Alternate Life-styles (Read Romans 1:24-28, 32)

16
SEPTEMBER

"Gross!" exclaimed Doug. "They're holding hands!" He pointed out the bus window to two men walking down the street. The other children stared and giggled. Some stood up to see better.

"Sit down!" the bus driver said when the traffic light turned green. "Respect their rights!"

Soon they were at school and in their classroom. "We saw a couple of gays," the children told their teacher.. "It was so gross," added Doug.

"You may think their way of life is gross, but everyone has a right to personal preference," said Mrs. Bala. "Don't mock others for choosing an alternate life-style. Just because it isn't your choice, that doesn't mean it's wrong."

Doug was still thinking about what Mrs. Bala had said when recess time came. Could she be right? He shrugged and joined some of his friends. Out on the playground, they ran through the girls' game of four-square several times. When the girls complained to Mrs. Bala, the boys defended themselves. "We didn't hurt them any," they said. "It's our playground, too. We have a right to be there." But Mrs. Bala made them stay in during the next recess.

That evening Doug and his family shared the experiences of the day, and Doug sulked as he complained about having to stay in at recess. "We have our rights," he repeated.

"You may have rights, but what you did was still wrong," Mom told him. "You know it was."

Doug also told his parents about the men they had seen. "I thought it was gross, but Mrs. Bala said they have a right to be that way," he said. "Do they?"

"They have about as much right as you had to bother those girls," Mom said.

Dad nodded. "You were punished for exercising your so-called rights," he added, "and those who choose a life-style other than what God commands will also be judged for their sin. In the world's eyes, they may have a right to an alternate life-style, but not in God's eyes." *N.E.K.*

HOW ABOUT YOU?

Do you realize that people supporting "alternate life-styles" are really saying it's OK to sin? Life-styles that contradict God's commands are always wrong.

MEMORIZE:

"Therefore a man shall leave his father and mother and be joined to his wife, and they shall become one flesh."

Genesis 2:24, NKJV

 "Alternate Life-styles" Are Sin

Darkness and Light (Read Matthew 5:13-16)

Debbie stomped into the house, threw her books on the table, and plopped down in the nearest chair. "Oh, I just hate living here, Mom," she said. "I don't think there's a single girl in my class at school who goes to church and tries to live right except me. The other girls use bad language, and they talk about going places where I'd never go. I sure need a Christian friend."

17

SEPTEMBER

"If you can win some of those girls to Jesus, you'll have some Christian friends," said Mother. "Do they know you're a Christian?"

"I don't know. I haven't said anything," admitted Debbie. "If I do, I just know they'll make fun of me. Oh, it was so much easier to be a Christian back in our old town. Why didn't God just let us go on living there?"

"Debbie, will you please get my flashlight?" Mother asked. "I need your help." When Debbie brought the flashlight, Mother told her to turn it on. "We're going to the basement to replace a burned-out bulb," said Mother. "Come along."

As they started down, it was easy to see why they needed the flashlight. The basement was very dark. After Mother replaced the bulb, she said, "Debbie, where was that flashlight needed—in the kitchen or in the basement?"

"In the basement, of course," answered Debbie. "That's where it was dark."

"That's right," agreed Mom. "Honey, the Bible says that Christians are to let their lights shine. Our light is needed most in dark places, like this town where we live now."

Debbie thought a moment before replying. "I suppose you're right, Mom," she said with a sigh. "Maybe I'll go give Karen a call and invite her to come to church with me on Sunday." *M.R.P.*

HOW ABOUT YOU?

Is it hard for you to live like a Christian and speak up for Jesus because there are so many unsaved kids in your neighborhood and school? Then there is much spiritual darkness around you, isn't there? That's exactly where you need to let your light shine.

MEMORIZE:

"Let your light shine before men, that they may see your good deeds and praise your Father in heaven."

Matthew 5:16, NIV

 *Let Your Light Shine*

Making Biscuits (Read 1 Corinthians 12:12-22)

18
SEPTEMBER

"We had fun at school today," announced Lisa as she bounded up the steps and into the house. "Miss Summers took us to the kitchen and helped us make cinnamon biscuits. We ate them while they were warm. They were delicious! And so gooey!"

"Well, good," said Mother. "Maybe you could help me make some at home sometime."

Lisa nodded. "That would be even more fun," she said, "because I'd get to do more. At school we each put in one ingredient and everybody volunteered so fast that I was the last. There was nothing left to do but put in the baking powder. I pretended I didn't care, but I would have liked to do the gooey part."

"Hmmmm," murmured Mother. "How much baking powder did you put in?"

Lisa frowned. "Only two teaspoons," she said. "It was such a little bit. The flour and shortening were a lot more than that."

"Were the biscuits fluffy?" Mother asked.

"Oh, yes!" Lisa's eyes sparkled. "Miss Summers said they were as light as they could be."

Mother smiled. "Without the baking powder, they would have been flat and hard," she said.

Lisa looked surprised. "Was the baking powder really so important?" she asked, and Mother nodded. "Then the gooey part wasn't the most important?" Lisa asked. She found that hard to believe.

Mother laughed. "All the ingredients were important, but it was your baking powder that made the biscuits light and fluffy," she said. She gave Lisa a hug as she added, "There is an important lesson for us here. You see, people are something like recipe ingredients. Each of us has different gifts and talents, so we're all needed. If we all work together, God can accomplish much through us. What appears to us to be a very small talent is as important as that baking powder." *D.R.O.*

HOW ABOUT YOU?

Do you feel hurt if you don't get what appears to be the most important job? Do you say you won't help at all then? Don't make that mistake. Remember that your contribution is important to God. So work hard for him—do something good, even if nobody else knows about it.

MEMORIZE:

"Let us consider how we may spur one another on toward love and good deeds."

Hebrews 10:24, NIV

 Use Your Talents for God

Hilary Agrees (Read James 1:5-8)

19

SEPTEMBER

Hilary couldn't seem to make up her mind about Bible class. "I know what you mean, Jill," her mother heard her tell one friend. "Bible is the most boring class we have. You'd think a Christian school would know how to make it interesting." That same afternoon, when another friend exclaimed over how much she liked the class, Hilary agreed. "It's the greatest—I love it, too," she said. But talking on the phone that evening, Hilary seemed to have changed her mind again. "You're right," Mother heard her say, "Bible class can be a drag." Hilary ignored the surprised glance her mother gave her.

"Mom, may I go skating with Janet's youth group tomorrow?" Hilary asked when she hung up the phone.

"Sure," Mother said. "I think that's a nice idea."

"You might fall and break your neck," teased Uncle Tom, who was visiting. "I don't think you should go."

"Oh, right," said Mother. "Tell Janet you can't go."

"Sounds like fun to me," observed Hilary's sister, Holly.

"Well, OK," said Mother. "Go ahead, Hilary."

"Then I'll have to do the chores by myself," grumbled Todd, Hilary's brother.

"That's right," murmured Mother. "You'd better not go."

"Mom!" exclaimed Hilary. "Every time somebody gives an opinion, you change your mind. What does it matter what they think? Can I go or not?"

Mother smiled. "You can go," she said. "I just wanted you to see what it was like to have someone be so easily swayed by the opinions of others. You see, I noticed today that you seemed to change your mind about Bible class each time one of your friends voiced an opinion. It makes me wonder if you might be that easily influenced when it comes to your faith in God or your convictions regarding the way to live for Christ. You need to stand firm. Don't shift just to fit in or to win the approval of other people, honey. Don't let anyone persuade you to compromise or doubt your faith for any reason." *N.E.K.*

HOW ABOUT YOU?

Do you say the same things your friends say, thinking it's what they want to hear? Decide what you believe, based on the Word of God, and don't change just to be accepted by others. Stand firm for the things that please God.

MEMORIZE:

"Stand firm. Let nothing move you. Always give yourselves fully to the work of the Lord."

1 Corinthians 15:58, NIV

 Don't Be Easily Swayed

Gretchen's Gift (Read Matthew 25:14-29)

20

SEPTEMBER

"I don't want to, that's all," said Gretchen impatiently when Mother reminded her that God would be pleased if she used her musical talent for him. "Can I go play?" Mother nodded, and Gretchen jumped up. "C'mon, Fritz," she called to the dog. "Let's run outside." She was tired of people trying to persuade her to play her flute in church.

When Gretchen opened the back door, Fritz raced out into the yard. Then he ran back to Gretchen. He jumped up playfully before racing through the yard once again. Finally, he stopped near his favorite tree and sniffed the ground. "Come play," Gretchen called, picking up a ball. But Fritz dug into the ground with his front paws and nose. "Quit digging and come play," Gretchen called again, walking toward the dog. But Fritz had uncovered a bone, and he lay happily chewing on it. "Silly dog," said Gretchen. She sat on the ground beside him and stroked his back.

"Fritz dug up a bone and played with it today, and then he buried it again," Gretchen told her mother when she and Fritz went inside. "Why do dogs bury bones?"

"I'm not really sure," replied Mother.

"Well, you're silly, Fritz," Gretchen told her pet. "When I have something nice, I don't hide it."

"Are you sure of that?" Mother asked. "I know of one gift that you take out and play with for your own pleasure, but then you hide it away when you're done—like Fritz." Gretchen was puzzled. "I'm talking about your gift from God, your ability to play the flute so well," explained Mother.

Gretchen's face felt flushed. "That's different from what I meant about Fritz," she protested.

"Yes, it is," agreed Mother. "A dog's bone is not going to bless other people the way music from your flute will. We gave Fritz the bone for his own pleasure and to strengthen his teeth. But God gave you talent to use in serving and glorifying him. You are hiding something that God wants you to share." *N.E.K.*

HOW ABOUT YOU?

Do you have a talent or ability that is "buried," kept a secret? God blesses us with gifts to use for his glory. When we honor God with our talents, he will honor us in return. Use your talents for him.

MEMORIZE:

"No one lights a lamp and hides it in a jar or puts it under a bed. Instead, he puts it on a stand, so that those who come in can see the light." *Luke 8:16, NIV*

 Share Your Talents

Sun Catchers (Read 1 Peter 2:9-12)

21
SEPTEMBER

Dirt and sand blew against the kitchen windows, but inside the house, Andrea hummed happily as she and Mother finished a gift for Grandma. Andrea mixed red food coloring with white glue and poured it all into a round plastic lid. "I'm glad I learned how to make sun catchers like this in school," she said. "Grandma will like these when I put them in her window!" Andrea checked the circles of blue and green glue in two other lids to see if they had begun to harden.

"The sun catchers will help brighten Grandma's days in bed," agreed Mother with a smile. "I hope she'll soon be feeling better. Time seems to go slowly for a sick person."

"Grandma could watch television to pass the time," said Andrea, "but she says she'd rather read." Andrea sighed as she looked at her mother. "She sounds like you. She says there's not much on TV that's worth watching. But it would give her something to do, so why couldn't she just ignore the parts of the programs that are bad?"

As Mother checked the sun catchers, she looked thoughtful. "Let's open the windows so these will dry faster," she suggested.

"Oh, no!" cried Andrea. "It's too windy out. Dirt and dust would get on them and stick to them. Then the sunlight wouldn't shine through as well."

"You need to protect them and keep them clean, don't you?" said Mother. "And it's even more important to protect your life and your mind. You need to be careful about what comes in through your eyes and ears. Many TV programs, books, and magazines have words and pictures that might dim the light of God within your life, just as dirt and dust would dim these sun catchers."

Slowly Andrea nodded. She hadn't thought of her life as being like a sun catcher—something that should be kept shiny and clean. *B.M.*

HOW ABOUT YOU?

Are you careful about what comes through the windows of your eyes and ears? Remember, your life is beautiful only if you let God's love shine through it. Words, pictures, or activities that would dim the light are neither good for you nor pleasing to God.

MEMORIZE:

"They [unbelievers] may see your good deeds and glorify God on the day he visits us."

1 Peter 2:12, NIV

 Keep Your Life Clean

Current Issues (Read Psalm 31:13-21)

22
SEPTEMBER

John liked the current issue discussions his class held, but he was very timid about speaking out for what he believed. "What do you think about murder and capital punishment?" his teacher, Mr. Lanham, asked one day. Opinions flew back and forth. John wanted to share what he'd heard in a recent message on the subject, but he didn't quite dare.

That evening, John and his father shot a few baskets in the driveway before dinner. "When I approach the basket, your defense is strong," Dad said. "You work hard to keep me from scoring. But when you approach the basket to shoot, you shy away. You need to work on building your offense. Be determined." John nodded and set to work.

During dinner, John described how he felt during current issues class. "You know, it doesn't bother me to be different from the other kids in what I believe or do," he said. "I mean . . . I'm never tempted to go along with their thinking, but I don't dare to tell them what I think, either."

Dad nodded, "Like in basketball, you have a strong defense," he said. "It's backed up by Scripture and prayer against the attacks of the world and the devil. But now it's time to get out there with a strong offense, determined to score victories for Jesus."

The following day, Mr. Lanham presented the current issue topic of abortion. "Any input?" he asked.

John thought of Dad's words. "Help me, Father," he prayed quietly, then he raised his hand. "Yesterday we talked about murder," he said boldly to the class. "Everybody agreed that murder was not right and wanted murderers punished. Well, we're talking about the same topic today, because abortion is murder. People make up all kinds of excuses to say it isn't, but that doesn't change it. It's still wrong in God's sight."

Some students agreed with John, but others poked fun at him and called him a "religious freak." John felt hurt, yet he was glad he spoke up. He was determined to score points boldly for Jesus.

N.E.K.

HOW ABOUT YOU?

Do you keep quiet when people promote ungodly positions on issues? Develop a strong offense for God. Speak up for the truth in a controlled, respectable manner. It needs to be heard. Ask God to help you be bold for him.

MEMORIZE:

"**Do not let me be ashamed, O Lord, for I have called upon You.**" *Psalm 31:17, NKJV*

 Speak Boldly for God

The Discontented Puppy (Read 1 Timothy 6:6-11)

23

SEPTEMBER

Every day after school, Monty begged to go to Tyson's house. "But Monty," Mother protested one day, "why don't you invite Tyson over here for a change?"

"There's nothing to do here," Monty complained.

Mother blinked. "Nothing to do? Your room is full of games and toys."

"Yeah, silly baby stuff," grumbled Monty. "Tyson has a computer and a robot. He even has a swimming pool."

Mother looked sadly at Monty for several seconds, then silently left the room. She looked hurt, and Monty was puzzled. *Why should it hurt her that I want to go to Tyson's?* he wondered.

"Monty," Mother called from the living room, "Friskie is over at the Parkers' house again."

"That silly dog!" Monty exclaimed as he stalked across the street. "Why doesn't he stay home? He's always running off." Monty stopped and watched. The Parkers' little boy was rolling and tumbling on the ground with Friskie. "Friskie!" Monty snapped his fingers. "Come home!" The puppy tucked his tail between his legs and whined. "Come here!" Monty commanded. Friskie looked at the little Parker boy, then at Monty. He whimpered.

Monty frowned, ran over, and picked up the puppy. "Can he stay and play?" begged the little boy.

"No," growled Monty. "He has a nice home. He should apprec—" He gulped. Now he knew what had caused that hurt expression on his mother's face. Just as Monty felt a little hurt that Friskie didn't seem to appreciate the nice home and the good care Monty provided, Mother felt hurt that Monty didn't appreciate the love and care and all the good things his parents provided.

As Monty put Friskie down in the hall, he called to his mother. "I think I'll see if Tyson can come over," he said. *B.W.*

HOW ABOUT YOU?

Do you thank God for your family and for all they provide for you? Or do you compare what you have with what others have and then complain because they have more? Stop and count the blessings that are yours to enjoy. Thank your parents for all they do for you. And thank the Lord for your home and family.

MEMORIZE:

"Giving thanks always for all things to God the Father in the name of our Lord Jesus Christ."

Ephesians 5:20, NKJV

🔑 *Give Thanks for Your Home*

Paul Revere (Read Ezekiel 3:16-21)

24

SEPTEMBER

"The British are coming, the British are coming!" cried Steve as he spurred his horse past Uncle Dave and thundered through the pasture back toward the barn. Uncle Dave soon caught up, and together they walked the horses the rest of the way. Steve grinned as he dismounted and led his horse inside to rub him down. "In social studies we learned about Paul Revere's ride," he told his uncle. "Boy! I wish I could have lived back then. That must have been really exciting! I mean, think about it! Riding at night to warn people that the enemy was coming, always wondering if you'd get captured or not."

Uncle Dave slowly nodded his head. "But don't you think it sounds pretty scary?" he asked. "I wonder how many of us would have really dared to do it?"

"I would," boasted Steve. "After all, somebody had to warn them, or they would have been captured."

"Hmmmm, yes," murmured Uncle Dave thoughtfully, "but since I sometimes fail in my job to warn people now, I still wonder if I would have done it back then."

Steve looked doubtful. "Huh? Who do you have to warn?" he asked. "And about what?"

Rubbing down his horse as he talked, Uncle Dave explained. "God has given his children a mission to warn people that they are sinners and need to repent," he said. "If we don't warn them, they'll spend eternity in hell."

"Oh!" Steve was a little embarrassed by the turn in the conversation.

"Do you think Paul Revere worried about whether people would believe him or would laugh at him?" asked Uncle Dave. Steve shook his head. "We worry about such things, though, don't we?" continued Uncle Dave. Steve nodded. "We have a message far more important than Paul Revere's, yet we allow people to embarrass us into keeping quiet instead of delivering the message God gave us."

J.B.

HOW ABOUT YOU?

How are you doing as a 'Paul Revere' for the Lord? God told Ezekiel to give a warning; apply those words to your life as well. Warn others of their need to accept Christ as Savior.

MEMORIZE:

"Hear the word I [God] speak and give them warning from me." *Ezekiel 3:17, NIV*

 Warn the Unsaved

The Birthday Gift (Read John 3:16; 10:25-30)

It had been a happy day for Tommy. He had spent the afternoon at his friend Jeff's birthday party. "Jeff really liked the truck I gave him," Tommy told his mother when she came to tuck him into bed that night.

25

SEPTEMBER

"Good," said Mother with a smile. "Now you need to settle down. It's time to pray and go to sleep."

As Mother turned down the covers, Tommy looked up with a puzzled expression. "Mom, how do you know for sure if you're really saved? I asked Jesus to be my Savior last spring, but sometimes I still wonder about it."

"Do you understand that Jesus died for your sins, and that you can't save yourself?" asked Mother with concern.

Tommy nodded. "Sure, I know all about that. But I still sin sometimes."

Mother picked up Tommy's Bible from the dresser. "Remember that truck you gave Jeff at the party today?" she asked. Tommy nodded. "Did you bring it home again when the party was over?" asked Mother.

"No. I gave it to Jeff," replied Tommy. "It's his."

"What if he's mean to you tomorrow?" asked Mother. "Then will you take the truck back?"

"Of course not!" said Tommy. "It belongs to Jeff now, not to me."

Mother nodded. "That's right, Son," she said, handing him his Bible and pointing to some verses. "Read this Bible passage to me." Tommy did so. (See today's Scripture.)

"God gave you the gift of eternal life when you asked Jesus to come into your heart," Mother said when Tommy finished reading. "You didn't earn it, just as Jeff didn't do anything to earn the truck you gave him. You gave it to him and he accepted it. And just as you gave it to him to keep, God gave you eternal life to keep. He doesn't take back his gift, either."

"Whew!" Tommy sighed with relief. "I'm glad I don't have to worry about that anymore." *D.F.*

HOW ABOUT YOU?

Do you sometimes have doubts that you belong to Jesus? If you really meant it when you accepted Jesus and asked him to forgive your sins, you are a Christian. God's gift of eternal life is yours. He won't ever take it back. Once you belong to Jesus, you will always belong to him.

MEMORIZE:

"I give them eternal life, and they shall never perish; no one can snatch them out of my hand." *John 10:28, NIV*

 **Salvation Is Forever**

The Right Fight (Read Psalm 76)

Mother knew something was wrong as soon as she saw Jeremy and Todd coming around the corner on their way home from school. She flung open the door. "Jeremy, your new jacket is all torn!" she cried, "and your lunch box is cracked! What happened?"

26
SEPTEMBER

"Some big boys grabbed my lunch box and tried to beat me up," wailed Jeremy. "But then Todd came along and made them stop. They tried to hit him, too, but he was bigger than them, and he chased them away."

Todd unzipped his jacket. "I didn't want to fight, Mom," he said, "but I had to because they were hurting Jeremy. I tried to tell them to stop, but they wouldn't listen. Sometimes you have to do things even if you don't want to."

Mother nodded as she helped Jeremy out of his tattered clothes. "Jeremy, last night you asked why there had to be war," she reminded him. "We know war is bad, but just as your brother had to fight against those boys who were hurting you, so our country must fight evil when others are being hurt. Todd fought because he loves you; our soldiers fight because they love our country. But do you know God is able to bring good out of anything—even a war?"

"Really?" asked Todd. "Where does it say that in the Bible?"

"Psalm 76:10 says that the 'wrath of man' will praise God," answered Mother as she gathered the torn clothes and headed for the sewing machine. "And Romans 8:28 says that 'all things work together for good to those who love God.' War often makes people think about God and realize how much they need him. That's good."

Todd nodded slowly. "I'm sure glad I live in a free country that stands for right," he said.

"Yeah," agreed Jeremy, "and I'm glad I have a big brother to fight for me!" *L.A.T.*

HOW ABOUT YOU?

Do you love your country's flag and respect its government? Are you glad for the freedom that allows you to go to the church of your choice and to study your Bible? Thank God for the freedom you enjoy and pray for your nation's leaders. Think of ways you can show your love today to your God and your country.

MEMORIZE:

"Surely the wrath of man shall praise You." *Psalm 76:10, NKJV*

 Love God and Country

Big Deal? (Read Psalm 51:1-13)

27

SEPTEMBER

"Oh, look, Tracy, a bargain rack!" exclaimed Barbara. "I'm glad Mom said I could choose my own dress. Maybe I'll find something here."

"Be careful," warned her older sister. "Did you see this?" She pointed to some small lettering on a sign above the rack. "Slightly stained—greatly reduced in price. All sales final," she read. She looked at Barbara. "You'd better look them over good."

"I will," Barbara assured her. "*Oh!* This one is just what I want for the church banquet." But sure enough, there was a small spot right on the front of the skirt. "I'll wash it out," declared Barbara. "No big deal."

Barbara bought the dress, but after two washings, the spot remained. "Good thing I didn't pay much for it," she said with a groan.

Mother nodded. "It sure is," she agreed. Then she frowned. "I saw Sandy at the store today," she added. "She said you told her there'd be no room in our car for her to ride to the banquet. Why did you tell her that? We'll have plenty of room."

"But Linda's coming with me, and we don't really want Sandy to go with us," mumbled Barbara. "It's no big deal."

Mother sighed. "Like the spot in your new dress?" she asked. "That small spot greatly reduced the value of the dress. That can happen to a Christian's testimony, too."

"What do you mean?" asked Barbara.

"Maybe what you told Sandy was no big deal to you. You might consider it only a little lie, only a small stain," said Mother. "But when Sandy finds out you lied, your Christian testimony with her will be greatly reduced. Do you think this will help her want to become a Christian?"

Barbara hung her head. She knew Mother was right. "It's not too late to do something about it," added Mother. "Why not call Sandy and tell her she can ride along with us?" Barbara nodded and headed for the phone. *M.R.P.*

HOW ABOUT YOU?

Even a small sin can greatly reduce your worth as a Christian in the eyes of others. You can't get that spot out yourself, but the blood of Jesus will wash it clean when you confess your sin to him. If you wronged someone else, be sure to make things right with that person, too.

MEMORIZE:

"**Make every effort to be found spotless, blameless and at peace with him.**" *2 Peter 3:14, NIV*

Sin Spots Your Testimony

The "Borrowed" Book (Read 1 Timothy 4:11-16)

Oh, no, Brett thought as he looked at the school library clock. *My time is up, and I haven't copied all the information I need from this book. I can't check it out because I haven't paid my fine from last week.* Brett's paper on the history of airplanes was due the next day. "I'll just take this book out to the study hall and bring it back when the bell rings," he decided. Mrs. Martinez, the librarian, was busy helping another student and didn't notice Brett as he left the room.

28
SEPTEMBER

In the study hall, Brett took his seat behind his friend, Craig. Brett worked swiftly, copying data about the Wright brothers and other flight pioneers. When Mr. Jordan, the teacher, went to the door to talk with the principal, Craig turned around and quickly took the book from Brett's desk. "Hey, I need that for my report," Brett whispered.

Craig opened the cover of the book and noticed that the library card was still in it. "I see you Christians steal books just like everybody else," he taunted.

"I didn't steal it. I just borrowed it until the bell," protested Brett. But he felt guilty. He had been inviting Craig to Sunday school, and now it was obvious what Craig was thinking.

"Well, I'll just borrow it from you then," said Craig with a smirk. Brett grabbed for the book. As he tried to pull it away from Craig's grasp, he realized that Mr. Jordan was standing beside them.

A few minutes later, Brett found himself being marched in to see the librarian. "Mrs. Martinez," said Mr. Jordan, "your books are so popular the students fight over them. Brett has something he wants to say."

Brett explained what he had done. "I didn't mean to steal it," he said, "but I can see that it amounted to the same thing since I knew I wouldn't be allowed to take it if I asked." He placed the book on the charge desk. "I'm sorry for what I did, and I'm ready to accept my penalty." *R.M.*

HOW ABOUT YOU?

Have you "borrowed" something without permission? At worst, that's stealing. At best, it's a poor example to others. If you've taken something that way and haven't returned it, be sure to do so right away. Then ask God to help you resist the temptation of "borrowing" without permission.

MEMORIZE:

"The wicked borrows and does not repay." *Psalm 37:21, NKJV*

 Don't "Borrow" without Permission

An Important Test (Read 1 Peter 5:6-11)

29
SEPTEMBER

Judy was in her room, trying to concentrate on her math lesson when her mother appeared in the doorway. "Hi, Mom," Judy greeted her with a sigh. "We're having a test tomorrow, and I can't seem to study—my mind is somewhere else. I've been like this ever since Dad left."

"I understand, honey. I miss him, too." Mother said. "Now that he's gone, we tend to forget your father's drinking problem and how he was always losing his temper and yelling at us. We weren't happy then, either, you know."

"I know," replied Judy. A tear slid down her cheek. "It makes me mad every time I think about how he treated us. Sometimes I think I hate Dad." She slammed her book shut. "Oh, Mom, I'm so mixed up—sometimes hating, sometimes loving. I'm miserable." Mother pulled up a chair and sat down, taking Judy's hands in hers. "Mom, why didn't God answer our prayers?" asked Judy. "Didn't we pray enough? Is it our fault Dad is still drinking and living with that woman?"

Mother shook her head. "No, Judy. We mustn't blame ourselves; we did all we could do. And we mustn't blame God, either. He wanted to answer our prayers, but when a person is determined to go his own way, God allows him to do it."

"But what about us?" cried Judy sadly. "Doesn't God care about us?"

"Judy, dear, the same God who gave his Son to die for us loves us just as much now as he always has," Mother replied. "I know it's hard, but just as we trusted Jesus to save us from our sins, we can trust him now to take care of us. Remember 1 Peter 5:7?"

Judy nodded. "'Cast all your anxiety on him because he cares for you'" [*NIV*], she quoted slowly. She sighed. "I'll try to remember that God cares, Mom. Then maybe I can settle down and study."

Mother nodded. "Passing the test of remembering God's promise is just as important as passing that math test tomorrow," she said. "And I think if you can manage the first, you'll manage the other also." *M.S.*

HOW ABOUT YOU?

Do you worry so much about a problem in your life that you forget how much God cares for you? Jesus wants to give you his joy and peace.

MEMORIZE:

"If God is for us, who can be against us?" *Romans 8:31, NIV*

 Jesus Cares for You

Robins on the Net (Read Matthew 6:25-34)

Eric washed the last plate and handed it to his mother to dry. Then he turned to look out the window. It had rained all morning, but now in the early afternoon the sun was shining brightly. The leaves on the big tree by the fence were golden and seemed to glow in the sunlight. *If only those leaves could be turned into real gold,* Eric thought, *Mom and I could solve all our problems.* He sighed. He couldn't help feeling worried since his mother had lost her job last week. Ever since Eric's father had died two years ago, it had been hard for them to manage. Now it would be even harder. Turning toward his mother, he asked, "What are we going to do about money, Mom?"

30
SEPTEMBER

"Don't you worry about that," said Mother. "I've been able to save a little, Eric, and I'll find another job soon. There are lots of jobs for computer operators." As she came to stand beside him at the window, three robins swooped down and perched on the badminton net in the backyard. Together Eric and his mother watched as the net sagged and swayed under the weight of the birds. Soon the thin metal poles that supported the net became uprooted, and everything crashed to the ground. Eric and Mom smiled in amusement as the frightened robins flew away.

"You know, Eric," said Mom, "money and material things are like that flimsy net. When we count on them to hold us up in times of trouble, they always fail. God never does, though. I'm thinking of a verse you learned in Vacation Bible School this summer, the one about the birds. Do you remember it?"

Eric nodded. "That's Matthew 6:26," he said. "'Look at the birds of the air, for they neither sow nor reap nor gather into barns; yet your heavenly Father feeds them. Are you not of more value than they?'" [NKJV]

"Very good," said Mom, giving Eric a big hug. "God will provide for our needs. We can be sure of that." *D.R.K.*

HOW ABOUT YOU?

Are you worried about your family not having enough money? Are you afraid because one of your parents is out of work? Pray that God will provide another job soon. Then trust God—not a job—to provide for your needs.

MEMORIZE:

"My God shall supply all your need according to His riches in glory by Christ Jesus."

Philippians 4:19, NKJV

God Supplies Your Needs

A Heavy Load (Read Matthew 11:28-30)

1

OCTOBER

Betty kicked some stones as she walked home from school. For some time she had lived with an ugly secret—something she wished had never happened. No one knew, except Uncle Ed, and he had warned her not to tell anyone. "But I must tell Mom," Betty decided finally. So when she got home, she said timidly, "Mom, I need to talk to you."

"Sure, honey," said her mother. They sat down on the sofa together. "What's the matter?"

"This is not going to be easy for me to talk about, Mom. I've been putting it off," said Betty with a slight tremble in her voice. "It's so terrible."

"Honey, if you've done something wrong, you can ask God to forgive you and he will. He loves you, no matter what you've done, and so do I," Mother assured her.

Betty dropped her head as she told her mother how dirty she'd felt ever since Uncle Ed visited the family that summer. "On the last night he was here, he came into my room in the night, and . . . Oh, Mom! It's so awful. I don't think I can say it."

Mother's face was grim, but she put her arm around Betty. "I think I know what happened, honey, and it makes me very angry— but not with you," she said. "I know it wasn't your fault."

Betty looked up at her mother. "You do? Uncle Ed warned me never to tell. I . . . I talked to Jesus about it, and that helped, but I needed to talk to you, too, Mom."

"You did the right thing in telling me. The Lord didn't want you to carry this burden alone," said Mother as she gave Betty a hug. "We'll talk to the Lord about this together. With his help, we'll work through the difficult times that may yet be ahead of you." She paused, then added firmly, "Uncle Ed will be dealt with, too. Only a person with a sick mind would act as he did. Maybe it will help us both to remember that." *M.S.*

HOW ABOUT YOU?

Has something happened that you need to discuss with someone? Do you feel guilty? Or upset? Or unclean? You can talk it over with Jesus. You will do well to talk also with someone else—one or both of your parents or a Christian friend. Don't wait. God wants you to take care of it today.

MEMORIZE:

"Come to me, all you who are weary and burdened, and I will give you rest." *Matthew 11:28, NIV*

 Tell Someone about Your Troubles

Mount Trashmore (Read Psalm 24:1-6)

It was the day before garbage pick-up, and Dad was helping Jimmy with his chores. "I hate this job," said Jimmy as he put the clean cans in one container and the clean plastic bottles in another.

"It would be easier if you wouldn't let things pile up for a whole week," replied Dad.

2

OCTOBER

"I liked it better when we just threw everything into one big plastic bag," grumbled Jimmy.

"Well, if we don't recycle what we can, there soon won't be any more room in the landfills," Dad told him.

Jimmy nodded. "I know," he said. "Our school bus goes past a landfill every day. There's a big mountain of garbage. The kids on the bus call it Mount Trashmore!"

Dad pointed to a brown paper bag. "What's that stuff over there?"

"Oh, those are things I wasn't sure how to sort," Jimmy mumbled, "but I'll figure it out."

"Let's see," said Dad. "Hmmmm. Records, some tapes, and magazines. Whoa! These magazines really are trash! Have you been reading these?"

"Some of the guys gave them to me," replied Jimmy. He was embarrassed.

"Do you enjoy these things?" asked Dad.

"At first I thought it was pretty grown-up to read them," admitted Jimmy, "but then I didn't like what I kept thinking about. I'm throwing the stuff out, and I'm not taking any more."

"I'm glad," said Dad. "Things such as this could cause your mind and heart to become so full of trash it would crowd out God."

H.A.D.

HOW ABOUT YOU?

Have you thrown out all the trash in your life? Make sure your books, magazines, tapes, and television programs are not the wrong kind. Ask God to tell you what to get rid of. He'll guide you as you pray and read the Bible. Don't build up a "Mount Trashmore" in your life.

MEMORIZE:

"Let us cleanse ourselves from all filthiness of the flesh and spirit, perfecting holiness in the fear of God."

2 Corinthians 7:1, NKJV

 Keep Your Mind Pure

Essential Attire (Read Ephesians 6:13-18)

3

OCTOBER

Emily flipped through a catalog with mild interest. Suddenly an outfit seemed to leap from the page at her. "Mother, look," she said as she pointed to her new discovery. "Can't you just see me in this outfit?"

"Why, yes, I can," said Mother, "and you do need a new outfit. Why don't we order it?"

"Oh, could we? Really?" Emily's eyes shone.

Mother helped Emily fill out the order blank; then she wrote out a check. Emily put a stamp on the envelope and took it out to the mail box on their street.

"I think you should also get a belt for your outfit, Emily," said Mother when Emily got back.

"You do?" asked Emily doubtfully. "I don't think it really needs one, and I already mailed the order." But she picked up the catalog and began looking for belts.

"You're looking in the wrong book for the belt you need," said Mother. She opened a Bible to Ephesians chapter six and handed it to Emily. "The belt you need is found in verse 14."

Emily didn't understand what Mom was getting at, but she read the verse anyway.

"Were you wearing the 'belt of truth' when you told me the bus was late yesterday?" asked Mother.

Emily dropped her eyes and blushed. "No, but Linda asked me to stop at her house," she whined. "I didn't want to tell her no, but I was afraid you'd be mad at me for not asking permission."

"I would have been disappointed," agreed Mother, "but I was far more disappointed when I talked to Linda's mother and she said you and Linda had baked cookies yesterday."

Emily nervously leafed through the catalog. She felt awful. Telling a lie had brought more complications than she had figured on. "I'm sorry, Mother," she said. Her eyes fell on the picture of the outfit she had ordered. "I'll wear the belt of truth from now on, I promise," she added. "My new outfit will remind me." *E.M.B.*

HOW ABOUT YOU?

Do you find it hard to tell the truth in some circumstances? The truth may get you into trouble, but lying will get you into even more trouble. It helps to pray sincerely each morning, "Lord, help me be honest and say only truthful things today."

MEMORIZE:

"The Lord detests lying lips, but he delights in men who are truthful." *Proverbs 12:22, NIV*

Wear the "Belt of Truth"

A Gift for Mrs. Morgan (Read John 15:9-12)

4

OCTOBER

Angela thought about her problem as she walked home from school. Fifty cents was all the money she had left, and that would not buy much of a gift for her sick friend and neighbor, Mrs. Morgan. Angela passed Mrs. Morgan's house. It was just the kind of day her friend liked—cool air and lots of bright sunshine. Angela hoped Mrs. Morgan had a window in her hospital room.

When Angela's father came home that evening, she was still thinking about her problem. "A penny for your thoughts," Dad said, so Angela told him about it. "I could give you some money," suggested Dad.

"But then it wouldn't really be from me," Angela protested. "I want to buy a gift with my own money."

"How about an advance on your allowance?" asked her father.

Angela hesitated. "I'd rather earn some money," she said, "but Mrs. Morgan is the only one who ever hires me to help her."

Dad smiled. "You realize, Angela, that there are many ways of giving," he said. "Your gift to Mrs. Morgan doesn't have to be purchased. The apostle Paul tells us to 'bear one another's burdens.' What do you think that means?"

Angela thought for a moment. "I think it means we should help others when they're going through hard times," she said.

"That's right," agreed her father. "Maybe your gift to Mrs. Morgan could be something that will show her that, in a small way, you're sharing in her troubles." He playfully tousled Angela's hair as he went out to the garage.

"Bear one another's burdens," Angela said to herself. Yes, she could imagine a little of what Mrs. Morgan must be going through now. She was a widow with no family living close by. Who would water her houseplants and weed her flower garden? Angela made up her mind. She would do those things! Wasn't this the kind of gift Dad was hinting at? Angela decided she would do all she could to help Mrs. Morgan while she was sick. She would give of herself.

D.R.K.

HOW ABOUT YOU?

Do you know someone who is sick and needs help? Maybe you can rake the leaves, shovel snow, or run errands. Whatever you decide to do will cheer your friend. It will please God, too.

MEMORIZE:

"Bear one another's burdens, and so fulfill the law of Christ."

Galatians 6:2, NKJV

 Help Others through Hard Times

The Right Source (Read Ephesians 5:1-8)

5

OCTOBER

Steve watched as his father worked on the car. "I hear you've been increasing your vocabulary," came Dad's muffled voice from beneath the hood. Steve felt a nervous quiver in his stomach, and he got busy searching in the tool box as Dad straightened up. "Coach Roberts tells me you've begun joining in the locker room conversation a bit more freely. As a Christian and a member of our church, he thought I should know about it."

Steve shrugged. "Well, you said yourself I was old enough to know more about girls and stuff like that."

Dad nodded. "I see." He looked at the spark plugs he held. "Run and get the owner's manual—that big book with the plaid cover. It's in the kitchen." Steve hurried away, surprised but glad his father had changed the subject. When he returned, he handed his dad the book. Dad began flipping through the pages. He smiled; then he laughed out loud. "I don't think I'll get much help from this book! It's your mother's cookbook, not the owner's manual," he said.

Steve laughed, too. "There were two books on the cupboard, and the covers are a lot alike." He went back to get the right one.

When Steve returned, Dad took the book. "It makes sense to get your information from the right source, doesn't it?" he said. "You wouldn't look in the cookbook for car repair information, or ask Miss White, the English teacher, for suggestions on skateboarding." Dad leafed through the manual. "You know," he added, "information about the relationships between men and women are a lot more important than a smooth-running car. Be careful about where you get information on that subject. Your friends may seem to know a lot, but for something this important, you need the best source of information you can get—God's Word and your own family." *C.R.*

HOW ABOUT YOU?

Do your friends try to impress one another with what they think they know about the opposite sex? Does listening to them seem more exciting than asking your parents? To prepare for the kind of marriage and home that is rewarding and lasting, get your information only from the proper source.

MEMORIZE:

"Let no one deceive you with empty words, for because of such things God's wrath comes on those who are disobedient."

Ephesians 5:6, NIV

 **Get Correct Information**

Old and Wrinkled (Read Psalm 71:9-15, 23-24)

"I sure had an interesting day at school today," Andrew told his mother, who was busy cleaning the refrigerator.

"Really?" asked Mother. "What did you do today?"

"We had a talk about euthanasia," said Andrew. "I thought euthanasia was some kids' group in China."

Mother laughed. "Tell me more about this talk."

"Well, Miss Grant, my teacher, asked what we should do about old people in our country," explained Andrew. "She said the cost of keeping all those people in nursing homes is getting to be a real problem. She wants us to write about what we think should be done. She did say that some people think we should stop paying for their care. They say we should put them to sleep with a drug—she called it mercy killing—when they get old and useless. That's what euthanasia is."

6
OCTOBER

"And what are you going to write?" Mother asked.

"I don't know," replied Andrew. "I think it's wrong but the people in favor of euthanasia say the old people don't want to live."

Mother thought a moment as she wiped the refrigerator shelf. Then she took out an orange from the refrigerator and held it out to Andrew. "Before you write that paper, have a little snack," she suggested. "Try this orange."

"Mother!" Andrew exclaimed. "How long has this been in there? Five years? It's old and brown and wrinkled!"

"Cut it open," suggested Mother.

Andrew obeyed, and to his surprise, the orange was juicy and tasted sweet. "Oh, this is really good!" he said.

"Right," Mother replied, "but you almost threw it away. You'd have missed a real treat."

"Mom, are you trying to tell me something with this orange?" asked Andrew suspiciously.

"When you write your paper, I just want you to remember that 'old' does not mean 'useless,'" said Mother. "Even a person who seems to be useless is valuable to God and can give us the chance to practice kindness and gentle, loving care. And God will reward us for it." *S.N.*

HOW ABOUT YOU?

Have you heard people talking about euthanasia, or mercy killing? That is murder. Remember that all human life is special to God.

MEMORIZE:

"You shall not murder."

Exodus 20:13, NKJV

 Protect the Elderly

Every Other Weekend (Read 1 Timothy 6:6-8; James 1:2-4)

7

OCTOBER

"I don't feel like going home today," Tim told his friend Brett. He kicked a stone on the pavement. "Nothing's going my way. I want to live with my dad, but it's been decided that we kids have to stay with Mom."

"So that's the problem," said Brett.

"Problem? It's a crisis!" cried Tim. "Dad always took time to do stuff with me. Y'know, guy stuff. Now I'll get to be with him only every other weekend."

"Well, you can talk to him on the phone, too, can't you?" asked Brett. "You still have a lot to be thankful for."

Tim noticed Brett's eyes were bright—were those tears? Suddenly he remembered that ever since he met Brett at the beginning of the school year, he had never seen or heard anything about Brett's father. "Does your dad live with you?" Tim asked.

Brett shook his head. "My dad died," he said softly.

"Oh," said Tim, not sure what else to say. "Sorry." Tim and Brett walked quietly. "How do you survive without ever seeing your dad?" Tim asked finally.

"It's not easy," Brett said, "but one day when I was trying to make a guitar with rubber bands and a long box, Mom helped me understand how she deals with it. Some rubber bands stretched and fit over my box easily, but others were tight and pulled out thin in order to get around the cardboard. A few even snapped," added Brett. He was still silent, remembering.

"What does that have to do with making it without your dad?" Tim asked.

"The ones that fit super-tight made the best music on my new guitar. And Mom said that as things happen in life, we're stretched, too—like those smaller rubber bands," explained Brett. "We may be uncomfortable, but we can choose to be content and make music, even during the hard times of our lives; or we can give up and snap and be useless. Mom and I decided to trust God to use this hard part of our lives for his good." *N.E.K.*

HOW ABOUT YOU?

Have things happened in your life that are hard to accept? God wants you to be content in all circumstances. With God's help, decide that you'll accept what he has allowed so that even your attitude may be a testimony for him.

MEMORIZE:

"Not that I speak in regard to need, for I have learned in whatever state I am, to be content." *Philippians 4:11, NKJV*

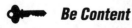 **Be Content**

Robert's Robot (Read Ephesians 3:16-21; 4:1-3)

8

OCTOBER

Robert watched proudly as his toy robot marched around the room. It was made of clear plastic, and Robert could see the working parts and flashing lights inside the robot's body.

"My robot's bigger than yours, Robert!" said his sister, Tonya. "It's prettier—it shines like gold, and you can't see all the ugly parts inside."

"Well, robots don't have to look pretty," argued Robert. "I bet mine can go faster than yours."

The children had begun a robot race when the lights went out. "What happened?" asked Tonya, trying not to sound worried.

"It must be the storm," said Robert. "I wish Mom and Dad were home. Let's go downstairs." They headed toward the door, but in the hall it was too dark to see. "Wait a minute," Robert said. Turning back, he managed to find his robot. He turned on the switch. The lights began to flash, and soon the children were downstairs, guided by the robot.

A little later, they saw car lights in their drive, and then Mom and Dad followed the beam of a flashlight into the living room. "Are we ever glad to see you!" exclaimed Tonya. "It was spooky alone here in the dark!"

"My robot helped, though," added Robert. He proudly demonstrated how his robot had saved the day. "Tonya was bragging about her big, shiny robot, but it was my ugly see-through one that gave us light," he said.

Mom chuckled. Then she said soberly, "Your robots remind me of Christians. There are those who appear to be big and important and attractive, but they don't let God's love shine out, and they don't seem to have much inner strength. When the going gets tough, they aren't good for much. Others may not look so good, but they're strong on the inside. You can always count on them! And you can plainly see the light of Jesus shining in their lives."

"That's right," said Dad. "That's the way Christians should be. They're filled with God's love and his Holy Spirit, and it should show." *J.L.*

HOW ABOUT YOU?

Are you the kind of Christian described in today's Scripture reading? What you look like on the outside is not nearly so important as what you're like inside—that's what God cares about. When you live as he wants you to, his light will shine out through your life.

MEMORIZE:

"Let your light shine before men, that they may see your good deeds and praise your Father in heaven."

Matthew 5:16, NIV

 Shine for Jesus

Two Mirrors (Read James 1:22-25)

"Don't forget to wash your face and comb your hair," said Mom when Joel got up from the breakfast table. "There's jam on your cheek, and your hair looks like you just got out of bed."

"OK," agreed Joel. When he got to his room, he looked at himself in his dresser mirror and saw that Mom was right. But by the time he found his books, he had forgotten about how he looked. Out the door he went, with his face dirty and his hair uncombed.

9
OCTOBER

When Joel arrived home after school that day, he found his sister, Claire, talking to Mother in the kitchen. "You should have seen Joel at school this morning," Claire told Mother. "He was a mess! His face was dirty, and I don't think he even combed his hair. My friends laughed at him and called him 'Sloppy Joel.' I was embarrassed!" She made a face at Joel.

"Well, I went and washed my face right after recess," Joel defended himself. "Combed my hair, too. So there!" He noticed Mother's frown. "I saw myself in the mirror before I left for school, but I forgot," he confessed. "From now on I'll be sure to clean up and comb my hair right away when I see I need it."

At family devotions that night, Dad announced, "Checkup time! We've been talking this week about the importance of Bible reading and prayer in our daily lives, and we all agreed that the verses we read convicted us about our need to be more faithful in those areas. So, Joel, how have you been doing with your personal, daily devotions?"

Joel blushed. "I still forget most of the time," he admitted.

"The Bible is like a mirror," said Mom. "It reveals our sins and shortcomings. But we must not only see what these are, we must do something about changing them—just as you should have washed your face and combed your hair right after looking in your mirror this morning."

"That's right," said Dad. "We must not only hear God's Word, but *do* it as well." *M.R.P.*

HOW ABOUT YOU?

Do you look into the mirror of God's Word each day? That's the way to see whether you're pleasing God. When you see things in your life that need correcting, take care of them at once, before you forget what they are.

MEMORIZE:

"To him who knows to do good and does not do it, to him it is sin." *James 4:17, NKJV*

Hear and Do God's Word

Laura's Accent (Read Romans 12:3-5, 10)

When Amy walked into her classroom one morning, there was a new girl sitting at the desk next to hers. Miss Taylor introduced her to the class. "This is Laura Dawson. Her family moved here just last week," she said, smiling encouragingly at the brown-haired girl who sat twisting her hands on the desk top. "She used to live about 500 miles from here, isn't that right, Laura?"

10

OCTOBER

Laura looked at her hands as she nodded. "Reckon so." Her words sent a giggle rippling across the classroom.

This should make school a whole lot more interesting! thought Amy. Leaning over, she whispered, "Hi. I'm Amy. If I can help you with anything, let me know, OK?"

"Shore thang," came Laura's soft answer.

That evening at the dinner table, Amy laughingly reported the story of the newcomer, imitating Laura's accent. "Laura didn't want to move here at first," Amy told them. "She said she 'bagged' her folks to just stay where they were." Amy went on, using several more of the words Laura pronounced in a different way.

"Bring her home sometime, Amy! Sounds like she'd be more fun than a barrel of monkeys," joked Jason.

Dad spoke up. "Did it ever occur to you that our way of speaking would sound funny in some parts of the country?" he asked. "Like in Laura's hometown?" He looked at them sternly. "If you're thinking of bringing Laura home just to laugh at her way of speaking, you'd better think again. Remember that God is no 'respecter of persons.' That means he doesn't consider one person better than another because of his money, clothes, accent, or anything else. And we shouldn't, either."

Amy's face turned pink. "Sorry, Dad," she said. "I thought it was funny, but I didn't intend to be mean. I really do want to be Laura's friend."

"That's my girl," her father said approvingly, "but be very careful. What seems funny to you may not seem at all funny to Laura. Make sure you're not unkind out of carelessness." *P.K.*

HOW ABOUT YOU?

Do you know someone who looks or talks different from you and your friends? Do you laugh at those differences? Be very careful not to hurt anyone's feelings. Remember that God loves everyone, and he wants us to show love to one another as well.

MEMORIZE:

"Be devoted to one another in brotherly love. Honor one another above yourselves."

Romans 12:10, NIV

Be Thoughtful of Others

Instant Replay (Read 1 Corinthians 13:4-9, 11)

11

OCTOBER

Brian and his father yelled at the football players on TV. Dad waved his arms as if the players could see him. But it was no use—the man they were cheering for was tackled. "That was a dumb move!" shouted Brian in disgust. "He didn't even see that guy coming at him!"

"No," said Dad, "but after he sees a replay of that move, he won't make that mistake again."

When the game was over, Mother had supper ready. "Hey, how come Gretchen gets a hot turkey sandwich and the rest of us get hot dogs?" asked Brian, glancing at his sister's plate as he came to the table. He yanked out his chair and bumped the table hard as he sat down. "You're just a spoiled brat," he complained to Gretchen. She began to speak, but Brian wouldn't listen. He roughly shoved his plate around, dumping his milk in the process, and he continued to grumble and complain.

"Son, I want you to go to your room and think about what you just did," ordered Dad. "Think about your words and your actions. They were not pleasing to us, and they certainly weren't pleasing to God. When you're ready to apologize, you may come back to the table."

Brian stomped off to his room, hungry and angry. He plopped down on his bed. And he did think. In his mind, he replayed what had happened. He knew he had made a mess and had hurt his sister's feelings. Then he thought of something else. He remembered that Gretchen had been sick when they had had turkey for dinner the day before. That was why she was getting turkey now. *What a dumb move*, Brian thought to himself. He asked God to forgive him and then went to apologize to his family.

As Brian again took his place at the table, he told the others how sorry he felt. Then he looked at his father. "Maybe if I watch replays of my actions more often, I won't keep making mistakes like that!" he said. *P.R.*

HOW ABOUT YOU?

Do you sometimes do things you regret later? Perhaps you've criticized a classmate for something he said, and then later you realized he was just trying to be helpful. Replay your actions each day in your mind so you don't keep making the same mistakes. Ask God to help you with this.

MEMORIZE:

"Thus says the Lord of hosts: 'Consider your ways!'"

Haggai 1:7, NKJV

 **Think about Your Actions**

A Guilty Secret (Read Galatians 6:1-10)

12

OCTOBER

Paul sighed in relief as he answered the last question on his test paper. He thought he'd done well, and it made him feel good to know his studying had paid off. Just then he noticed a movement in the next row. His friend Jeff was sliding a small paper out of sight, before jotting down some figures. Then Jeff took another secret glance at it before finishing his test and handing it in to Mr. Baylor. Paul's heart sank. *Oh no!* he thought. *Jeff cheated!*

All afternoon Paul wondered what he should do. Should he tell Mr. Baylor? Accuse Jeff? Forget he'd ever seen anything? Walking home later, he still was confused.

The crisp fall air chilled him. He looked up when he heard the familiar sound of geese honking as they flew south for the winter. He remembered what Mr. Kent, his Sunday school teacher, had told them last week—that the honking of the geese seemed to encourage those who lagged behind or got out of line. Paul had heard that the geese took turns leading, too, and that they helped each other stay strong and united for their long journey. Mr. Kent said Christians need to help each other like that.

Suddenly, Paul knew what to do. He walked over to Jeff's house and rang the bell. Jeff answered the door.

"Hi, Jeff," Paul said. "I need to talk to you. I saw what happened during the test today."

Jeff nodded miserably. "I don't know what got into me," he muttered. "I've never cheated before. I feel awful about it. It's just that math is so hard for me!"

Paul looked at him sympathetically. "What are you going to do?" he asked.

Jeff sighed. "I guess I'll have to tell Mr. Baylor what happened, and that I'm sorry," he said.

"I'll go with you, if you want," offered Paul. "Maybe he'll let you take the test over. I'll help you study, Jeff. Maybe then you'll pass because you understand it—not because you cheated." Slowly Jeff nodded. *J.B.*

HOW ABOUT YOU?

When someone does something wrong, do you get angry and accuse him or tattle on him? Or do you take the easy way and pretend nothing happened? God wants his children to help each other do what is right. It's hard to do, but it will make you happier when you lovingly help someone overcome sin.

MEMORIZE:

"Bear one another's burdens, and so fulfill the law of Christ."

Galatians 6:2, NKJV

 Help Others Do Right

Tina's Pity Puddle (Read Psalm 40:1-3, 16-17)

13

OCTOBER

Tina's face was even gloomier than the falling rain as she sat gazing out the kitchen window. "I tried so hard to make the honor roll this time. I wanted you and Dad to be proud of me," she said as a tear escaped and trickled like a raindrop down her cheek.

"Dad and I are proud of you, Tina, even if you didn't make the honor roll. We know how hard you worked," replied her mother in a soothing tone. "Besides, you can try again next time."

"No, Mom, I'm through trying," declared Tina. "It's no use anyway."

Just then Billy, a neighbor boy, went running up his driveway. Tina and her mother gasped as Billy stumbled and fell. He landed on both knees in a mud puddle, but in a flash he was back on his feet. "I wonder why Billy got up so quickly," said Mom. "Why didn't he just stay there in that puddle awhile?"

Tina's eyes grew almost as round as the chocolate-chip cookies her mother had just set on the table. "Mom, why would he do that?" she exclaimed. "He'd get even more wet and dirty—and maybe even sick!"

"Well, you seem to be in a puddle, too, Tina," Mom pointed out, "but instead of jumping up to get out of it, you plan to stay and wallow in it."

"What do you mean, Mom?" asked Tina in surprise.

"Disappointment and discouragement lead to self-pity," said Mom, "and self-pity is very much like a mud puddle. You can lie in it and be miserable and bogged down. Or, with God's help, you can jump right out of that puddle and keep on going."

Tina thought for a minute. "You're right, Mom," she said, munching on a warm, chewy cookie. "I'm going right upstairs to do my homework. Maybe I'll never make the honor roll, but with God's help, I'll at least do the very best I can." *J.L.*

HOW ABOUT YOU?

Do you keep trying even if you don't get an *A* or win a contest? Don't feel sorry for yourself and spend time in a "pity puddle." Ask God to help you go on and be a winner by doing the best you can.

MEMORIZE:

"I can do all things through Christ who strengthens me."

Philippians 4:13, NKJV

 *Don't Give Up*

God's Jewels (Read Matthew 7:21-23; John 3:36)

14

"Welcome to my lapidary shop, boys," Mr. Williams greeted his Sunday school class. Since his shop was close to church, and since he wanted to use some of his things as an object lesson, the class was meeting there.

"Wow, look at all the neat stuff!" exclaimed Daniel, walking over to a counter full of jewels.

Mr. Williams smiled. "As you know, I'm a lapidary—a gem cutter," he said. The boys looked around and pointed out the gems they liked best. "Boys, did you know that if you're saved, you're one of God's jewels?" asked Mr. Williams. "In Malachi, God says those who fear him are his jewels. The word means 'special treasure.' Isn't that great?"

"If I'm a jewel, I'd like to be one of those," said Tim, pointing to a beautiful diamond set in a ring.

"Not me," said Daniel. He pointed to another ring. "I think this one's the best."

Mr. Williams took out both rings. "These two stones will be just right for today's lesson," he said. "One of them is a real diamond, and the other is just glass—a fake. Can you tell which is which?"

The boys examined the rings carefully, but they couldn't see any difference. Mr. Williams picked up Daniel's choice. "This is the fake," he said. He grinned at Daniel, who made a face at having chosen the fake one. "It's not surprising that it looks real to you, but I can easily tell the difference, because I know jewels." Then Mr. Williams became very serious. "Boys, some people fake being God's jewels by trying to look, act, and talk like Christians. Often we can't tell a 'pretend Christian' from a real one, but God can never be fooled. His jewels are those who have believed in Jesus as personal Savior. One day he's going to gather them all together and take them to heaven to be with him. But the 'pretend Christians'—the fakes—will be left behind. Don't be among them. Accept Jesus now!" *M.R.P.*

HOW ABOUT YOU?

Have you been claiming you're a Christian, when deep inside you know that you've never received the Lord Jesus into your heart? Then you're not one of God's jewels, are you? Won't you trust him today?

MEMORIZE:

"'They shall be Mine,' says the Lord of hosts, 'on the day that I make them My jewels.'"

Malachi 3:17, NKJV

 Become One of God's Jewels

God's Jewels (continued from yesterday) (Read 1 Peter 1:3-7)

15

OCTOBER

The boys in Mr. Williams's class were again meeting at his lapidary shop. Taking them to the back of the shop, Mr. Williams showed them a rough, uncut diamond. "Most diamonds look dull like this when taken from the ground," he said. "Before this diamond will flash and sparkle, I must cut many little sides, or facets, in it. Each one must be just the right size and be placed at exactly the proper angle to bring out its full beauty. Let me show you." As Mr. Williams began to work, he explained a little more about diamond cutting. "See how much better this is beginning to look?" he asked after cutting and polishing the diamond with abrasive wheels. He turned toward the boys. "Now, here's what I want you to remember: God is doing lapidary work on his jewels, too. What do you suppose I mean by that statement?"

"Is it that he works on us to make us better Christians?" suggested Daniel.

Mr. Williams nodded. "When you're first saved, you're something like a rough, uncut gem," he said. "Then, in your day-by-day experiences, God begins to develop your Christian character. Often he needs to use troubles and tough times to polish you and make you more like him. But there's a big difference between me cutting and polishing a gem and God polishing you. Can you guess what that might be?"

"God never makes a wrong cut? He never makes a mistake," suggested Tim.

"Great!" exclaimed Mr. Williams. "And another difference is that you're not lifeless like this diamond is. You can fight back and become bitter about your troubles, or you can let the Lord shape your life, remembering that he does know what he's doing. He knows what is best for you, even though the cutting and polishing may hurt. As you yield to him, he will use each of life's experiences to make you what you ought to be." *M.R.P.*

HOW ABOUT YOU?

Have you been complaining about your troubles, or have you been letting God use a difficult time to shape you into what he wants you to be? Don't become angry at God and quit reading your Bible and praying. Instead, allow him to use the troubles to cut and polish you so you'll become more like him.

MEMORIZE:

"For it is God who works in you both to will and to do for His good pleasure."

Philippians 2:13, NKJV

 *Let God Polish You*

God's Jewels (continued from yesterday) (Read 1 Peter 5:4-11)

It was the last class session to be held in Mr. Williams's lapidary shop. "Here's the diamond you saw me cutting and polishing last week," said Mr. Williams as the class began. "When I worked on it this week, I discovered something—a flaw. See it there?" He showed the spot to the boys, using a large magnifying glass. "It's caused by a bit of mineral that doesn't belong there," he said. "The purity and the value of the diamond will be lessened by it. What do you think I should do about it?"

16

OCTOBER

"Can you cut it away?" asked Daniel.

Mr. Williams nodded. "Yes, I can still have a beautiful jewel by cutting away the flaw," he told them. "Boys, what makes flaws in God's jewels?"

Tim spoke up. "It's sin."

"That's right," agreed Mr. Williams. "This is another reason God must cut on his jewels—to remove sin. We must be willing to confess any known sin. Then God will cut it away." He set the flawed diamond aside and opened a drawer. "A lady brought this birthstone ring in to be cleaned and made bigger," he said, pulling a box from the drawer. "It's an amethyst. She said it used to be real pretty, but it doesn't shine very much anymore. Let's see what we can do about that." Mr. Williams brought out a jewel-cleaning solution and dropped the ring into it. In a few moments he held it up, sparkling clean.

"Wow, that's beautiful!" exclaimed Mark.

"That stone was still an amethyst, even though it was dirty, wasn't it?" asked Mr. Williams. "It was like a sinning Christian—still saved, but dirty. We don't like dirty jewels, and the Lord doesn't want his jewels to be dirty, either. What is his cleaning solution?"

"I know—Jesus' blood," answered Tim.

Mr. Williams nodded. "If we sin, we must confess it to God and turn from it," he said. "Then God will cleanse us through the blood that Jesus shed for us. He'll make us glow with his beauty once again." *M.R.P.*

HOW ABOUT YOU?

Have you thought, said, or done something that doesn't please God? If you're God's child, you're still his jewel, but your sin has made you a flawed, dirty jewel. Confess your sin, and let God cut it away. He will make you all sparkling clean again with his cleaning solution—the blood of Jesus Christ.

MEMORIZE:

"The blood of Jesus Christ His [God's] Son cleanses us from all sin." *1 John 1:7, NKJV*

 Christ Cleanses from Sin

The Dimmer Switch (Read Colossians 3:12-17)

17

OCTOBER

John's feet dragged as he went up the front steps. He tried to open the front door quietly, but Mother was coming down the stairs. "Well, today was report card day, wasn't it?" she asked cheerfully. "How did you do, John?"

John slowly handed her the report. "Good work," she said after looking it over. "Most of these are not bad grades. In fact, if they're your best, they're all great! But a *D* in reading? I'm sure that isn't your best! Last time you got a *B* in that subject."

John shrugged. "It's boring." He shuffled into the family room and switched on the TV. When his father came home, John stayed in the family room. He was sure his parents were discussing his report card, and he just wanted to forget about it.

Soon Mother called him for supper. "It's too dark here," he grumbled as he pulled out his chair. The lights of the chandelier over the table were dim. "I can't even see what we're eating! Can't we have brighter lights?"

"From looking at your grades, John," said Dad, "I got the impression that you like working at less than full power. It seems to me you're turning on only part of your brain-power when it comes to schoolwork. After all, working hard in school is one way to do your best for God."

John stared at his plate. "I suppose," he admitted, sighing.

Mother reached for the light switch. At once the room brightened. "What an improvement!" exclaimed John, hoping to change the subject. "Supper looks yummy!"

"That's because the lights are shining to their full potential," observed Mother. "And I think it's about time your light shines to its full potential, too. Ask God to help you knuckle down and study harder."

John nodded. "OK, I will," he promised. "I'll study hard for my test tomorrow. You'll be proud of me!"

"Just do your best," said Mother, "and we'll be happy with the results. And God will be, too." *D.F.*

HOW ABOUT YOU?

Are you working at full power? Are some subjects in school boring or hard? Maybe getting all *A*s, or even all *B*s, is not possible. God doesn't expect you to be perfect, but he does expect—and deserve—the best you can give him in all areas of your life. That includes schoolwork!

MEMORIZE:

"And whatever you do in word or deed, do all in the name of the Lord Jesus."

Colossians 3:17, NKJV

Do Your Best in School

Beautiful Feet (Read Isaiah 61:1-3)

18
OCTOBER

"I hate my feet!" declared Susan. "They're too big."

"Well, not everyone can have small feet," replied her older sister, "and I don't think you'd want to do what the Chinese did—wrap up your feet so tight they can't grow."

Susan glanced down at her long feet and frowned. "Did they really do that?"

"Yes, they used to." Christine nodded. "In school this week, we read a story about a Chinese lady. She had her feet bound when she was very young, so they hardly grew at all. She was proud of them. But when she was older, she had to be carried a lot of places. Her feet were too delicate to walk over rough or uneven ground."

"That might not be too bad," Susan said, still staring at her feet. "Maybe mine should have been bound."

"Well, you wouldn't be able to go skating or skiing or even run," said Christine. "You wouldn't like that." She grinned at her sister. "But you know what?" she asked. "You can still have beautiful feet."

"Who? Me? You're kidding!" exclaimed Susan.

Christine laughed. "No, I really mean it. Remember the Chinese lady? Well, she found out that smallness doesn't make feet beautiful, but something else does." Susan looked doubtful as Christine continued. "To make a long story short, she became a Christian. After she got married, she and her husband became missionaries to the Chinese people."

"And?" prompted Susan.

"Don't you see? She was using her feet to spread God's Word, and the Bible says that people who witness have beautiful feet," explained Christine.

"Where does it say that?" Susan asked.

"Somewhere in Romans," said Christine. "Let's go ask Mom to help us find it." (For this verse, see today's memory verse.) *J.B.*

HOW ABOUT YOU?

Do you witness for the Lord when you're at school, at play, or even at home? That's what makes beautiful feet in God's sight. God wants you to use your feet to tell others about his wonderful gift. Tell someone today about Christ.

MEMORIZE:

"**How beautiful are the feet of those who preach the gospel of peace, who bring glad tidings of good things.**" *Romans 10:15, NKJV*

 Witness to Others

Christy and the Spiders (Read Psalm 37:1-9)

19

OCTOBER

"Maggie and Beth are so nasty," grumbled Christy as she leaned against a tree during recess, "but they always blame someone else. They get away with everything. It's not fair!"

"Yeah," agreed Dana. "I wish they'd get caught once!"

Christy nodded. Suddenly she jumped. "Ooooh!" she gasped. "A spider!"

Dana laughed. "My brother collects them, so they don't scare me," she said. "Look, it trapped a fly."

"The fly is caught in the web, but the spider isn't," observed Christy. "Just like those girls. They get others into trouble, but they go free." Christy thought about the spider so much that she almost called the girls "spiders" during class.

"Why don't some people get caught when they do wrong?" she asked Mother that evening. She told Mother about the problem at school. "Those girls never get caught. They're like spiders who make webs and catch other insects while they stay safe."

"I've heard that it's possible for a spider to get caught in its own web," said Mother. "I don't know if that's really true."

"Well, I hope those 'girl spiders' get good and stuck," grumbled Christy.

"Someday they will," Mother assured her. "All sin will one day be judged by God. But I wouldn't be surprised if those girls get tangled in their own web before then."

"Good!" Christy said angrily.

"You should be angry at injustice and sin," Mother said, "but don't allow so much bitterness in your heart that you want people to suffer. It would be more pleasing to God for you to want them to know his grace and mercy."

"If I were a fly in a spider's web, I wouldn't want that spider to get any mercy," protested Christy.

Mother smiled. "But you're not a fly," she pointed out. "You are a Christian in a world run by the devil. Be angry at the devil, but pray for those who are under his power. Don't allow their sin to cause you to sin, too, by becoming bitter over what has happened."

N.E.K.

HOW ABOUT YOU?

Do you get angry when other people get away with doing wrong? That's understandable, but be careful that it doesn't produce a sinful attitude in your own life. Learn to pray for those who are sinning. They need God's mercy.

MEMORIZE:

"Evil men will be cut off, but those who hope in the Lord will inherit the land." *Psalm 37:9, NIV*

 Pray for Sinners

Good Listener (Read Psalm 46:1-11)

20

"Andrea makes me mad," declared Leslie as she came into the house. "When we're playing, she never listens to any suggestions other kids make! And she always whispers in class! I wish she'd be still for one minute!"

"Well, just be sure you don't allow anyone to keep you from listening when your teacher is speaking," advised Mother. "Listening is your responsibility."

After dinner, it was Leslie's turn to read a selection for family devotions. She hurried through the Bible verses before offering a quick prayer. "Does anyone have any comments?" she asked, sitting on the edge of her chair. "If not, I have a phone call to make."

"That was quick," Dad said. "And, yes, I have a note of praise to share. This morning, I knew in my heart that the Lord was telling me to forgive a man at work for something he had said about me. I prayed about it, and then when I saw the man, I told him that I forgave him. It was hard to do, but I feel so much better now. I'm thankful to the Lord for gently speaking to my heart about that matter and helping me make things right."

"How does God speak?" asked Leslie. "He never speaks to me like that."

"Could it be you don't take time to listen?" Dad asked.

"I listen!" protested Leslie. "My teacher says I'm one of her best listeners."

"You may be a good listener at school," Mom told her, "but do you really listen for what God wants to tell you?"

"Take this evening, for instance," said Dad. "You raced through the Bible reading and prayer before you had the slightest chance of hearing God's message for you. You need to meditate on what you read—carefully think about it. Then ask God to help you know how and where you need to apply it to your life."

"Remember how you wished your friend Andrea could be still for one minute?" Mom asked. "I think God would like you to be still and listen to him, too." *N.E.K.*

HOW ABOUT YOU?

Are you a good listener when others are talking? Be sure that you take time to listen to God, too. Read—and reread—the Scriptures. Meditate (think) on what they say, and be still enough to listen to God.

MEMORIZE:

"Be still, and know that I am God; I will be exalted among the nations, I will be exalted in the earth!" *Psalm 46:10, NIV*

 Listen to God

Poor Ricky! (Read Luke 10:30-37)

21

It was almost supper time, so Mollie and Joy Barton started walking home from their friend's house. As they passed an empty lot, they heard the sound of crying. And there, in the empty lot, was Ricky Taylor—"Icky Ricky," the children called him. Not only was he usually dirty and smelly and looking like he needed a bath, he was also the school bully. Yet there he was, crying like a baby! Nearby, a rather badly wrecked bike lay in a heap. The boy had a skinned knee and some blood on his nose. The girls looked at him and hurried on by, both secretly glad that finally "Icky Ricky" had gotten what was coming to him.

When they arrived home, the girls hurried to wash up for supper. Soon they heard their father coming home. When they returned to the kitchen, they were amazed to find Ricky Taylor being helped into the house by Dad.

"Look what happened to this poor young man!" Dad said, pulling up a chair for Ricky. Mom quickly began cleaning Ricky's knee and nose. The girls hung back near the wall as their dad got a phone number from Ricky and called his grandma. Soon Ricky and his wrecked bike were on their way home in Dad's car.

"Well! It surely was nice for Ricky that your dad came along," declared Mom. "Not everyone helps people out like your father does. He's really a Good Samaritan."

"A Good Samaritan?" asked Mollie guiltily.

"You mean like in the Bible?" added Joy. Both girls had heard the story many times and now felt ashamed.

"That's right." Mother nodded. "You know God is pleased when we show his love to others—even to those who seem unlovely to us." *C.G.*

HOW ABOUT YOU?

Do you help other people whenever you can—even when they seem "icky" to you? God loves them, and he wants you to love them, too. He wants you to treat them as neighbors and to love them as you love yourself. That's loving quite a lot, isn't it?

MEMORIZE:

"You shall love your neighbor as yourself." Matthew 19:19, NKJV

 Love the Unlovely

The Broken Promise (Read Genesis 9:8-17)

22

OCTOBER

"Uncle Tom promised to take me to work at the airport with him today," pouted Larry. "How can he change his mind all of sudden? He promised!"

"Something came up, honey. This stormy weather delayed airplanes, and he's going to be too busy to have you along," explained Mom. "He'll take you another time."

"But he broke his promise!" insisted Larry.

"I'm not sure he actually promised," said Mom, "but in any case, I think you should try to understand. He can't help it that his plans had to be changed. It's kind of like last week when I said I'd be home from shopping by five o'clock, but then I got in a traffic jam and didn't get home until almost six. You forgave me because you knew I couldn't help it that something happened to change my plans."

"Well, I hate things that change plans," grumbled Larry. He watched out the window as the rain poured down. He had looked forward to this special day at the airport.

A little later, Larry's face brightened. "It's still raining, but the sun's coming out!" he exclaimed. "Maybe Uncle Tom will come and get me now."

"Your uncle will still be too busy," said Mom.

The frown returned to Larry's face. "I hate broken promises," he said, "even when they're caused by a change that wasn't planned."

"Keep looking out that window," suggested Mom. "Maybe you'll see the sign of a promise that will never be broken—a sign that God gave."

"There it is already," said Larry, pointing to the beginning of a beautiful rainbow. "That's the sign God gave when he promised to never again destroy the earth with a flood. We learned that in Sunday school."

"That's right," said Mom, "and it always reminds me that God will always keep all of his promises. Why don't we go look up some of God's 'forever' promises and get your mind off the one you feel your uncle broke today." *N.E.K.*

HOW ABOUT YOU?

Has anyone ever broken a promise to you? Have plans or events changed, leaving you disappointed? It hurts when promises are not kept, but you'll never know that kind of disappointment with God. His Word never changes. He always keeps his promises.

MEMORIZE:

"He who calls you is faithful, who also will do it."

1 Thessalonians 5:24, NKJV

 God Keeps His Promises

Computer Printout (Read Matthew 12:33-37)

Danny sat at his family's home computer and typed a sentence for each of his spelling words. "Looks good," he thought as he printed his work onto a sheet of paper. He leaned back and turned on his radio.

23

OCTOBER

"Turn that off," his mother called. "I asked you to use better judgment when listening to your radio. I don't want that kind of music in this house again." Danny scowled, but he turned the radio to a different station.

Later that evening, Danny packed his book bag for the following day. "I can't find my spelling sentences," he said. "I've looked everywhere, Mom. I don't want to have to write them all over again."

"Well, you did your homework on the computer tonight, didn't you?" asked Mother. "Did you store it in the computer's memory?"

"Oh, that's right!" exclaimed Danny. "I forgot. I'll just print out another copy."

After school the next day, Danny and his mother went out to rake the yard. "There's no meaning to this life anyway, so do what you want; want what you do; make your meaning, make your meaning, make it," sang Danny as he worked.

"What are you singing?" Mother asked.

"Oh!" Danny was startled. He hadn't meant to sing those words right out loud. "Nothing important. I hardly realized I was singing," he replied.

"Well, you were," said Mother, "and I didn't like the words." She was thoughtful as she raked. "Your mind is like a computer," she said. "You need to decide just what kind of printout you want your life to have."

"What do you mean?" asked Danny.

"Well," replied Mother, "like a computer, your mind stores the things you put into it, and those are the things that also come back out. You may think it doesn't hurt you to listen to ungodly music, but when you put that into your mind, wrong messages are almost certain to come out through your mouth." *N.E.K.*

HOW ABOUT YOU?

What kind of material do you store in your memory as you listen to music? Be careful to fill your heart and mind with music that glorifies the Lord. Then what goes in and what comes out will be pleasing to God.

MEMORIZE:

"Out of the overflow of the heart the mouth speaks."

Matthew 12:34, NIV

 Choose Music Carefully

Merging Traffic (Read Luke 6:31-38)

24

OCTOBER

"I guess Jana's OK, but it's hard to have a new kid join your class in the middle of the year," complained Kara as she and her mother drove away from the school. "I mean, we're in the middle of our science projects, and we have our parents' night skit almost all practiced, and we have nice, even teams in gym. And now somebody new comes along, and we have to make room for her. It just spoils everything."

"Surely adding one to your group can't be that bad," replied Mother as she slowed the car to turn onto the ramp leading to the highway.

Kara shrugged. "Well, it's not fun," she insisted. She braced herself as Mother slowed almost to a stop. "It's nothing personal. It's just that we're already set with our groups." She frowned as the cars on the highway roared by in the lane Mother needed to use. Mother had to come to a complete stop. "Hey!" said Kara. "What's with all those drivers on the highway? They're not moving over to let us in. We shouldn't have to stop. Don't they know they're supposed to let us merge in?"

"They should know," said Mother. "There's a sign on the highway back there to tell them. But I guess they're so busy doing their own thing, they don't want to bother with anyone new in their lane. I imagine you can understand that. I'm sure it's nothing personal." Kara blushed as she glanced at her mother.

Finally, they were able to move out onto the highway. "It doesn't feel very good when no one wants to make room for you, does it?" asked Mother.

Kara didn't answer immediately. "I guess we need some Merging Traffic signs in our class," she said finally. "I guess I better be the one to let Jana in."

Mother nodded. "That would be great," she said. "It will make Jana happy, and I know you'll feel happier yourself. Best of all, it will please the Lord." *H.M.*

HOW ABOUT YOU?

Is there a new person in your school or neighborhood? Has anyone "let him in"? Perhaps God wants you to be the one to make room for the newcomer. Think about how you would feel if you were new. How would you like to be treated? God says you should treat others that way, too.

MEMORIZE:

"**And just as you want men to do to you, you also do to them.**"

Luke 6:31, NKJV

 *Accept New People*

The Way Home (Read John 14:1-6)

25

Mark squirmed as his mother talked to him. She had recently become a Christian and was trying to explain how he could receive Christ as Savior, too. "I want you to be in heaven with me someday," she said.

"Don't worry, Mom," answered Mark. "Uncle George says I'm such a good boy that if anybody makes it to heaven, I will."

"Uncle George is a very smart man, but he's mistaken about the way to heaven," Mom replied. "It's not your goodness that will take you there. Jesus is the only way."

Mark turned toward the door. He didn't want to talk about salvation anymore. "I have to go finish my paper-route collections now," he said, hurrying out of the kitchen.

As Mark was busy on his route, he saw a girl and a little boy. "Don't cry, I know how to get to 102 Shelby Street," he heard the girl say. "You go that way one block," she said, pointing north, "and turn right. That's Main Street. Then go three blocks and you come to Shelby. Your house is right there on the corner." Mark frowned. Those directions weren't right!

As the girl went into her house, Mark met the boy. "You're Jimmy Jones, aren't you?" exclaimed Mark. "I deliver papers to your house. Remember me?" The little boy looked at him and nodded. "That girl gave you the wrong directions," said Mark. "You have to turn left at Main Street, not right." Jimmy's lip began to tremble, and Mark took his hand. "I'll take you home, OK?" Mark asked. Happily, Jimmy nodded, and soon Mark had delivered him to his family.

On the way home, Mark thought about what had happened. Suddenly he realized that he was just like Jimmy! He was trying to follow directions to heaven that were given by someone who didn't know the way. He needed to listen to what God said in his Word, and God said Jesus was the only way. *I was Jimmy's way home because I took him there,* he thought. *Jesus is the way to heaven. I want him to be my Savior and take me there. M.R.P.*

HOW ABOUT YOU?

Are you following the right directions to heaven? God knows how you can get there. His directions are found in his Book, the Bible. He says you must trust in Jesus, the only way to heaven. Trust Jesus today.

MEMORIZE:

"There is a way that seems right to a man, but in the end it leads to death." *Proverbs 14:12, NIV*

Jesus Is the Way to Heaven

A Bigger Tree for Travis (Read Psalm 27:5-14)

26
OCTOBER

There was so much arguing going on inside the house that no one heard Travis slip out the back door. He ran across the yard to his favorite tree. Somehow sitting in that big, old tree made Travis feel better—safe from things like noise and hurt. This tree was his hiding place and escape.

Travis stayed in the tree for a long time. He listened to happy birds chirp and sing. He watched small, quick squirrels run around the yard. The day looked better from high up in his favorite hiding place. There were no problems there. Still, his heart was very heavy.

"Travis! Travis!" Mom called out the back door. "Where are you?" Travis saw that his grandmother was with her, so he climbed down and walked slowly toward the house. Grandma had come to take him home with her for a while.

"That must be a very special tree to you," Grandma said as they got into the car. "Your mom says you spend a lot of time in it."

"I like it up there," Travis said. "Away from everything." He sighed. "But it's almost winter," he added. "Then I won't be able to hide in my tree anymore."

"Hmmmm," murmured Grandma. "Then you'll need to find a new hiding place, won't you? And you know what? There's a better place—a bigger 'tree,' so to speak—where you can take shelter from the things that trouble you."

Travis was surprised. "There is?" he asked. "Where?"

"Where?" repeated Grandma. "Well, it could be most anywhere you want it to be. You see, it's in the Lord's presence. If you'll go to him with your problems, he'll help you through them. You can talk to him anywhere, at any time. Sometimes it's good to actually get right down on your knees and ask God to hold you safe. As you focus your attention on him and think about his power and love, you'll find yourself safe in his care." *N.E.K.*

HOW ABOUT YOU?

Where do you go when you are hurt, sad, afraid, or disappointed? When you need to get away and hide, remember that God wants to protect you. Think about him. Talk to him. Ask him to hold, keep, and comfort you in the bad times—and in the good times, too!

MEMORIZE:

"You shall hide them in the secret place of Your presence . . . from the strife of tongues."

Psalm 31:20, NKJV

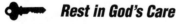 **Rest in God's Care**

An Hour Early (Read Psalm 57:7-11)

27

OCTOBER

"Get going, gang. Let's get ready for church," Dad said. "We don't want to be late."

"Dad says that every week," Ben told his sister, Nance. "Some Sunday we should get ready early just to see if Dad's really talking or if it's a recording." Dad grinned.

When they drove up to the church, they saw that there were no cars there. "Whatever could . . . ," began Dad. Then he stopped. "Oh, how silly!" he said. "Remember last spring when we moved the clocks ahead? Well, last night we were supposed to set them back."

"We're not late this week," said Mom, "we're an hour early!" Everyone laughed.

"Well, let's get ready for church," suggested Dad.

Nance giggled. "But we are ready. We got up, ate breakfast, cleaned up, got dressed—we're not only ready; we're early!"

"We prepared our bodies," agreed Mother, "but we should also prepare our hearts for worship."

"We can't feed our hearts breakfast," said Ben, grinning.

"Sure we can," replied Dad, opening his Bible. "Let's feed on God's Word for a few minutes."

"Well, we can't wash our hearts," said Nance next.

"Sure we can," Dad said. "Let's each take a few moments to confess our sins to God. He'll cleanse our hearts."

The car was silent for a few minutes. Then Ben spoke up again. "We can't dress our hearts," he said positively.

"Sure we can!" Nance exclaimed before Dad could answer. She looked up at him. "But how?" she asked.

"By praising God," suggested Dad. "Dressing nicely helps put us in the right mood for attending church, and singing praises to our heavenly Father should help set our mood for worship." So the family joined in some songs of praise.

"We should do this every Sunday and really get ready for church," declared Nance as the first cars began to arrive.

"Is that my recording I hear?" Dad asked, and they all left the car smiling. *N.E.K.*

HOW ABOUT YOU?

Do you prepare your heart for Sunday worship? Get up early enough to read some Scripture and praise God so your heart will be ready to listen and worship at church.

MEMORIZE:

"Lord, You have heard the desire of the humble; You will prepare their heart; You will cause Your ear to hear."

Psalm 10:17, NKJV

 Prepare Your Heart for Worship

9-1-1 (Read Psalm 136:1-9, 23-26)

28

OCTOBER

"Grandpa!" exclaimed Gary as he opened the door to his grandfather's house and saw Grandpa lying on the floor. His sister, Patti, came running up the steps and into the kitchen. "Grandpa's not breathing," gasped Gary, "and I can't find a pulse. I'm going to call 9-1-1!"

"Dear God, please let Grandpa be OK," Patti prayed as Gary dialed the number. "Help us know what to do."

When the call was answered, Gary quickly explained the problem. "Do you know CPR?" asked the 9-1-1 operator.

"No, but I've seen it done on television," Gary answered. "My sister's here, and she can help, too."

"Good. Now listen carefully and do exactly what I tell you," replied the operator. "Your sister can breathe while you pump." Carefully following directions, they were soon hard at work. As Gary pumped and counted, Patti listened closely for her cue to breathe. "One–one thousand, two–one thousand, three–one thousand, four–one thousand, five breathe. . . ." The cycle continued on.

Finally, they heard the sirens coming closer, and Patti ran to let the paramedics in. The trained men took over, and soon Grandpa was on his way to the hospital.

That evening the children were very happy to hear that Grandpa was doing well. "You saved his life," Dad told them. "I am so proud of both of you."

"It was a lot like that rescue program we watched last week," said Patti. "On that show everyone got together at the end to say thank you to those who helped."

"Could we do that, Dad?" asked Gary. "I'd really like to thank the 9-1-1 operator who helped us."

"That's a great idea," agreed Dad, "but isn't there Someone else you should thank, too? Didn't you give Someone else a call? Seems like I remember you told me you prayed."

"We sure did!" exclaimed Patti, "even while we—Oh! You mean we should thank God!" She grinned. "I've already thanked him."

"Me, too," said Gary, "but I think I'll thank him again." *S.S.*

HOW ABOUT YOU?

Do you say thank you to those who help you? It shows them you appreciate what they do. Do you also thank God for helping you—do you tell him that you appreciate him? Why not stop right now and say, "Thank you, Lord," for something specific that he's done for you.

MEMORIZE:

"It is good to give thanks to the Lord." *Psalm 92:1, NKJV*

 **Say Thank You**

Switch Channels (Read Philippians 4:6-9)

29

OCTOBER

Tiffany pushed the food around on her plate. "I've got so much stuff on my mind that I can't eat," she said with a sigh. "I didn't sleep very well last night, either."

"What kind of stuff?" asked Mom.

"You know, about Dad divorcing you and marrying someone else," replied Tiffany. "And Dad going to court to try and get custody of me. I don't want to live with him." Tears welled up in her eyes.

"Well, you're not at fault for the things that have happened, and you can't do anything to change them," Mom said. "But you can do something about having peace inside." Mom put down her fork and stood up. "Come with me," she said. Mom led Tiffany into the living room and turned on the TV. She motioned for Tiffany to sit down.

"Why are we watching this?" asked Tiffany after a moment. "You never watch these shows, because the bad words and actions upset you."

"You're right," agreed Mom. "What do you suppose I could watch to make me feel good?"

"You could switch to the Christian channel," said Tiffany, and Mother did so. Tiffany looked at her mother suspiciously. "Does this have anything to do with me?"

"Yes, it does," answered Mom. "I want you to see that you can switch channels, too. You don't need to keep listening to the things that trouble you. The Bible says we'll have perfect peace if we keep our mind on the Lord and trust him. Keeping your mind on your troubles makes you worried and depressed. You need to 'switch channels' in your mind."

"You mean I should quit thinking about all the bad things and think about God instead," said Tiffany slowly.

Mother nodded. "First, tell your problems to the Lord," she said. "Tell him that you believe him and trust him to meet your needs. Then start praising him for the many good things he's done for you. You just can't praise him and worry at the same time." *M.R.P.*

HOW ABOUT YOU?

Are you letting your problems keep you from being happy? Switch channels! Turn your mind off your troubles and begin thinking about the Lord. It's not easy to do, and it's something you'll work at throughout your life. But it always works. Keeping your mind on the Lord gives you peace.

MEMORIZE:

"You [God] will keep in perfect peace him whose mind is steadfast, because he trusts in you." *Isaiah 26:3, NIV*

 *Think about God, Not Your Troubles*

Balancing Act (Read Jeremiah 29:11-13)

30

OCTOBER

"Well, Son, how did you like the circus?" asked Mom as Joey ran into the house ahead of his father.

"Oh, Mom! The tightrope walker—you should have seen him!" exclaimed Joey excitedly. "I couldn't believe my eyes! I want to be a tightrope walker when I grow up."

"Why did you find the tightrope walker so thrilling?" asked Mom as Dad entered the kitchen.

"He was so high up!" exclaimed Joey. "On TV they don't look that high. The man at the circus was so high up his head almost touched the top of the big tent. He swayed back and forth up there—sometimes it seemed like he was going to fall." Joey demonstrated, waving his arms about as he pretended to walk the tightrope.

"Do you know why he didn't fall?" Dad asked.

"Not really," Joey answered thoughtfully. "I should think he would, with the crowd screaming and everything. But he didn't seem to notice. He didn't look around when they screamed. He just kept looking straight ahead."

"That's right, and that's why he didn't fall," replied Dad. "He never took his eyes off the rope in front of him."

"In a way, Christians are tightrope walkers, too," observed Mother. "A Christian who doesn't keep his eyes on God loses his balance and falls."

"But we can't see God," objected Joey.

"We can't see him physically," agreed Dad, "but we can see his work in nature. And we can see his work in our life. We 'see' him in the Bible, too."

Mother nodded. "When we read it, he uses it to bring balance into our life. His balance keeps us from falling into sin."

Joey thought about that. Then he grinned. "I guess that means I don't have to wait till I grow up to be a tightrope walker!" he said.

S.A.H.

HOW ABOUT YOU?

Have you been reading the Bible every day and letting God speak to your heart? When you do that faithfully, the troubles or temptations in your life won't be too strong for you. The Lord is waiting and ready to help you balance your life.

MEMORIZE:

"And you will seek Me and find Me, when you search for Me with all your heart."

Jeremiah 29:13, NKJV

 God Brings Balance to Life

Light in the Darkness (Read Psalm 119:105-112)

31

OCTOBER

Jeremy's heart raced. He had been excited about his new bedroom in the basement, but he hadn't planned on having to get up in the middle of the night. Now he was somewhere between his room and the steps leading to the bathroom upstairs. Jeremy felt for the wall, but it wasn't there. He took a couple of steps forward, then stopped in his tracks. He was almost sure he had seen something move in the corner! He was six now, so he no longer believed in ghosts or monsters. Still . . . Jeremy turned around quickly, but he tripped over something on the floor in front of him, and he fell. His scream echoed throughout the house.

Soon Jeremy was safe in his mother's arms in the well-lit kitchen. He was finally able to laugh about how he had ended up in the laundry room and fallen into the clothes basket. "Why didn't you turn the light on?" asked Mother.

Jeremy shrugged. "I couldn't find the switch," he said.

Mother got up, opened the drawer, and took out a flashlight. "Jeremy, would you like to have this flashlight in your room?" she asked. "Then if you need to get up, you can use it to help you find your way."

Jeremy grinned and nodded. He flicked the flashlight on and off a couple of times. "Mom?" he asked, "Do you ever get scared?"

Mother smiled. "Sure I do," she said.

"Do you use a flashlight, too?" Jeremy asked solemnly.

"In a way I do," said Mother. "God says in the Bible that his Word is like a light to our path. It helps us as we go on our way. For example, when I get scared, I think about verses like Joshua 1:9. It says, 'Do not be afraid . . . for the Lord your God is with you wherever you go' [*NKJV*]. That helps me." She gave Jeremy a hug. "That would be a good verse for you to remember, too," she added. Jeremy nodded, and they repeated it together several times.

Jeremy's flashlight shone brightly on the steps back to his room. He repeated the verse to himself. He felt safe with his flashlight and his "lamp"—God's Word—to guide him. *A.J.S.*

HOW ABOUT YOU?

Are you sometimes afraid of things? Are you unsure about what you should do when you have a problem? Turn to God's Word, study it, and use it to direct you. Let the Bible be your light.

MEMORIZE:

"**Come and let us walk in the light of the Lord.**" *Isaiah 2:5, NKJV*

 *Let God Guide You*

Helpful Light (Read 1 John 1:5-7)

"Hey, Mom, what are you doing?" asked Mary. She stood beside her mother at the linen counter in the department store. Mother was holding a napkin up toward the light.

"These are 'seconds,' Mary. That means they cost less, but it also means there's some flaw in them," said Mother. "When I hold them up to the light, I can see what's wrong and if it's serious or not."

"Oh," said Mary. "How can you tell?"

"The light shines through the material so that I can see if there's a thin, weak spot," explained Mother. She pointed out one of the flaws. "Most of these aren't very bad, so I think I'll buy some." Mary helped her mother inspect and choose several napkins.

1
NOVEMBER

That evening, Mary told her father what she had learned. "Light is a great help, isn't it?" said Dad as Mary pointed out a flaw in one of the napkins. "You know, this reminds me that Jesus is the light of our life. When we stay close to him and to the light of God's Word, the flaws in our life show up. Then we can correct them."

"Remember when you were angry with your friend Christy, and you wanted to get even with her?" asked Mother. "We looked up some Bible verses, and you were able to see that it was wrong to want to pay her back."

Mary nodded. "I know. The Bible says to repay evil with good, and at first I didn't want to do that. But when I did, it worked! Now Christy and I are best friends."

"That's great," approved Dad. "Sometimes it's hard to let Jesus' light shine through. We'd rather not hold some parts of our life up to his light, but the only way to truly live for Jesus is to let his light show us where we are wrong. I hope you'll always do that, Mary."

L.W.

HOW ABOUT YOU?

Are you willing to let Jesus' light shine through your life? Listen carefully to what he says in his Word. Let him show you the flaws in your life—the unkind words or feelings, the lack of obedience, the desires to do wrong things. Then ask him to change these things and make you what you ought to be.

MEMORIZE:

"He who follows Me shall not walk in darkness, but have the light of life." *John 8:12, NKJV*

 Walk in Jesus' Light

Broken Beads (Read Ephesians 4:29-32)

2

NOVEMBER

"That dumb old Debbie!" cried Glenna, slamming the door. "I'll never play with her again."

Mother held a broken cup. "What's the matter?" she asked. "I thought Debbie was your best friend—and even if she isn't, I don't want you talking about her like that."

"Some friend!" exclaimed Glenna. "She broke the shell beads Grandma sent me from Florida. Look!" She opened her hands to show her mother the pile of tiny shells.

"Hmmmm," murmured Mother. "The shells don't seem to be broken—only the cord they were on. We can restring them good as new. Was Debbie angry about something?"

"No," admitted Glenna. "I just let her try them on, and when she straightened them, they broke. The shells went all over the floor. She should have been more careful! I was so mad, I just scooped them up and came home."

"I see," said Mother. After a moment she added. "Maybe we shouldn't go to Faith Church anymore, either."

"Why not?" asked Glenna in surprise. "We've always gone to that church. I have lots of friends there—I like going there."

"But look at this." Mother held up the broken cup. "Pastor Howard stopped by, and I gave him a cup of coffee. When he set the cup down, the handle came off. I could glue it back on, only—"

"But, Mother, that's silly," protested Glenna. "He didn't mean to break it. It was an accident. Why would . . . Oh!" She saw her mother's slight smile and the twinkle in her eye. "You tricked me," giggled Glenna, "but I get the point. I'm being as silly as you—maybe worse. OK. I'll forgive Debbie—if there's anything to forgive, that is. I guess the broken beads were an accident, too."

"I think so," agreed Mother. "It's funny how much easier it is to see that someone else is acting foolishly than it is to see that you are. Next time you begin to feel angry at someone, think about how it looks to other people—and more importantly, how it looks to God." *L.M.W.*

HOW ABOUT YOU?

Has someone made you angry by ruining something of yours? Did you stop being friends because of it, or did you say mean things about that person? Think carefully now—are you being foolish? Why not ask God to forgive you, and then make things right with your friend, too.

MEMORIZE:

"**Be kind and compassionate to one another, forgiving each other, just as in Christ God forgave you.**" *Ephesians 4:32, NIV*

 *Forgive One Another*

Memory Quilt (Read Isaiah 55:6-11)

3

"That's going to be neat when it's done," said Arlene as she watched her mother work on a patchwork quilt.

Mother smiled. "I hope so," she replied. "This project is very special to me." She picked up a few of the fabric squares. "Do you recognize these pieces of material?"

"Some of them are scraps from dresses I used to wear, aren't they?" asked Arlene.

Mother nodded. "Yes, and they remind me that God's way is best," she said. "You see, I used to become very disappointed and angry when I didn't get my way. I would even get upset with God when he didn't answer my prayers the way I wanted him to."

"Really?" asked Arlene, eager to hear her mother's story. "How do these quilt pieces remind you of that?"

"Well," said Mother, "before you came to live with us, I wanted a little baby very much. I prayed that we'd be able to adopt one right away. But it didn't happen. Your father and I prayed and prayed, and we waited and waited. I sometimes felt angry at God for not giving me my way."

"But then you got me," Arlene said.

"That's just the point," said Mother with a smile. "I didn't get my way. I got God's way, and it was much better. He taught us so much during those years we were waiting. We learned a lot about patience and about trusting God to work out his best for us. And then, as you said, we adopted you."

"If you had gotten a baby earlier, you might not have gotten me," Arlene said.

"That's right," agreed Mother. "That's why this quilt is such a special project to me. I'm sewing together little remembrances from your life. It's my way of reminding myself how wonderful God's way was—and is—for me."

"Whenever I begin to feel unhappy because God doesn't do things my way, I'll try to remember that, too," promised Arlene with a smile. *N.E.K.*

HOW ABOUT YOU?

Are you patient when you don't get your own way? Or do you want what you want when you want it? Ask God to help you to want and accept his ways. Trust him, knowing that his way is best.

MEMORIZE:

"For as the heavens are higher than the earth, so are My ways higher than your ways, and My thoughts than your thoughts."

Isaiah 55:9, NKJV

 **Desire God's Way**

The Box of Paints (Read 1 Corinthians 12:27-31)

Why didn't God give me musical talent, too? thought Melissa as she listened to her family give a musical program. "I couldn't carry a tune if it were in a bucket."

After church, she complained out loud. "It's not fair. All of you can play and sing, and I can't," she grumbled. "I feel stupid sitting there—the only Miller not in the program. I wish I could have a part, too."

4
NOVEMBER

"We'd like you to join us, Melissa, but . . . we don't know how to use a bullfrog," teased her brother.

"That was uncalled for, Bill," said Mother, noticing the hurt look on Melissa's face. "Melissa may not have a musical talent, but she has other talents." She turned to her daughter. "You like to draw pictures," she reminded Melissa. "That's a special talent God has given you."

"That's nothing," protested Melissa. "I want to be musical, like all of you."

The next afternoon when Dad came home, he handed Melissa a box. "Here are some paints for you," he said.

"Thanks, Dad," squealed Melissa. Quickly she opened the box. "There must be a mistake," she wailed. "There's only blue here. I can't paint pictures with only one color."

"It takes different colors to paint pretty pictures, doesn't it?" agreed Dad. He handed her another box.

Melissa nodded as she eagerly looked over the variety of colors in the second box. "But why did you give me only blue at first?" she asked.

"I wanted you to see how interesting it would be if all people were just alike," answered Dad. "God gives each person different abilities for doing his work. How dull it would be if we were all the same."

Slowly Melissa nodded. "Like having only one color to paint with," she said. "I guess God would rather have me paint than sing. So I'll try to be the best artist I can." *M.R.P.*

HOW ABOUT YOU?

Have you discovered your own special talents? Maybe you can't sing or paint, but perhaps you're good at math or writing. Whatever your abilities are, develop them the best you can. God may have a special use for them someday.

MEMORIZE:

"Whatever your hand finds to do, do it with all your might."

Ecclesiastes 9:10, NIV

 Use Your Talents

The Best Team (Read Ephesians 1:2-7)

Jerry shifted nervously from one foot to the other, wiping his sweating palms on his jeans. How he wished his gym teacher would just assign teams for the various games they played, but once again they were choosing sides. Jerry was smaller and slower than the other boys in gym, and he was usually left till last. It just wasn't fair! Why did God make him so small? He was close to tears, and his heart roared in his ears. Already there were only six boys left to be chosen.

"Tim," called Brent, the biggest team leader.

"Justin," barked Clint, the other leader.

"Fred."

"David."

Jerry licked his dry lips nervously as Brent and Clint looked at each other and grimaced. "Byron," Brent called, motioning to the boy beside Jerry.

"All right, Jerry, come on," Clint called grudgingly.

Fighting tears, Jerry walked over to the team. Then throughout the game, though he tried his very best, he didn't do very well and got nasty looks from other team members.

After school, his tears fell on his peanut-butter sandwich as he told his mother about his problems. She spoke tenderly. "I know it hurts very much not to be chosen until last," she said. "Maybe it will help a little if you remember that you have been chosen for a team that's more important than all others, and whose team captain is over all other team captains."

Jerry wiped his eyes. "I have?" he asked hopefully. "What team is that?"

"God's team—and size doesn't count, either!" said Mother triumphantly. "God says in the Bible that he has chosen each of us!" She gave Jerry a bright smile. "And you're made just to order for the part you'll play on his team!" *D.E.*

HOW ABOUT YOU?

Do you sometimes wish God had made you differently because you don't fit in a sport or musical activity? God does not make mistakes. He has a very wonderful plan for each life. Follow him daily, and you'll find the reason you were made in your own special way.

MEMORIZE:

"You did not choose Me, but I chose you and appointed you that you should go and bear fruit." *John 15:16, NKJV*

 God Made You Just Right

The Flower Kit (Read Psalm 119:33-40)

6

NOVEMBER

"This dumb thing!" snapped Lauren in disgust, throwing the flower kit across the table. "None of the pieces will go together."

"Calm down," Dad said. "Getting angry and out of control won't help." He picked up some of the items from the kit. "Aren't you missing something?" he asked. "Whenever your brother and I assemble a model, we use the directions to guide us. Did this kit come with directions?"

"I already read them," Lauren said, "but I couldn't understand them." She rummaged through the wastebasket. "Here they are," she said, handing a paper to Dad.

"Maybe you read too much at once," suggested Dad. "Let's just take one step at a time. Let's see . . . it says to bend the green pipe cleaners in half to look like diagram A." He waited while Lauren took the pipe cleaners and bent them. "Now it says to put them aside and wrap the yellow yarn around the small spiral wires." Lauren and Dad began wrapping the yarn. "Next we wrap red yard around the longer spirals." Lauren and Dad spent the afternoon together, reading the directions and following them closely until the flowers were completed.

"Thanks, Dad," said Lauren, holding up the finished project. "It just wouldn't come together for me. Those directions were too hard to understand."

"We needed them, though, didn't we?" replied Dad. "This is a good example of how important it is to read the directions. And did you know that it's even more important to read the directions God has given to help us in our daily life?"

"You mean the Bible," Lauren said. "Sometimes I can't understand it, either."

"I know," said Dad, "but I hope you won't just toss it aside. Instead, ask God to show you what his Word means."

"And you can help me with understanding God's directions, too," Lauren said. "Like you did today."

Dad nodded. "I'll be glad to help whenever I can." *N.E.K.*

HOW ABOUT YOU?

Do you ever feel that the Bible is too hard to understand? Don't quit reading. It's important to find out what God desires of your life. You don't need to read it all at once, but you should find something in it each day that you can apply to your life. Ask for help in understanding the more difficult passages.

MEMORIZE:

"Open my eyes that I may see wonderful things in your law."

 Psalm 119:18, NIV

 **Read the Bible**

Words and Actions (Read Matthew 21:28-32)

"You'd hardly know Jay Snider lately!" Mark reported enthusiastically at the family dinner table. "He quit going to all those drinking parties on weekends, and he even carries a Bible with him to church now."

"Well, Laura Perry is just the opposite," said Mark's sister, Lisa. "She's always gone to church, and she talks like a Christian in Sunday school and youth group. But now she's started going to those same parties that Jay quit. You should hear the stories she's been telling about how much she can drink and everything. So now Jay, the drinker, goes to church and Laura, the churchgoer, goes out drinking. Seems odd, doesn't it?"

7

NOVEMBER

"Well," said Mother thoughtfully, "do you remember when I asked you to empty the dishwasher the other night, Lisa? You said you would, but then a friend called and you took off without getting it done. I was frustrated with you, and I asked Mark to do your job. Mark told me he couldn't because he had some important home-work to do."

"That's true," put in Mark defensively, "but then I realized it was just an excuse, and so I did it anyway."

"So . . . who emptied the dishwasher? The child who said yes or the one who said no?" asked Mother.

"I guess it was the one who said no," said Lisa a little sheepishly.

"That's right," said Mother. "And that's the kind of thing I see happening with your friends."

Dad nodded. "Laura has always gone to church, and she seemed to have said yes to God. But now her actions seem to show that she never really said yes in her heart. We need to pray that Laura will come to a true yes to God and show it by her life. On the other hand, Jay said no to God for several years, but once he said yes, he meant it; we know that by his actions."

"We all need to be sure our lives show that we're saying yes to God by the things we do," added Mother. *L.W.*

HOW ABOUT YOU?

Have you said yes to Jesus in words? That's good, but what are your actions saying? Do they show that your yes was genuine? Does your language reflect it? Remember, actions often speak louder than words. Make sure your actions are a testimony for Jesus.

MEMORIZE:

"Be doers of the word, and not hearers only." *James 1:22, NKJV*

 Say Yes to God by Your Actions

Temper Tantrums (Read Jonah 3:10–4:11)

8

"Lord, I can't believe you didn't let me get picked for chorus. It isn't fair!" Jenelle accused the Lord. "I'm a good singer. You know how much I wanted to get in. Sometimes I think you just don't care or something, because if you did, you'd change things." She fumed all the way from school to Mrs. Johnson's home, where she was going to baby-sit the rest of the day.

When she arrived, Mrs. Johnson explained what she would need to do. "Brandi will be two years old soon," Mrs. Johnson said. "Sometimes she throws temper tantrums when she can't get her way. If she does that, don't give in to her. We want her to learn that temper tantrums don't work."

After Mrs. Johnson left, Jenelle stopped Brandi three times from sticking her fingers into the slot of the VCR. Finally she carried Brandi away from it and set her beside her toys. Brandi threw herself down, wailing and banging her head on the floor.

"I'm sorry, but you can't put your hand in the VCR. Here—look at this," said Jenelle, trying to interest the baby in a jack-in-the-box. But Brandi just screamed louder and kicked her feet. Jenelle grabbed a magazine and pretended to read it, ignoring the little girl. It worked. Soon Brandi quieted down and started to play with her blocks. She looked at Jenelle, and Jenelle smiled at her.

Jenelle picked up the TV remote control. As she flipped through the channels, her mind went back to her disappointment in not getting into the school chorus group. Then she heard somebody on TV say, "You're acting just like a two-year-old!"

Suddenly Jenelle realized that she had been acting like a two-year-old with God. She had been throwing a temper tantrum, too. "I'm sorry, Lord," she said as she watched Brandi playing with her toys. "I guess I can find something else to do, too, just like Brandi did." *M.K.N.*

HOW ABOUT YOU?

Do you accept what God sends, or do you get angry with him when things don't go your way? Jonah did that (see today's Scripture), but God didn't give in to him. God wants what's best for you. He wants you to grow up to be like Jesus. He won't give in to temper tantrums.

MEMORIZE:

"A man's own folly ruins his life, yet his heart rages against the Lord." *Proverbs 19:3, NIV*

 **Accept God's Way**

Hamburger for Babies? (Read Hebrews 5:11-14)

"Baby Janie sure drinks a lot of milk," observed Laura one day. "She drinks it all day!"

"That's true," Mother answered. "Maybe she's getting tired of milk. Shall I feed her a peanut butter sandwich and an apple?"

"No!" Laura laughed at Mother's joke. "She can't eat that! She isn't big enough yet, and she hasn't got any teeth to chew with."

9
NOVEMBER

"You're absolutely right." Mother smiled. "But before too long she'll be able to have some soft rice cereal and some juice. And then maybe we'll mash a few bites of banana for her."

"How about hamburgers?" suggested Laura.

"Not for quite some time," said Mother. "She's got a lot of growing to do before she'll be big enough for them."

Dad held up his roast beef sandwich. "Well, I'm glad I'm big enough to have this," he said with a grin. "But you know what, Laura? Just as babies slowly grow big enough to eat different things, baby Christians do, too."

"Baby Christians?" Laura asked.

Dad nodded. "When a person asks Jesus to become his Savior and take away his sins, he's called a 'babe in Christ.' We older Christians help him understand the 'milk' of God's Word—the easiest verses and stories. Then as he grows bigger, we share the meat of God's Word—the deeper truths of Scripture that are harder to understand."

"Oh," murmured Laura. She thought for a moment. Then she grinned. "I don't think I'll ask you at what stage you think I am," she decided. "I don't think I'm at the 'milk' stage anymore, but I'm probably not quite ready to chew the 'meat' of the Bible, either. You'd probably say I'm at the 'mashed banana' stage, and that sounds horrible."

"As long as you're growing in Christ a little every day, it's great, not horrible," said Mother. "The only horrible thing would be if you stopped growing altogether." *C.G.*

HOW ABOUT YOU?

Maybe you're ready now for some of the harder things Christians must learn. Listen to the sermons at church, and read God's Word for yourself. You won't understand everything at first, but don't get discouraged. The more you grow in Christ, the more you will understand.

MEMORIZE:

"But solid food is for the mature, who by constant use have trained themselves to distinguish good from evil."

Hebrews 5:14, NIV

 Chew the Meat of God's Word

Double Topping (Read Proverbs 6:20-23; Ephesians 6:1-3)

10
NOVEMBER

After school, Marcella waited when her friend called to her. "Come to my house," Cathy invited, but Marcella shook her head. "Oh, I forgot," moaned Cathy. "Your mom wants you to stay home till she gets home from work. You don't have any fun!"

"I have lots of fun!" protested Marcella. "Tonight I'm going to start supper, and I'm surprising Mom by making dessert, too! I found an easy recipe for chocolate cream pie." They reached her home, and she unlocked the door. "I'll tell you tomorrow how it turned out!"

"I'll help," offered Cathy, but Marcella again shook her head. "I know you're not supposed to have anyone over, but your Mom will never know. Please?" pleaded Cathy.

Marcella hesitated. "I can't, Cathy!" she said. "Mom trusts me to do what she says. See you tomorrow!"

Marcella changed her clothes and went to work in the kitchen. "There!" She scooped the last bit of pudding into the crust. "All I need now is the topping!" She slapped her forehead as she realized she had forgotten to get topping. "Oh, no! Mom's pie will be so . . . plain!"

Marcella sat at the kitchen table, head in her hands, and thought about her problem. "I could run to the store," she murmured, "but then I'd be disobeying. Besides, like I told Cathy, Mom trusts me. That settles it. She gets a plain pie. Some surprise!"

Tears of disappointment spilled down Marcella's cheeks as her mother walked in the door. "What's wrong, honey?" Mother cried. After hearing the whole story, she hugged Marcella tight. "Your surprise is much better than you think!" she said.

"My surprise has no topping," moaned Marcella.

"Marcella, the topping was that you obeyed me! Even though you thought about breaking my rules to do a good thing for me, you chose to obey! That makes me happier than a hundred pies!" Marcella grinned as Mother hugged her again. "Actually, Marcella, it's a double topping!" added Mother. "When you chose to obey, you not only pleased me, you pleased the Lord!" *D.L.L.*

HOW ABOUT YOU?

Have you ever wanted to do something really nice for someone, but you'd have to disobey to do it? There is no gift you can give, and no deed you can do, that is better than obedience. By obeying, you set a good foundation for your own future, and you bring glory to God.

MEMORIZE:

"Children, obey your parents in all things, for this is well pleasing to the Lord."

Colossians 3:20, NKJV

 *Choose to Obey*

The Soldier's Story (Read Isaiah 53:3-6)

11

NOVEMBER

The somber black wall, engraved with rows and rows of names, filled Paul with awe. He was visiting Washington, D.C., with his family, and he was standing in front of the monument honoring those who had fought in Vietnam. All the names were of those who had died in that war.

A soldier stood near the wall, dressed in uniform, with medals on his chest. He seemed to be looking for something as he read the names. Then he placed a finger on one of the names and began tracing the letters. Over and over the soldier traced the letters of that name.

Curious, Paul edged closer. He was surprised to see tears wetting the soldier's cheeks. He hadn't imagined that a soldier would cry. The soldier noticed Paul, and feeling embarrassed, Paul backed away.

"It's all right, young man," said the soldier. "Come here and let me explain the reason for these tears." He squatted down and looked Paul in the eye. "The name I was tracing belongs to a man who fought with me in Vietnam. We were together when a grenade landed right beside us. Glenn threw himself on top of it and took all the fury of the explosion. He died for me. Because of him, I'm alive today." The soldier gave Paul a trembling smile, and Paul felt tears filling his own eyes as he watched the soldier walk away.

Later, Paul told his parents what the soldier had said. "That must be a strange feeling, to know that somebody died to save your life," Paul added.

Dad nodded thoughtfully. "Actually, that happened to you, too," he said. "Someone did give his life for you."

"When?" asked Paul in surprise. "Who did that?"

"The Lord Jesus did," replied Dad. "All that he suffered on the cross was for you, Son—it was to pay for your sins, as well as for mine, Mom's, and those of the whole world."

"Oh, that's right!" said Paul. "I'm so glad I know him as my Savior." *C.Y.*

HOW ABOUT YOU?

Have you accepted the sacrifice that Jesus made for you? By his death on the cross, Jesus took the punishment for your sins, so you can have eternal life with him in heaven. If you've never asked him to forgive your sins, do it today.

MEMORIZE:

"He [Jesus] was wounded and bruised for *our* sins."

Isaiah 53:5, TLB

 Jesus Died for You

A Puppy for Lisa (Read Matthew 25:14-27)

12

NOVEMBER

Rex was angry. His little sister, Lisa, was in the living room playing with her new puppy, but he was sulking in his bedroom. If Lisa could have a puppy, he didn't see why he couldn't have a kitten! "Rex," said Dad when he saw his son's unhappy face, "you don't have any excuse for acting this way. You had the same chance to have a kitten that Lisa had for a puppy. If you had taken good care of your goldfish, we'd have allowed you to get a kitten. Instead of caring for the fish, you failed to clean its bowl and feed it. Lisa had to take over its care."

"But I don't like goldfish!" wailed Rex.

"You didn't have to like the fish," said Dad, "but you did have to take good care of it if you wanted a kitten. If we can't trust you to take care of something small, how can we expect you to take care of something bigger and more complicated like a cat?" Dad paused, then added, "You know, this is often how God works as well."

"What do you mean?" asked Rex. "Are you saying I shouldn't ask him for a kitten?"

"No, but I'm saying that God generally first trusts his children with small tasks," replied Dad. "I've known people who had dreams of doing great things for God, but they lacked the discipline to follow through on small things—like reading the Bible and praying, helping a neighbor, or doing a good job where they were. We need to do well in small things before God is likely to trust us with bigger tasks—such as going out and saving the world."

Rex thought about his father's words. "Dad?" he said after a few moments.

"Yes, Son?"

"Could I have my goldfish back?" asked Rex.

"Hmmmm," said Dad with a smile, "I suppose we could give it another try." *L.W.*

HOW ABOUT YOU?

Do you do your best in small things? Do you do a good job with your chores? With your schoolwork? Be faithful in whatever God gives you to do now. Then you can be trusted with even greater things.

MEMORIZE:

"Now it is required that those who have been given a trust must prove faithful."

1 Corinthians 4:2, NIV

Be Faithful in Small Things

The Shark's Bite (Read Psalm 3)

13

NOVEMBER

Lou Ann stood still outside the aquarium door. "I don't want to go in there," she protested. "It's full of sharks!"

"Oh, come on, Lou Ann," said Jeff. "The sharks are behind thick glass walls. There's no way they can get out."

"It's perfectly safe, honey," encouraged Dad.

"Well, I won't like it," Lou Ann said stubbornly, but she joined her family as they entered the aquarium.

On the other side of the aisle, glass walls rose from floor to ceiling, and beyond them was a magnificent view of life beneath the sea. Lou Ann felt like she had sunk to the floor of the Atlantic—hundreds of glittering fish swam about. "Oh, look!" she exclaimed. "There's a giant sea turtle." She stepped forward and pressed her nose against the glass as she watched the turtle swim away. She did not see a dim shadow emerge from the depths of the tank. It grew larger and larger as it swam toward her. A shark! Lou Ann screamed and darted back as the creature glided by right before her eyes.

Dad put an arm around his shaking daughter. "There's nothing to be afraid of, honey," he said. But Lou Ann was glad when they left the aquarium.

That evening there was a lot of excited chatter as the family discussed the events of the day. "I still don't like those sharks," stated Lou Ann.

Dad smiled. "That type of shark doesn't worry me as much as the 'sharks' that prey upon our family every day," he said. He reached for a devotional book and his Bible.

"I bet you mean the devil," said Lou Ann.

"Yes, I do," agreed Dad. "Satan would like nothing better than to sink his teeth into us. But God is like the thick glass that keeps the sharks away. He acts as a shield and protects us."

Mother nodded. "We stay behind that shield by learning and following God's Word. If we ignore God's will, it's as though we step out from his shield and become easy prey for the 'shark.'"

Lou Ann shivered. "I plan on staying behind God's shield forever!" she declared. *E.C.O.*

HOW ABOUT YOU?

Are you staying behind God's shield? Read your Bible every day. Learn and follow his guidelines for living. You'll save yourself from receiving some nasty "bites."

MEMORIZE:

"But You, O Lord, are a shield for me." *Psalm 3:3, NKJV*

 Stay Behind God's Shield

The Want List (Read 1 Chronicles 16:25-29)

14

NOVEMBER

"Can I stay home from church tonight?" asked Ben one Sunday evening. "I want to watch the big game on TV."

"No," said Dad firmly. "Worshiping God is more important than any football game."

"But we already went to church once," Ben grumbled. "Where does the Bible say we have to go twice?"

Dad sat down. "That's a fair question," said Dad, "but the answer might be hard to understand. As you know, the Bible says believers should meet together. Also, the early Christians met together as often as possible, even every day. But God didn't give us an exact amount of time we should spend in worship—in church or by ourselves."

"Why not?" asked Ben. "If it's so important, why didn't he spell it out?"

"Perhaps it's because he wants us to serve him out of love, not just from obligation," suggested Dad.

Still grumbling, Ben got ready for church. When he returned, Dad handed him a paper. "While you were getting dressed, I wrote something for you," he said.

Ben read it aloud. "Fishing line, hunting socks, cologne, typing paper . . ." He looked up. "There's twenty things on this list," he said. "What's it for?"

"It's my gift list—I want you to buy those for me," explained Dad. "Get me the first thing for Christmas, the next for my birthday, the next for Father's Day, and so on."

"But, Dad!" Ben frowned. "If I get you something because you say I have to, it won't seem like a real gift."

"That's true," agreed Dad. "Now perhaps you see what I was trying to say earlier about why God hasn't told us exactly when, where, and how to worship him. If he had, our worship might be more out of duty than out of love." He chuckled. "Do you think I would really want you to buy me a gift just because I told you to?"

"No," replied Ben, "and I see what you mean, Dad." Then he grinned. "I'm glad I don't have to follow this list, but I'll keep it. I just might want some ideas sometime." *S.K.*

HOW ABOUT YOU?

Do you complain about learning Bible verses, spending "quiet time" in prayer, or going to church? Do you worship only when you "have to"? If so, you're probably not really worshiping God at all. He is so wonderful and has done so much for you. Worship him out of love, with your whole heart.

MEMORIZE:

"Give to the Lord the glory due His name; bring an offering, and come before Him. Oh, worship the Lord in the beauty of holiness." *1 Chronicles 16:29, NKJV*

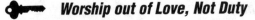 *Worship out of Love, Not Duty*

Stair Steps (Read Psalm 37:23-31)

"Oh, boy! Fried chicken!" exclaimed Jim. "I'm glad you invited me for dinner."

His grandparents smiled. "I noticed you went forward at the end of the service this morning, Jim," said Grandpa as he passed the chicken. "Was there a special reason?"

15

NOVEMBER

"Yes, sir," said Jim. "You know how I've always wanted to be a doctor?" Grandpa nodded and Jim continued, "Even though I'm just a kid, I really feel the Lord wants me to be a missionary doctor someday. Today I said yes." Grandma's eyes filled with happy tears, but Jim frowned slightly as he grabbed a biscuit. "I just don't know how I can ever do it, though. Mom says it costs a lot of money to get a doctor's training, and we're pretty poor since Dad died. I may not be smart enough to be a doctor," he added doubtfully.

"With God all things are possible," quoted Grandma softly.

After dinner, Grandpa asked Jim to go upstairs and get a book for him. "And let's see you leap up there in one bound," he added. "There are seventeen steps to the top."

Jim laughed. "I can't do that," he said.

"You have to take one step at a time, don't you—or maybe two steps since your legs are getting so long," said Grandpa. "It seems to me that reaching your goal of being a missionary doctor is like reaching the top of the stairs. God doesn't expect you to get there all at once. He expects you to take one step at a time."

Jim looked up the stairway thoughtfully. "I guess sometimes a person can't even see how to take one step."

"That's where faith comes in," answered Grandpa. "If the Lord says to step, you lift your foot, trusting him to make your way possible."

"I guess I took my first step today when I said yes," said Jim. "What do you suppose the next one will be?"

"Probably to study hard," suggested Grandpa. "And maybe the third will be to get a part-time job and save your money."

Jim grinned. "I better go home and start on my second step," he said. "I've got a test tomorrow." *M.R.P.*

HOW ABOUT YOU?

Do you feel God wants you to do something that seems impossible? He can help you study, witness, be kind, obey—anything! Be sensitive to what he wants you to do, both now and in the future. Don't be afraid to say yes to God. If he wants you to do something, it's not impossible.

MEMORIZE:

"With God all things are possible." *Matthew 19:26, NIV*

 You Can Do What God Asks

Basketball Blues  (Read Romans 12:1-8)

16

NOVEMBER

Joey yanked the door open, bounded into the house, and fell dramatically into an overstuffed chair in the living room. Behind the newspaper, his father watched Joey from the corner of his eye. "So, Joe. How was your day?" Dad asked his usual before-supper question.

"Fine," Joey muttered as he stared out the window.

Joey's father folded up the paper and laid it down beside him. "You don't seem very happy tonight," he said. "Is there something bothering you?"

Joey opened his mouth as if to speak, but then closed it, changing his mind. He sighed. "It's basketball that I'm bummed about," he said finally. "I didn't make the team."

"I didn't know you were going out for the team," said Dad. "Do you enjoy playing basketball that much?"

Joey shrugged. "All my friends are on the team," he said.

Dad reached over and picked up a sculpture of a bird.

"Will your friends like you less if you're not on the team?" he asked as he turned the bird over in his hands.

"No," Joey replied, "but I want to be like them. I just want to fit in."

"Let me ask you this, Joe," said Dad. "If your friends decided to rob a bank, would you still want to fit in?"

Joey laughed. "Of own course not, Dad," he replied.

"Even though you wouldn't be like them if you didn't?" said Dad.

Joey sighed. "I guess I just feel clumsy," he replied. He looked at the bird sculpture Dad was holding. "I remember making that," he said. "Sixth-grade art class."

"Apparently God didn't make you a great basketball player," observed Dad, "but he did give you a gift for art. And you enjoy it."

"Yeah," agreed Joey. He took the bird and examined it closely. "You know, Dad, maybe I'll sign up for an art class next year!"

"What about your friends?" asked Dad.

Joey laughed. "Maybe I'll carve them a basketball!" *V.L.R.*

HOW ABOUT YOU?

Do you try to fit in with your friends even if it means doing things you don't care about doing? God has given you special talents of your own. Don't try to copy what others do if it's not right for you. Be honest with yourself. Whatever your talent might be, find it and put it to use!

MEMORIZE:

"Having then gifts differing according to the grace that is given to us, let us use them."

Romans 12:6, NKJV

 ***Develop Your Own Talent***

The Fastest Balloon (Read James 2:1-9)

Kelly was helping decorate for a Sunday school party. Mrs. Brown, her teacher, filled each balloon with helium, and then Kelly tied a string around the end. "Do you suppose those new kids will come?" Kelly wondered out loud. "You know, those Harper kids that came last Sunday? They're kind of different."

17

NOVEMBER

"People are all different," Mrs. Brown pointed out.

"I guess so," admitted Kelly, "but those Harper kids wore such funny, worn-out clothes."

"Hmmmm," murmured Mrs. Brown as she handed another balloon to Kelly. "Well, I think I have just enough helium in the tank for two more balloons. Why don't we each choose a color and see which color will rise up faster."

"I'll have a blue one," said Kelly. "I like blue ones best."

"Then I'll take this purple one," said Mrs. Brown. "I bet it will go up to the ceiling faster than your blue one."

"Not if you fill them up the same," said Kelly.

"We'll see." Mrs. Brown inflated the balloons. After Kelly had tied long strings to both, she held the ends of the strings and watched the two balloons rise side by side.

"See, it's the helium in the balloon that makes them rise," said Kelly, "not the color."

"So it's what's inside that counts?" asked Mrs. Brown. Kelly nodded, and Mrs. Brown continued. "You're right, of course," she said. "I think that could also apply to people."

Kelly looked at her teacher. "I know a person's color isn't the important thing," she said.

"Good." Mrs. Brown nodded. "But outside appearance versus what's inside can apply to other things, too."

"Like the kind of clothes kids wear?" Kelly asked slowly.

"Exactly," agreed Mrs. Brown. "You see, Kelly, the way a person looks doesn't make him what he is, any more than the color of the balloon determines how fast it will rise or how high it will go. The important thing is not so much how people look, but what they are." *S.L.S.*

HOW ABOUT YOU?

What's important to you? Skin color? The right kind of clothes? Good looks? People come in all shapes, sizes, and colors. But everyone has feelings, and everyone deserves to be treated kindly. More importantly, every person has a soul, and that soul is precious to God. The inner person is what you should care about.

MEMORIZE:

"If you show favoritism, you sin." *James 2:9, NIV*

 Don't Show Favoritism

The Blank Page (Read Romans 6:12-18, 22)

18
NOVEMBER

"Hi, Mom," said Jason as he came into the house. "Want to see the picture I painted at school today?" He held out a paper with a scene of mountains and trees.

"This is really good, honey!" exclaimed Mother. "You're a good painter."

Jason beamed. "I think I'll be an artist when I grow up," he said. "I just love to paint." He went to a drawer and took out a fresh piece of paper and some paints.

"Well, that would be great," said Mother with a smile, "if that's what you feel the Lord wants you to do." She pointed to the paper that Jason had spread out on the kitchen table. "Have you ever looked at your blank paper and wondered what it will look like when your painting's done?" she asked.

"Sure." Jason grinned at his mother. "Sometimes I do good, but other times I mess it all up."

Mother nodded. "Our lives are like this blank paper," she said. "Our actions are like the brush that applies the colors to the page, making something beautiful or something ugly."

"But the brush can't paint by itself," said Jason. "It's up to the artist to choose the colors and paint the picture."

"That's right," agreed Mother. "And we can let either Satan or the Lord be the artist holding the brush—controlling our actions."

Jason looked at the blank page. "Well, I don't want Satan to be in charge of my life," he said. "He'd make a mess out of it."

"Yes," agreed Mother. "We need to give each day to the Lord," she said, "and constantly yield to him. Then we'll be pleased with the pages of our life—and he will, too." *M.R.P.*

HOW ABOUT YOU?

Is God pleased with the pictures on the pages of your life? Do they show kindness, obedience, and God's love? If you've messed up, ask the Lord to forgive you and make the ugly pages clean again. Ask him to help you do the things that please him. Let him, in his own way and time, make your life beautiful.

MEMORIZE:

"Do not offer the parts of your body to sin . . . but rather offer yourselves to God."

Romans 6:13, NIV

 *Let Christ Control You*

The Measuring Stick (Read Romans 3:9-12)

19

NOVEMBER

Calvin stood next to a wall, holding himself as straight as possible. His father made a chalk mark just above his head. When Calvin stepped aside, Dad began to measure the distance from the floor to the mark. "Let me do it," pleaded Bernie, Calvin's little brother. Bernie was studying measurements in school, and he had been running around measuring things all week.

A few minutes later Bernie whistled. "Wow!" he marveled. "You're ten feet tall."

"What?" asked Calvin. "That can't be right. What kind of measuring stick are you using, anyway?"

"It's one I made," said Bernie, looking at the stick he held. "I thought it looked about right."

"Well, it's wrong," said Calvin scornfully. "You have to use a regular yardstick, don't you, Dad?"

"Correct," agreed Dad. "An improper measuring stick will give the wrong measurements. You can't use your own ideas about how long a foot is." He was thoughtful as he measured Calvin's height again. "A lot of people use their own self-made measuring sticks," he added.

"They do?" asked Calvin. "I don't know anybody who made a measuring stick . . . except Bernie."

"I wasn't thinking of an actual measuring stick," explained Dad. "I was just thinking of how so many people expect to get to heaven because they consider themselves to be good. But do you know how they measure their goodness? By their own rules. God's rule is the Bible. It says, 'All have sinned and come short of the glory of God.' We all fail to measure up to God's glory. That's why we need Jesus to save us. It's only by accepting him as Savior that we can measure up to his requirement for entering into heaven." *M.R.P.*

HOW ABOUT YOU?

What are you using to measure your life? God measures according to his glory, and everyone comes short of his standard. But when you receive Jesus as your Savior, God will declare you to be just as righteous—or good—as Jesus is. Trust him now.

MEMORIZE:

"For there is not a just man on earth who does good and does not sin." *Ecclesiastes 7:20, NKJV*

 Use God's Standards

The Oyster and the Pearl

(Read James 1:2-4; 1 Peter 1:6-7)

20

NOVEMBER

"It's just not fair," complained Kimberly, pointing to the cast on her leg. "Why do bad things always happen to me?"

"Trials come to all of us," answered her mother. "You see, no one's perfect, and we all need help in developing Christian character."

"Well, couldn't I get more help for my character at school and church than lying here?" asked Kimberly.

"We have to leave that sort of thing to God," replied Mother. "He knows what you need. I want to show you something," she said. She left the room but soon returned with a small box. She opened the lid, and Kimberly peered inside.

"Oh, the pin Grandma used to wear!" exclaimed Kimberly. "It's so pretty. Is that a real pearl?"

Mother nodded. "Do you know how this pearl was formed?"

"Sure," said Kimberly. "Something—maybe a grain of sand—got inside an oyster's shell and hurt him. So he made some stuff to cover the sand. And after a long time, it was a pearl."

"That's right," said Mother. "An oyster makes something beautiful out of any object that irritates it. Don't you think we should follow that principle?" She paused, then added, "Perhaps you could start letting your broken leg help you make your life more beautiful."

"Whew!" said Kimberly with a frown. "My leg really hurts! How can I make anything beautiful from that?"

"Maybe this is a good time to learn patience," suggested Mother. "The Bible says, 'The testing of your faith produces patience' [James 1:3, *NKJV*]. You do need more patience, you know."

Kimberly sighed. "Yeah, I guess I do get all upset when things don't go right," she admitted. "OK, I'll work on doing better. But how long am I going to have to wear this stupid cast? It's so—" Kimberly stopped. Then she grinned. "There I go again! Maybe I have to wear it just long enough to grow one tiny pearl of patience—or I might even try for a whole string of pearls." *M.R.P.*

HOW ABOUT YOU?

Do troubles make you cross and upset? Everything in a Christian's life is there for a purpose. God may use trials to teach you patience and endurance or to teach you to trust him or to make you a better Christian in some way. Learn to be joyful as he develops beautiful pearls from your troubles.

MEMORIZE:

"Count it all joy when you fall into various trials." *James 1:2, NKJV*

⚷ Trials Can Beautify Your Life

Deleting Mrs. Trembley (Read Isaiah 56:5-7; Luke 10:20)

21

NOVEMBER

Sandy swallowed hard. Ever since Dad had helped her set up her paper route accounts on the computer, she had worked very hard, keeping the records up-to-date. But now she appeared anything but businesslike as her fingers hovered over the delete key. The name on the computer screen glowed with a special brightness—or so it seemed to eleven-year-old Sandy. As she stared at it, she tried hard not to cry. "Elizabeth C. Trembley, 288 Fiftieth Street, Grand Rapids, Michigan." Sandy swallowed again, and then punched the key. The computer screen turned instantly blank and the name was gone forever—just like Mrs. Trembley.

A tear slid down Sandy's cheek as her mother came into the room. "Why, honey, what's the matter?" asked Mother.

"I . . . I erased Mrs. Trembley." Sandy gulped. She gestured toward the family computer on the table behind her as she brushed a tear away with the back of her hand. "I feel so bad, Mom. Mrs. Trembley was the nicest lady on my paper route. And she always paid me right on time, too." Mother nodded. Mrs. Trembley had been a real friend to Sandy. But the kind, elderly woman had died of a heart attack two weeks earlier. "When I pushed the delete button, I felt like I was the one erasing Mrs. Trembley's life," added Sandy faintly.

"Wasn't Mrs. Trembley a Christian?" asked Mother.

Sandy nodded. "She told me she accepted Jesus when she was a little girl."

"Then Mrs. Trembley is safe with the Lord," Mother told her. "Her name is written in the Lamb's Book of Life, and it will never be deleted. You deleted her name from the computer, but no one will ever erase her name from God's records."

Sandy thought about that. She sighed but she nodded. "I'm glad of that," she said with a little smile. *C.B.*

 Make Sure You're Saved

MEMORIZE:

"Everyone who conquers will be clothed in white, and I will not erase his name from the Book of Life, but I will announce before my Father and his angels that he is mine."

Revelation 3:5, TLB

Vera's Sadness (Read Psalm 145:17-19)

22

NOVEMBER

"The house will be so empty without Bobby," Vera said, wiping tears from her eyes. "Why didn't God make him well? How can we manage without him?" Vera and her parents were driving home from the funeral home, where her baby brother's body lay in a tiny casket.

Mother put her arm around Vera. "Honey, there are some things we can't understand, but we know God cares," Mother said softly with tears in her eyes. "Remember, the doctor told us when Bobby was born that he might not live even a month? Of course, we'll miss him, but we can be thankful we had him for three months—and that he's with Jesus now."

"I know," replied Vera, "but I still feel awful." Mother hugged her a little closer.

Daddy pulled into the driveway and turned off the motor. "Vera, do you remember what Pastor Hughes said this evening?" he asked as they got out of the car. Vera stood silently thinking. Then she squealed as Daddy suddenly scooped her up in his arms and carried her into the house. "That's your clue," he said, putting her down.

Vera looked at her father with a little smile. "Now I remember. Pastor Hughes said when we feel too sad to go on, God will carry us. But I don't know what that means."

"It means God cares for us and will comfort us," Daddy explained. "He'll help us through the sad times in our life."

Mother nodded. "We need to learn to trust him," she said. She smiled at Vera. "Now," she added, "shall we read a bedtime story together? We must not let our sadness keep us from doing the things we've always enjoyed."

Vera knew Mother was right. And she knew that somehow she and Mother and Daddy would manage to be happy again as they waited for the day when they'd be reunited with little Bobby in heaven. *M.S.*

HOW ABOUT YOU?

Do you feel sad about something that happened in your life? Do you wonder why God let it happen? When you can't understand why certain things happen, you can trust God to help you. He loves you and doesn't want you to hurt. Thank him that he will carry you through your difficult times.

MEMORIZE:

"He heals the brokenhearted and binds up their wounds."

Psalm 147:3, NKJV

 *God Comforts the Sad*

Super Glue (Read Romans 8:31-39)

23

NOVEMBER

Crash! Philip's mother looked up from her sewing and listened. "Oh, no!" came a wail from the kitchen. "What am I going to do?" A moment later, Philip shuffled into the sewing room holding a coffee mug with a broken handle. "I just broke Dad's favorite mug," he confessed. "I didn't mean to. It just fell when I was going to rinse it."

Mother took the cup and looked it over. "I know it was an accident," she said, "and Dad will understand. But I think we can fix it good as new. Come with me."

In the kitchen, Mother grabbed a small yellow tube. She took off the cap and squeezed a tiny bead of clear glue onto each end of the handle. Then she pressed the broken handle to the mug and held it for a few seconds. Setting it on the counter, she looked at it. "You can't even tell it was broken," she said with a smile.

Philip looked at the once-broken mug. "What happens if the glue gets wet? Won't it come unstuck?" he asked.

Mother shook her head. "If this glue is as good as the man at the hardware store says, nothing will be able to break the handle apart from the mug."

"Well, that's a relief," said Philip with a sigh.

Mother smiled as she started back to the sewing room.

"All this reminds me of some verses in the Bible," she said.

"The Bible!" exclaimed Philip. "You're kidding! I'm sure the Bible doesn't talk about glue! They didn't have glue back then."

Mother laughed. "No, but the Bible says that nothing can separate us from the love of God. Once we've received Jesus as Savior, it's like we're permanently stuck to him."

Philip grinned. "That's neat," he said.

Mother nodded. "Yes, it is," she agreed. "Now, go finish the dishes—and try not to break anything else." *L.S.R.*

HOW ABOUT YOU?

Aren't you glad that, as a Christian, the love of God is yours for keeps? No matter what you do, God loves you! No matter what problems you face, God loves you! He will help you through them. No matter what happens in this world, God loves you! What a wonderful God!

MEMORIZE:

"Neither death nor life, neither angels nor demons, . . . nor anything else in all creation, will be able to separate us from the love of God that is in Christ Jesus our Lord."

Romans 8:38-39, NIV

 God Always Loves You

Missing Guests! (Read Hebrews 5:12-14)

24
NOVEMBER

"Do we have to go to church this morning?" Brent asked his mother. "Can't we stay home and get ready for the Andersons?" Some former neighbors from another town were coming for a visit.

Mother surveyed the house. "Everything is ready," she said. "The roast is in the oven, the table is set, and the house has been cleaned from top to bottom."

"But maybe they'll get here early," persisted Brent. "Shouldn't we be here to greet them?"

"We are going to church this morning," Dad said firmly as he got his coat out of the closet. "I'm a little concerned about your attitude lately, Brent. You didn't want to go to church last week either." Brent just shrugged.

After church, Brent and his family hurried right home, looking forward to their visitors. While they waited, Dad turned on the telephone answering machine to see if there were any messages. Brent heard the familiar click. Then he heard Mr. Anderson's voice. "I'm sorry we won't be able to make it today," said Mr. Anderson. "It's been a very busy week, and we just don't feel up to making the fifty-mile trip."

"What kind of lame excuse is that?" protested Brent. "Poor Mom! She spent all that time cleaning and cooking—and we all helped, too—and now they're not even coming!"

Dad looked at Brent thoughtfully. "This reminds me of someone else who prepared a special meal, but the guest didn't want to come," he said.

"Really?" asked Brent. "Who didn't want to come?"

"You," replied Dad. He went on to explain. "Pastor Mueller is a man who loves the Lord and cares about teaching the Bible. Each week he spends many hours in study, preparing a message that's like a spiritual meal for us. The choir and those giving the special music help prepare that spiritual meal by spending a lot of time in practice. Think how they feel when people give silly reasons for staying home from church." *L.W.*

HOW ABOUT YOU?

Do you often stay home from church or youth activities to watch a special television show or because you're tired? Many people spend time preparing for each meeting. Be there so you can "eat" the spiritual food that comes from God's Word and from fellowship with Christians. As a result, you will grow in the Lord.

MEMORIZE:

"Oh, taste and see that the Lord is good; blessed is the man who trusts in Him!"

Psalm 34:8, NKJV

Attend Church Activities

Songs of Thanksgiving (Read Luke 17:12-19)

Great-Aunt Jennie had a tiny yellow canary in a shiny brass cage. Carrie loved to watch and listen as the bird fluttered around, pecking seeds and singing his happy songs. Great-Aunt Jennie said she figured the bird sang because he was thankful. "You know, dear," she said in her scratchy voice, "the Bible says in Deuteronomy 8:10 [NKJV], 'When you have eaten and are full, then you shall bless the Lord your God.'" Great-Aunt Jennie had a Bible verse for almost everything, even happy canaries.

25
NOVEMBER

Carrie perched on a high stool, listening while the little bird poured cheerful notes into the sunny kitchen. "Aunt Jennie," said Carrie thoughtfully, "at our house we don't always pray when we eat. Sometimes Dad calls and says he'll be late, so Mom fixes a tray for me to eat in the family room while she feeds Timmy in his high chair."

Great-Aunt Jennie's smile softened the directness of her answer. "Well, no matter where you're eating, you can thank Jesus for your supper tray. The Bible says we're not to forget our benefits." Carrie didn't answer, so Aunt Jennie asked, "Do you remember the story about Jesus healing the ten lepers, but only one returned to thank him?"

"Yes," Carrie nodded.

"Even Jesus seemed surprised that the others forgot, didn't he?" Great-Aunt Jennie looked toward the cage. "You notice, no one has to remind my canary to be grateful—he just naturally is. It's almost as if he's trying to teach us how to be thankful, isn't it?"

Carrie watched the old lady's blue eyes twinkling behind her glasses. She knew the sweet smile and contented manner reflected a thankful heart.

"Because Jesus is my Savior, Carrie, I've found that a prayer of thanksgiving is as natural as a canary's song," added Great-Aunt Jennie. "I believe God wants us to learn from this little teacher."

"I'll remember," Carrie promised with a smile. "And wait till I tell Dad and Mom I had a lesson from a canary. Won't they be surprised?" *P.K.*

HOW ABOUT YOU?

Does thanksgiving come naturally to you? Do you remember to thank the Lord for your blessings every day—not only on Thanksgiving? He asks us to be grateful for all things. Be sure you are—and tell him.

MEMORIZE:

"In everything give thanks."
1 Thessalonians 5:18, NKJV

 *Thanksgiving Should Be Natural*

A Little Syrup (Read Psalm 37:1-9)

26

NOVEMBER

"Are we going to set up all the trees today?" asked Gary as his father drilled a hole into the trunk of a maple tree. "This will take forever."

"Making maple syrup does take a long time, and it's hard work," agreed Dad, "but it's worth the effort."

Gary helped his father until all the maple trees had buckets hanging from the pipes, ready to collect the sap that would drip out during the week.

Back in the house, Gary slumped into a chair. "What a lot of work," he said with a sigh. "In a week we'll be out there gathering all those buckets of sap. But no, we won't have syrup yet! We'll have to dump the sap in that big container and gather wood to build a fire under it. And then we have to boil and boil, and we'll stir it and stir it, and finally, what will we have? Gallons and gallons of syrup? No! By the time the water is out of the sap, we'll probably have one measly little quart of syrup. Making maple syrup takes too long. Wouldn't it be a lot easier to buy some?"

"Yes, but it wouldn't be nearly as good," said Mother. "We're going for quality!"

"Well, I hate waiting," grumbled Gary.

"Hmmmm. Do you suppose God thinks and feels like that, too?" Dad asked.

Gary frowned. "God?" he asked. "I've never thought about what God thinks of maple syrup."

Dad smiled. "I wasn't talking about syrup," he said, "but it occurred to me that it sometimes takes us a long time to make some very small steps toward godliness. And God waits."

Mother nodded. "It's a slow process for lives to be 'boiled down,' like the sap," she agreed. "And after all the 'water,' or negative things in our life, is removed, it might look like there's very little left."

"God patiently waits for us to make those little steps," added Dad, "because when the result is quality, a little means a lot."

N.E.K.

HOW ABOUT YOU?

Do you feel like you'll never get control of your temper? Or learn how to witness to your friends? Does it seem like you're making very little progress in your Christian walk? Sometimes what looks "little" has great value. Trust God to turn your life into quality "syrup," slowly making you more like him.

MEMORIZE:

"Being confident of this very thing, that He who has begun a good work in you will complete it until the day of Jesus Christ."

Philippians 1:6, NKJV

 **Be Patient**

A Way to Visit (Read Hebrews 4:12-16)

Carrie's eyes filled with tears, and she rubbed at them angrily. "Bethany, you just can't move away!" she wailed. "You're my best friend."

But Bethany did move away, and soon the two girls were carrying on a lively correspondence. They "visited" each other through letters, and whenever their mothers would let them, they also called one another on the phone.

27

NOVEMBER

One day, Carrie took one of Bethany's letters to share with her Sunday school class. The teacher, Mrs. Lemon, let her read it aloud before the lesson began. "I really miss Bethany," said Carrie after she read the letter, "but we write each other a lot, and we visit on the phone. When Bethany left, I thought I'd never see her anymore, but we're going to get together sometime soon."

Mrs. Lemon smiled. "Girls," she said, "you remember that Jesus went back to heaven after his resurrection. I'm sure his disciples missed him very much, just as Carrie misses Bethany. Two angels told them that he'd return someday. We look forward to that time, too. But tell me, how can we 'visit' with Jesus now, even though we can't see him? How does he talk to us?"

Carrie raised her hand. "Through the Bible," she said. "It's like he wrote letters for us to read."

"That's right," said Mrs. Lemon. "Someday we'll see him face to face, but right now he talks to us when we read his Word." She looked at Carrie. "Would you ever consider putting one of Bethany's letters aside and never reading it at all?" she asked.

Carrie shook her head vigorously. "I'd like to read a letter from Bethany every day," she said. "We should read something from God's Word each day, too, shouldn't we?"

Smiling, Mrs. Lemon nodded. "And don't forget that we can talk with him in prayer," she added. *S.E.F.*

HOW ABOUT YOU?

Do you miss a special friend who has moved away? Do you still visit your friend through letters and phone calls? Jesus has gone to heaven, but he still wants to speak to you through the Bible. Do you let him do that? Do you talk with God in prayer each day? He wants to visit with you in these ways.

MEMORIZE:

"I will listen to what God the Lord will say." *Psalm 85:8, NIV*

 "Visit" with God

The Coach's Voice (Read 1 Corinthians 2:9-16)

28

NOVEMBER

The referee's whistle for time-out sent Dave and his team-mates to the sideline. "Dave, stay outside where you get your best shots," said the coach. "Tom will pass to you. Jerry and Bob will handle rebounds, and Ted will be free to move. Listen closely for my directions."

When play started, the crowd shouted advice. "Dave! Get under the basket!" he heard. "Get the rebounds, Dave!" It was hard not to listen when he heard his name. He concentrated on one voice, the voice of his coach, calling directions. Dave's two baskets carried his team to a lead at halftime.

Dave sagged onto a bench, feeling weak from playing two full quarters. "Jerry, you look like you just started," he said, watching his friend pacing the locker room.

"I feel great!" Jerry said. He leaned closer. "My mother has these pills she takes when she needs a boost. I take 'em on game days," he confided. "I could run forever!" He laughed loudly. "Do you want one? It'll do you good. It might be the difference between winning and losing."

Thoughts filled Dave's head like the voices of the crowd. He thought about how tired he was and how much his team was counting on him. He thought about how great Jerry looked. A voice in his head shouted, "Take a pill! Take it!"

Then, just as he had made a decision to listen to his coach and ignore the advice of the crowd, Dave decided to listen to the voice of God speaking to him. It wasn't as loud in his mind as the other voices, but sure enough, it was there when he listened. "You were bought at a price; therefore glorify God in your body" (1 Corinthians 6:20, *NKJV*).

Dave looked at Jerry. "I don't want any," he said.

"Aw, c'mon," Jerry coaxed. "The coach wouldn't care."

"My Coach would," Dave said. "He told me so!" *C.R.*

HOW ABOUT YOU?

Does it seem like everyone tries to give you advice? Does that advice sometimes contradict what you have learned from the Bible? God wants to lead you in the right path. Listen for his voice, and he will speak to you. He will guide you with his Word and through the Holy Spirit.

MEMORIZE:

"When He, the Spirit of truth, has come, He will guide you into all truth." *John 16:13, NKJV*

 *Listen to God*

The God of Ninevah (Read Jonah 3:1-10)

29

Roger and his sister Michelle looked at the floor as their mother told Dad what had happened that afternoon. "Officer Johnson from the police department called," reported Mother. "Roger and Michelle were caught with a group of kids who were shoplifting. Our kids didn't actually take anything, but the police had taken them in for questioning, along with the others—most of whom were guilty of shoplifting."

"Shoplifting?" asked Dad, surprised.

"We never took anything, Dad," Roger said quickly. "We know it's wrong to steal."

"Did you know what the other kids were doing?" Dad asked. The children didn't answer, and Dad shook his head. "You shouldn't even be with kids who shoplift," he told them. "Some people would consider you to be guilty by association. In other words, they figure if you're with that crowd, you must be a part of what's going on."

Michelle began to cry. "I'm sorry. I'll never, ever go with them again," she promised.

Dad looked at Roger. "Me neither," said Roger, looking down. "I'm sorry I ever went with them in the first place."

"Hmmmm," murmured Dad. "I'll have to think about your punishment. Let's read from the book of Jonah and see how God disciplined the people of Ninevah for their sin."

When they finished reading, Michelle smiled. "The people were sorry," she said, "so God didn't punish them."

"Does that mean you're not gonna punish us?" Roger asked hopefully.

"You both said you were sorry and you wouldn't run around with those kids again," said Dad, "so I'll show mercy this time, just as God did. I believe you're sorry and have learned something."

"We have," Michelle agreed.

"Yeah—and thanks, Dad," added Roger with relief.

Dad smiled. "You're welcome," he said. "Now, let's thank God for his great mercy, too, shall we?" *S.N.*

HOW ABOUT YOU?

Do you know that God is a God of mercy? He doesn't enjoy punishing you. He would rather have you repent and turn away from your sin when you're warned, like Ninevah did. Thank God for his mercy and try to obey him always.

MEMORIZE:

"Who is a God like you, who pardons sin. . . . You do not stay angry forever but delight to show mercy." *Micah 7:18, NIV*

 God is Merciful

The God of Ninevah (continued from yesterday)

(Read Nahum 1:1-3; 2:8-10; 3:7)

30
NOVEMBER

Michelle came home from school by herself. "Where's your brother?" asked Mother as Michelle came in the door.

Michelle hesitated. "Uh . . . well . . . he went to the drugstore with some friends," she said slowly.

"What friends?" asked Mother suspiciously. "I hope it's not the same group that was caught shoplifting." Michelle didn't answer. "Is it that group?" demanded Mother, and finally Michelle admitted that it was.

When Roger came home about an hour later, Dad was already home. "Where have you been?" asked Dad.

"Oh, I was just in town at the drugstore," Roger replied.

"Who were you with?" Dad asked him.

"Uh . . . nobody," answered Roger sheepishly.

"That's funny," Dad said. "Michelle tried to get out of telling, but when Mother insisted, she admitted that you were with some other kids. The same ones, in fact, who were caught shoplifting last week."

Roger stared at the floor. "All right," he finally said with a sigh, "but nobody shoplifted anything today. Besides, I'll never go with them again. I promise. I really mean it!"

Dad reached for his Bible. "I think we need to read about Ninevah again," he said, "only this time we'll read in the book of Nahum. This book was written 150 years after the book of Jonah."

As Dad began reading, Roger squirmed in his chair. "That's talking about God's destruction of Ninevah," said Dad when he had finished. "Earlier, God showed mercy. But the people sinned again, and God had had enough of their sin." Dad looked at Roger and shook his head. "I'm afraid I can't be merciful with you this time, Son. You didn't learn your lesson when I was merciful, so now you must be disciplined." *S.N.*

HOW ABOUT YOU?

Do you know that God hates sin? He is a God of holiness as well as of mercy. When people will not turn from their sin, he must punish them.

MEMORIZE:

"The Lord disciplines those he loves, and punishes everyone he accepts as a son."

Hebrews 12:6, NIV

 **God Is Holy**

On Earth, Peace (Read Luke 2:8-16)

"This house is like a war zone," fretted Mother. "Fussing, arguing, quarreling. Oh, for some peace and quiet!" Just then, Amy slammed the door behind her as she came into the room. "Now what?" Mother asked.

"Guess who got the part of Mary in the Christmas play?" Amy asked sarcastically. "Holly, of course. And she said she didn't even want it! I'm the Reader . . . again!"

1

DECEMBER

Dad looked up. "Isn't Holly your best friend?"

Amy curled her lip. "She *was* my best friend," she corrected. Scowling, she went to her room.

As four-year-old Sandy helped Mother decorate cookies, a little later, she practiced her part for the Christmas program. "Glory to God in the high . . . highest, and on earth, peace, good . . . good will toward men," she recited. Then she asked, "Mommy, did Mary get Jesus' baby clothes at the Goodwill store?"

Mother laughed. "No, honey. They didn't have Goodwill Industries in Jesus' time," she said.

"Mom," said Amy, coming back into the kitchen, "when are Aunt Edna and Uncle Carl coming?"

Mother frowned. "They aren't," she replied shortly.

"Not coming?" cried Amy. "Why not? It won't be like Christmas without them!" When Mother didn't reply, Amy looked at her suspiciously. "Haven't you spoken to Aunt Edna since Great-Grandmother's funeral?" she asked. "Are you still mad about that album?"

"I'd rather not discuss it," Mother answered icily.

"You're mad at Aunt Edna," observed little Sandy. "And Amy's mad at Holly. I don't know who I'm mad at." She went back to practicing her lines. "On earth peace, good will toward men."

Mother sighed. "On earth peace, good will toward men," she repeated softly. "I could use some peace." She went to the telephone. "I'm going to call Aunt Edna. It's still not too late for them to come for Christmas."

Amy smiled. "Really? Then I'll call Holly," she decided. "Maybe she can come over and help decorate cookies." *B.W.*

HOW ABOUT YOU?

Do you have bad feelings in your heart toward someone? Is there someone you need to make peace with? Jesus came to bring peace on earth. He wants you to have peace in your heart and be at peace with others.

MEMORIZE:

"Live in peace with each other." *1 Thessalonians 5:13, NIV*

 Live in Peace with Others

Beware of Little Foxes (Read Matthew 18:15, 21-22)

2
DECEMBER

Mandy burst through the door and dropped her books noisily on the kitchen table. Her mother looked up in surprise. Seeing the angry expression on her daughter's face, she asked gently, "Something wrong, honey?"

"Yes, something's wrong!" Mandy's words burst out. "I'm never going to speak to Laura again!" Laura was Mandy's best friend. "Kim told me she heard Laura and Ginny talking about the roller skating party last Friday night. I had to baby-sit that night, and Laura told me she wasn't going skating if I couldn't go. Now I know what kind of a friend she is!"

"Now, Mandy, surely you girls can share your friendship with others," reasoned Mother. "It's foolish for you to be so tied to one another that one of you can't go somewhere unless the other goes."

"It's not so much that Laura went, Mom, but that she didn't tell me," Mandy said sadly.

"Why don't you call Laura and talk this over?" Mother advised softly. "It could be just a misunderstanding and not what you think at all. You know, in the Bible there's a verse that speaks of the 'little foxes spoiling the tender vines.' Do you want to let a couple of little foxes named 'Gossip' and 'Jealousy' spoil the tender vine of your long friendship with Laura?" The chime of the doorbell interrupted Mother's words.

Mandy opened the door, and there stood Laura. "Hi, Mandy," said Laura eagerly. "Has Ginny talked to you yet?" Mandy shook her head. "She's inviting us to her birthday party Friday night—it's going to be a skating party," continued Laura. "She talked to me at school, and she's going to call you tonight."

"Oh, really?" asked Mandy. "I . . . I thought . . ."

"Come in, Laura, and have a cookie," Mandy's mother broke in. She poured two glasses of milk. "I'm sure you girls have a lot to talk about," she said as she left the room. "Enjoy your snack."

P.K.

HOW ABOUT YOU?

Do you allow little things to spoil friendships? Believe the best about your friends. Even if they do hurt you sometimes, forgive them. Show your love for God by the way you love others.

MEMORIZE:

"Be kind to one another, tenderhearted, forgiving one another, even as God in Christ forgave you." *Ephesians 4:32, NKJV*

 *Be a True Friend*

Special House, Special Person

(Read Matthew 5:14-16)

3

DECEMBER

"Oh!" gasped Alyssa. "Look!" She and her family were driving around the city, taking their annual "Christmas lights tour." Dad pulled to the side of the street so they could look at the house that had won the award for the best lights. They admired it for a few minutes, then continued on their way. But none of the other places could compare to the house that won the award.

The next day was the first day of Christmas vacation. "I'm glad school's done for a little while," declared Alyssa at the breakfast table. "I can't do anything right in school. I don't read well. I can't spell. I do crummy in math." She let out a long sigh. "I try hard, but I just can't do it. I'm a failure," she added dramatically.

Dad looked at Alyssa for a moment. "Go get your coat on," he said as she finished her breakfast. "I want to take my little 'failure' for a ride."

Alyssa and her father went out to the car. "Where are we going?" Alyssa asked as they drove through the city.

"You'll see," said Dad. Soon he pulled up to the side of the street. "Recognize this place?" Alyssa shook her head. Dad pointed. "That's the house we saw last night," he told her.

"You mean the one that had all the beautiful lights?" asked Alyssa, surprised. "It doesn't look like much now!"

Dad smiled. "You're right—it's when we see the lights that it looks beautiful," he said. "I thought about that when you were telling us you can't do anything well. You see, as Christians we may not always be able to do things as well as we'd like. But the important thing is that people see the light of Christ in us." He paused as he smiled at his daughter. "Alyssa," he added, "though you struggle in school, I can say this: The Lord surely does shine through you. This is a special house, and you're a special person."

Alyssa smiled. "Thanks for the encouragement, Dad," she said as she gave him a big hug. *S.N.*

HOW ABOUT YOU?

Do you feel like a failure? Like you can't do anything well? Do you feel that you don't have any great talents or special abilities? If you're a Christian, you have a great ability and a great responsibility—that is to be a light and witness in the world.

MEMORIZE:

"You are the light of the world."

Matthew 5:14, NKJV

 Be a Light in the World

A Wonderful Gift (Read Philippians 2:3-8)

4

DECEMBER

"Oh, Mother, I can't wait until Dad gets home," said Marcia, full of enthusiasm. "I've waited so long for a Christmas tree—I'm so anxious to decorate it!"

Mother hesitated. "Marcia, honey, I'm not sure . . ." She left the sentence unfinished.

"Dad will bring one," Marcia said confidently. She pressed her nose against the window to watch for Dad. Finally he came into view, but his head was down, and he carried no tree. As he entered the house, he brushed past Marcia with a quick greeting. She couldn't believe it. Her father let her down!

Although Marcia knew that Christmas was the time to remember the birth of Jesus, she didn't feel like celebrating. She felt more like sulking in her room, which was what she did. The sound of voices soon interrupted her thoughts.

"I feel so terrible that I can't afford to get Marcia a Christmas tree," Dad sounded even more sad than Marcia felt. She couldn't hear Mother's reply. Immediately Marcia had a plan.

After their conversation ended, Marcia joined her parents. "Dad, could we get out that little artificial tree we used in Grandma's hospital room last year?" she asked. She pretended to be thrilled. As Marcia helped her father decorate the little tree, she continued with her cheerful act. "I remember when you and I bought this ornament," she said as she hung the bird on the tree.

The angel from years past overwhelmed the tiny tree, but Dad placed it on the top anyway. "Your mother and I bought this for your first Christmas," he said, as he had every year.

By the time they finished working and talking, Dad's spirits had lifted. And Marcia was surprised to discover that she no longer had to pretend to be happy. Her joy was real.

At bedtime, Marcia thanked God for his love in sending Jesus to be her Savior. On Christmas morning she would open her presents. She didn't expect to get many, but that didn't matter. She had already received a wonderful gift—the joy of making another person happy. *E.M.B.*

HOW ABOUT YOU?

Is there something you could do to make someone's Christmas happier? Express greater appreciation? Reduce your own "want list"? Hide a disappointment? Remember, the greatest joy of Christmas is giving to someone else.

MEMORIZE:

"It is more blessed to give than to receive." *Acts 20:35, NIV*

Learn to Give

Too Big a Bite (Read Mark 4:3-20)

5

"Tomorrow evening is the mission rally at church," Dad reminded his family as they were eating at their favorite restaurant.

"I have play practice at school," said Marla.

"The last time we had a special service you had a band concert," Mother reminded her. "Perhaps we've allowed you to do too much at school."

"Why, hello." The voice of Marla's Sunday school teacher interrupted them. "I missed you Saturday morning, Marla," said Miss Willis. "We had such a good time at the nursing home." After chatting a few minutes, she left.

"Why didn't you go to the nursing home?" asked Dad.

Marla answered, "I was making student council posters."

Mother frowned. "It seems to me that you are too—"

"What's wrong with that man?" interrupted Marla, pointing to another table.

Dad jumped up and dashed across the room. "Are you choking, sir?" he asked. The man nodded frantically. "I'm going to help you," said Dad. He stood behind the frightened man and put his arms around him. With his clenched fist, he gave a couple of sharp upward thrusts. The man gasped for air, and a moment later he was breathing normally again. Everyone applauded.

"Oh, thank you," said the man when he was able to talk. "I guess I tried to eat too fast. I was in too big a hurry."

On the way home, Marla's family talked about what had happened. "We're so busy, we even eat in a rush," observed Dad. "That makes it easy to choke. And it's very easy to get choked by the cares of life, too. We can get involved in so many things that we choke out our spiritual life."

Mother nodded. "There are a lot of things we can get involved in that are not wrong," she said. "They may even be good, unless they consume our time so much that we forget God."

Marla was sure her parents were thinking of her. "Maybe I've bitten off more than I can chew," she admitted. "Maybe I'll drop some activities." *B.W.*

HOW ABOUT YOU?

As you get older, you will find many things crowding into your life. Do you still have time for prayer, Bible reading, and church? Be sure you don't get so busy with the cares of life that your spiritual life is choked out. Let your life be used for God.

MEMORIZE:

"Take heed to yourselves, lest your hearts be weighed down with . . . cares of this life."

Luke 21:34, NKJV

 Don't Get Too Busy

No Sissy (Read Isaiah 41:10-13)

6

DECEMBER

"It's icy, Eric," said Dad as he walked with his little son one wintry day. "Let me hold your hand."

"No," protested Eric, but soon he slipped and fell. "I'll hold your coat," he told his dad.

After a few more steps, Eric fell flat again. That hurt, so, holding back the tears, he said, "I guess you'd better hold my hand, Daddy." The next time Eric slipped, he didn't fall because his father's hand held him firmly.

Several years later, some boys at school made fun of Eric for refusing to join them in telling dirty jokes. "Baby!" they said. "Sissy!" Eric said nothing, but that night he promised himself that if the boys teased him again, he'd be brave and witness to them. It happened the next day—"Sissy! Baby!" the boys chanted. Eric's knees shook. He opened his mouth, but no words came. The boys walked away, laughing.

That night Eric told his father what had happened. "Eric," Dad said, "you may not recall this, but one day long ago, you fell on the ice two times before you finally let me hold your hand. You couldn't walk by yourself on the icy spots. You needed my strong hand to hold you up." Dad smiled as he remembered. "I think you're trying to go it alone again. You need God's help, Son. He'll hold your hand, if you'll let him."

When Eric saw the boys the next day, he prayed, "Lord, please help me to be a brave witness." When the boys approached him and asked if he'd grown up enough to join their gang, Eric took a deep breath. "I don't want to join it," he said. "And I'd like to tell you why. I'm a Christian, and God wouldn't be pleased if I did some of the things you do." He took another deep breath and hurried on. "Why don't you join me instead?" he asked. "I'm going to Bible Club tonight—you'd like it."

The boys sneered. But as they walked away, Eric heard one boy declare, "He's weird—but he's no sissy!" *M.R.P.*

HOW ABOUT YOU?

Are you weak-kneed and tongue-tied when others want you to take part in wrong activities? Is it hard for you to witness at school and in your neighborhood? Trust the Lord to "hold your hand"; then stand up and be counted for Jesus.

MEMORIZE:

"For I, the Lord your God, will hold your right hand, saying to you, 'Fear not, I will help you.'" *Isaiah 41:13, NKJV*

 **Let God Help You**

Dial-A-Fortune (Read Isaiah 47:12-15)

"Who made these expensive phone calls to this 900 number?" Mother asked Liz and Garth. She and Dad were discussing the phone bill.

"We did call a number advertised on TV," admitted Liz.

"You called ten times this month!" exclaimed Mother.

"It was 'Dial-A-Fortune,' and when some things came true, we figured there must be something to it," explained Liz, "so we called back to find out more."

"It's no big deal," added Garth.

7

DECEMBER

Dad frowned. "It's a very big deal," he said, "not just because you made these calls without permission, but also because fortune-telling is against God's Word."

"Let's try something," suggested Mother. She wrote on some cards, then scattered them face down on the floor. "Pick a card to find out about yourself," she told Liz.

Liz picked a card. "You're a man," she read.

Dad tried it. "You hate ice-cream," he read. Ice-cream was Dad's favorite dessert. "Your turn," he told Garth.

"This is dumb—Mother can't tell fortunes," mumbled Garth, but he took a card. "Your name is Garth," he read.

"It worked! I must really be a fortune-teller!" exclaimed Mother. "Draw another card—find out more."

"It worked once by chance," grumbled Garth. "Two out of three times you were wrong."

"So you're saying that if anybody believed these cards offer truth just because of one coincidence, they'd believe lies most of the time?" asked Mother. Garth nodded.

"You're right about that," said Dad, "and that's the way it is with fortune-telling, too. Most information given is lies devised by the devil. Sometimes they may appear to be correct, but they're really a scheme to trap people into believing false messages."

"Stick to the Bible," advised Mother. "Its messages are true."

"Yes," said Dad. "And as for the phone bill, money will be taken from your allowance until these calls are paid for. Did the fortune-teller mention that?" *N.E.K.*

HOW ABOUT YOU?

Have you ever been curious about fortune-telling? Don't look to people, the stars, or crystal balls for help. Depend on God's truth for the real answers. Trust him for the future day by day.

MEMORIZE:

"I will put an end to all witch-craft—there will be no more fortune-tellers to consult."

Micah 5:12, TLB

 Listening to Fortunes Is Sin

The Worrywart Hamster (Read Matthew 6:25-34)

8
DECEMBER

"I have a treat for Chester," Dad announced after supper. He pulled a box out of a paper sack as Nancy came running to see what he had brought for her pet.

"Dog biscuits?" Nancy was amazed. "Those are as big as Chester! How can he eat them?"

"The man in the pet shop told me that hamsters need to gnaw because their teeth never stop growing, as ours do," Dad said. He placed a single dog biscuit on the floor of the animal's cage. "Have a dog treat, Chester!"

Nancy watched as her pet sniffed the new treat. "Dad, he can't decide what to do with it," she said. She giggled as Chester moved the huge "bone" from one corner to another. "That's a good place for it, Chester!" she said. "Oh, no! Now he's moving it back to the first corner again. Will he ever stop carrying it back and forth?"

"I guess he's afraid we might bother his treat, so he's looking for a really safe place for it," said Dad.

"What a silly little animal," said Nancy with a laugh. "Why would we want to take an old dog biscuit?"

Dad chucked. "When you think about it, Chester's a little like us, isn't he?" he asked. "We fret and worry about silly things now and then, too. Or don't you do that?"

Nancy grinned. "Oh, no. Not me!" she said, joking. "Like a song we used to sing in our youth group says, 'Why worry when you can pray?'"

"Did you stop worrying about going to a new school after you had prayed?" Dad asked.

"Well, no," Nancy admitted. "But I should have." She pointed to the hamster, which had finally decided on a resting place for his huge snack. "God took care of the problems I was worrying about."

Dad nodded. "He always does," he said. "We need to trust him and stop worrying." *D.F.*

HOW ABOUT YOU?

Are you a worrywart? Whether your problem is illness, getting used to a new school and friends, or just remembering to do your chores, tell God about it. He is able to handle it. He may not solve it instantly, but in time you will see his answer. Tell him your problems; then stop worrying.

MEMORIZE:

"Don't worry about anything; instead, pray about everything; tell God your needs, . . . If you do this, you will experience God's peace." *Philippians 4:6-7, TLB*

 **Don't Worry; Trust God**

Popcorn Tongue (Read Ephesians 4:29-32)

Suzie watched eagerly as her grandmother began to pop some corn. "Tell me about school, Suzie," said Grandma. "Do you have lots of new friends?"

Suzie sighed. "Not really," she said. "It's not easy to move to a new town and go to a new school."

As Suzie talked about the kids she had met, Grandma noticed she complained about them a lot. "God says in Proverbs that if we want friends, we need to be friendly. Are you friendly?" asked Grandma. Suzie shrugged as Grandma poured the popcorn into a bowl and held it out. With a smile Suzie dug in. She stuffed a handful of popcorn into her mouth. As she began to chew, her smile vanished. "Would you like some more popcorn?" Grandma asked.

Suzie shook her head. "It doesn't taste good," she said.

Grandma smiled. "Do you think perhaps you're something like this popcorn?" she asked.

"This popcorn?" asked Suzie. "What do you mean?"

"Well, I think the reason you don't like the popcorn is because I didn't add any salt," replied Grandma. "Without salt, there isn't much flavor. Colossians 4:6 tells us that our speech needs salt, too."

Suzie laughed. "So I should carry a saltshaker and sprinkle some on my tongue before I talk?" she asked.

Grandma laughed, too. "No, but you need to recognize that if the things you say are negative or complaining, people won't care for any more after the first taste. On the other hand, if you 'add a little salt'—if you say things that are positive, things that make people feel special—they'll like talking with you and will be back for more," explained Grandma as she sprinkled salt on the popcorn.

"I'll take some of that popcorn now," Suzie said. She reached toward the bowl and put some in her mouth.

"I'll be back for more," said Suzie. "Salt does make a difference." She grinned at Grandma as she added, "I'll try using a little 'salt' at school tomorrow, too." *S.S.*

HOW ABOUT YOU?

We all spend a lot of our day talking. Do you spend that time complaining, putting others down? Or do you look for a chance to say something kind? Take God's advice and add a little "salt" to your words by saying nice things. Then the people around you will be back for more.

MEMORIZE:

"Let your speech always be with grace, seasoned with salt." *Colossians 4:6, NKJV*

 Say Positive Things

Inside-Out Times (Read Romans 8:31-39)

10

DECEMBER

"But why did Buster have to die?" wailed eight-year-old Craig. Buster was the family's loyal old dog. "He was a hero. Remember when Billy got lost, and Buster found him playing in the woods? And remember when I was so sick? Buster stayed in my room every day until I was better. Even you weren't there as much as Buster was, Mom. Why did he have to die?"

"I wish we could have kept Buster longer, too," Mother answered sadly, "but he was very old, and his body just wore out. Let's try to be thankful for the time we had him."

"But . . ."

Craig had just begun another hard question when his four-year-old brother, Billy, burst into the room. *"Varo-o-o-om!"* Billy called as he zoomed between the living room chairs and stopped in front of Craig and his mother. He wore a yellow and blue shirt with the name and mascot of the local school. But Billy's shirt showed a jumbled mass of colored threads instead of the bright picture.

"Your shirt is inside-out, Billy," Craig snapped, upset over being interrupted.

"Yes, it is, but look closer, Craig," suggested Mom thoughtfully. "Maybe Billy's shirt can answer your questions about Buster." She gently told Billy to hold still so they could see his shirt better. "These knots and loose threads on the inside-out part show how the disappointments in life look to us. When someone we love dies, or when something happens that we think is bad, the whole design looks like an ugly mess," she said.

Mom turned the shirt over. "But look what God is doing on his side," she said. "He's using the same threads to make something beautiful. Each mistake and each disappointment works together to form a beautiful design. God says that 'in all things God works for the good of those who love him.'" *J.J.*

HOW ABOUT YOU?

Has a friend or family member gone away and left you feeling lonely? Maybe school hasn't been going well this year, or you weren't picked for your favorite team. Such things hurt, but let God teach you through these "inside-out" times. Trust him to use them to make something beautiful of your life.

MEMORIZE:

"And we know that in all things God works for the good of those who love him, who have been called according to his purpose." *Romans 8:28, NIV*

 *God Works for Your Good*

Enough Love (Read 1 Corinthians 13:4-11)

11

"You love Katie more than me!" Jennifer accused her mother one day. "Katie gets more attention than I do, and more meals, and . . ."

Jennifer pulled away as Mother tried to hug her. "Honey," Mother said gently, "we need to talk. But first, let's make a list." She took a sheet of paper. "On one side, list the good things you get to do. On the other side, list Baby Katie's privileges." Jennifer stared at the paper, frowning. "For example," said Mother, "you get to go skating—you can write that." Jennifer did.

Just then Katie toddled toward the bookcase. "No, no, Katie," warned Mother. But Katie just shook her head and grabbed a book. "Time out," Mother told her firmly, placing her in the playpen and setting the beeper on her watch for one minute.

"Out!" Katie demanded, beginning to cry.

Jennifer looked at her, smiling. "I get to touch all the books— and the TV and VCR and remote control," she said, writing that on her list.

When Jennifer was finished, she showed the list to her mother. "You didn't write much on Katie's side of the paper," Mother said with a smile. "Did you decide you have more privileges than Katie?"

Jennifer nodded. "A lot more," she said.

"Hmmmm," murmured Mother. "Well, now maybe you should make a list of the times you get attention and the times Katie does. See how that comes out."

Jennifer thought about that for a moment. Then she shook her head. "I get just as much," she decided. "Katie takes two long naps, and I get to stay up and do things with you." She laughed. "Katie has baby privileges, but I have better ones."

Mother lifted Katie out of the playpen. "God knows what you need at every age," she said, "and he provides people—usually parents—to take care of your needs. They have plenty of love to go around." She smiled at Jennifer. "Katie's privileges are all she needs right now, and I believe yours are right for you, too. They'll change and grow along with you." *D.A.L.*

HOW ABOUT YOU?

Have you ever been jealous of a new baby? Remember that your parents love you just as much after the baby is born as they did before. They just show their love for you and the baby in different ways.

MEMORIZE:

"When I was a child, . . . I thought as a child; but when I became a man, I put away childish things."

1 Corinthians 13:11, NKJV

 Thank God for Parents' Love

The "Who Cares" Attitude (Read Revelation 3:14-16)

12
DECEMBER

"Mom!" called Sandra, jumping up and down while looking out the window. "It's snowing! Hip, hip, hooray!" Sandra ran to the living room to look out the big picture window. "Dad! Look at it coming down. Maybe we won't have school tomorrow!" Sandra hurried to the family room. "It's snowing, Ann," she told her sister.

"So?" said Ann, staring at the television screen.

"I just love snow! Snow, snow, snow," sang Sandra. "Maybe we'll get a snow day and have off from school tomorrow."

"So?" repeated Ann, not at all moved.

"Well, I'm happy," Sandra said, skipping out of the room and back to the kitchen. "I love snow, but Ann doesn't like it."

"I didn't say I didn't like it," grumbled Ann, coming into the kitchen to help set the table.

"Well, you sure aren't happy," said Sandra.

"I'm not happy or unhappy," said Ann. "I just don't care one way or the other." Sandra didn't bother to reply.

After dinner, Dad took out the Bible and read a passage of Scripture. "How can we use these verses this week at work and school?" he asked. Ann made a few suggestions, and Dad nodded. He turned to Sandra. "What about you, Sandra?" asked Dad. "Sandra?" But Sandra's mind had wandered, and she hadn't even heard the question. Dad frowned. "It seems to me you seldom pay attention during devotions," he said. "Don't you like devotions?"

"They're OK, I guess," Sandra said with a shrug.

Dad frowned. "I've noticed that you don't seem much interested in several things lately," he said. "Things like Sunday school lessons, church attendance, and devotions."

"You were frustrated with Ann's 'who cares' attitude about the snow," observed Mom, "but you seem to have that same attitude when it comes to your Christian life."

Dad nodded. "I enjoyed seeing you dance around the house earlier this afternoon," he said. "Wouldn't it be great if we all had the same kind of enthusiasm for the Lord?" *N.E.K.*

HOW ABOUT YOU?

What does your Christian faith mean to you? Are you excited and busy working for the Lord? You should be. You have a lot to be excited about.

MEMORIZE:

"So then, because you are lukewarm, and neither cold nor hot, I will vomit you out of My mouth." *Revelation 3:16, NKJV*

 Be Excited about the Lord

Poinsettia Bouquets (Read John 3:1-7, 16)

13

"Gram," said Ellie, "I think Mrs. Craft is a Christian, don't you?" Ellie was referring to a next-door neighbor.

Grandma looked up. "Well, I don't know, but I'm afraid not," she said. "I've talked with her about the Lord, but just last week she told me she believes that anybody who does his best to live a good life will surely go to heaven."

"But she's so nice," said Ellie. "She's a lot nicer than some of the Christians in our church."

Grandma sighed. "I guess that's true," she agreed, "but you know that being nice is not what makes a person a Christian."

"I know," admitted Ellie. "But it just seems that somebody like Mrs. Craft would have to be OK."

Grandma's glance fell on the poinsettia plant standing on the dining room table. She turned it around. "This is a pretty nice plant, isn't it?" she said. "But this isn't the prettiest poinsettia I've ever had. Do you know where I received the prettiest poinsettia of all?"

"In Tripoli," answered Ellie. She knew the story of how Grandma had so enjoyed unusual poinsettia bouquets years ago when she taught school in the faraway city in Africa.

Grandma nodded. "Yes," she said, "we used to buy huge bouquets of poinsettias. They were so lovely! They always died and had to be thrown out, though." She looked at the plant on the table. "I've had this plant a number of years. Why do you suppose it has lasted so much longer than the beautiful bouquets we used to buy?"

"Because those were cut flowers," said Ellie. "This one is rooted in the soil, so it goes on living."

"Exactly," agreed Grandma. "It's like that with people, too. They may live in such a way that we consider them to be 'beautiful people.' But unless they're rooted in Jesus, they cannot live forever in heaven. Mrs. Craft, like all the rest of us, needs to trust in Jesus." *H.M.*

HOW ABOUT YOU?

Are you a "good" person? So was Nicodemus. Jesus told him, "You must be born again." You may be a nice, pleasant, lovely person, but that's not enough. Unless you accept Jesus, too, that loveliness will wilt and die. Don't let that happen. Trust Jesus today.

MEMORIZE:

"No one can see the kingdom of God unless he is born again." *John 3:3, NIV*

 *Trust in Jesus*

Pearl Diving (Read James 2:1-9)

14

DECEMBER

"You'll never guess what happened to me at the Trade Fair, Aunt Oleta," squealed Ronda, bursting through the front door. She shook the brown curls away from her ears and revealed two pearl earrings.

"Ohhh!" breathed Aunt Oleta. "You must have spent your whole savings to buy those! Or did Uncle Frank buy them for you?"

"We didn't exactly *buy* them. I got them at a pearl diving booth," explained Ronda, laughing. "Every shell was guaranteed to have a pearl inside. 'Buy an oyster— take home a gem' the sign said. So from a large glass bowl, I picked out the smallest, ugliest one I could find. When the man in charge opened it, guess what? Twins!"

"There were two pearls?" Aunt Oleta asked.

Ronda nodded. "And Uncle Frank paid to have them made into earrings," she said. "He said it was an extra Christmas present."

"Well, well! And they were inside the ugliest shell of all," said Aunt Oleta, shaking her head in disbelief. "I bet people had been shoving that shell aside all day. Just goes to show you that you can't judge value by outside appearances."

"I'll never, ever judge that way again," declared Ronda.

"Oh, by the way," said Aunt Oleta, "Maggie Somebody-or-Other called while you were gone. She wants you to come to a party."

Ronda scowled. "I hope you said no," she told her aunt. "I don't think anyone will go to her party. She's the ugliest kid in my Sunday school class, and she wears the dumbest clothes!"

"Then maybe she's the nicest, sweetest girl around," Aunt Oleta said quietly. Ronda stared at Aunt Oleta, puzzled.

"Maybe you should go to the mirror and take a look at those earrings again," Aunt Oleta suggested. "They should remind you of what you promised to never, ever do again."

Ronda blushed as she recalled what she had said. "It sounds to me like you're letting Maggie's 'shell' hide her real beauty," continued Aunt Oleta. "Inside she may be a wonderful and unique person." *J.R.G.*

HOW ABOUT YOU?

Do you judge a person by the way he or she looks or dresses? Do other people's opinions influence whom you will be friendly to? Every person is precious in God's eyes, no matter how he or she may look to you. Each one has potential and value that God can shape to glorify him.

MEMORIZE:

"**God does not show favoritism.**" *Romans 2:11, NIV*

🔑 *Don't Judge by Appearances*

Words and Actions (Read Luke 16:10-13)

15

DECEMBER

"Mr. Henry sure rushed out after the services this morning!" observed Dennis one Sunday afternoon.

"He was having trouble at the farm," said Dad. "Thousands of baby chicks arrived yesterday, and last night the heaters in his chicken house went on the blink. I heard he actually slept in the chicken house last night."

"Talk about dedication!" exclaimed Dennis, making a face at the idea. Then he excused himself.

"Where are you headed, Son?" asked Mother.

"Over to Barry's," replied Dennis. "The guys are all going sledding on his hill." He paused and looked anxiously at his father. "I can go, can't I?" he asked. "You've said how much they need my Christian influence."

Dad smiled. "I think that will be all right," he agreed.

When Dennis arrived home, his face was cold and his clothes were soaked. "Take those boots off outside," ordered Mother. "And hurry—it's almost time for church."

"I can't go tonight," Dennis said. Then he saw his father's frown. "I mean, may I please stay home tonight? The guys are going back to Barry's to play Ping-Pong on his new table." He could see Dad shaking his head. "You said my friends need my Christian influence," Dennis argued. "If that's the case, I need to be with them."

"Wasn't it you who marveled at Mr. Henry's dedication when you heard he'd slept in the chicken house last night?" Mom asked. "Mr. Henry didn't say a word to you, but his actions impressed you quite a bit."

"Well . . . yeah." Dennis wasn't sure where this conversation was leading.

"People who watch Mr. Henry can tell he's committed to farming. Because of that commitment, many people find it easy to trust him for advice," explained Dad. "That principle holds true in regard to Christians, too. Telling others about being a Christian is good, but it has more impact when they can see our commitment to God."

"That commitment to God shows in our faithful church attendance," added Mom, "so . . . go get ready for church." *N.E.K.*

HOW ABOUT YOU?

Are you committed to God? Can others see that commitment by the way you live and by what takes first place in your life? Others will see the Lord through your actions as well as your words.

MEMORIZE:

"Commit your way to the Lord, trust also in Him, and He shall bring it to pass." *Psalm 37:5, NKJV*

 Be Committed to God

Blanket of Peace (Read Luke 6:27-36)

"Tracy hates me!" Ann sobbed. Her hand trembled as she held the Christmas card out to her mother. "Look what she sent me!"

Mother took the card and looked at it. The cover had a picture of an angel announcing the message "Peace on earth, good will toward men!" Then she opened it and read aloud, "Merry Christmas from your ex-friend!" Mother's face turned grim. "Oh, that's too bad," she said. "Tracy shouldn't have sent this to you."

16

DECEMBER

"I told you she hates me," cried Ann. "We were best friends until Sara moved next door to her. Now she only likes Sara—she won't play with me anymore." Ann burst into tears, and Mother held her tightly until she calmed down.

"What Tracy did was wrong," Mother said quietly. "It makes me angry, too. But, honey, you can't change other people; you can only pray for them. Do you think you could pray for Tracy?"

"Pray for her?" Ann asked stonily. "I don't ever want to talk to her again! Why should I pray for her?"

"Look out the window," suggested Mother. "Do you see how the snow is beginning to fall?" Ann nodded. "The ground is dark and frozen—like the feelings you and Tracy have for each other just now," continued Mother, "but it will soon have a blanket of snow to cover it and make it beautiful again. Prayer works something like that. When you pray and tell God about your angry feelings, he understands. He is called the Prince of Peace; he brings the gift of 'peace on earth, good will toward men.' Wouldn't you like to have it?"

Solemnly, Ann nodded her head. "Good," said Mother. "God also gives you wisdom about how you should act. When you bless those who hurt you, God can change their feelings, too." *A.L.*

HOW ABOUT YOU?

Are you hurt because someone has been cruel to you? Do you find it hard to forgive and forget? You can choose to pray for your enemies just as Jesus did. Then God will help you find peace.

MEMORIZE:

"But I tell you: Love your enemies and pray for those who persecute you." *Matthew 5:44, NIV*

Pray for Your Enemies

Daddy's Girl (Read Romans 8:12-17)

"Mom, who do I look like?" Theresa asked while watching her mother fix her hair.

"What do you mean, Theresa?" asked Mom. "Duck," she added, aiming the hair spray.

"I look like a duck?" Theresa laughed, knowing Mom meant "move or get sprayed." Mom laughed with her. "You know, do I have your eyes, or Dad's nose, or what?" asked Theresa.

17
DECEMBER

Mom took a long look at Theresa's face, then at her own reflection in the mirror. "I'd say you look more like your father—more so every day," she said thoughtfully. Theresa's father had died when she was very small.

"You remind me of your dad very much. You not only resemble him, you act like him, too. You eat just as fast as he did," teased Mom, as they walked to the kitchen to eat breakfast.

"Isn't it strange," said Theresa as she set the table, "that I hardly knew Dad, but now I look like him and act like him? I even like the same foods he used to eat—asparagus, and beets, and pickle-and-peanut-butter sandwiches! How can I be so much like him when he's not here to show me how?"

"I believe you come by those things naturally because you are a part of Dad," said Mom as she poured the orange juice. "And then, too, I've shared my memories of Dad, you've read his letters to me, and you've seen our photo albums." She smiled at Theresa as she added, "Being a child of God is something like that. We don't see God, but we act like him because we are a part of him, and he is a part of us. We read about him in his Word, we see glimpses of him in other Christians, and we talk about what he has done." Mom squeezed Theresa's hand. "Let's ask God to help us be more like him today!" *D.E.M.*

HOW ABOUT YOU?

Can others tell who your Father is by looking at you and your actions? Is it easy for them to see that you're a child of God? Ask the Lord to help you be like Jesus, so others will see your heavenly Father in you.

MEMORIZE:

"That you may become blameless and harmless, children of God without fault in the midst of a crooked and perverse generation, among whom you shine as lights in the world."

Philippians 2:15, NKJV

 Act like a Child of God

"Old Fogey" (Read Romans 6:11-14; 1 Corinthians 6:19-20)

18
DECEMBER

"Can't we go faster, Dad?" grumbled Paul. He looked through the windshield at the falling snow.

Dad kept his eyes on the road. "It's too hard to see," he said. "It would be risky to pass anyone."

"Look! Someone's passing us!" Paul said. "If he can pass, so can you. You're driving like an old fogey!"

"Old fogey or not, I'm staying in this lane," declared Dad. "It's very slippery." Dad held the wheel tightly as the car swerved a little. "From what I hear, you're on a slippery road yourself. Is it true that you smoke pot?"

Paul made a choking sound. "Did Cindy tell you that?"

"Your sister is worried," said Dad.

"I only tried it once," Paul said quickly. "Some older guys meet us on our way home and offer us the stuff. They make us look like jerks if we don't try it. It was free, so I figured it wouldn't hurt to try it once. I just wanted to get them off my back."

"And now that you've tried it, have they left you alone?" asked Dad. Paul shook his head, and Dad continued. "First they get you to try it, then they want you to try it again and again. Once you're hooked, they sell it to you."

"I have seen some kids give them money," admitted Paul. "Some of them are younger than I am."

"You've got to say no to them, Paul, even if it means looking like a jerk. That's a lot better than getting hooked and destroying your life," said Dad as traffic came to a halt. When they finally started creeping again, they saw a lot of cars parked along the median strip. One car was in a ditch, upside down, with the wheels spinning.

"That's the car that passed us!" exclaimed Paul.

Dad nodded. "To tell you the truth, Paul, I wanted to take off after that car when it passed us," he admitted. "I didn't like being called an old fogey. I didn't give in, though. We all have to do what's right."

"I'll do what's right, too," promised Paul. "I'll tell those guys to get lost." *H.A.D.*

HOW ABOUT YOU?

Drugs will destroy your life. You should avoid them no matter how much others pressure you to try them. And if you're a Christian, there's another reason to avoid drugs: your body is the temple of the Holy Spirit, and you must treat it well. God will help you handle the pressure put on you by those who sell drugs.

MEMORIZE:

"In God I trust; I will not be afraid. What can man do to me?" *Psalm 56:11, NIV*

 *Just Say No*

The Dual Thermometer (Read Revelation 3:1-6)

"Look at that!" exclaimed Jimmy. He was standing at the window of his grandparents' kitchen. "One of these thermometers says 40 degrees, and the other says 72. And they're right beside each other." He pointed at one of them. "This one must be wrong," he decided. "It's warmer than 40 in here."

19

DECEMBER

"Nope. They're both right," said his grandfather. He pointed to a small tube running from one thermometer out through the window. "One of them shows the temperature outside by means of this tube. The other one shows the temperature of this room. That's why they can be side by side and have two very different readings." Grandpa's brow wrinkled.

"Oh, oh!" said Jimmy with a grin. "Grandpa's about to give us a mini-sermon. I can tell by the look on his face."

Grandpa playfully boxed his grandson's ears. "I was just thinking," he said, "that this is like the difference between some Christians. They may be standing side by side, but one has warmth and love and enthusiasm for the things of God while the other is cold and uninterested and far from God."

"But what makes the difference?" asked Jimmy. "Why is one warm and another cold?"

"I think the warm Christian is the one who spends time with the Lord and with other Christians," replied Grandpa. "He gets fired up for God through Bible reading, prayer, church attendance, and being with Christian friends. The cold one has come to know the Lord, but he still keeps close contact with the world. He's probably often involved in the things of the world, hanging out with the wrong crowd." Grandpa took his Bible from a kitchen shelf. "Time for our daily Bible reading," he said. "Time to get warmed up a bit once again." *M.R.P.*

HOW ABOUT YOU?

What is your spiritual "temperature"—hot or cold? Is your life filled with enthusiasm for serving the Lord? With cheerful obedience? With love for those around you and for God? If not, perhaps you're not spending enough time with the Lord and with other Christians. Become a warm Christian.

MEMORIZE:

"**Because of the increase of wickedness, the love of most will grow cold.**" *Matthew 24:12, NIV*

 Be a Warm Christian

Two Kinds of Kernels (Read 2 Corinthians 5:14-21)

20

DECEMBER

"We will pop the corn tonight," sang Gail merrily as the corn popped on the stove. "Pop! Pop! Pop!" She was at a Sunday school class party.

Her sister, Nan, joined in and they finished the song together. "See the kernels big and bright. Pop! Pop! Pop! They are dancing all about. 'Tis great fun without a doubt. They are asking to come out. Pop! Pop! Pop!"

Gail and Nan laughed at the face one of the girls made. "Our great-grandmother taught us that song when we were little kids," explained Gail. She stuffed some popcorn into her mouth. "Ummmm. Good!" But a moment later, she removed a hard kernel. "Oops!" she added. "This one didn't pop. It's no good."

Shortly before the party ended, the teacher called the girls together for devotions. She held two kernels of popcorn in her hand, one small, hard, and dry and the other puffed and snowy white. "I was just wondering," said Miss Martin, "how many popped kernels we have in this class and how many hard kernels are left." She smiled at the puzzled expressions she saw on each face. "You see," she continued, "we're something like this popcorn. When we put it on the stove and heated it, moisture inside the kernels turned to steam and caused many of them to explode. They changed a lot, didn't they?"

The girls nodded. "But how is that like us?" one girl asked.

"Well, when people hear the gospel and respond to it by accepting Jesus as Savior, an 'explosion' takes place within them," explained Miss Martin. "A great change takes place in their lives, making them more useful and lovely people. God says they become 'new creations' in him." She looked around the group. "Have you experienced a change, like this fluffy, white kernel?" she asked. "Search your heart, and if you're still unchanged, like this hard one, won't you accept Jesus tonight?" *H.M.*

HOW ABOUT YOU?

Has your life been changed by God? If you haven't been changed, you need to be. Trust Jesus as your Savior.

MEMORIZE:

"If anyone is in Christ, he is a new creation; old things have passed away; behold, all things have become new."

2 Corinthians 5:17, NKJV

 Become New in Christ

The Clean Slate (Read Psalm 51:1-10)

21

DECEMBER

Ginny dipped a sponge into the water and then squeezed it out carefully. "I like washing my chalkboard instead of just erasing it," she told her mother. "Look how brand new it looks." She stepped back and admired her work.

During family devotions that day—and on each of the next few days—Ginny confessed to God a sin she had committed. It was something for which her parents had already punished her. "Please forgive me for lying to Mom and Dad," she prayed. "I'm so sorry I did that. Please help me not to do it again." Ginny's parents assured her over and over that the sin was forgiven—by them and by God. But Ginny wasn't sure. "When someone asks me to forgive him for something, I sometimes have trouble really forgetting it," she said. "I just want to be sure God knows I'm truly sorry."

"Ginny, before you go to bed tonight, I want you to wash your chalkboard so it's nice and clean," said Mother.

"I washed it already," replied Ginny. "It's clean."

"Why not do it again, just to make sure," suggested Dad.

"But I haven't used it since I washed it," Ginny protested. "If it had only been erased, there would probably be smears left from the old chalk. Sometimes you can even figure out what words were erased. But now it's washed—it looks brand new."

Dad nodded. "When we confess our sins to people and they forgive us, it might compare to the board being erased, but when we confess our sins to God, they are totally removed," he told her. "God cleanses you, and the slate is clean. Every bit of the sin is washed away—just like when you wash the blackboard."

Ginny liked the sound of that. And when she prayed the following night, she stopped repeating her confessions. God had forgiven her sin and forgotten it, so she decided to stop reminding him. *N.E.K.*

HOW ABOUT YOU?

Do you ever feel like you need to keep apologizing for a sin you committed? God forgives you the first moment you sincerely confess a sin. After that, all you need to do is thank him.

MEMORIZE:

"**The blood of Jesus Christ His [God's] Son cleanses us from all sin.**" *1 John 1:7, NKJV*

 God Forgives Completely

Whose Fault? (Read Romans 5:6-11)

22
DECEMBER

"Oh, no!" groaned Dana as she and her mother stood looking at the dent in their car. "What happened?"

"Apparently someone backed into the car while we were shopping," replied Mother. "Whoever it was didn't leave a note admitting his fault." She sighed. "Well, there's nothing to be done, I guess, but I suppose we should make a police report."

After the report was made, Dana and Mother hurried home to tell Dad about the accident. "Well," he said as he looked at the car, "this isn't major damage, but the body work will be expensive. I'll call our insurance agent—I think this will be covered."

"The person who did it ought to pay the bill," declared Dana. "It was his fault."

"Yes, but we can't get him to pay the bill when we don't know who he is," replied Mother, "so if the insurance doesn't cover it, we'll just have to take care of it ourselves."

"Well, you shouldn't have to pay to get the car fixed," Dana insisted. "That isn't fair!"

"No," said Mother, "but there's not a whole lot we can do about it."

"I know one thing we can do," said Dad. "We can all be thankful it's just a car that's damaged. Nobody got hurt."

Mother nodded. "I'm also thankful that the damage is so minor that the car can still be driven," she added.

"I'm thinking of something else, too," said Dad. "We can use this as reminder to be thankful that Jesus paid the price for sin even when he knew who was at fault—us. I must admit I'm not happy about paying for repairs that are someone else's fault, but Jesus willingly paid the price when the fault was ours. Let's never forget to thank him for that." *N.E.K.*

HOW ABOUT YOU?

Does paying the price for something that was someone else's fault make you angry? That's natural. But just think, Jesus died willingly to pay the price for our sin. His love for you is that great! If you haven't already accepted what he did for you, do so today.

MEMORIZE:

"But God demonstrates his own love for us in this: While we were still sinners, Christ died for us." *Romans 5:8, NIV*

 Jesus Paid for Your Sin

Not Dummies (Read James 3:5-10)

23
DECEMBER

Gina and her mother stopped at the central square in the mall and watched a ventriloquist perform. "That was fun!" Gina said later. "I know that man was really doing the talking for the dummy, but I couldn't even see his lips move. It seemed like the dummy was actually talking."

That evening, Gina had a big argument with her brother, Lyle. "You pig!" Gina shouted at him.

"Gina," Mother said, "watch your tongue! You know how I feel about name calling."

A little later, Gina and Lyle were fighting again. "You're an ugly rat!" grumbled Gina.

"Gina!" Mother called sternly. "Come here right now and sit on this chair for a while." Embarrassed, Gina did as she was told. "Where are those words coming from?" asked Mother after a little while. "Do you forget that you're a Christian?"

Gina sighed. "I just say them without thinking," she said. "But why doesn't God stop me? I don't understand why he lets bad words come out of my mouth."

"Well," said Mother, "God isn't a ventriloquist in the sky, you know."

"You mean like the man at the mall?" Gina asked.

Mother nodded. "The man at the mall worked that dummy like a puppet and spoke for it. But God lets us move our own mouth and choose the words we speak."

"We're not dummies, are we?" murmured Gina.

"If you were, you wouldn't be a free child of God serving him out of a willing, obedient heart," replied Mother. "Instead of spouting out whatever you want, you can choose to say words that are pleasing to God. Ask him to help you do that." *N.E.K.*

HOW ABOUT YOU?

Are you careful to say only things that are pleasing to God? When you say unkind words, you're making a poor choice. Ask God to help you speak for him.

 Watch What You Say

MEMORIZE:

"Do not let any unwholesome talk come out of your mouths, but only what is helpful for building others up according to their needs, that it may benefit those who listen."

Ephesians 4:29, NIV

A Christmas Tradition (Read Psalm 62:1-8)

24
DECEMBER

Every Christmas, Nathan's family visited Grandma and Grandpa Talbot in Minnesota. To Nathan, the best part of the week was Christmas Eve breakfast. He and Dad would rise at dawn, bundle up, take a skillet, food, and matches, and walk to a nearby lake. At first it would be cold, but then they'd get the fire going and the food cooking, and Nathan would soon be toasty warm. This year, though, the temperature dropped to a record-breaking low.

"Can we go for our breakfast, anyhow?" Nathan asked anxiously. "We don't want to break tradition."

"Sure," Dad agreed. "We'll have a real adventure."

So early on Christmas Eve they headed for the lake. Wind whipped snow every which way, stinging Nathan's cheeks. Sometimes he couldn't see more than a few feet in front of him, but finally they made it to the lake. Nathan was so cold! "Maybe we shouldn't have come," he yelled to his dad over the wind.

"No problem," Dad assured him. "Head for that huge boulder over there. We'll be OK."

Behind the towering rock, Nathan instantly felt warmer. Within minutes, they had a fire going, and slowly they began to warm up. "I can't even feel the wind here," said Nathan.

"That's true," agreed Dad as he put the bacon in the frying pan. "We can hear it blowing all around us, but the rock protects us." He cracked open some eggs. "This rock is a good picture of what it says in the Bible—that the Lord is our Rock, our strength and our protection. He keeps us safe from the confusion that's all around."

"My Sunday school teacher talks about that sometimes," said Nathan, "but I never knew what it meant until now."

Dad put the bacon and eggs on plates, and Nathan poured hot chocolate from the Thermos. Then Dad asked Nathan to pray. "Thank you, Lord, for this neat breakfast with Dad. Thank you for the protection of this rock. And thank you for being our Rock and Strength." *L.W.*

HOW ABOUT YOU?

Have you ever stood behind a big rock to get out of the cold or wind? Have you hidden from someone behind a rock? Rocks can protect you in many ways. The Lord says he is your Rock. Lots of bad things go on around you every day, but you are safe in the shelter of the Lord, the Rock of your salvation.

MEMORIZE:

"He only is my rock and my salvation; he is my defense; I shall not be moved."

Psalm 62:6, NKJV

The Lord Is Our Rock

Candy Cane (Read Isaiah 53:1-6)

"May we have a candy cane?" Josh begged as he looked at the candies hanging on the Christmas tree.

"Yeah, may we?" echoed his sister, Amy.

Mother smiled. "All right," she agreed, "but as you eat them, I want you to think of a way they can remind you of the reason we celebrate Christmas."

25
DECEMBER

"OK," agreed the children, and they each selected a cane from the tree. They sat down, unwrapped them, and began to eat. For a few minutes, no one spoke. Josh held his candy at arm's length and stared at it. "Hey!" he yelled. "Our Sunday school verse last week said, 'by His stripes we are healed,' so the stripes can remind us of how they whipped Jesus." Then he frowned. "But that doesn't have anything to do with Christmas, does it?" he added.

Mother smiled. "Oh, indeed it does," she assured him. "The reason Jesus was born was to grow up and suffer and die for our sins—to be a Savior to anyone who believes in him and accepts him."

Amy looked up, her eyes sparkling. "Then the red stripe on the candy cane can stand for the blood Jesus shed for us when he died on the cross," she said. "I'm glad he came to die for us." *J.B.*

HOW ABOUT YOU?

Do you get so excited about Christmas candy and presents that you forget the real reason for Christmas? On this special day celebrate the fact that Christ was born so he could save you from sin. Accept the wonderful gift he offers you—the gift of salvation.

MEMORIZE:

"But He was wounded for our transgressions, He was bruised for our iniquities; the chastisement of our peace was upon Him, and by His stripes we are healed." *Isaiah 53:5, NKJV*

 Christ Was Born to Save You

The Silly Monkey (Read Colossians 3:12-17)

26

DECEMBER

"Fight! Fight!" several children shouted, and Jeff and Steve did. But the scuffle didn't last long. They exchanged only a few blows before they were separated by Mrs. Hansen, their Sunday school teacher. "I'm surprised at you, boys," she said. "Why were you fighting?"

"Steve called me clumsy and stupid, and a bunch of other bad names," complained Jeff.

"That's because you tripped me," retorted Steve.

"I couldn't help getting in the way of your big feet," grumbled Jeff.

"You boys remind me of a story I heard from a missionary in Brazil," Mrs. Hansen said. "He saw a monkey sitting on a log, cracking nuts with a stone. The monkey looked up and saw the missionary watching him. This caused him to miss the nut and instead hit his tail with the stone. The monkey got so mad, he threw his stone at the missionary and then ran off. Evidently he blamed the missionary for his pain. Aren't you boys like the monkey—blaming each other for something that was really your own fault?"

The boys looked at the floor as Mrs. Hansen continued. "When we're tempted to fight, we should think about how Jesus told us to treat one another," she said. "Jesus said, 'Love one another as I have loved you' [John 15:12, *NKJV*]. How much did he love us?"

"Enough to die for us," answered Steve hesitantly.

"That's right," agreed Mrs. Hansen. "And Paul wrote, 'If anyone has a complaint against another; even as Christ forgave you, so you also must do.' How does Christ forgive? Jeff?"

"Well, he forgives completely," said Jeff slowly. He looked at Steve with a sheepish grin. "I'm sorry, Steve. Will you forgive me?" he asked.

"Sure," replied Steve, "and you forgive me, too, OK?"

Mrs. Hansen smiled. "Good," she approved. "It's nice to see you acting like Jesus rather than like a silly monkey." *M.R.P.*

HOW ABOUT YOU?

Do you blame someone else when things go wrong? Stop and think before accusing someone else—maybe that person isn't at fault. Even if he is, follow Christ's example. He died for you, even though you sinned against him. He freely forgives when you ask him, and he never holds a grudge.

MEMORIZE:

"If anyone has a complaint against another; even as Christ forgave you, so you also must do." *Colossians 3:13, NKJV*

 *Forgive As Christ Does*

Daily Bread (Read Deuteronomy 8:1-6)

"You missed!" Jenny sang out as she ducked the flying snowball. "Say, Abby, let's go sliding down the big hill behind your house."

"OK," agreed Abby. "You ask your mother, and I'll check with mine. Meet you there in ten minutes?"

27

DECEMBER

"Sure," Jenny called as she ran up her driveway. She found her mother cleaning out the refrigerator. "Hi, Mom," Jenny said, "can I go sledding with Abby?"

"Hi, honey." Mother smiled at her. "Sledding will be fine, but didn't you tell me you planned to have your quiet time with the Lord right after school?"

"Well, yeah . . . but I can skip it and catch up on it at the end of the week," Jenny answered. She sniffed the air. "What's for dinner tonight?"

Mother smiled. "I told the church shut-in committee I'd fix a meal for Mrs. Green tonight. That makes me really busy. Would you mind if we just skipped dinner here tonight? If we could eat just a couple of times a week it really would save me a lot of time. Or maybe I can fix us a special meal on Sunday instead of eating every day."

Jenny stared at her mother in astonishment. Why, she just had to be kidding! Suddenly she knew what her mother was really saying. "Oh, Mom!" said Jenny. "I get the point. If I don't have my quiet time with God each day, it's like not eating spiritually, isn't it?"

Mother nodded. "That's right, Jenny. It's when we feed on the Word of God that we grow spiritually. We need spiritual food every day."

"Well, I guess if I have my quiet time now I'll still have time to play outside, too," Jenny decided. "I'll call Abby and tell her I'll join her in half an hour. Oh, and Mom . . . may I invite her to dinner tonight? Uh . . . you *are* going to fix dinner, aren't you?" Mother laughed and nodded. *S.B.*

HOW ABOUT YOU?

Do you spend time in God's Word each day? Or do you try to get by with learning about God only on Sunday? Just as your body needs food to grow, your soul needs the food of God's Word, the Bible, to help you grow spiritually. Make Bible reading an everyday habit.

MEMORIZE:

"Man does not live on bread alone, but on every word that comes from the mouth of God."

Matthew 4:4, NIV

 Read Your Bible Every Day

All One Team (Read Ephesians 4:4, 11-16)

28

DECEMBER

Danny was excited. Uncle John, who raised sled dogs, had promised to teach him how to drive a team of dogs. "Danny, which dog is the most important?" Uncle John asked when the team was harnessed to the sled and ready to go.

"The one in front," said Danny promptly.

Uncle John smiled. "That's the lead dog," he said. "Which do you think is the least important?"

"Well, I guess this one way in the back," replied Danny. "He probably can't even see where he's going." Uncle John stepped to the last dog and unbuckled the harness. "Now which is the least important?" he asked. When Danny pointed to one of the smaller dogs, Uncle John unharnessed that one and asked the question again. This continued until there was only one dog left—the lead dog. "We'll leave this one," said Uncle John. "You said he was most important. Let's get going!"

Danny looked puzzled. "But, Uncle John," he protested, "doesn't he need all the other dogs to help pull the sled?"

"You mean the ones I let go?" asked Uncle John. "You said they weren't important."

"Well, not as important as the leader," said Danny, "but he needs help. He can't do it alone."

"You're right," agreed Uncle John. "But if the others are needed, aren't they as important as the lead dog?"

"I suppose so," admitted Danny. "It just seems like the one in front would be more important."

"That's because he's in a prominent position," said Uncle John, "but always remember that the smallest or least-noticed member of your team is as important as the biggest member. If they don't all work together, nothing gets done. People are a lot like that," he continued. "Sometimes we think only leaders are important, but that's not so." Danny wondered if his parents had told Uncle John that he thought other kids were given more important things to do than he was. "Always remember, Danny, that in God's sight you're just as important as anybody else," added Uncle John. *D.M.*

HOW ABOUT YOU?

Do you realize that you're important even though you may be too small to do some things, or even if you don't do things that everyone sees? God can use anyone for his service; all it takes is a willing heart.

MEMORIZE:

"From him the whole body, joined and held together by every supporting ligament, grows and builds itself up in love, as each part does its work." *Ephesians 4:16, NIV*

 *You Are Important*

Hot Cookies and Ski Trips (Read Romans 13:1-5)

29

Opening the oven door, Marianne removed a pan of cookies. As she set them on the table, her small brother darted into the kitchen. "Cookie!" exclaimed Peter, reaching toward the hot pan.

"No!" cried Marianne, quickly pulling him aside. Peter howled and kicked furiously. "That's hot! You'll get burned if you touch it," Marianne told him.

"What's going on in here?" asked Mother, coming into the kitchen and taking hold of Peter.

"Peter's mad because I stopped him from picking up the hot cookies," said Marianne. She went to answer the telephone while her mother dealt with Peter.

A little later, Marianne slumped down in a chair as Mother took more cookies from the oven. "That was Leslie," said Marianne. "She was telling me about all the rules Pastor Dan has made up for our youth group's trip. We've been looking forward to going, but I'm not sure it's gonna be any fun! Leslie says there'll be room-cleaning requirements, chaperons, and even a curfew! It's totally unfair!"

"Just like Peter thought you were unfair for not letting him touch the hot cookies?" asked Mother.

Marianne looked surprised. "I don't mind if he has some cookies," she said. "I just didn't want him to get burned."

"And Pastor Dan doesn't mind if you have fun," said Mother, "but he doesn't want you to get hurt. Pastor Dan is head of the youth division; therefore, he's God's servant for our good, and God holds him responsible for every person in the group. God will hold you accountable to obey the guidelines Pastor Dan sets whenever you're under his care."

Marianne sighed. "I suppose," she said as the oven timer buzzed. She grinned at Peter, who was sitting quietly, staring at the cookies. "Come on, little brother," she said, "let's have cookies and milk. They've cooled down, and they'll be great now—you'll see. And I'll try to remember how good the ski trip will be if I follow the rules." *J.R.G.*

HOW ABOUT YOU?

Do you sometimes balk at rules? God says you are to obey those who have authority over you. When you choose to do that, it will not only benefit you, it will also delight your heavenly Father.

MEMORIZE:

"Submit yourselves for the Lord's sake to every authority instituted among men."

1 Peter 2:13, NIV

 Obey Those in Authority

Bumper Stickers (Read Titus 2:6-15)

30

DECEMBER

"Let's read bumper stickers," suggested Jason on the last day of their vacation, "and try to decide what kind of people are riding in the cars."

Melody was the first to spy a sticker. "Hey, I see one on that truck," she called out. "It says, We're Spending Our Children's Inheritance. They must be retired and rich."

Mom laughed. "Well, rich or not, their children won't inherit whatever they do have," she said.

Dad tapped the horn. "Wave to the people in that car when we pass them," he said. "Their bumper sticker says, Honk If You Love Jesus. I'd guess they're Christians."

Soon Jason saw a sticker. "That one doesn't make sense," he said with a frown. "It says, 'I' and 'New York,' but there's no word in between—just a drawing of a heart."

"I know what that means," declared Melody. "The heart stands for love. So that says, I Love New York. Those people have a Florida license plate, but maybe they used to live in New York."

"Uh-oh! I'm not going to read that one out loud," said Jason, pointing to a truck that was speeding by.

"I should hope not," said Mom. "The words are filthy. They shouldn't be allowed in public places."

"Then the driver must not love Jesus. Isn't that right, Dad?" asked Melody.

"He certainly doesn't give evidence of it," agreed Dad. "You know, children," he continued, "we've been judging people by their bumper stickers, and I believe we've made some pretty good guesses as to what they're like. But do you know how the world judges you, as to whether or not you're a Christian?"

"Well, we don't go around wearing stickers," said Jason, "but I think I know what you mean. Other people judge us by the way we live, don't they?"

"Yes, they do," agreed Dad, "so we need to be careful about what we say with our life. Wouldn't it be great if everyone could see that we have a great big heart of love between ourselves and the Lord Jesus?" *M.R.P.*

HOW ABOUT YOU?

What do people think about you as they watch your life? Do your actions show that you're God's child? Only God can see your heart; people judge you by your outward life. Ask God to help you make it always say, "I love Jesus."

MEMORIZE:

"Declare the praises of him who called you out of darkness into his wonderful light."

1 Peter 2:9, NIV

 **Act like God's Child**

Something Inside (Read 2 Corinthians 4:7-10)

31

DECEMBER

"Is Uncle Bob going to be OK?" asked Mark when his parents picked him up at his grandmother's house. They had gone to the hospital as soon as they heard about Uncle Bob's accident.

"We don't know for sure yet, but at least he's stable for now," replied Dad wearily. "We're going home to get some rest. They'll call us if anything changes."

"Well, I don't get it," declared Mark, climbing into the car. "Uncle Bob is a Christian, but what difference did that make? God let that drunk driver hit him anyway." He frowned. "Oh, I know he'll go to heaven if he dies," he added impatiently, "but being a Christian didn't stop the accident. So what difference does it make now?"

"Why, it makes a lot of difference, Son," began Mother, but Mark just scowled as his parents tried to explain.

When they arrived home, Mark noticed a box on the kitchen table. "What's in the box?" he asked.

"It's a can crusher," replied Mom. "It's supposed to make recycling a little easier. Let's try it out."

Mark opened the box, and they read the instructions. Then he grabbed a couple of empty cans, set them in place, and pushed the lever of the can crusher. "Hey! It works great!" he said.

"Try this one," suggested Dad, handing him another can.

Mark gave him a puzzled glance when he felt its weight, but he pushed down on the lever anyway. "I can't crush this one—it's full," he said.

Dad smiled. "I think what happened to the cans shows us the difference being a Christian makes—even though bad things still happen to you," he said. He picked up a flattened can. "People who don't know Jesus are often like this one," he said. "They can be easily crushed when bad times hit. On the other hand . . ." Dad held up the full can. "Christians should be like this. Ephesians 5:18 says we are to be filled with the Holy Spirit—we have the power of God's Spirit within us. Even though hard times may still push down on us, we won't be crushed by them." *S.S.*

HOW ABOUT YOU?

It's easy to trust God when everything is going great, but what do you do when difficult things happen? The next time a problem tries to crush you, choose to trust Jesus. Let his strength hold you up. If you're a Christian, you're not empty. You have Jesus within.

MEMORIZE:

"We are hard pressed on every side, yet not crushed."

2 Corinthians 4:8, NKJV

 Trust God's Strength

Index of Topics

September 23,
October 28,
November 25

Videos/movies
January 17,
February 3,
June 19,
August 14

Witnessing
January 20,
February 20,
April 9, 29,
July 26,
August 3, 27,
October 18,
December 6

Index of Scripture Readings

Nahum 1:1-3; 2:8-10; 3:7
   November 30

Matthew 4:1-10 *September 14*
Matthew 4:1-11 *January 26,*
   June 2
Matthew 5:13 *February 20*
Matthew 5:13-16 *September 17*
Matthew 5:14-16 *December 3*
Matthew 6:19-24 *August 19*
Matthew 6:22-24 *August 14*
Matthew 6:25-34 *September 30,*
   December 8
Matthew 6:26-34 *July 8*
Matthew 7:1-5 *May 19, June 18*
Matthew 7:13-14 *July 21*
Matthew 7:21-23 *October 14*
Matthew 9:36-38 *August 3*
Matthew 10:24-25, 32-34,
   38-39 *March 22*
Matthew 11:28-30 *September 5,*
   October 1
Matthew 12:33-37 *October 23*
Matthew 12:35-37 *June 11*
Matthew 18:6-7, 10-14 *March 30*
Matthew 18:15, 21-22 *December 2*
Matthew 18:21-22 *August 4*
Matthew 20:1-15a *February 26*
Matthew 21:28-32 *November 7*
Matthew 23:25-28 *June 9*
Matthew 24:36-42 *March 7*
Matthew 25:1-13 *April 6, May 18*
Matthew 25:14-27 *November 12*
Matthew 25:14-29 *September 20*
Matthew 25:34-40 *August 5*
Matthew 26:69-75 *September 8*
Matthew 28:1-9 *January 8*
Matthew 28:16-20 *January 20*

Mark 2:1-12 *August 24*
Mark 4:3-4, 13-15 *March 6*
Mark 4:3-20 *December 5*
Mark 13:27-37 *May 27*
Mark 13:32-37 *January 9, March 2*

Luke 2:8-16 *December 1*
Luke 6:27-35 *July 6*
Luke 6:27-36 *December 16*
Luke 6:31-38 *August 4, October 24*
Luke 6:40-46 *May 7*
Luke 6:47-49 *May 2, June 17*
Luke 10:20 *November 21*
Luke 10:29-37 *June 29*
Luke 10:30-37 *October 21*
Luke 11:1-13 *April 14*
Luke 11:5-13 *February 1*
Luke 12:1-3 *January 25*
Luke 12:16-21 *May 20*
Luke 12:22-31 *August 26*
Luke 14:15-23 *April 3*
Luke 15:3-10 *August 28*
Luke 15:11-17 *April 12*
Luke 15:18-24 *April 13*
Luke 16:10-13 *December 15*
Luke 17:11-19 *May 5*
Luke 17:12-19 *November 25*
Luke 18:1-8 *June 3*

John 1:14-18 *June 8*
John 3:1-7, 16 *December 13*
John 3:16; 10:25-30
   September 25
John 3:36 *October 14*
John 6:30-35 *February 15*
John 6:32-35 *April 29*
John 8:31-36 *July 4, July 7*
John 10:1-5 *June 16*
John 10:7-10 *August 13*
John 13:34-35; 14:2-3 *February 4*
John 14:1-6 *October 25*
John 14:1-6, 16-17 *February 14*
John 14:13-17, 25-27
   September 10
John 15:1-6 *March 24*
John 15:1-7 *May 14*
John 15:9-12 *October 4*

Acts 1:6-9 *August 9*
Acts 2:42-47 *March 13*

Index of Memory Verses

Matthew 10:32 *March 14, March 22*
Matthew 11:28 *October 1*
Matthew 12:34 *October 23*
Matthew 12:37 *June 11*
Matthew 15:14 *January 7*
Matthew 18:20 *May 25*
Matthew 19:19 *October 21*
Matthew 19:26 *November 15*
Matthew 21:22 *April 14*
Matthew 23:26 *June 9*
Matthew 24:12 *December 19*
Matthew 24:31 *March 7*
Matthew 24:44 *January 9, May 18*
Matthew 25:13 *April 6*

Mark 1:17 *April 29*
Mark 11:26 *August 4*
Mark 13:35-36 *May 27*
Mark 16:15 *August 9*

Luke 6:31 *October 24*
Luke 8:16 *September 20*
Luke 8:18 *May 24*
Luke 11:9 *February 1*
Luke 18:1 *June 3*
Luke 19:10 *August 28*
Luke 21:34 *December 5*

John 1:14 *June 8*
John 3:3 *December 13*
John 4:35 *January 20*
John 6:35 *February 15*
John 8:12 *November 1*
John 8:36 *July 4*
John 10:9 *August 13*
John 10:10 *March 6*
John 10:27 *July 13*
John 10:28 *September 25*
John 13:35 *May 12*
John 14:6 *January 8*
John 14:15 *September 6*
John 15:4 *March 24*
John 15:5 *May 17*

John 15:13 *February 4*
John 15:16 *November 5*
John 16:13 *November 28*

Acts 5:29 *June 15, July 14*
Acts 17:26 *April 26*
Acts 17:28 *May 26*
Acts 20:35 *December 4*
Acts 24:16 *March 8*

Romans 1:16 *September 12*
Romans 2:11 *December 14*
Romans 5:8 *March 16, December 22*
Romans 6:13 *November 18*
Romans 6:23 *January 10, April 30, June 6*
Romans 7:23 *February 12*
Romans 8:1 *February 2*
Romans 8:2 *May 14*
Romans 8:15 *July 20*
Romans 8:28 *May 23, December 10*
Romans 8:31 *September 29*
Romans 8:38-39 *November 23*
Romans 8:39 *January 12*
Romans 10:14 *June 13*
Romans 10:15 *October 18*
Romans 10:17 *June 16*
Romans 12:1 *March 18*
Romans 12:6 *February 21, November 16*
Romans 12:10 *October 10*
Romans 12:15 *March 17*
Romans 12:18 *February 23*
Romans 13:14 *July 16*
Romans 14:7 *February 8*
Romans 14:10 *July 9*
Romans 15:4 *September 7*
Romans 15:6 *March 21*
Romans 15:7 *May 30, June 29*

1 Corinthians 2:12 *January 14*
1 Corinthians 3:11 *April 11, May 2, June 17*

2 Timothy 2:22 *February 22,*
June 22

Titus 3:2 *May 19*

Hebrews 5:13 *April 22*
Hebrews 5:14 *November 9*
Hebrews 10:24 *September 18*
Hebrews 11:6 *June 25*
Hebrews 12:2 *April 18*
Hebrews 12:6 *November 30*
Hebrews 12:11 *May 1*
Hebrews 13:1 *August 12*
Hebrews 13:5 *February 14*

James 1:2 *November 20*
James 1:8 *April 7*
James 1:22 *January 24,*
November 7
James 2:9 *August 8, November 17*
James 2:10 *May 8*
James 4:7 *June 2, August 18*
James 4:8 *April 12*
James 4:17 *October 9*
James 5:16 *July 15*

1 Peter 1:3-4 *August 16*
1 Peter 1:18-19 *March 31*

1 Peter 2:2 *February 3, March 19*
1 Peter 2:9 *December 30*
1 Peter 2:12 *September 21*
1 Peter 2:13 *December 29*
1 Peter 3:10 *February 10*
1 Peter 3:17 *April 4*
1 Peter 5:7 *September 5,*
September 10

2 Peter 3:14 *September 27*
2 Peter 3:18 *August 7*

1 John 1:7 *October 16, December 21*
1 John 1:9 *June 12, July 27*
1 John 2:1 *September 4*
1 John 2:28 *March 2*
1 John 3:2 *May 16*
1 John 3:10 *May 7*
1 John 4:1 *April 1*
1 John 4:4 *September 15*

Revelation 1:5-6 *March 11*
Revelation 3:5 *November 21*
Revelation 3:16 *December 12*
Revelation 3:19 *June 19*
Revelation 19:9 *April 3*
Revelation 22:12 *April 21*